The Complete

ENCYCLOPEDIA OF CATS

Esther J. J. Verhoef-Verhallen

CHARTWELL
BOOKS, INC.

© 2003 Rebo International b.v., Lisse, The Netherlands

Text: Esther J. J. Verhoef-Verhallen
Photographs: Furry Tails/Esther J. J. Verhoef-Verhallen
Layout and Typesetting: AdAm Studio, Prague, The Czech Republic
Cover design: AdAm Studio, Prague, The Czech Republic
Translation: Alastair and Cora Weir for First Edition Translations
Ltd., Cambridge, Great Britain
Proofreading: Joshua H. Joseph, Jarmila Pešková Škraňáková

This edition published in 2005 by
CHARTWELL BOOKS, INC.
A division of BOOK SALES, INC.
114 Northfield Avenue
Edison, New Jersey 08837
USA

ISBN-13: 978 0 7858 1998 1
ISBN-10: 0 7858 1998 3

Printed in Slovenia.

Contents

Foreword

In recent years, cats have enjoyed a steadily increasing popularity. More cats than dogs are kept as pets and the number of cat owners is still rising. Surprisingly, the popularity of pedigree cats is also increasing by leaps and bounds. A few decades ago, there were far fewer fanciers and owners of pedigree cats than there are now. People used to think of pedigree cats as an elitist luxury only for those who already had everything. This is odd, considering that pedigree dogs were becoming an established feature of the urban landscape at the same time. But cats? You could pick them up any weekend from the nearest farmer!

It seems that the tide has turned in favor of pedigree cats. Increasingly, people are realizing that pedigree cats, like pedigree dogs, have an appearance and temperament typical of their breed, which may or may not appeal to them. A pedigree cat is much less of a surprise package than a kitten of unknown provenance although, of course, both can be lovable and beautiful! A growing number of people do, however, want to know how their new pet—which is, after all, going to be a member of the family for at least fifteen years—will eventually grow up and what kind of temperament it is likely to have.

A large part of this encyclopedia is therefore devoted to descriptions of the dozens of breeds and varieties that are now available to choose from. What kind of temperament do they have? What do they look like, and what colors and kinds of coat can they have? What should you look out for in any specific breed? What is its origin and history? In addition, whether it is a pedigree cat or just an "ordinary" household cat, it will of course need care, food, and attention. Accommodation, food and drink, and care and maintenance are comprehensively covered, together with the most common diseases and indispositions that can afflict a cat.

I would like to close by thanking everyone who has assisted in this extensive project. Without the help of literally hundreds of people, including breeders, photographers, show judges, vets, and genetic experts, this encyclopedia could never have appeared in this form. I do hope that you, the reader, will take pleasure in looking at and reading this book, and that you will find it a valuable addition to your library.

Esther Verhoef

Part 1: General

Cats through the ages

Caracal

Early ancestors

Present-day researchers cautiously proceed from the assumption that the domestic cat is the descendant not of a single small wild cat, but of several varieties. Among others, *Felis lybica* (African Wildcat), *Felis silvestris* (Wild Forest Cat), *Felis chaus* (Jungle Cat), *Felis margarita* (Sand Cat), and *Felis caracal* (Caracal) have been suggested. To this day, it is still not known precisely how and when cats were first domesticated—in other words, when the wild animal became a pet. Researchers used to start from the premise that cats were first domesticated in Ancient Egypt, somewhere around 2000 B.C. More recent research has, however, rejected this: some finds indicate that domestication may have taken place much earlier. For instance,

European wild forest cat

excavations in the Jordan valley and in Cyprus have indicated that small cats with domesticated characteristics already existed in the year 7000 B.C. In itself, this is not really surprising, because it was in that period that man started to cultivate and store grain. Stored food attracts rats and mice, which in their turn attract cats. It is possible that the people of that time, the New Stone Age (Neolithic), realized the usefulness of cats. Perhaps on occasion a motherless wild kitten was taken into a home and "tamed;" we will probably never know exactly how it happened, only that there is evidence that cats have been part of our lives for at least nine thousand years.

The Ancient Egyptians

Cats occupied a special place in Ancient Egypt, at least from the year 900 B.C. onward. In excavations in Egypt, countless images of cats—mummified cats, pictures of cats, and paintings of them in tombs—have been found. It is clear from all these finds that cats, together with a few other animals, had a high, more or less sacred, status. They were regarded as incarnations of gods, and cats were incarnations of the goddess Bastet. Several temples were built and dedicated to this goddess, the largest and most famous of them being in the town of Bubastis. Certainly at that time respect for cats was so high that the penalty for killing one, intentionally or not, was death. It is estimated that particularly the cats living in and around Bastet's temples were well cared for and, after their deaths, mummified and buried together. Cats' mummies have also been found with mummified

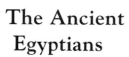

Mummified cat
from Ancient Egypt

Egyptian Mau

mice—food that the cat could take with it on the long voyage to the hereafter. Mass graves, in which hundreds of thousands of mummified cats have been found, were discovered in the early twentieth century by the British who, unfortunately, did not, to say the least, appreciate the archaeological value of their discoveries. The mummies were shipped back to England as ballast, where they were ground up into fertilizer for agriculture. Regrettably, only a few of the original millions of mummified cats have survived, in various museums across the world. In fact, these mummies are rarely cat-shaped: they were arranged to look like Bastet, who had a long human body with a cat's head.

Egypt: the reverse side

It is not wise, however, to over-romanticize the Egyptians' veneration of cats. New research methods, by which mummies can be closely examined without damaging them, have revealed that many of the preserved mummies did not die a natural death. This applies particularly to mummies after the year 330 B.C.—the date when Alexander the Great conquered Egypt. One of the things known of this period is that mummified cats were bought

A Bedouin and a cat in
the desert, Egypt
(Sahra'Esh Sharqiya)

by pilgrims as offerings to the gods. The demand for these mummies may have been greater than the supply, thus creating an important additional source of income for the less ethical of the Egyptian priests who looked after the temple cats.

The Middle Ages

After the Egyptian period, cats came to be regarded in a more usual way. They lived with people and did what they were good at: keeping houses and barns free of rats and mice. This changed, however, during the Middle Ages (A.D. 500–1500). Particularly in the last few centuries of this period, cats came to be thought of as familiars of the devil. The infamous persecution of cats, and black cats in particular, with the consequent superstitions that endure to this day, have their roots in the fourteenth century. At that time, the Catholic Church suffered a decline in influence, for which two things were to blame. Firstly, there was the debauched lifestyle of many holders of high ecclesiastical office and the luxury in which they lived, which was in stark contrast to the poverty of the common people. Secondly, the Church could offer no solution to the countless problems facing the population, such as the outbreak of plague, which held half Europe in its grip from the mid-fourteenth century onwards and wiped out a quarter of the population (about 25 million people). In these turbulent times, people were more in need of an anchor than ever, and with the failings of the Church in this regard "heathen" beliefs mushroomed. Women featured strongly in many of these, especially through their asso-

In the Middle Ages cats were often dealt a poor hand

Cats were associated with witchcraft

ciation with fertility and birth. Many of the "new" beliefs also harked back to the earlier worship of cats, which were associated with the feminine gender. This was, for many reasons, offensive to the Church. In seeking not only to retain but also extend its power, it mounted a severe counter-attack on these diverse religions, which degenerated into a comprehensive smear campaign. This resulted in a black period for both Europe and the cat, which left its traces long after the Middle Ages ended.

Cats and the persecution of witches

In 1484, two German Dominican monks (Heinrich Kramer and Jacob Sprenger) persuaded the then Pope, Innocent VIII, to publish a papal decree, giving the inquisition the right to root out "witches." They wrote a book, published in 1487 under the title of *Malleus Maleficarum* (the Hammer of Witches), which described how a witch could be recognized, interrogated, and killed. The book was used as a manual by many holders of high office, at a time when people still

9

An eighteenth-century Hungarian print

knew little about natural phenomena and science was in its infancy. Most were illiterate, with reading and writing skills confined to the upper classes and clergy, and it was therefore quite easy to influence the "common people." The persecution of witches—and cats—lasted a long time. In most countries and regions, witch hunts ended around 1700, although Holland ceased the practice much earlier, in 1610. It would, however, be the nineteenth century before the persecution of witches was brought completely to an end. The large-scale persecution of cats, however continued. For instance, an American newspaper reported in 1929 that, due to a wave of witch phobia, there were no black cats to be found in the whole of York County, Pennsylvania. In view of the extended period in which cats were regarded unfavorably, it is perhaps not surprising that many superstitions linger to this day.

Luxury positions for luxury cats

Although the persecution of cats was widespread in Europe, there were plenty of cats that did not suffer, and led a life of luxury. These were rarely ordinary, shorthaired cats, but cats with a special appeal to the upper classes. We know that the first Turkish Angora cats were brought to Europe from Turkey by Italian merchants in the early seventeenth century. These cats, often with a white coat and blue eyes, were enthusiastically welcomed by the nobility of Europe. They feature regularly in paintings, beside highborn ladies, their children, and the little "lapdogs" of the time. Because these luxurious-looking, longhaired animals were particularly in vogue at the French court, they were also called "French cats." It is known that the ancestors of the French

The Chartreux was described
as early as 1756

The (white) Turkish Angora was a popular breed at the French court

shorthaired blue pedigree cat, the Chartreux, were recorded in the sixteenth century both in Rome and in France. The name of the Chartreux breed appears first in the eighteenth century as the name for the blue shorthaired cats that were popular in Paris, but which had originated in an isolated mountainous region of France (Grande Chartreuse). Apart from nonpedigree cats, it is therefore these two breeds that had the honor of being described by Buffon in his voluminous *Histoire naturelle*, which appeared in 1756. In this comprehensive work, the (Turkish) Angora was given its Latin name *Felis catus angorensis*.

The first cat shows were held towards the end of the nineteenth century

Cats in the early twentieth century

The twentieth century was an important time for cats, particularly pedigree ones—they were discovered as domestic pets on a wide scale. The first cat shows were held in the late nineteenth century, the earliest of these being a particularly British phenomenon. Because of its many colonies, Great Britain was familiar with exotic plants and animals; its sailors brought unusual plants and animals back with them to England, where they were put on display in botanical gardens and zoos. In the late nineteenth century, unusual-looking cats, such as the blue-eyed color points (the Siamese, from what was then called Siam) and longhaired cats with a silver-colored undercoat from India (the forerunner of the Chinchilla Persian), came into the hands of the English upper classes, who decided to breed from these animals. The first major show, organized by Harrison Weir, was held in London in 1871 in the Crystal Palace. Of course, there were not as many breeds represented at the earliest shows as is the case today. The first breeds of cat were the Siamese, the Longhair (also called Persian, Persian Longhair), Manx, Abyssinian, and Shorthair (now British Shorthair). Blue shorthaired cats, such as the Russian Blue and the Chartreux, were exhibited simply as "Shorthair Blue," with no further distinction

The Book of the Cat, a luxuriously produced book about cats published in 1903

being made—only later did cat fanciers begin to realize that not only a specific coat color and length characterized a breed, but that other external characteristics, related to the region from which they originated, distinguished cats of a particular breed. It was also in Great Britain, around this time, that the rescue of stray cats began. These early animal shelters were financed by private individuals.

Details of a cat show in England in the early twentieth century

Pedigree cats "for everyone"

With increasing prosperity, and particularly after the Second World War, ownership of a pedigree cat was no longer confined to the upper classes. Certainly from the 1950s onwards the appeal of cats—including pedigree cats—as pets, for breeding, and for showing, grew rapidly. The Siamese breeds reached their peak during this time, followed by the Persian Longhair, which was particularly popular in the 1970s (when it still had a normal-length nose). Existing breeds, such as the British Shorthair, the Persian Longhair, and the Siamese were perfected and shown across the globe. Cat associations proliferated, and the breeding of pedigree cats became a favorite hobby throughout the social ranks. The limited number of existing breeds was now rapidly expanded— sometimes with cats that already existed in a particular region, but were only now recognized as a breed, such as the Norwegian Forest Cat and the Turkish Van in the 1960s; sometimes with breeds created deliberately by crossing existing breeds; and sometimes by the discovery of a cat with a particularly unusual characteristic on which a new breed could be based, such as the Scottish Fold and the various Rex breeds.

The Cornish Rex is one of many popular breeds developed in the mid-twentieth century

Around 1900 cats were still shown on a lead

The Norwegian Forest Cat was identified as a breed in the 1960s

Harrison Weir, an Englishman, was one of the first prominent cat fanciers

Pedigree cats versus pedigree dogs—two different worlds

Pedigree dogs and pedigree cats are often mentioned in the same breath, but their history and development run on far from parallel lines. Breeds of cat, cat organizations, and associated matters are in practice still in their infancy, compared with, for example, horse and dog breeds. Pedigree dogs have been bred seriously for much longer and most breeds of dog can boast a long, if not centuries-old, history. There is a reason for this: dogs have traditionally been bred for specific purposes. People realized very early on that dogs could be helpful to mankind in a variety of ways. Slender, wiry greyhounds were developed for hunting hares; heavy, savage breeds for use in wars and

Sphinx

revolts; sled dogs (in the days before snowmobiles existed) to act as convenient draft animals in snowy areas; pointers and retrievers to retrieve shot game for their masters. In the development of these and many other breeds and groups of breeds, not only was there strong emphasis on character traits and talents that the dog needed to carry out one specific task, but also the bodily structure, coat, and sometimes even color were often essential equipment for that task in its specific environment. In this way, hundreds of

Black tortoiseshell ticked and white female

countries created the opportunity. As a result, and particularly through the 1960s to the 1980s and 1990s, many new breeds of cat appeared. The pedigree cat world currently consists, therefore, mainly of breeds that are relatively recent, and of which quite a few are still in the development stage. Breeders of pedigree cats, and those interested in them, have, moreover, only a limited amount of early documentation on which they can draw, compared with the enormous amount of information which their dog- or horse-breeding colleagues have at their disposal. Altogether, the development of pedigree cat breeds and its related associations and organizations are still very much works in progress.

breeds of dog originated across the world, whose appearance and characteristics are a reflection of the task for which each specific breed was originally intended (and sometimes still is today). When technology made the help of dogs redundant in many fields, people concentrated on retaining the breeds. The rules governing the breeding and showing of these dogs are often strict and focused on breed preservation. Experiments aimed at setting up new breeds of dog have been relatively few, particularly in the last fifty years, and have rarely led to the official recognition of a new breed.

The world of pedigree cats

The cat, on the other hand, has traditionally had only one function: combating vermin. The animals were kept as companions or pets to a considerably less degree. In any case, keeping luxury pets was the preserve of a handful of people with sufficient time, money, and space to do so; the bulk of the population worked hard for long days and basic wages, with little scope for pastimes such as breeding and showing pedigree cats. It is not surprising, therefore, that interest in pedigree cats only increased in the second half of the twentieth century, when improved standards of living and leisure time in western

Black striped Oriental Longhair and a "streamlined" German Dog

A cat as a domestic pet

2

A cat is good company, but also creates more work

Preliminary considerations

When thinking of a cat as a pet, it is often only the advantages that are taken into consideration, but the disadvantages must also be recognized. Keeping a cat as a pet means taking on responsibility for a dependent animal that will need care and attention for a period of up to twenty years, if not longer. This is a substantial period of time, during which the cat will need to be wormed regularly and kept free of fleas, its litter tray will require emptying every day, good food—which is not cheap—will have to be provided for daily, and inoculations will be neccessary on average once a year. Care of the coat,

particularly with longhaired cats, is also a regularly recurring chore, as is checking the teeth and hearing and, if necessary, cleaning the eyes. In addition, it means more housework. Both short and longhaired cats shed their hair, which will stick to your furniture and clothes. A cat may also sometimes leave a fur ball on your carpet, scratch at your wallpaper or your upholstery, or accidentally knock over an ornament or vase, with the inevitable consequences. Whenever you go away on vacation, or just for a weekend, a solution must be found for your four-footed residents, such as a cattery or a cat sitter in your home. It is to be hoped that it never happens, but a cat can become ill or be involved in a road

Guess who will get to pick up the pieces!

Japanese Bobtail

accident. In any such event, it would be completely dependent on you for nursing. You would have to get veterinary help, the cost

Will it be a pedigree cat, such as the unusual Devon Rex?

of which can sometimes run into hundreds, if not thousands, of dollars. Such less pleasant occurrences are also part and parcel of keeping a domestic pet. It is important that you should be fully aware of all this before you take a cat into your family.

Pedigree cats versus non-pedigree cats

Non-pedigree cats are far more popular than pedigree cats will ever be. This is partly the result of the easy availability of non-pedigree kittens, but also because many people appreciate the unpretentious charm of an ordinary cat. In spite of this, there has in recent years been a noticeable increase in the interest in pedigree cats. The expense of a pedigree cat has become easier to bear for increasing numbers of people, particularly young couples with two incomes. In addition, the popularity of dogs as pets appears to be decreasing in comparison with cats, particularly pedigree cats. This is

House cats are in no way inferior to pedigree cats as far as beauty is concerned

An older cat, too, will easily get attached to its new owner

Kitten or older cat?

possibly because people are taking more vacations—many people go away several times a year, insted of just once. It is easier to find a good cat sitter than someone to look after a dog, which demands more work. On the other hand, it may also be because taking a dog out is becoming increasingly troublesome, as more and more places are barred to dogs and owners are expected to clear up any mess. A nice cat, with a friendly and affectionate character, then becomes an attractive compromise. A pedigree cat has several advantages over an ordinary house cat. It is often easier to predict the character of a pedigree cat and, as its appearance is to a large extent established, it can be less of a surprise than a non-pedigree. In addition, serious breeders have their breeding stock tested for infectious diseases, such as Feline Aids (FIV) and viral leukemia (FeLV), so that the kitten you have bought will be free of these fatal infections. Although the purchase price of a non-pedigree cat is nowhere near that of a pedigree one, however, the daily and recurring costs for their care and maintenance are the same.

Most people choose a kitten rather than an adult cat, often because they enjoy watching the new member of their household grow up, but sometimes, too, because they think that

The temperament of a non-pedigree kitten is more or less a surprise package

British Shorthair, tom with heavy jowls

an older cat will have difficulty adjusting to a new family environment. This last argument is not supported by the facts, however. In most cases, an older cat will adapt just as well to a new environment as a kitten, and the ties you develop with it will be just as close. Some people opt for a kitten because they think that it will be more tractable. The character of a cat, however, is determined partly by heredity and partly by the environment into which the kitten was born, and the way the breeder treated his animals. In the end, the efforts of the new owner will indeed have some influence, but the character of a kitten is to a large extent established by the time it comes to you, and all you can do is teach it your house rules and polish up its behavior here and there. After all, a young kitten will not know automatically what is allowed in your house and what is not, and to teach that you will have to invest time in this new member of your family. For some people, therefore, a slightly older cat, which has had a good basic training somewhere else and has learnt what is and what is not acceptable behavior, may be a better choice. Both cases obviously depend a great deal on the previous history of the cat in question.

Male or female?

An important difference between male and female cats is in their general appearance. In many breeds, the males are often much larger, heavier, and more impressive than the females, and they have wider heads. This is also often the case with non-pedigree cats, though in their case it is more difficult to assess how they will later develop as usually little or nothing is known of their ancestry. If, for example, you come across a large breed and find a large cat beautiful, you may well choose a male. Females are in general finer in build, lighter in weight, and smaller, so that people who like their cats slim and elegant often choose a female. Here too, however, the difference is often a function of the breed and, within the breed, a function of the family (there are bloodlines in which the

Black striped Persian Longhair

females are as large and imposing as their male partners, or the males as slim and elegant as the females). The difference in character is not as divergent as some people think. There are easy-going males and catty females, and vice versa. If you choose a pedigree cat and want to show it, then it matters little whether you choose a male or a female. There are, after all, separate classes

Cats enjoy company, like these two Singapuras

at shows for males and females, as there is a separate class for neutered cats. If you want to get a pedigree cat with the intention of breeding a litter from it, then acquiring a female is the most obvious solution. The male will nearly always start spraying as he reaches sexual maturity, and it will be almost impossible to keep him indoors. A female, however, can be taken to a great many places to be covered, with more choice and possibility of alternative arrangements than with a stud male.

The cat is not a solitary animal

People sometimes acquire cats because they assume that they can more easily be left alone in the house than dogs. Broadly speaking, this is true. A cat does not need to be taken for a walk and you can sometimes quite happily leave it on its own for a night. There are, however, too many people who think that cats are solitary animals and are best off when they are the only pet in the house. Yet the opposite is usually the case. Cats that have grown up "wild," or semi-feral on a farm, are taught by their mother to stand on their own feet. The mother cat stops giving her kittens food and no longer tends them once they are about eleven weeks old. Over a relatively short period, they are made independent of their mother and the young cats grow up as solitary animals. If a kitten is born among people, however, it is never cast out. We look after the animal's coat by stroking it and brushing it, thereby copying the care that a mother cat gives her kittens. In addition, we give them food, just as their mother would do when they were little. Because of this nurturing, pets are to a large extent kept psychologically at the "kitten" stage, at which they have a great need for companionship. You are, therefore, letting a house cat down if it is labeled as solitary animal. Owners of two or more

If you are often away from home, a feline playmate is very welcome

Kittens are generally more easily accepted

and companionship it needs, is it reasonable to have only one cat in the house.

An extra cat

If you already have a cat and would like to get another one, in theory it makes no difference whether your new housemate is male or female. Two males (or neutered males) can often get on just as well with each other as a male and a female, or two females. Equally, it may be that these same combinations do not mix. In general, it can be said that a kitten is more readily accepted than a full-grown cat, although that in itself is no reason to make such a choice. A mature cat that got on well with other cats in its previous home will normally cause no problems in your family either. If you have a friendly, sociable cat and you want to get another, equally sociable adult, there is a good chance that things will work out well without too many adaptation problems. Within a couple of weeks, its acceptance may well be complete. In other cases it may take a little longer—it is not unheard of for a whole year to pass before some cats will trust each other and share a basket.

cats often observe how their pets become attached to each other and make lifelong friendships. Certainly, if its owners are away from home a lot, a cat will be pleased if it can share its house with a feline playmate. It is also well-known that kittens that have been left alone from a young age, perhaps by owners who are not at home much, can start to display behavioral problems later on. This is why many pedigree cat breeders will not sell a kitten as the only cat in the house to people who are out all day. Only if you are at home a lot, and can give your pet the attention

It looks fearsome, but usually it is mostly show

Acquiring a non-pedigree cat

A non-pedigree cat—why?

Most people opt for a non-pedigree cat as a pet. The acquisition of such a cat could not be easier. Everyone knows someone who at some time has had a litter of kittens for which they wanted to find good homes. Often such kittens can be acquired for very little, or free, and in looks

Temperament is inherited—sweet-tempered parents are likely to have lovable kittens

There is always someone around who has a litter of kittens

they are certainly in no way inferior to pedigree cats. If you want to take a non-pedigree kitten into your family, however, there are a number of points you should look out for.

The character of the parent cats and their everyday surroundings

Character is, to no small degree, an inherited trait. People who want a cat as a pet often look for a friendly cat with a stable character that likes being stroked and will interact with other

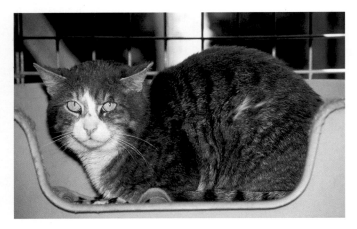

A cat that has not been around people will always be suspicious of them

ticularly among such "outdoor cats," it is more or less a matter of survival of the fittest. The cleverest, most skilful, most careful, and toughest cats have more chance of survival than cats whose nature is all too trusting. In fact, it is these cats that also have the best chance of reproduction. If a kitten from a "half-wild bloodline" learns from its mother to avoid people, it will go on being suspicious of them for the whole of its life. Such an animal will rarely grow up into an affectionate lap cat and will often go on looking at its "own" people with suspicion.

members of the household. Such qualities depend partly on heredity, and partly on experience, imprinting, and socialization in early youth. To begin with, therefore, it is important that the kitten should have inherited the desired characteristics from its father and mother. Kittens from a farm or the offspring of feral cats can sometimes have a less affectionate and trusting character than kittens born from good-tempered, well-cared-for, lovable parents that have lived as family pets. This is because, par-

A kitten's age

Non-pedigree kittens are often taken from their mother at too early an age, at between six to eight weeks. Kittens should, however, be at least ten, preferably thirteen, weeks old before you take them home. Sadly, taking the kittens away at an earlier age can result in a range of behavioral problems that, in the most positive cases, an owner can learn to cope with, but which frequently result in the animal being disposed of or put in a cat's home, where its regressive behavior makes it difficult to rehome. Kittens learn

Kittens learn valuable social lessons with their litter mates

Pedigree kittens are not handed over until they are 13 weeks old—only then have they had sufficient inoculations and are "ready" socially

important skills between the sixth and eleventh week of their lives. They learn where the boundaries of acceptable behavior lie by playing around and having fights, real or pretend, with their litter mates. The mother cat has an important influence in this development, since she has the "upper paw," as it were, and is the only one capable of correcting a kitten, sometimes quite sharply, when it oversteps the mark. Consequently, kittens that have been taken away from their mother much too young, and also bottle-fed kittens that have been brought up separately from their litter mates and their mother, can have problems with boundaries. They bite and scratch too hard when playing with "their" humans, and also have difficulty in adapting to the rules of society observed among cats themselves.

Worming and inoculations

If you buy a kitten from a private individual, ask if they will have your kitten inoculated against cat's distemper (FIE) and cat flu, and have the animal wormed. If this presents a problem, ask if you can take the kitten to the vet yourself. All kittens are infected with thread worms, whether or not the mother cat has been wormed regularly. Moreover, the resistance to disease that kittens derive from their mother's milk suddenly disappears around the age of eight weeks. To prevent your kitten falling sick, it makes sense to have it inoculated. It is wise to wait for a week after the inoculation before taking the kitten home. The body of a newly inoculated animal is already under stress through producing antibodies against the disease for which it has been inoculated; if the trauma of a house move is added, it can reduce resistance and thereby cause a reaction to the inoculation.

Parasites

Always inspect a kitten carefully. Has it any discharge from the nose or eyes, dirty ears, or traces of diarrhea? These are not good omens. It is best to leave kittens with these symptoms where they are, because they may be harboring a disease. Other problem signs include tummies that are too round and bald patches in the coat, which can have various unpleasant causes. It is also better not to choose the "runt" of the litter, because there are often good reasons why it is so much smaller and less able-bodied than the others.

A Norwegian Forest kitten

Getting a cat from a feline rescue center

The obvious place to find a kitten or a mature cat is, of course, a feline rescue center or animal shelter. There are people who think that cats

Mother cat and offspring

have one or more cats of your own, then it is a good idea to ask whether the rescue cats are tested for Feline Aids (FIV) and feline leukemia (FeLV). These fatal diseases are not always reflected in the behavior, or state of health, of an animal that has been infected, but there is still the possibility that they will be passed on to other cats. In some regions, the percentage of free-roaming cats that suffer from one or both of these diseases is estimated at five to twenty percent. Blood tests to determine whether newly arrived cats are suffering from one of these diseases are, because of their high costs, regrettably not a matter of course in all rescue centers.

from these homes are problem cats, but this need not be the case. Most rescue cats have a normal character and are in the home because of circumstances that have nothing to do with them. The staff at these shelters will be very pleased to talk to you and tell you what they know about any particular animal, including any "care label" attached. If you acquire a rescue cat, and already

Black classic and white female from a cat's home

There is rarely something wrong with a cat from an animal shelter—they have just had bad luck

Obviously, few pedigree cats are on offer from such homes. This is partly due to the fact that there are relatively more non-pedigree cats than pedigree ones. In addition, there is often someone to be found in a cat-owner's circle of friends or acquaintances who would like to have a "luxury" pedigree cat, so that there is no need to take the animal to a shelter. Also, cat clubs often have their own safety net for pedigree cats that need a new home.

Acquiring a pedigree cat

What breed is best suited to our family?

There are many different breeds of cat and all of them, in addition to the external features linked to the breed, have character associations. Cats of some breeds, for example, tend to be very active and playful, while others would rather lie for hours on a window sill and let themselves be pampered. Representatives of other breeds are very happy to be allowed to go their own way undisturbed, while yet others need lots of attention and would rather sit on your shoulder and

Not everyone is cut out for such an inquisitive and active breed as the Abyssinian

To keep a Persian Longhair so well-groomed requires intensive daily care

Black-silver classic Scottish Fold female

behold, but every owner of a Persian knows that a beautiful coat needs considerable daily attention. They also know that, if it is neglected, the coat will become tangled in a very short space of time, with the knots having to be cut out. It could be months before the animal looks presentable again. This encyclopedia not only examines the external features of each breed, but also (as far as possible) describes the typical character traits of a particular breed and, in addition, considers the amount and nature of care that specific breeds require.

Interpretation of terms

It would not be sensible to base your choice of a breed solely on what has been written about it. These descriptions may well agree about the image of that particular breed, but the interpretation of them can vary from one individual to another. Thus an "affectionate breed that needs a great deal of attention" can be understood by some people as meaning "an importunate breed that does not give you a moment's peace and gets on your nerves." A "peaceful, phlegmatic breed" can, in reality, be a "very boring cat that sleeps all through the day and does not want to play." So before you make a final choice, it is important to talk to people who own the breeds you are interested in. For this, you can go to a cat show. Apart from meeting all the cats there in real life, you can benefit from discussions with the breeders and fans of these breeds. A breeder may even invite you to their home, so that you are able to form a better and fuller picture of the breed and its behavior in its home environment.

stick their noses into everything you do. Some breeds are known for their sociable dispositions, while others do better in a family with two or, at most, three companions of the same breed. It is a personal choice, in which there will be certain characteristics that you seek, and others that you wish to avoid, in the new member of your family. It is therefore important that, in your choice of a pedigree cat, you look not only at physical features, but also inform yourself about the character associated with that particular breed. If you do not, you may come to regret it afterwards, perhaps because you misjudged the amount of attention the animal would demand, or it turned out to be very playful and wild or, conversely, too lethargic and "boring." The care of its coat is also a factor worth considering. A well-groomed Persian Longhair is a delight to

Munchkin, a black ticked tabby

Red point Cornish Rex kitten

Where do I buy my pedigree cat?

A cat show is traditionally a first-class place to get a picture of the various breeds and to con-

Burmilla kittens

journals. A medium that is increasingly consulted when people are looking for a pedigree kitten is the Internet. Many breeders of pedigree cats have a website showing photos of their cats, explaining their views, and presenting themselves and their cats to you. Careful scrutiny of a website will often reveal how a breeder treats his cats—for instance, how many cats does a breeder have and how quickly did he acquire them? How many litters does he or she breed per year? How are the animals accommodated? Is there evidence of love and knowledge in the text of the website or is the whole site dedicat-

A male Norwegian Forest Cat, black smoke and white

tact their breeders. These events are often announced in the media, but you can also contact a cat society to ask if there is a show planned in your area. In addition, almost all cat associations and breed clubs run some form of kitten information or kitten agency. The people who run these services have an up-to-date list of kittens from their own membership. You will find the addresses of cat associations in most animal

ed to the sale of as many kittens as possible? Through such a website you can get in touch with the breeders by e-mail, which is often followed by a phone call and eventually a visit. Via the Internet you can quietly compare all the cats, breeders, and their opinions with each other at your convenience, so that you are rather

A rare breed such as the La Perm is not often seen at small national shows

better prepared when you actually make contact with a breeder.

Showing and breeding

If you want to purchase a pedigree cat and do not want to rule out showing it or breeding a litter from it some day, you should be rather more critical than if you just want the animal as a companion. Not every kitten with a pedigree is suitable to breed from and/or to show. Furthermore, not every breeder is an expert well-informed on all aspects of the breed in general and the qualities and weaker points of the parents and grandparents of the available kittens in particular. It is better to spend a little more time beforehand collecting the information yourself than to realize later that you have acquired a kitten that will never show or breed suc-

British Shorthair, tom

cessfully. The kitten may stem from a not completely pure-bred line or have "faults" that prevent you showing or breeding from it. You can read up information on the Internet yourself, so that you have some idea in advance which breeders, cats, and catteries attract you most. Then you should visit various shows. It would also make sense to join one of the pedigree cat associations or even a breed club before acquiring your first kitten. There is often a wealth of information on background and new developments in the association newsletters, which you will not necessarily find in general publications and literature. When you visit the breeder, tell

Sphinx

A future prize winner?

him in advance that you are not immediately looking for a kitten, but just want to get an idea of the breed. A dedicated breeder will gladly accept you as a prospective fancier of the breed, even if you are not offering him the immediate prospect of a kitten sale. Do not be shy about visiting a number of different breeders, in order to compare them. You can then make a well-informed decision based on the way the animals are treated, the breeder's knowledge, and, of course, the animals themselves. For the acquisition of a kitten you want to breed from or show, it is usually best to go straight to an experienced and serious breeder who can tell you everything about the bloodlines from which your kitten stems, advise you properly about breeding, and will generally be happy to help you.

will only produce top kittens—the combination of bloodlines must "click" to some extent. The absence of championship titles in the pedigree says just as little about the quality of the kittens. It means only that the owner of the cat involved has not shown the animal, or has not done so very often. That may be because of the character of a cat that does not like to be shown, but it can also mean that the breeder himself simply does not enjoy showing his cats.

Champion kittens?

Do not forget that, even when you acquire a very promising kitten descended from outstanding parents and grandparents from a well-known, established breeder, there is no guarantee that it will

Descended from champions?

As soon as you start looking at the bloodlines of pedigree cats you will notice that most of them include one or more champions. Of course, this says something about the general appearance of the cats in the pedigree, but it says nothing about how your kitten will develop. This in fact depends entirely on the combinations of parents and bloodlines the breeder has achieved; it is not the case that a top cat mated with a top cat

Promising Norwegian Forest kitten, but no breeder can guarantee if it will grow up to be a champion

Sometimes there are longhaired kittens in litters of British Shorthair cats

grow up to be a champion. It is in fact extremely difficult to forecast how a kitten will develop. There are plenty of kittens that at a young age

This odd-eyed white Russian is beautiful, but its eye color is not recognized everywhere

would not have won a beauty pageant but have grown up into stunners—and vice versa. A study of the parents and grandparents can, however, give some indication, and environmental factors also play a role, in respect of the food and care the animal enjoys from you. So never believe a breeder who assures you that his or her kittens will become champions; no one can give you such a watertight assurance.

Maine Coons? Or common longhaired house cats? Without a pedigree you cannot be sure

"Second choice" kittens

Although a breeder can never guarantee that the kitten you choose will grow into a show champion, the opposite is often the case. Sometimes when a kitten is born, the breeder can see, even at an early stage, that it will not completely satisfy the breed standards. This is mainly the case among breeds in which the markings are important, such as, among others, British Shorthairs, Ragdolls, "sacred" Birmans, and Persians—too large or too small an amount of white, or the "wrong" positioning of that white, is already visible at a young age. These white markings are, of course, obvious, but usually the

Some house cats are longhaired

House cat with blue point markings

Red Persian Longhair

minor differences that make a cat suitable or not for a show career are hardly discernible to a layman. As such, you may just as easily be charmed with the minor faults of your cat. Kittens that possess such beauty faults are usually sold under the label of "pet quality" for an appreciably lower price than their litter mates, which do display the desired markings and/or other characteristics. Such kittens are, however, from the same good stock as the "top" ones from the litter, so you are assured of an animal that is sound in other aspects. If you have no interest in breeding or showing, but are looking for a pet with unusual features, then such a kitten may suit you very well. Some breeders ask you to sign a form whereby you agree to have the animal neutered at the appropriate time. This insures the breeder against any faults in the kitten being reproduced in later generations.

Pure bred cats without a pedigree

A pedigree cat is not cheap, and for this reason many people choose a pure bred cat without a pedigree. After all, they do not need a pedigree certificate if they are not going to breed or show. Furthermore, pure bred cats without a pedigree often cost only half as much—maybe less—than their pedigree peers. So it is a good thing to know that many "pure breeds" without pedigrees

are, in fact, not pure breeds at all, but only look like them. In some cat shelters, for example, it is the practice to call longhaired cats with a rather round head "Persians," and the same longhaired cats with a rather long nose "Maine Coons" or "Norwegian Forest Cats." In the same way, a cat with Siamese markings is often called a Siamese. In reality, these are almost always crossbreeds of longhaired, non-pedigree cats. Sometimes, too, kittens of a particular breed are offered for sale without pedigrees. This is usually the case with kittens of very popular breeds, such as the British Shorthair. These, too, often prove in practice not to be pure bred cats, but crosses. In the case of pure breeds, it is also odd, to say the least, if no pedigree comes with them.

Ocicat

There is, after all, no reason why a breeder should not apply for pedigrees for his litter of pure breed kittens—the pedigree costs only a fraction of the kitten's price. Moreover, a breed association rarely refuses to issue a pedigree for kittens. They only do so when the parents have not been tested, or test positive, for FIV and FeLV, when a breeder allows a female to have more litters than is good for her health (normally three litters every two years is the maximum), or when the breeder has several stud cats and does not know which of them has fathered the litter. As a rule, you would do better to save up for a carefully bred kitten from good, tested parents and from a good, dedicated breeder, than acquiring a cheaper kitten that may have something wrong with it.

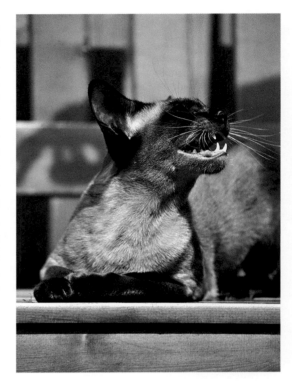

The Tonkinese loves contact and company

Maine Coon with the cross facial expression so typical of the breed

Relocated cats, problem cats?

If you are looking for an older pedigree cat, then you can apply to the breed association that looks after the interests of that breed. In these associations, there is often someone whose job it is to put people who want an older cat in touch with those looking for a new home for their cat. This is usually done through the kitten information service or kitten agency. These people will tell you the facts, because they have the interests of the breed at heart and it is not to their advantage if their attempts at mediation end in disappointment. There are, in fact, many people who think that they only deal with problem cats, but this is certainly not the case. Usually it is just the opposite. There can be many reasons for parting with an older pedigree cat. Divorce, death, emigration, or other personal circumstances can sometimes make it necessary for people to part with a pet, usually for reasons that have nothing to do with the animal itself. It can also happen that one particular cat at a breeder may not get on well with the other cats. That cat will then be better off at an address where it is the only cat, or can live in a smaller group of cats. Very occasionally, breeders are on the look-out for new homes for cats from which they are no longer breeding, because they only have limited accommodation and cannot afford to keep on neutered animals. This again says nothing against the cat itself. It is different when the cat has to be re-housed because it is aggressive, excessively shy, chronically displays unsanitary behavior, or develops some other objectionable character fault that is difficult to live with. In fact, a cat often displays behavior linked to a specific location. A cat that refuses to be house-trained at a breeder's establishment need not do so in your home because the circumstances there are different. If you are considering acquiring an older cat and do not know enough about cats yourself, it would be sensible to take someone with you who has rather more experience in the matter and can advise you. It is also sensible to reach an agreement with the original owner that you can return the cat if, for any reason, it does

Cats used for breeding should simply join the household

not settle in your home. In respect of price, a mature cat will cost about the same as a neutered animal.

Take note of the way the breeder treats his or her animals and how the animals react to the breeder

Lively and well-socialized kittens will find your visit interesting

Good hygiene is very important

What should I look out for?

When you visit a breeder to look at a litter of kittens, watch out for the following points:

Are there too many cats?
Most breeders have several cats, both indoors

A dirty coat, a dripping nose, and watery eyes—
this kitten is not well

and possibly living in runs outside. It can also be that a breeder has only one or two. There are people who think that a cattery should be on a large scale, but that is not in fact desirable. It is not a good sign if the place is literally and figuratively crawling with cats. Cats need attention and care, which will be in shorter supply as numbers increase.

How are the animals housed?
It may be that a number of cats, permanently or temporarily, are kept in a run outside. This is often the case, for example, with male cats that keep spraying. For their social development, however, kittens need to be brought up indoors and not in a barn, outside run, or in a spare room where they do not share in the daily life of the house. Kittens that grow up in isolation are socially disadvantaged in a way that may be very difficult or impossible to put right later in life. As kittens pass the most important phase of their life—the stage at which they are imprinted—at the breeders, it is important that breeders train their kittens properly and let them grow up amongst the family. This will accustom the kitten to a variety of situations, people, and animals, so that it can respond in any future encounters with equilibrium.

How do the kittens react to your visit?

Observe how the kittens react to your visit. Unless they are sleepy, healthy kittens should regard your visit as a welcome change in the normal daily routine, and certainly not as frightening or threatening. They should therefore approach you freely, and will probably display their playfulness. Kittens that have been brought up in a separate room and are only allowed in the living room for your visit are often rather less forthcoming in these, for them, unfamiliar surroundings. They may appear rather nervous and uninterested in the visitor.

What about hygiene?

Always take note of the hygiene. It may not smell quite as fresh at a breeder's place as it does at home, which is almost certainly the case if there is an unneutered male present that does not live in an outside run, but may come into the house. There is no excuse, however, for dirty litter trays, cats with tangled coats or dirty eyes, a filthy floor, dishes with old scraps of food, or anything else that indicates a limited degree of care. Such neglect is a breeding ground for bacteria and other problems.

Do the kittens look healthy?

It may happen to the best breeders that on one or more days the kittens have a weeping eye or some small infection. Until this is under control, however, a serious breeder will rarely let any outsiders come to look at the kittens. So if you spot any discharge from the nose or eyes, dirty ears, a ragged coat, or signs of diarrhea on the hairs under the tail, these are not good omens. Do not let yourself be seduced into acquiring a kitten showing these kinds of symptoms, even out of pity, since it may be harboring a disease. Other signs that all is not well include tummies that are too round and hard (worm infections) and bare patches in the coat (ringworm).

Some breeds tend to suffer from inherited disorders—always ask for test reports

All are sweet—an experienced breeder knows which kitten is the most promising

What about documentation and test certificates?

Some breeds can have inherited problems, and tests are now available for many of these problems, varying from a simple blood test to ultrasound scans. Good breeders who have the welfare of the breed at heart will not spare money or effort in having their breeding stock tested for such conditions and, if necessary, the kittens, too. A serious breeder of a breed that has no known inherited problems will at least have his parent cats tested for cat leukemia (FeLV) and Feline Aids (FIV), for which no safe vaccines have so far been developed. If you have informed yourself well in advance, you will know what problems may arise with the breed of your choice. You may then specifically ask the breeder for a sight of the test results. A serious breeder will be only too pleased to show them to you.

Do not visit several breeders on the same day

Although the hygiene and health precautions at most breeders are first class, you are advised not to visit more than one breeder on the same day. There is always the risk that you will unwittingly carry germs to the next cattery.

Your choice

Everyone who has ever been to look at a litter of kittens will know how difficult it is to make a choice. They all look lovely and adorable. If you want a kitten for yourself and have no aspirations in the area of breeding or showing, then the best advice is to follow your instinct. Emotional choices usually turn out very well. If you want to show or breed, then the opinion of the breeder should also influence your choice. Certainly, experienced breeders will recognize the refinements that can give that little extra to one particular kitten. Kittens, however, can also have their preferences, and may decide that they like you—or not. If you and that one kitten somehow do not "click," it is better to wait for the next litter. After all, the cat will be a member of your family for fifteen years or more.

Cats at home

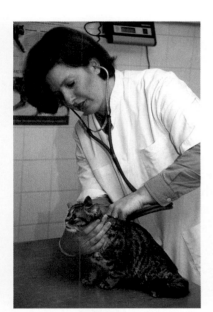

It makes sense to have the newcomer checked by a vet first

Kitten in the house

By the time a kitten comes into your home, it will be about ten weeks old. Pedigree kittens are often only allowed to leave at the age of thirteen weeks. If it is a pedigree kitten it will probably be delivered to your house. Then the breeder can see where his or her carefully bred kitten is going and the kitten can learn about its new home (and its inmates) while the familiar breeder is still around. The pedigree should be handed over to you with your pedigree kitten, together with a vaccination record showing when, where, and against what your kitten has been inoculated. Before your kitten arrives, ask the breeder or previous owner what kind of food the kitten is accustomed to eating and the sort of cat litter it is used to, to ensure that you have these ready in the house in advance. A change of home can be stressful for a cat and stress reduces its resistance, so that the animal will be more vulnerable to diseases. So it is best—certainly in the first few weeks—to make as few changes as possible in its diet, the times at which you feed it, or its cat litter. Many breeders work with a sales contract setting out the rights and obligations of the buyer and the seller. Make sure the contents of the contract are reasonable before you sign it.

Blue-cream and white Cornish Rex

A newcomer in the house—a critical moment you must leave to the cats to sort out among themselves

Outside, too, territorial boundaries have to be set

If there is already a cat in the house

If you already have one or more cats or other pets, it is a good idea to let the kitten first explore some part of the house, such as the living room, by itself in peace for a few hours. First put the animal down on a clean litter tray, so that it knows where to go when it needs to. Give it the opportunity to have a drink and perhaps to eat something (though it is rare for cats or kittens to start to eat immediately in a new environment). Only after this introduction should you let it meet its new housemates. In this way, the animal does not have to take in too many new impressions at once and finds itself less threatened, because it has had the chance to learn something about its new surroundings.

Accustoming cats to one another

Whether the newcomer, adult or not, will get on with any other pets you already have, is dependent both on the character of the animal concerned and the attitude of your existing animals. If you already have one or more cats, these may

sometimes at first decide to adopt a "dog-in-the-manger" attitude and not accept the newcomer, but usually any problems are resolved within about a month. This is usually the case if there is sufficient space and if certain preconditions (see below) are satisfied, although it does not always happen. There are cats that will not tolerate a newcomer, which they can show in such ways as abandoning their house-training or becoming hypersensitive, withdrawing to a

In this way cats can get used to each other quietly and safely

quiet spot in the house and refusing food or, on the other hand, by always provoking fights. Sometimes the difficulties will ease in the course of time, but it can also happen, on rare occasions, that you have to find a new home for one of them. It is sometimes said that a kitten is accepted more easily, but this should in no way prevent you acquiring a fully grown cat, since there are just as many examples of animals that have made firm friendships at a later age. Also, in practice it matters little whether the newcomer is male or female. There are females who make friends with females, males who make friends with males, and cats of opposite sexes who make friends, just as there are animals of the same or different sexes that cannot stand the sight of each other. Just like humans, cats can

Some breeds, such as the Oriental Shorthair and the Siamese, have a natural affinity for each other

learn to like each other or take a dislike to each other. It is not always possible to predict on which side the scales will come down. In any event, during the settling-in period peace and patience are perhaps the most important factors of all. If you jump up every time a cat hisses or growls, you will contribute to making an already unstable situation even more unsettling—and it can start to escalate. It is better to let the cats work things out among themselves as much as possible and try not to react when there is any hissing going on. Go on stroking the old cat or cats as usual, or take them in your lap as you once did. Try to ignore growls, hissing, and even cuffs among the cats as much as possible—except, of course, when they really go too far.

Extra requirements—the preconditions

An extra cat almost certainly means some adjustments to be made in the house and, in most cases, there are some essential requirements.

Extra cat-litter tray

Urine and feces have a function of signaling "this is mine." Cats mark out their territory via these. A newcomer may sometimes not dare to leave its visiting card in the domain of an existing cat. It can also work the other way round, however: the older cat may no longer feel comfortable with a tray that is also being used by the newcomer. So an extra litter tray is no superfluous luxury. Preferably put it in another room, or quite a long way from the existing tray, so that you do not start any "boundary disputes."

Extra scratching places

Cats that never go out particularly benefit from the opportunity to scratch, climb, and sharpen their claws. Existing climbing or scratching posts, however, will be full of the scents and marks of the old cat. A newcomer is sometimes not accepted there, at least not before the ani-

An extra litter tray is no luxury when there is an extra cat in the house

A newcomer is not always accepted near the scratching post

Special aids

To speed up the process of familiarization, you can buy special sprays from the pet shop or from your vet that release scents that are reassuring to cats, such as pheromones. The use of these sprays can be helpful in speeding up the settling-down process, particularly with cats that are nervous or lack confidence.

If there is a dog

If the dog in the house is used to cats and is gentle in its dealings with them, then it will normally also accept the newcomer in your home. There are also dogs that will chase cats outside the house, but will never harm a hair of the household cat to which they are accustomed. A strange cat in the garden is, after all, an offence to virtually every dog, even for a dog that gets on very well with its own cat. You will have to know your dog well to know how it will react to

mals have become used to each other. So the new cat may go and scratch somewhere else in the house, and will go on doing so—from their point of view there is just no other option, since the only scratching post in the house is, after all, reserved for the other cat. So an extra scratching post is in fact just as essential as a second litter tray.

Food and drink bowls

To begin with, do not give the animals food next to each other or from the same bowl. For food and drink, the same rule applies—the newcomer can feel overawed by a member of the old guard in the house and dare not let itself be seen in its eating place. So put food and water down in separate places in the house. As time passes and the animals become used to one another, they will often quite happily eat out of the same bowl, or side by side from different ones.

A dog smells quite different!

An extra food tray prevents angry scenes

a cat, and it is self-evident that, if you have any doubt, you will take care that your dog and cat are not left alone at first, and that the cat has sufficient bolt holes where the dog cannot reach it. In some cases, it may be that you just cannot have a cat. It can sometimes be easier to take an older cat, which is already used to dogs, into your family. Kittens—as they squeal, play, spit, or run away—are clearly fascinating to some dogs. Never hold the cat when the animals first make each other's acquaintance; there is always the risk that it will want to get away and scratch you in its panic, after which the dog will immediately start chasing after the panic-stricken cat—with inevitable consequences.

Guiding the process

You might be able to guide this process of acclimatization by giving the dog something nice to eat every time he or she behaves well towards the cat. In this way, the dog will at some stage link the presence of the cat with rewards and so begin to see the cat as a positive contribution to its life instead of as an intruder. At the same time, the dog learns that good behavior is rewarded; this behavior meaning that the cat is left in peace and treated as a friend. For the same reason, it is not a good idea suddenly to start telling the dog off as soon as the kitten or cat comes into the house, or laying down the law, which in practice only results in all the animals

Starting young is the best way for cats and dogs to learn to get on together

Acclimatization

It is sometimes convenient to let your cat and dog get to know each other gradually. This is particularly the case when you have a big dog, or when you think that the dog and/or cat may perhaps display aggressive behavior towards each other, or have never met another dog or cat before. In that case, let the cat get used to the situation by keeping it in a separate room and just putting it in a protective pen in the living room for half an hour a day. Give the dog its food in the living room at the same time and also give the cat something nice to eat in its pen. This is important in creating a positive association. The advantage of the pen is that the animals cannot hurt each other; nor can the cat run away, which might provoke the dog to give chase. Do this for at least a week and watch how the animals

Cats and dogs can become the best of friends

in the house getting nervous. It is better to keep a subtle eye on how things are going, stay calm, and only interfere if you think things are really going wrong. Continue to give your dog the attention he or she has always had from you, and do not depart from the routine to which your dog is accustomed.

If a dog is used to cats, it will often accept a newcomer without a problem

react to each other. If they hardly notice each other or react in a positive way, you can open the pen and let the animals meet. You will previously have allowed the cat to find its way round the living room, so that it knows any possible escape routes. A less labor-intensive possibility is available to you if you have a separate room adjoining the living room (such as a conservatory or outdoor run), separated by a glass or trellis partition. Let the cat live in the conservatory or outdoor run and put no further emphasis on it. You must give your dog the impression that it is the most natural thing in the world for there to be a cat in the house. As soon as the dog and the cat approach each other in a friendly way, you can leave the door open a crack and let the animals meet each other. Generally, both animals will get used to the new situation within a few weeks, but it is all dependent on good, calm guidance and, of course, the character of the animals.

Their body language is almost the opposite and offers plenty of scope for misunderstandings

The body language of cats and dogs

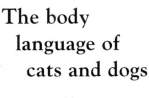

It takes a while to get used to a new house

One problem a cat owner is faced with is the difference in the body languages of dogs and cats. If dogs and cats do not grow up together from a young age, it is very probable that they will not understand each other's body language. Dog and cat languages tend to be the opposite of each other. A cat holding its tail up straight indicates by so doing that it is pleased and relaxed. A dog holding its tail up high, however, can express domination, aggression, or tension. If a cat folds its ears back, it is frightened or feeling aggressive, whereas dogs folding their ears back are in fact being submissive. It is not surprising, therefore, that cats and dogs that have not learned in their youth to understand each other's body language can find it difficult to live together when they are fully grown.

Cats and small pets

Living with small pets such as birds, fish, hamsters, or baby rabbits can be a problem, but does not have to be. In such cases, much depends on the character of the cat. A breed such as, for example, the Turkish Van, which is still close to its natural state, will not let a single unguarded moment be wasted in disposing of smaller animals—its natural prey. There are plenty of breeds, however, such as Persians and "Sacred" Birmans, which appear to have little interest in small pets and will never do them any harm. How this works out with non-pedigree cats is difficult to forecast, because their characters are so various. In general, it can be said that cats that love playing wild games also love hunting. Play is, after all, a form of hunting. In any case, the new member of your household is and remains a predatory animal and there are very few of them that can really be trusted with pets that, in the normal course of events, would form their natural prey.

A cat for the children

Many pets first join a family because the children want them, and there is nothing wrong with that. It is very good for the social development of children to grow up with animals and thereby learn to take some responsibility for a living creature. Moreover, a lovable house cat

Children are often fond of cats—whether the reverse is true depends on the guidance they have from their parents

Cats are predators

can be a great comfort to a child; it is an animal that has no prejudices, but only reacts to the way in which it finds itself treated. A companionable cat that likes being stroked and cuddled can have a salutary effect on children who are unhappy or who are hiding some childish secret. After all, a child can confide everything to the cat, which always has a listening ear and will never betray the confidences entrusted to it. Never assume, however, that your children, particularly young ones, will be able to take on the whole care of the cat. Children do not possess a

fully-developed sense of responsibility and, with a few honorable exceptions, the novelty will soon wear off, with the care of the cat ending up on your shoulders. In view of the relatively great age a cat can reach, it is not unlikely that the children will have left home while the cat is still in the prime of life. Complete responsibility for a pet cannot be expected from children under the age of perhaps eleven or twelve. Up to that age, children are still very playful and cannot foresee the long-term consequences of their actions. From the age of four upwards, a child can sometimes be asked to put out a bowl of water or food for the cat. Its parents should, however, not blindly assume that the child will actually do it. This is not from disobedience or cruelty on the part of the child—he is just not yet ready intellectually to bear the responsibility. Later, a child can help with cleaning out the lit-

American Curl, kitten

Many people get cats because the children would like to have one

ter tray and brushing the cat (provided it is a peaceful one). If you acquire a cat, never do so just for the children; you should also want it yourself.

The role of the parents

When your child nags for a kitten, start with the realization that you as a parent will always have to bear the responsibility for the proper care of, and food for, the animal. Furthermore, it is you as a parent who has to teach your child respect for the animal—that it is not a rag doll that can be dragged around everywhere and that it would like to eat in peace, wants privacy on its litter tray, and will sometimes want to withdraw to sleep or rest. The role of the parent in all this is

Japanese Bobtail

Always make sure that the cat has a hide-out

very important, because otherwise the relationship can become much less harmonious, particularly for the cat. If a cat is never left in peace and is always being picked up and disturbed in whatever it is doing, it will very quickly acquire an aversion for the child or even become afraid of it. A responsible parent will therefore take care that the child knows how to approach the cat and pick it up, and that it must not be chased after. Even with the best brought-up children, however, it is sensible for the cat to have an escape route—somewhere the child cannot go and where the animal feels safe. This may be on top of a cupboard or a tall scratching post, or a cat flap through which it can get into the garden. Apart from that, it is sensible to take extra care when you have both children and cats. Check the drier or the washing machine well before you switch them on—there may be a cat inside—and teach the children that a door should only be shut when the whole of the cat, including its tail, has gone through. Many vets could write volumes about cats' tails that have been irretrievably damaged in this way. Small children do not yet understand such things properly. This is the responsibility of the parents, who have to be alert. Also teach a child that it must keep away from the cat's water and food. This is not because dry cat biscuits are not good for children—no child has yet been made ill from eating cat food—it is so that the cat does not feel the child is a competitor for its food. When the child has a birthday party, it is best to put the cat in a separate room. In all the excitement, it is impossible for the parents to keep an eye on everything, and the whole experience may prove too stressful for the cat.

Cats and children— playing together

Teach the child how to play with the cat without being hurt by it. Some cats, for instance, are

Teach your children to respect cats

Children and the choice of breed

Not all cats have the disposition necessary for family life. For nervous, shy, and unstable cats, it can be far too hectic. If you have children and would like to have a cat, choose by preference a well-balanced, self-confident animal. Such a cat will enjoy interacting with the children and not be concerned when the house becomes a little noisy. If you go to inspect a litter, choose an animal that walks up to you openly and freely and is playful and inquisitive. Do not take any kitten that is nervous, hisses at you or the children, or has to be "caught"; such kittens rarely adapt

If the cat is asleep, it should be left in peace

so absorbed by their game that they forget that children's hands and faces are also involved. Let them play together with, for example, scrunched-up balls of paper—every cat loves it when these are "launched" for it. The toys known as "cat teasers," sticks with a bunch of feathers or a small rattling ball at one end, are relatively safe provided the child knows what to do with them. Also, of course, you can regularly trim the sharp points of your cat's claws so that it will not do too much harm if it plays too wildly.

This Oriental Longhair kitten takes playing with a "cat teaser" very seriously indeed

Exotic, golden tabby

to households with children. If you choose a pedigree cat, do not forget that character is not only breed-linked but sometimes also family-linked. Some bloodlines of predominantly well-balanced breeds can be rather less stable, and vice versa. It is therefore advisable to visit several different breeders to look at the characters of the parents and prospective parents, and not just decide on the first kitten you are offered. You may also consider getting a stable older cat, which is used to children. Local cat shelters can give you objective advice on this. You can also turn to the various cat associations that are sometimes seeking new homes for adult cats.

There is very little risk of a well-cared-for cat infecting a child with a zoonosis

Zoonoses

Zoonoses are diseases that can be passed from animals to people. Among cats, too, several zoonoses are known. It can unfortunately sometimes happen that a cat is disposed of when a woman is expecting a baby. Some women think the risk of a toxoplasmosis infection too great. This is a pity, since it has recently been discovered that, if the cat's litter tray is cleaned out every day and the expectant mother wears gloves to do this, the risk of infection is virtually nil. There is a much greater risk of infection from eating meat that has not been cooked through, such as rare sirloin or *filet americain*, or from working in the garden without wearing gloves. If a

A litter of Bengals

woman is pregnant and has a cat, then it is sensible during the waiting time to teach the cat that the baby's room is "out of bounds." It is not

You have to teach a kitten what is and what is not allowed in the house

that cats deliberately suffocate babies, but a baby's cot is naturally very attractive and soft, and the baby very small and delicate. The cat can certainly sleep with the child when it is big enough to push it away should that be necessary. Usually children reach that stage when they are about two years old. There are a few other things you also ought to consider if you have cats and children. Ringworm, for instance, can also be passed on to humans. Avoid your cat having trouble with this as much as possible by preventing contact with potentially infectious ani-

mals and always be on the lookout for symptoms, which in people include red, round patches on the skin. It is also necessary to have your cat or cats wormed very regularly. Do not forget that the positive aspects of living with cats far outweigh the extremely small risk of a healthy and well-cared-for cat infecting your child with worms or ringworm.

Upbringing

A great deal of a kitten's upbringing comes from its mother and its litter mates. In the litter, the kitten learns how it should behave towards other cats. It learns, for instance, not to play too hard. As soon as a kitten arrives in your home, you will have to impart your house rules. What these rules are varies from house to house; some people do not like the cat to get on the table, on the kitchen worktop, or into the beds, while others think that it perfectly acceptable. Try to draw a consistent line with the other people in the house, because flexible rules are confusing.

Young cats are mischievous

"No!"

thing it should not, treat it to a jet of water. This need not be directed at the cat itself, but can go near it, depending on how steely the cat's nerves are. Take care that the cat should not associate the jet of water with you, but with the place where it is or what it is doing. If you do this consistently, the kitten will learn that sitting on the worktop results in a jet of water—and will stop doing it. For cats that are not impressed by the water (and there are plenty!) there is still the possibility of shooting paper pellets or making a loud, irritating noise, such as the noise of a football rattle. With a little ingenuity, there are plenty of devices you can find in toyshops to can use for this. Of course, you must offer the kitten or adult cat plenty of opportunities to play and indulge itself in devices specially made or acquired for it.

"No!"

You should punish your cat as little as possible, and punishments should always be well thought out. Obviously, you will feel inclined to shout at a kitten that gets on your worktop when it is forbidden, to say that it should not, and, if it still does not listen, to be angry with it. All a kitten learns from that is that it should not get on the worktop if you can see it. It will go on doing so when you are not there. If you get angry with the kitten and give it a slap, then there is a great risk that the kitten will not trust you any more and will avoid you or be afraid of you. You can prevent this by "punishing" without making the kitten associate the punishment with you. This will take time and demands understanding. Many cats do not like water, and a sudden jet of water shocks them and makes them stop what they are doing. So get yourself a plant spray (or a water pistol) with which you can produce a fine, thin spray of at least three or four meters. Each time your kitten or adult cat does some-

"Yes?"

Accommodation

The dangers of an outdoor life

Until a few decades ago, cats by definition ran loose outdoors, except for expensive pedigree cats whose owners were afraid that the animals might get lost or be stolen. Cats were, after all, valued mainly for their capacity as mouse catchers; their function as a companion was less common. Today, it is the other way around: in the first instance, the cat's function is that of a companion, and we usually feel more responsible in our dealings with them than our parents or grandparents did. It is not only the function of the cat and the average cat lover's view of cats that has changed in the course of time, however. Society as a whole has been subject to change. There are now more people living per square mile than before. Perhaps this increased population density is partly to blame, but tolerance of each other and of each other's pets has diminished. Many people are annoyed by cats ranging free because, for instance, they are a threat to birds in aviaries, scratch or leave dirty footmarks on car enamel, or because they do their business in someone else's garden. Many quarrels between neighbors are the result of pets, including cats, and people's intolerance of them. Social pressure can therefore be so great for some people that they decide not to let their cat run

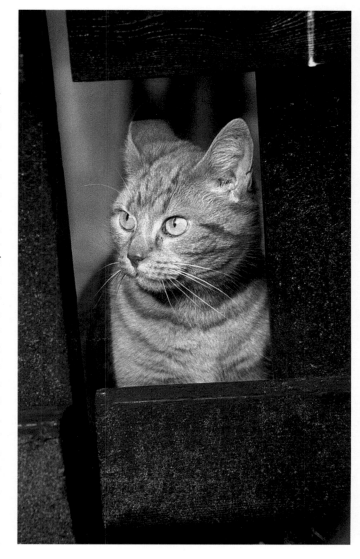

free outside any more. For most people, however, it is not actually social pressure that is the deciding factor in keeping their cat indoors, but the dangers a free-ranging cat can encounter in its path.

Traffic
Traffic has become heavier and more hectic and is probably the number one cause of death among cats. In practice, cats that do not yet have much experience of life and those that are ruled by their hormones seem to be particularly prone to accidents.

In spring young toms are often the victims of traffic accidents

Poisoning and ill treatment
There have always been cat haters, and any free-ranging cat can on a bad day be "cleared out of the way" or ill-treated by such a person. When a cat is poisoned, this need not, of course, always indicate the presence of a cat hater in the neighborhood. It can also happen that cats eat the corpses of mice that in their turn have been poisoned, or ingest poisonous plants. Among cats that live in agricultural areas, symptoms of poi-

Eating a poisoned mouse will poison the cat

soning can occur when pesticides have been sprayed. Even at home the use of some cleaning materials or paints can cause problems, as well as poisonous houseplants, such as Dieffenbachia and Poinsettia.

This farm cat lost an eye in a fight with a rat

Cats can get lost, too

Dogs

Fortunately, the risk of a cat being injured or killed by a dog is steadily diminishing, because most people nowadays keep their dogs on a leash. During its wanderings, however, your cat may well venture into a garden with a dog that is not cat-friendly. Rats, particularly large ones, can also be dangerous.

Getting shut in

It frequently happens that cats accidentally get shut up in a shed or garage, without anyone noticing. With a bit of luck the owner of the shed or garage will come back the same day, giving the animal the opportunity to escape, but it

Sometimes a cat decides to go and live with someone else

does sometimes happen that cats remain shut in for a considerable time.

Getting lost

Under normal circumstances, cats are extremely good at finding their way back home to their own territory. Sometimes, however, there are circumstances to prevent that. A cat can be extremely shocked by fireworks or, through some other cause, become distanced from its own territory. Cats that know the neighborhood well and spend a lot of time outside will find their way home better than cats that seldom or never go out, or cats that normally are only allowed in their own garden.

Feline distemper is one of the illnesses a cat may
pick up outdoors

Diseases

Some life-threatening cat diseases are spread by fighting or mating. It is not for nothing that many cat breeders have their pedigree cats tested for certain infectious diseases before they breed from them. A number of cat associations even make tests for these diseases (FeLV and FIV) compulsory. In addition, there are equally serious diseases that a free-running cat can pick up more easily than one that only lives in its own house and garden, such as feline distemper (FEI). Coming in contact with one of these feared diseases is certainly not just a theoretical risk. Every vet, both in country and town, can give you instances of them.

A change of address

A cat with an unusual appearance has an irresistible attraction for some people. This attraction is sometimes so great that they will take a cat away—"it has no collar, so it has no owner." It can also happen, however, that a cat feels more at home somewhere else than it does with you and simply decides to live with somebody else.

Most cats love going outside

The advantages of your cat running free out-of-doors

Obviously, there are advantages in letting a cat run free. It means less work at home and you will usually have to clean out its litter tray less frequently. Some of the behavioral problems that occur with "indoor cats," such as unhygienic habits or aggression, can be resolved when the cat is allowed to roam free. With some cats, the restricted space of a house, which may also have to be shared with other cats, can be a reason for them to feel unhappy. Of course, most cats think it is wonderful to go outside and enjoy all the new impressions there. If you do decide you want to give your cat free access to the "wicked world outside," however, first ensure that it is neutered and chipped or tattooed. Neutered cats are less inclined to stray and are also much less liable to get involved in fights where they might pick up infections. Moreover, the owner of a chipped or tattooed cat can always be traced by virtue of its registration number. This need only be a consideration, however, if you have a lot of space around the house and there is no heavy traffic nearby. So look at the conditions in your neighborhood before you decide whether you can responsibly let your cat go out, or whether you should restrict its movements.

A cat run

If you do not want to run these risks with your cat, then a cat run offers an ideal opportunity for it to get a breath of fresh air. Join the run up to a window or door, perhaps the back door, then the cat can go out without a problem when it feels like it. You can screen off a balcony with netting so that it can enjoy being outside without the risk of falling. Such arrangements are not cheap, but anyone good at DIY can, with a little creativity and not too big a budget, go a long way. Some people screen off their gardens in such a way that it becomes very difficult for the cat to escape their boundaries. A little electric wire along the top of the hedge, or a high fence bent back at the top, is enough to dis-

A compact cat run

This "Sacred" Birman is perfectly happy in its outside run

A completely covered and fenced-in garden

An electric fence does not keep all cats "within bounds"

courage most cats. A cat flap in the door lets the cat go in and out when it feels like it.

Staying indoors

Most cats can be quite happy if they are kept indoors. This is particularly true for those that are by nature peaceful. If your home is not very large and you cannot offer your cat any access to the outside world, it would be sensible for you to choose a quiet one or to make sure that you have a good scratching and climbing post for it at home and enough toys for the cat not to get bored and into mischief. For the majority of cats it is clear that, once they have become accustomed to an indoor life as a kitten, they no longer hanker after a free existence, but obviously this does not apply to all cats. Because a house still has to be aired, and open doors and windows give excellent opportunities for escaping, it is a good idea to fix good strong screens across the windows. The soft kinds of insect screens are not always cat-proof, so only get the tougher varieties. If your windows are "tip-up" ones that open inwards at the top, beware. The opening at the side gets narrower towards the bottom. It has occasionally happened that a cat

A balcony, too, can be made "cat-proof" with a few simple measures

has tried to get out of such a window, but got stuck between the window and the frame—the animal drops by its own weight to where there is even less room. Many cats have lost their lives in this way.

Moving an adult cat to a new home

Most cats get upset if they have to go and live in a new home. If you are moving house, make sure that this event causes as little extra stress as possible to your cat. It is a good idea to put the cat in a separate room in the old house, with the door closed or locked. Only when you have completely moved into your new home and everything has been unpacked and put in its place, can you take the cat to the new home and let it explore everything there. In practice, it is most convenient only to let it loose in the new house when anyone else who may have been helping you move has gone home, and no more drilling or joinery is going on; it is also sensible to wait until any possible paint smells have gone, because these can be harmful to your cat and cause bare patches in its coat, and other problems. As soon as you let the cat out in the new house, make sure that all the doors and windows are shut. It can be so stressed by the new impressions that it escapes and tries to find its way back to the old house—that is, after all, where its old familiar territory is, with the scents it has put there itself (by muzzling up against things, scratching, and urinating).

Going out for the first time

It is hard to say when it is safe to let a cat go out for the first time after moving to a different house. Normally speaking, a period of at

Many cats are perfectly happy indoors

55

If your kitten has been kept indoors from a young age, it will not yearn for the great outdoors later in life

Maine Coon

running away, and trying to find its way back to its old house.

least three weeks is advised and, for rather nervous cats, an even longer period of familiarization is highly recommended. There is a reason for this. If you are in the habit of letting your cat out, it will now have to claim its place in its new environment. Each of the neighboring cats will have its own territory, and it is very probable that your garden will be part of the territory of one of the local cats. So your cat, which has just moved to a new home, will have a tough time on its first outing: it must put its markings over those of the established order in the new neighborhood, and this can cause tension for the cat. Once the cat feels completely settled in, it will be able to win its place outside more easily than if it is not sure of its position at home. When a cat does not feel comfortable, there is considerably more risk of it

A cat that has just moved house has a busy time marking out its new territory

Essential requirements

A litter tray with a raised edge

small filter in the hood helps to control some of the unpleasant smell. When you buy a litter tray, make sure that it is easy to use: ideally the hood should be easily removable and the tray deep enough for a good quantity of litter, so that excrement and urine is slower to reach the bottom where it can corrode the plastic. Also consider the overall size—a cat litter tray can never be too large.

Litter tray

A litter tray is something you cannot do without. These items are available in various forms, sizes and models, from very cheap open trays to larger trays with a hood and odor filter. Trays without a hood are usually not so convenient and are actually only suitable for kittens. A cat, after all, buries its urine and feces and, when it tries to cover it, some of the litter may easily spill out of the tray. There are also cats that sit in the tray itself, but regularly deposit their excrement over the edge of it—a hood will prevent this. A

Oriental Longhair

For kittens a small, low litter tray is ideal

Japanese Bobtail

Cat litter

There are many different kinds of cat litter, varying from clump-forming kinds to ecologically sound litters made of wood, corn waste, or paper. Consequently you will find that there are great differences in price. For cat litter, the maxim "buying cheap is costly" almost always applies. More expensive cat litters usually scatter fewer bits around, absorb liquid more efficiently, and are better at preventing unpleasant smells. Often more expensive litter lasts much longer and that prevents unnecessary lugging of heavy sacks—and waste—around. The most economical litters are the clump-forming ones. These are available in both fine and coarse grains. Clump-forming litters are so called because the cat's urine turns into solid clumps in the tray. Hence, the grains around them stay clean and dry, the litter does not have to be changed so often, and the smell is limited. Provided there is a good layer of litter in the tray, the

urine does not sink to the bottom, but can simply be scooped out of the tray with a strong, coarse-meshed cat-litter scoop. The remainder of the litter in the tray stays clean. This only works well when the tray is really checked every

Ocicat, chocolate

day. With other kinds of litter, which are also made of clay or brick, the urine sinks to the bottom and is often only partly absorbed by the porous surface of the grit. These kinds are the cheapest to buy, but you will need more of them, so that they work out more expensive in practice. Litters based on wood, corn, or paper are not harmful to the environment and can be used as compost in the garden, but these, too, are not always so economic and do not always absorb smells and liquid well. If you have a large garden, however, you can make good use of the biologically degradable type of litter as fertilizer. It is then sensible not to put too thick a layer in the litter tray and to fill the tray up again every day. The latest generation of litters consists of little balls that absorb urine and odors. You do not have to clean the tray often and the smell is usually kept under control. Which cat litter you choose depends partly on what the cat was used to at the breeders and partly on your personal preference. It is in any case advisable to start with the kind and the brand of litter the breeder used. If you find this litter inconvenient, you can always change it later. Most people find the clump-forming litters, consisting of fine grains, the most convenient and most economical to use.

Food and drink bowls

There are so many different kinds of food and drink bowls that the choice depends mainly on your own taste and budget. The better bowls are of porcelain, glazed earthenware, or stainless steel. These are more easily cleaned than, for instance, plastic ones and they are also more hygienic in use. This is important because, for instance, it is known that plastic bowls can sometimes cause or aggravate acne on cats' chins. If a cat has acne on its chin, it

Stainless steel food and drinking bowls with a base

Food and drinking bowls with integrated base

Some cats play wild games with a toy mouse

If you have more than one cat a food silo is a hygienic solution

Play is an essential part of life, certainly for kittens

Sometimes an extra scratching post is an essential
piece of equipment

looks as if it has grains of soil in it; unglazed earthenware bowls also sometimes hold dirt and can be a source of bacteria. The other disadvantage of earthenware bowls, glazed or not, is that they are easily broken. So in practice stainless steel bowls are the best choice. They last a long time, cannot break, are very easy to clean—they can even be boiled—and are relatively cheap. You may also need some kind of stand to prevent the bowl from sliding on the floor when the cat eats from it.

Toys

Toys are a must for every cat. Every cat is different, however: one will find soft mice made of rabbit's fur terrific fun, another will love to chase after a ball, and yet another will prefer dangling toys. If you want to splash out, you can go ahead and get several kinds, and let the cat decide which it likes best. Do make sure, however, that the toys are safe. Screwed up balls of paper are very good, but balls made of aluminum foil can produce problems if the cat swallows bits of them. Nor is every toy from a pet shop guaranteed safe. So keep an eye on how the cat is get-

Climbing and scratching posts are often in constant use

ting on with its toy and whether that toy can in fact stand up to the way your cat plays with it.

Scratching post

Cats like to scratch and will not stop doing so. They do this for a variety of reasons. For instance, by scratching they can remove the old layer of horn from their claws. Every cat owner has come across flakes from the outer layer of hard cuticle on their cat's claws. They also scratch to mark their territory or to impress other cats. Scratching is often instinctive, so that you cannot teach a cat not to do it; it is integral to its nature. To prevent the cat exercising its instinct on the furniture, it is important to ensure that it has sufficient places where it can scratch, and that it uses these from the start. Cats are, after all, creatures of habit and, once a

particular spot has become a favorite scratching place, it is no use trying to make them think differently. If from the start they have a sturdy scratching post or plank, then most of them will give that preference and will not attack your sofa or doorposts. If you hold the front paws of your kitten and make scratching movements with them at the scratching device you have acquired, then it will usually realize the intention. A frequently heard complaint is that the cat takes no notice of its scratching post. The reason is usually that the post is too small and not steady enough. Scratching posts must be high enough for the cat to scratch with its forefeet when it is standing at full stretch on its back legs. If it cannot do that, the post is too short. Also, it is important that the scratching post should be as sturdy as possible. A scratching post that always gives way when the cat scratches it, or even falls over, is not suitable. The cheap scratching posts with only one seat on them are usually only suitable for kittens. They should be replaced after a few months with a larger one. It is usually advisable to start by buying a larger, sturdier scratching post, even if it is more expensive. Certainly for cats that never go out-of-doors, such a scratching post is an excellent investment. If a cat has a good scratching post and does not use it, it may help to sprinkle special bait on it. Suitable baits can be purchased at cat shows and pet shops.

A climbing post can never be too large

Scratching is an instinctive need

Other scratching places

A scratching post has other functions than just to be scratched. Cats also love climbing and playing on them. They usually place a high value on their scratching post. If there is no budget, however, for a comprehensive "cat's playground," which would generally cost as much or more than the average pedigree kitten, then there are other, cheaper solutions for keeping the urge to scratch under control. Scratching boards are a good alternative. There are cheap, throwaway scratching boards of cardboard, but also more durable boards with a scratching surface of sisal or some other tough material. You can fasten these boards against the wall in various places about the house. Coconut matting is also highly appreciated by most cats and is very

suitable as a scratching place. You can fasten it to a wall, or simply leave it lying on the floor.

Combs and brushes

A cat's standard equipment should include a brush suitable for the structure and length of its coat. If you have a pedigree cat, ask the breeder which kind of comb or brush he or she uses. The breeder will probably have tried a variety of brushes and should be able to tell you which kind is most suitable. You will notice that grooming the coat of your cat takes up much less time and is far more efficient if you work with tools suitable for that specific type of coat. For longhaired cats that will often be an ordinary brush as used by people, with metal bristles covered with a layer of plastic. A flea comb is actually only necessary if you have a shorthaired cat, because the teeth are so close to each other that a longhaired coat would only be damaged by it. For shorthaired cats, it is useful to have a small, rubber brush in the house. At molting times, the dead undercoat can be very simply and effectively removed with such a brush.

Nail clippers

You need the right tools to do a job properly, and that is certainly true of clipping a cat's claws. Sometimes scissors or nail clippers designed for humans are used for this, but they are not suitable. They are rarely sharp and strong enough, so that more force is necessary to finish the job properly and pressure is often put on the quick, which can be painful. What you need is a pair

A useful brush for (semi) longhaired cats

A flea comb is only useful for shorthaired cats

of very sharp nail clippers made specifically for animals. "Guillotine clippers" in particular are strong, extra sharp, and very accurate. You can get them from pet shops. Try the clippers out in the pet shop and choose ones that do not stick or are not too stiff.

Anti-flea preparations

As soon as you have a hairy pet in the house, there is a good chance that fleas will also find their way there. So anti-flea preparations should be a standard part of the cat's equipment. The pros and cons of various anti-flea preparations are set out in the chapter on Parasites.

Nail scissors

Travel carrier

Anyone who has a cat needs a travel carrier. Carrying a cat about loose is quite impossible and, moreover, unsafe. There are various kinds of travel carriers for cats. The best are plastic carriers that are easy to clean—some cats defecate and urinate in their carriers from shock. When you buy a travel carrier, check all its fastenings and make sure that these are strong enough to withstand rough handling. The same applies to the door. Wickerwork baskets are still sometimes offered and bought, particularly because they look nice, but the doors hardly ever shut properly and their fastenings are often poor. Moreover, wicker travel baskets are difficult to clean. It speaks for itself that the travel carrier you buy should be properly ventilated, but at the same time not too open—the cat must feel safe in it. Open wire cages are therefore less suitable as travel carriers for a cat. The most convenient carriers are plastic ones with the door on the top. This makes it easier to take the sometimes frightened or resistant cat in and out of the carrier when you take it to the vet. When you choose one, you should also bear in mind that your cat may still grow, and it is obvious that you will need a bigger carrier for a cat the size of a British Shorthair or Maine Coon than for an Oriental Shorthair or Burmese.

Harness

For cats that have a very strong objection to traveling in a carrier, a harness may be a possible option (see also Chapter 8: Care). Some-

A carrier that will open on top

For large breeds such as the Maine Coon standard-size carriers are too small

If you do buy one, make sure that the harness fits the body well. It is sometimes necessary to go back to the pet shop a few times before you find the right model and size. It is useful to warn the pet shop of this in advance and make sure that there will be no problem in changing them. In the course of time you will probably have to get more harnesses. Older, fully-grown cats are quite capable of learning things, but it is best to start accustoming them to a harness as early as possible. Young cats and kittens that are still growing are better able to adapt in this way than older, adult cats. A harness suitable for a kitten is rarely also suitable for a grown-up cat. You should never fasten a harness so loosely that the cat can wriggle free, but neither should it be too tight. If it is, the cat will, understandably, find the harness very objectionable, and that is not the intention.

times cats are taken camping, perhaps to a permanent campsite or on a boat, in situations from which they can run away and get into difficulties if they are not on a leash. It can also make sense to accustom a kitten to a harness and leash.

The need for identification

It is obviously sensible to provide your cat with something to identify it. If it runs away or gets lost, you can be traced as its owner by the iden-

A harness can be very useful

painful and often the ink used fades, so that after a few years the code is no longer easy to read. For that reason, people are increasingly having their animals chipped.

Chipping

The latest development for identifying a cat is inserting a microchip subcutaneously. This is a metal chip about the size of a grain of rice, which is inserted under the skin by a vet, using a hollow needle. The chip has a unique code, which is registered in various databanks. Using a registration form you fill in at the vet, the cat's code is linked to your data. All vets, animal ambu-

A collar with an address canister

tification it carries. There are various ways of doing this and all of them have their advantages and disadvantages. The most popular method, but sometimes also the most inconvenient, is a small metal canister on the collar. The canister will usually contain a sheet of paper on which the owners can write their name and address. In practice, these canisters do not always close very well and the note with the details can fall out of them. A medallion with your address engraved on it is therefore a better choice. You can order these in most pet shops. Both solutions do, however, have the disadvantage that the cat must wear a collar for them and, if the collar gets caught in something and breaks—as all good cat collars should—your cat will lose its identification. In some countries, cats are tattooed. Thanks to a unique code in its ears, animal rescue organizations can then find out where the cat belongs. These tattoos can however be

A microchip cannot be seen or felt, and a cat is not hindered by it

lances, and animal shelters have readers that can read the code. The corresponding owner's data can be requested from a central databank, so that you can be informed that your cat has been found. The microchip has many advantages: your cat does not have to wear a collar, it does not have to suffer a painful tattoo, and it is impossible for its own unique code to get lost or become unreadable because it is safely stored under the skin. There are obviously also arguments against the chip: for example, it has to be inserted by a vet, and of course this costs money.

Many cats prefer a warm surface to lie on

For air transport a special carrier such as this one is used

Another disadvantage is that, in a very small percentage of cats, it has been found that the microchip does not remain between the shoulder blades, but "drifts." This, however, only happens occasionally. A third disadvantage is that the cat carries no externally visible identification and people unfamiliar with the microchip, or who know nothing about it, may think your cat is a stray and take it home. Yet chipping animals is increasingly gaining ground and is, for instance, now common practice for thoroughbred horses and pedigree dogs. The disadvantages are far outweighed by the great advantages of this form of identification.

BASIC REQUIREMENTS

- FOOD AND DRINK BOWLS
- LITTER TRAY
- LITTER
- LITTER TRAY SCOOP
- CAT FOOD
- CLIMBING POST OR SCRATCHING BOARD
- ANTI-FLEA PREPARATIONS
- GOOD NAIL CLIPPERS
- BRUSH AND COMB
- TOYS
- GRASS
- TRAVEL CARRIER AND/OR HARNESS

A doormat is good for scratching

Care 8

The importance of care for the coat

With the exception of a number of virtually hairless or sparsely coated breeds, all cats have a coat. They will instinctively look after it themselves. With cats that do not molt too much and have a smooth, short coat, this is often no problem. It is different when the cat has a rather thicker coat, a longhaired coat, or molts heavily. Then it is up to the owner to help it look after its coat, for the following reasons:

A cat can swallow a great deal of hair while grooming

An extremely longhaired coat needs thorough and skillful maintenance

Fur balls

Cats have tiny, barbed hooks on their tongues, facing backwards. These cause all the hairs that end up in its mouth while grooming itself to be swallowed. If too much hair is swallowed, it forms a fur ball (or hairball) in the stomach, which in extreme cases may have to be removed surgically. A cat that can roam free outside will now and then eat some fresh blades of grass that act as a natural emetic, so that the hair is removed from the body by vomiting. If your cat cannot run free outside, it would be sensible to grow some of your own grass. In the absence of grass, your cat may well start nibbling at your

If there is no grass available, the cat will start eating plants

will come to light much earlier. It might not be immediately noticeable to a casual observer if a cat has a tick on its skin, but its owner is bound to come across it during a brushing session. Flea infections will also be noticed more quickly, and the same goes for any damage to the skin, bare patches, or abscesses.

Felting and skin problems

For longhaired cats it is important to groom the coat regularly. Particularly in cats with a soft coat structure, such as Persians, the first tangles can appear within a matter of days, if the owner does not regularly groom the coat. Long-term neglect will result in the coat forming felted patches on the skin, which in their turn will cause all kinds of problems, such as skin irritations and rashes, and you may even get bare patches, or painful abscesses.

houseplants and, apart from the fact that you will probably not approve of that, many house-plants are poisonous to cats. To spare your cat's stomach, you should also brush and comb the cat rather more frequently when it is heavily molting. Scientists claim that cats not only eat grass as an emetic, but probably, too, because it contains the folic acid that they require every now and then. Some cats are troubled with fur balls more than others. If a good brushing does not help, it is worth knowing that there are also special cat foods called fur-ball pastes, which ensure that the fur balls are excreted through the intestines and so do not have to be spewed out.

A female Turkish Angora with a felted coat

Parasites or medical problems

If an owner combs or brushes his or her cat regularly, then any problems

Burmilla kitten

Strengthening mutual bonds

Cats that get on well with each other wash each other. We can emulate that by stroking the animal, but many cats regard grooming in the same way and like to be brushed or combed—even if it is only for the attention and the

Grooming a cat's coat reinforces the mutual bond

ual of brushing and combing and to make it as pleasant as possible for the animal. So begin very early and do not force it. Brush its coat now and then as it lies in your lap and give it something nice to eat afterwards. You can then gradually build up the brushing sessions, always stopping before the animal has had enough. Getting used to this from an early age is really important with cats such as Persians: if you have a cat with a badly tangled coat, and it really objects to being groomed, then sometimes there is no other solution than to have its coat shaved off or have the tangles and felted places removed under an anesthetic. Furthermore, because it does not change the animal's aversion to being groomed, this will be a regularly recurring chore.

Washing

People who show their cats will not only brush and comb them regularly, but also wash them frequently. Shows are, after all, beauty contests, and well cared for animals usually do better than cats that look as if they have just been plucked out of the garden. Most show cats are used to being washed and do not make a fuss about it. If possible, choose a shampoo that suits the color of the cat's coat. There are, for instance, shampoos that will make a cat look whiter, or a deeper black. Wash the cat at least three or four days before the show, so that the coat has time to

strengthening of the mutual bond between you and the cat.

Early learning lasts a lifetime

Certainly with longhaired cats it is advisable to accustom a kitten at a very young age to the rit-

If a Persian is not groomed, its coat may start felting badly within a week

Shorthaired cats such as these need hardly any grooming

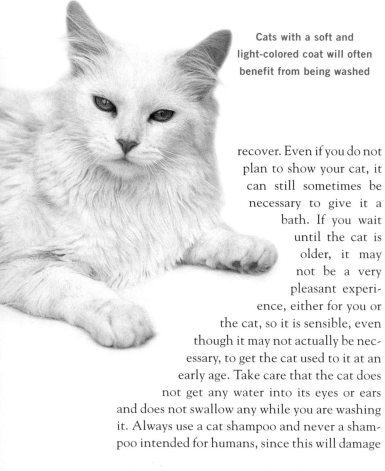

Cats with a soft and light-colored coat will often benefit from being washed

the structure of the coat and the fatty layer of the skin. You can dry your cat with a hairdryer, but if it reacts nervously to this you can rub it dry with a coarse hand towel and put it in a warm and draft proof place to finish drying off.

Washing with dry shampoo

Some cats persistently offer strong resistance to being washed. In such cases, their coats can also be cleaned with a fat-free, unscented powder that attracts dirt and excess oil. This powder, better known as dry shampoo for cats, can be obtained from larger pet shops and at all cat shows. Sprinkle the powder into the coat against the direction of the hair growth and massage it well in before brushing it out until not a trace of powder can be seen in the coat. Talcum powder is not suitable, as it contains elements that can cause irritation.

recover. Even if you do not plan to show your cat, it can still sometimes be necessary to give it a bath. If you wait until the cat is older, it may not be a very pleasant experience, either for you or the cat, so it is sensible, even though it may not actually be necessary, to get the cat used to it at an early age. Take care that the cat does not get any water into its eyes or ears and does not swallow any while you are washing it. Always use a cat shampoo and never a shampoo intended for humans, since this will damage

Cats largely look after their nails themselves

British Shorthair, blue-silver classic

Care of the claws

From a medical point of view, cats' claws need never be trimmed. Sometimes, however, it is better to do so if, for instance, you have a cat that likes to climb into your lap and then makes kneading movements with its razor-sharp claws. Very sharply pointed claws also make deeper scratches in the furniture. Cats that are shown

Scottish Fold kitten

are required to have had their claws trimmed recently and the same goes for a queen in season that is taken to a stud. Never trim more than one or two millimeters off the claw, but only just the tip. You will then be well away from the quick. Cats' claws grow back quickly, so that trimming them is a regularly recurring job. For that reason, it is important to get the cat used to its claws being trimmed as early as possible. If a cat is used to it from a young age, and it is done properly and quickly, it will rarely cause problems when it is an adult.

Claw removal?

The scratching behavior displayed by cats is instinctive—you cannot stop this. Make certain, therefore, that your cat has its own scratching post, or perhaps a sisal or coconut doormat. Some people are so irritated by their cat's scratching that they take them to a vet to have the claws removed surgically although, in most countries, the removal of a cat's claws is illegal. After all, its claws are an essential part of a cat. Cats without claws are simply handicapped. The saddest consequence of removing them is that, in spite of this intervention, they instinctively go on scratching in order to sharpen their non-existent claws. Because they no longer have any claws, many of these cats will scrape the soles of their feet until they bleed.

Cornish Rex kitten

Care of the ears

Most cats will have little trouble with ear problems throughout their lives, without their owner

American Curl kitten

Care of the eyes

A cat's eyes rarely need any care. A little dirt in the corner of the eyes can be carefully removed with a damp Kleenex. Always wipe towards the nose. Cats with a flat face, such as Persians, Exotics, and related breeds, often need more attention to their eyes. These cats sometimes get weeping eyes, which can lead to ugly, dark tear lines in the creases of their face. Try as much as possible to prevent the dark discoloration of their facial creases, as in most cases neglected tear stripes will remain visible. Daily care of the eyes and facial creases prevents this. You can clean them with a Kleenex damped with boiled water or a special cat's eye lotion, obtainable from larger pet shops and at all cat shows.

Care of the teeth

Persians and Exotics can sometimes suffer from weeping eyes

ever having to clean out their ears. Cleaning the ears or, rather, the auditory canal is rarely necessary. Too much cleaning can also cause problems, so only clean out the auditory canal if the ear is dirty. Do not use Q-Tips for this—they will just push the dirt further into the auditory canal, with possible inflammation deeper in the canal as a result. It is better to drip some special eardrops for cats into the auditory canal and massage them in. The dirt will then soak off and come out, and you can simply wipe it away with a Kleenex. Of course, you can also use Q-Tips for this, as long as they do not go right into the auditory canal. If your cat is troubled with an evil-smelling, dark, grainy discharge from the auditory canal, this indicates infection by ear mites. Your best course is to contact a vet, because ordinary eardrops will not kill these mites.

Teeth need to be checked regularly. Cats change their kitten teeth for their permanent adult teeth between the fourth and sixth month of their life. It is a good habit to check on this process from time to time. Sometimes a first tooth is left in place and the new tooth coming through below it grows crooked. If you have any doubts, always

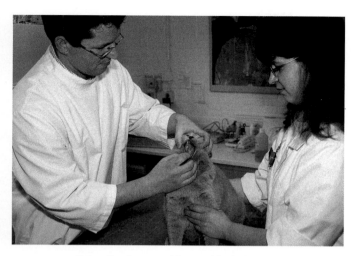

Cats often have problems with their teeth

out; certainly in summer, perishable food becomes a breeding ground for bacteria, which can soon make your cat ill. Moreover, never put food, perishable or not, in the full sun.
- Wash food bowls every day, particularly if you have given canned food or meat. Bowls in which dry food has been put can be washed up twice a week.
- Make sure that fresh air can get into the house. Air the house every day for at least an hour.

A hygienic environment prevents diseases and other problems

go to the vet. Tartar, which is visible as a dark-colored deposit on the teeth, can lead to decay and ultimately to teeth falling out. So try to prevent tartar by regularly giving your cat hard (larger) chunks or other food on which it has to use its teeth, such as a good piece of beef heart, or a day-old chick. Never give a cat bones; apart from the risk of splintering, they may get stuck in its jaw. If your cat has tartar, it is best to have this removed by a vet (see also: Diseases and disorders of the skeleton and teeth).

Hygiene

Hygiene is very important. The absence of a hygienic, well-ventilated living environment can result in problems.
- The litter tray should be attended to daily, and at least once a week—depending on how much it has been used—emptied, disinfected, and filled with fresh cat litter. In summer, it does no harm to clean it more frequently.
- Fresh drinking water should be provided every day. Rinse drinking bowls out well and wash them at least once a week. In summer, put the drinking bowl in the shade.
- Perishable food, such as canned food, meat, or fish, should be removed one hour after it is put

- Do not neglect normal hygiene: wash cloths and similar items once a week and vacuum daily.

Black classic and white longhaired non-pedigree cat

This Norwegian Forest Cat is embarking on a boat trip

Hairless cats need to be washed at least once a month

Transport

Every cat has to be moved at some time in its life. Many cats object to this. In spite of that, there are many cats that accompany their families on a boat, to campsites, or to a cat show, without any trace of stress. An objection to traveling and to a strange, unknown environment is therefore certainly not a universal character trait of cats. How the cat reacts to being moved can depend on the innate character of the cat itself. Human-oriented, self-confident, and inquisitive kittens and cats are much more receptive of new impressions than kittens and cats that do not have these characteristics. The latter are often stressed by travel and new impressions, while the former may even enjoy it. Some cats can only be put into a travel carrier by force, and then cry pitifully all the way, or are even so upset that they urinate or get diarrhea (which is why the travel carrier has to be easy to clean). If a cat has an objection to travel, it need not be blamed on its character, but there is always the possibility that the animal associates the travel carrier itself with something upsetting (e.g., a visit to the vet or car journey). So if you have a kitten, it is a good idea to make the travel carrier part of its daily life. Simply put the carrier down in the living room, kitchen, or utility room—wherever the cat spends much of its time. From time to time, you can put a toy or a treat in the carrier. You will see that your cat occasionally lies down in it and does not regard it as something sinister, but as a familiar feature of its environment. If you then want to take your cat anywhere, it will feel much safer in its own, familiar travel carrier, than if you only produce it when the cat has to go to the vet or the boarding home for a holiday. Some people use special scents, such as valerian, which they sprinkle in the carrier to make the cat feel more at ease. This does not, however, work with all cats. You will just have to experiment.

A harness

Some cats object strongly to being shut up in a travel carrier. As soon as its door is closed, they try with all their might to get out of it and express their dissatisfaction very loudly. This is, of course, extremely stressful both for the cat and its owner. Taking the cat with you loose is not an option, however, because it could take

your best plan is to build up the training very slowly and try to distract your cat as much as possible. Start by putting the harness on only indoors, where the cat cannot escape. In the first week, do not leave it on for more than about five minutes at a time, and never more than twice a day, always distracting the animal by food, a cuddle, or its favorite toy. What method of distraction you use must depend on your cat's prefer-

A harness may be a solution if the cat
dislikes its carrier

Hardly any cat enjoys wearing a harness for
the first time

fright at any moment and try to run away, with inevitable consequences. These same cats often have no objection if you take them with you in a harness; they just do not like the idea of being shut up in a small space. If you want to teach your cat to come with you on a leash, you should always start by getting a harness without a collar. A cat struggling against a collar can very easily be injured if all its weight and pressure is concentrated on its neck. Of course, not every cat has the disposition necessary for a leash and harness.

ences—you know your cat best and know what it is most keen on. The distraction is necessary to prevent it becoming obsessive about the harness and developing negative associations with it. If you approach it correctly, after a week or

Getting used to a harness

Hardly any cat likes a harness the first time. It will very much want to get out of this "abomination." To prevent a battle, but above all any possible permanent aversion to the harness,

Avoid force—it is better to entice the cat to come along

two your kitten will be more or less used to wearing the harness and associate putting it on, not with something annoying, but with something nice. So do not make the mistake of trying to do it too quickly, as that will certainly have the opposite effect.

Learning to go for a walk in a harness

The introduction of a leash that restricts the cat in its freedom of movement should take place indoors too. You should also build up the use of the leash gradually and go on distracting the cat with something it likes. Never force it to go for a walk with you, which would provoke strong opposition. It is better to lure it on with kind words, a treat, or by stroking it, as long as it is necessary. When eventually your cat walks peacefully along with you, then you can gradu-

ally decrease the treat. As soon as it is used to it, you can expand the training sessions a little, which in this case means that you exercise with it successively for a longer period of time. If this also works, then you can take your cat outside with you for short walks, but do not forget to check first that the harness is a good fit. In the end, your cat will experience the harness and leash as something completely normal or even enjoyable, and you can then take it with you in this way without a problem. You should, however, only fit the harness during training sessions or later on, when you are really going to take the animal for a walk. If you cannot keep an eye on it, there is a risk that the harness may get caught up on something, with potentially harmful consequences.

Care of an older cat

Cats can reach an age of twelve to eighteen years. There are also even older cats: there have been, though this is admittedly rare, reports of cats in their late twenties or early thirties. When a cat dies, it is often attributed to its age, though in fact no animal actually dies of "old age;" the cause of death is always an ailment that cannot be cured by its aging body or by the veterinarian. Certainly among older cats a matted coat and loss of weight is often seen as a natural deterioration, which is to be expected with age. In reality, it is likely that the cat in question has an underlying medical problem about which something can be done. If you notice that your elderly cat is no longer comfortable, then it is sensible to ask the veterinarian to check its blood and urine. This should disclose whether some bodily functions are no longer working properly, which can often—though unfortunately not always—be helped by medication. It may be useful to give an elderly cat special food for older cats that makes less heavy demands on its digestive system.

Older cats need more care

Ailments in general

General

Cats often grow old without any particular problems. Their resistance and resilience is greater

If a cat looks ill, it really is ill

Aggression or bad behavior may be the result of a medical condition

than that of many other kinds of animals. In spite of this, they can suffer from a wide diversity of diseases and complaints, although owners often fail to spot the symptoms as cats are adept at concealing bodily discomfort. In general, you can assume that, if a cat looks ill, it really is ill. Whereas with other kinds of animals we might watch them for a few days before we consult a veterinarian, this is really not a responsible approach with a sick cat. In practice, it still often happens that the owner does not realize in time that there is something wrong with the animal. A cat that suddenly abandons its house-training, but otherwise looks healthy, need not be a cat with a territory problem: it might have a bladder infection or a kidney disorder. Bad behavior toward its owner or other animals in the house is sometimes nothing more than the expression of discomfort and pain; because the animal is in pain, it does not want to be touched, or at least not in the places where it hurts. Sometimes such an animal displays no other symptoms and the owners may overlook a possible illness. To spot a disease or problem is clearly very important although this can be difficult, as feline illnesses are not often overtly displayed or, if they are, by only slight modifications in the animal's behavior. It is therefore important to be familiar with the normal behavior of your cat. You will then be alert to any changes and can take your pet to the veterinarian for a checkup.

The right vet

The training to become a veterinarian is long and intensive, but it is not focused only on cats. A qualified vet has to know all about every kind of ailment, disease, or problem which can occur among almost all domesticated animals, including cattle, poultry, and rodents. From the symptoms you describe, or which he or she observes in the animal, a vet will have to consider which complaints and diseases can be ruled out. Then, by means of blood samples, x-rays, or in some other way, a diagnosis is reached, so that the animal can be treated. Here the vet can be com-

Thai kitten

Good vets are worth their weight in gold

pared to a family doctor, except that the family doctor only gets one species of animal in his consulting room: *homo sapiens*. Vets get all kinds of pets to treat, each with its specific biological and chemical makeup. In addition, vets also func-

tion as surgeons—they must be able to turn their hand to anything. It is quite obvious, therefore, that a vet really cannot know everything. These days it is becoming increasingly common for a vet to specialize in some direction, or to concentrate on one particular kind of animal. Clinics, too, which feature a range of specialties, are fortunately becoming more and more

Young red house cat

The chances of picking up a disease are greater
in a large group of cats

Prevention is better than cure

Many diseases and problems among cats are preventable to a certain extent. Animals are more susceptible to diseases if they suffer from stress (overcrowding, a noisy environment, moving house, too little attention), are badly fed (not enough variety, too few high-value nutrients), and if they have to live in unhygienic conditions. If you acquire a kitten or a full-grown cat, only do so from a reliable address where hygiene is observed and the animals enjoy good care and are properly fed. If you buy a pedigree cat, inform yourself first about the possible weaknesses that can occur in the breed and only do business with a breeder whose stock has been tested for such weaknesses.

common. If you take your cat to your local vet, you cannot really know whether he or she is familiar with all the latest research on feline disorders and keeps up to date with the professional journals, or has in fact more affinity with quite a different kind of animal, perhaps dogs. For the annual injection or routine operations, such as neutering, this obviously does not matter. The question of expertise only becomes significant if your cat develops a less usual complaint, so it does no harm to enquire among cat fanciers about the vets they have found the best. Breeders in particular have a great deal to do with veterinarians, because their animals have to be regularly tested for the presence of possible disorders. They also have to call in a vet rather more often than the average cat owner for the birth of a litter.

Plenty of room, fresh air, little stress, and good food are the
ingredients for a healthy life

Good hygiene at home is also important. The cat's litter tray in particular can be a source of infection or re-infection and must be kept properly clean. Moreover, avoid stress— solitary cats that get too little attention or cats that have to share their environment with too many other animals are subject to stress, which lowers their resistance. This does not mean that animals that become ill all lead a stressful life, are badly fed, or are not cared for, but only that the best environmental factors can help to maintain better resistance, with the consequent prevention of illness and problems.

THE DISEASES AND PROBLEMS DISCUSSED IN THIS ENCYCLOPEDIA DO NOT COVER ALL THE PROBLEMS THAT CAN OCCUR AMONG CATS. THEY ARE THE MOST COMMON PROBLEMS. IT IS THEREFORE SENSIBLE ALWAYS TO CONSULT A VETERINARIAN IF YOU HAVE ANY DOUBTS ABOUT THE HEALTH OF YOUR CAT.

Some common symptoms of illness are:
- Diarrhea (not in all cases)
- Great difficulty urinating and defecating
- Feces or urine of an unusual color
- Frequent urinating
- Third eyelid visible
- Discharge from nose or eyes, or vulva in females
- Rise in temperature (normal is 101.3° to 102.2° F)
- Sudden unsanitary behavior for no apparent reason
- Abnormal eating behavior (eating less or not at all, drinking more)
- Abnormal behavior (very quiet, withdrawn, or shy)
- Eruptions on the skin
- Sudden loss of hair or bald patches
- Patchy, tufted fur
- Dribbling
- Cat hardly ever grooms itself
- Loss of weight
- Poor condition generally
- Swollen stomach
- Difficulty with walking
- Signs of paralysis
- Frequent vomiting of food (not to be confused with fur balls)

Maine Coon, black tortie and white

Parasites and fungal infections

10

A cat may have fleas without your being aware of it

Fleas: has my cat got them?

Fleas are parasites that live on the blood of living creatures. There are many different kinds of flea, but virtually all fleas we find on cats (or dogs) are "cat fleas" (*Ctenocephalides felis*). For every flea living on the cat itself, there are ninety-five relations in its vicinity, whether in the egg, the larva, or chrysalis stage. So it is no use just treating the cat against fleas, as there are numerous sources of re-infection all around it. A cat can have fleas without you noticing—fleas can jump a long way and move extremely fast. Moreover, they are sensitive to light; as soon as you begin to search the coat they hurry off somewhere else. The simplest way to see whether your cat has fleas is from the latter's droppings. You will find these particularly on your cat's back, towards the tail, and they look like little black grains. Because these grains can also look confusingly like grains of sand or earth, remove some from your cat and put them on a damp piece of paper towel. If they are flea droppings, then you will see a reddish ring appear round them, as flea droppings are blood waste. If you actually see fleas on your cat, you must assume that it is offering board and lodging to a multitude of them.

Ocicat

Cats with fleas will try to rid themselves of their tormentors by scratching and biting

Fleas—harmless?

Almost every animal suffers from fleas sometimes, so it is certainly nothing to be ashamed of if your cat has them every so often. It is, however, harmful if you do nothing about it. In very young kittens a heavy flea infection can lead to anemia and even the death of the animal. Moreover, the flea acts as an intermediate host for the tapeworm. Cats often have trouble with fleas and will try by scratching and biting to get rid of their unwelcome guests. Too much scratching and licking can harm their skin and make the cat more vulnerable to other problems. So fleas must always be controlled—you cannot just let things drift.

Fleas—their life cycle

Female fleas lay eggs as soon as they have drunk blood. Without first drinking blood, they are unable to lay their eggs, which are extremely

small—mostly no larger than half a millimeter long—and white in color. They usually fall out of the cat's coat and land in the immediate surroundings. Depending on circumstances, the eggs hatch after one day or up to ten days after they are laid. It is not a flea that emerges, but a larva. The larva is also white and very small, usually only a few millimeters long. Because the larvae are so thin and shy of light, they often go unnoticed in floor coverings or cracks. Flea larvae eat mostly flea droppings, but also flakes of skin and suchlike. Eventually the larvae turn into chrysalises. When each one does so depends on circumstances, but on average it is between five and ten days after it has emerged from the egg. From the chrysalis stage the larva develops into a flea, which comes out of its cocoon as soon as it senses that the circumstances are favorable: a very damp atmosphere, warmth, and vibration. The latter in particular encourages the flea to emerge, because it can indicate the presence of a warm-blooded host. The cocoon offers the creature good protection for a long time: depending on circumstances,

Sphinx

Persian Longhair, blue tabby

whatever stage, are almost insensitive to cleaning materials, and the damp produced by mopping is simply a blessing for them. In addition, there must be enough food for the larvae, which live chiefly on flea droppings, skin flakes, and house dust. If you do not vacuum often, they will have more than enough food. Larvae are also shy of light—sunlight can dry them out. They instinctively seek out dark chinks and seams. You make it rather more difficult for the flea if you have a smooth floor, such as linoleum,

fleas can live for more than two years in their protective cocoon. After they have left the cocoon they jump on to a host as quickly as possible to drink blood; if they do not succeed, however, they can still survive without food for several days. Female fleas can lay their own eggs within two days of sucking blood. They are very productive at this; in their life, which lasts several months, female fleas can produce thousands of eggs. As long as they can go on drinking blood, they can go on producing eggs.

Fleas—the ideal living conditions

To understand why fleas can be particularly troublesome in summer, it is important to appreciate their ideal living conditions. Eggs, larvae, and chrysalises all flourish in a warm, damp, and preferably dark environment. Generally speaking, the warmer and damper it is, the faster they develop. A cold environment and, above all, dry conditions, can lead to slower development and even premature death, particularly of the larvae. The adult flea, however, can survive very well when the external temperature drops, so long as it is sitting warm and snug in the coat of its host and is able to drink blood. From this it is apparent that frequent mopping, particularly in summer, is a kindness to fleas. The creatures, at

American Curl, longhaired kitten

which you rarely mop but vacuum frequently, and if there is plenty of direct sunlight in the house.

Controlling fleas

Unfortunately it is not enough to adjust your living conditions to make it more difficult for

Cats may suddenly start biting into their coat in
reaction to a fleabite

the fleas to reproduce. All you are doing is harassing them. The use of chemical preparations is still essential. Here it is important that all other possible hosts in the house are treated, together with the cat. At the same time you should treat the surrounding area, as this is where the largest concentration of fleas will be found, whether in the egg, larva, or chrysalis stage. If you are looking for anti-flea prepara- tions, the best place to get them is the vet's office. There is a reason for this. In the course of time, fleas develop immunity to a particular active ingredient (the active ingredient is the particular substance that kills the flea, with the others just assisting it). New flea treatments, with a new active ingredient against which the flea has not yet been able to build up immunity, are for a period of time always first sold to vets. It can be several years before they are offered on the open market, during which time the flea has often developed some degree of immunity. If you have an anti-flea preparation that does not appear to be working, check the package for the active ingredient and look for something with another, more modern, active ingredient. There are also preparations that render female fleas infertile; these have to be used at regular inter- vals, and always in addition to the more direct flea treatments, but in the long term they offer very good results.

Norwegian Forest Cat, red and white kitten

Somali kitten

FLEA CONTROL

- DIRECT SUNLIGHT
- VACUUM FREQUENTLY
- PUT ANTI-FLEA PREPARATION IN THE VACUUM CLEANER BAG
- DO NOT MOP FLOORS (OR ONLY WITH ANTI-FLEA SHAMPOO)
- TREAT ALL DOGS AND CATS WITH AN ANTI-FLEA PREPARATION
- TREAT THE SURROUNDINGS WITH AN ANTI-FLEA PREPARATION

Worms

Worms are internal parasites, which means that they actually live inside the animal. Various kinds of worms are known to live in cats, the most familiar being the pink and white roundworm (*Toxocara cati*) that can grow to about ten centimeters long, and the (white) tapeworm (*Dipylidium caninum* and *Taenia taeniaformis*) that can reach a length of a meter, or even longer when fully grown. These species of worm live in the cat's digestive system and eat the half-digested food present in the intestines. There are other kinds of worm that nestle in the lungs, the heart, or even the eyes, but these are not common, although a worm that normally lives in the digestive system can sometimes find a path through other organs to get to its destination, causing damage on the way. Worms, particularly in large numbers, can be a problem, especial-

ly in cats with low resistance. The swollen, round bellies of kittens with a serious roundworm infection are often coupled with patchy coats and diarrhea. A worm infection can undermine the resistance of a very young or elderly animal to such an extent that it dies. Among strong adult animals the symptoms are hardly noticeable, apart from an occasional slight loss of weight or a patchy coat. Sometimes segments of the tapeworm can be seen in the cat's excrement, or sticking to the coat round the anus. These segments are about the length of a grain of rice and are often slightly flattened. Each segment is full of dozens of tapeworm eggs that can be picked up by fleas and thereby re-infect the cat.

Heartworms

Heartworms occur particularly in the United States, but relatively recently this kind of worm has also been found in parts of southern Europe. The worm, which nestles in the heart and surrounding blood vessels of cats (and dogs), is passed on by the bite of a particular kind of mosquito. The infection can impede the effective working of the heart, which at some stage will stop. Your vet has special preparations that can prevent infection by heartworms, inhibiting the development of the parasite so that it dies before causing a problem. It is unfortunately not yet possible to cure a heartworm infection.

Predatory animals are more prone to worm infections

Worm infections

Kittens become infected with roundworm through their mother's milk, even if the mother cat has been regularly treated against worms. A serious breeder will therefore have his kittens treated against worms every two weeks and repeat this treatment before the kitten comes to you. If you have found a kitten from a farm, or a stray kitten, it is very likely to have worms and you should treat the animal as quickly as possible with an anti-worm preparation. Worm infections can also be picked up from contact with infected excrement or through the consumption of prey (e.g., mice) that is infected with worms. Moreover, it is known that roundworm eggs can survive for years in grass and soil; if they are licked up they have the opportunity of completing their development in their host and reproducing themselves. Cats that roam free outside and regularly catch and eat prey will therefore run a greater risk of worm infections—and hence acquire them more often—than animals that never go out. A well-known intermediate host of the tapeworm is the flea. A cat that is host to fleas runs the risk of acquiring a tapeworm infection as well. A cat with fleas should not only be treated for the fleas, therefore, but should also be given an anti-worm preparation.

Kittens are infected with roundworms through their mother's milk

Worms and humans

Worm infections can be passed on to people, particularly to children. This can happen whenever cats, or other hosts to worms, excrete in a sandpit, or the child has very close contact with an infected animal from which it swallows some worm eggs. The eggs can seldom develop into their adult form in the human body, but their larvae drift through the body and in this way can cause damage. These larvae, usually of the species *Toxocara*, are called "*larvae migrans*." In children, a worm infection can cause a variety of complaints. Well known is the (fortunately extremely rare) blindness in one or both eyes caused by migrating larvae in these organs. The only way to prevent worm infections in children is to ensure good hygiene (keep the sandpit covered up, and wash hands after playing outside or cuddling a strange animal). You can, of course,

Worm infections can transfer to people, particularly children

keep your own animals free of worms by preventive treatment. It is recommended that this should be done at least four times a year.

Worming preparations

For worming preparations, as for flea preparations, you are advised to go to your vet's office, where you will find the latest kinds of treatment and the best advice. The vet can also give you special treatments for kittens, which often have to be wormed for the first time at the age of four weeks. You can also, in discussion with your vet, assess how often your animals should be wormed. This rather depends on the way you keep your cats—normally four times a year is enough, but cats that spend a lot of time outside and eat what they catch may need worming more often. Usually the vet will provide a broad-spectrum treatment, which should be effective against all kinds of worms regularly occurring in cats, and not against only one or two specific kinds.

Ticks

Ticks are far from harmless parasites: they live on the blood of humans and animals. They are

Cats pick up ticks in high grass

Cats that are often outside will need worming more often

spider-like creatures with eight legs, about the size of a pinhead. They live in long grass and shrubs, waiting for warm-blooded passers-by so that they can fasten themselves to their skin. Once they have attached themselves, these parasites suck themselves full of blood and are easy to recognize as round, shiny, gray warts on the skin—they can grow to a centimeter in diameter, but more often no larger than half that size. When they have eaten enough they drop off

their host. Apart from the skin irritation they cause, ticks are in themselves relatively harmless. However, the pathogens they carry with them are not. It is estimated that about fifteen to twenty-five percent of ticks are infected with the pathogen that can cause Lyme's disease, a disease that can bring with it chronic health problems for the tick's host, including people. In

Anti-tick preparations are advisable for cats that roam free

Bengal kitten

Ear mites make the ears itch

southern climates ticks can pass on Babesiosis, a potentially fatal disease. A cat that never goes out will not get ticks. For all other cats, prevention is better than cure. There are special tick collars and tick sprays that protect your animal against tick bites. If in spite of this you find a tick on your cat, remove it as quickly as possible. If it is removed within twenty-four hours, infection is virtually ruled out. You remove a tick by grasping it as close as possible to the bite in the skin with special tick pincers or simply between your finger and thumb, and pulling it off with a single twist. Then disinfect the wound with iodine. In the past it was recommended first to render the tick insensible with alcohol, but it has now been discovered that this only increases the likelihood of infection. Ticks are particularly active in warm, damp regions and seasons.

Ear mites

If your cat has black or brownish grains in its ears that have an unpleasant smell, it is probably an ear mite infection. Ear mites are very small, white, spider-like creatures that feed on earwax. An ear mite infection should not be left untreated. Apart from the fact that these parasites often trigger off an itch, causing a cat to start scratching its ears (and possibly injuring them as a result), a neglected infection can lead to inflammation of the ear. Moreover, ear mites can infect other cats. Treatments for ear mites are available from every vet, but not all preparations work

Young Chartreux, female

equally well. An ear mite infection can therefore be very persistent.

Mites

Mites, also known as fur mites or itch mites, are very small parasites that live mainly on or in the host's skin. There they dig tiny grooves and in this way cause a great deal of itching and discomfort. The animal starts to scratch itself, thereby damaging its skin, which becomes scabby and scaly, and its coat, which can finally lead to inflammation. The most usual kind of mite in cats is *Cheyletiella blakei*. If it is suspected that a cat has mites, the vet will take swabs from various places on the skin. Under a microscope it is possible to see whether in fact a mite infection is involved. At the same time the vet can see what kind of mite it is. Depending on these findings, treatment can be started, mostly consisting of weekly washings with a special shampoo. Sometimes the animal will be treated with injections and sometimes its environment will have to be treated as well. Because mites are very infectious, the treatment rarely involves only one animal but all those in the household that are susceptible to that kind of mite.

Lice

Although it is a rare occurrence, cats can contract lice (*Felicola subrostratus*), which cause itching and loss of hair. They are passed on either by direct contact or indirectly, through shared use of brushes or blankets. Lice fasten on the cat's skin, as do their eggs, which are called nits. An obvious symptom of louse infection is that the coat smells musty. The vet can help you with a treatment to control lice, but in addition the cat's bedding and brushes, etc., will have to be thoroughly cleaned. Generally speaking, lice result from poor hygiene. They are host-sensitive and stay faithful to their own host, in this case the cat.

Seal point Devon Rex

Toxoplasmosis

In cats, an infection with the single-cell parasite *Toxoplasma gondii* usually runs its course without any signs of sickness. Cats are the original host of this parasite, but many other animals, including sheep, pigs, and cattle, can act as intermediate hosts. The cysts of the parasite are excreted with the cat's feces and, particularly if there is sufficient moisture in the atmosphere, they can survive for a long time in vegetables, grass, the soil, and so on. Cats can become infected

La Perm, red classic and
white male

Ringworm—
a parasitic fungus

Ringworm is a fungal infection resulting in a feared and very infectious skin disorder, which is almost always caused by the *Microsporum canis*. This fungus lives on the keratin in the hair and skin and rarely causes itching. Dogs and people (particularly children) can also be infected by it. The incubation period is usually only one or two weeks, but can extend to six weeks.

through eating the prey they catch, or raw meat, but also through eating grass, by which they swallow the cysts. Cats are rarely troubled by a Toxoplasmosis infection. This also goes for people—adults or children—who often only display some flu-like symptoms before building up sufficient resistance. Very occasionally, however, the infection is more serious and someone dies. Toxoplasmosis is also very dangerous for unborn children, but only if an expectant mother is not immune to it and comes into contact with it for the first time during her pregnancy, when it can result in permanent damage to her unborn child. For this reason, pregnant women are advised to let someone else clean the cat's litter tray, or only to do this wearing gloves. The cat is in fact not the only animal to spread *Toxoplasma gondii*; it can also be caught by working in the garden or by eating infected vegetables (including salad) or underdone meat. Research has shown that more than half of Europeans carry antibodies to Toxoplasmosis, and that the largest source of infection is not actually cats, but raw meat and vegetables. Cats only spread it for three weeks after being infected with *Toxoplasma gondii* cysts.

Cats may be infected with toxoplasmosis, among other things,
by eating grass

This fungal infection classically shows itself by bare patches, round or oval in shape, usually round the neck or near the ears, but also on the legs or elsewhere on the body. This is, however, only one of the typical symptoms. Not all cats coming in contact with ringworm actually get bare patches. Moreover, some cats that have once gone through a fungal infection, but have themselves recovered from it, can still carry the infection. They show no symptoms, but can infect other cats. These cats are carriers. Particularly in catteries and rescue centers, where

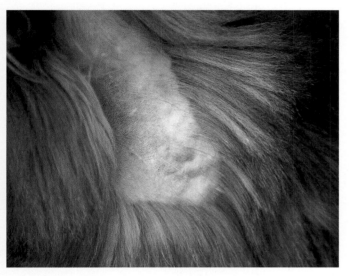

Ringworm rarely causes the skin to itch and often produces "clean" bald patches

there is a higher risk of infection (e.g., through pregnant females, skin damaged by fights or mating, and young kittens) a fungal infection can affect a large number of animals in a very short time.

Ringworm—the diagnosis

Because the symptoms can vary from cats that show no ill effects or only a small bald patch, to cats that have lost almost all of their coat, ringworm cannot be diagnosed only by symptoms. Sometimes a ringworm infection can be shown by holding the affected animal in a dark room in front of a Wood's lamp. Some of the fungal

spores (thirty-five to forty percent) look greenish under this lamp. A more reliable method of diagnosing ringworm is by cultures of hair and skin samples. For this, the vet will take samples from all the cats present (including those showing no symptoms), often with a clean, new toothbrush (MacKenzie method). This has to be done very thoroughly, because otherwise there is a possibility that only those places where there are in fact no spores on an infected animal are examined. Normally a culture will begin to grow within ten days, but it can take up to three weeks after the treatment has started before it shows results and the vet or laboratory can give an answer. Treatment is usually started straightaway, even though there is only a suspicion of ringworm.

Preventing ringworm

Ringworm cannot always be prevented. To start with, it is spread by miniscule spores that are capable of causing new infections for years and can remain active almost anywhere—in the car, under the soles of the feet of visitors, and so on. If a cat has been diagnosed with ringworm, its owners should therefore not visit other people who have pets. Catteries where ringworm has been found are closed until the problem has been eliminated. During the period of eradicating the infection, there will be no mating, no shows will be visited, and no animals bought or sold. In most cat associations there is an obligation on breeders to declare a ringworm infection. Ringworm can to some extent be prevented by plenty of fresh air (good ventilation) and by ensuring dry and light living conditions—ringworms do not like fresh air, sunlight, or dryness. You should also guard against your animals suffering undue stress.

Controlling ringworm

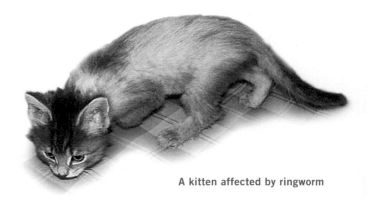

A kitten affected by ringworm

Until a few years ago there was little one could do other than shaving all your animals and washing them thoroughly—weekly or even more frequently—with a special anti-fungal shampoo, cleaning out the entire house and surroundings thoroughly, and replacing anything that could not easily be disinfected (upholstered furniture, floor-coverings, etc.). In addition, the animals were given a treatment (such as Griseofulvin), which was often aggressive and had serious side effects, particularly for unborn kittens. The more expensive Sporonox was also regularly used, because it had fewer side effects. Often this treatment was combined with fumigating the cat's living quarters with special smoke candles (also used by commercial rabbit breeders, among others, but not easily available in all countries), so that the ringworm spores were properly killed and re-infection prevented. It was altogether an extremely labor-intensive and also very expensive procedure, which sometimes drove breeders and managers of cat shelters to despair. Particularly for breeders whose social life was largely conducted among cat fanciers, a ringworm infection meant a long period in which only telephone contact could be maintained with friends and acquaintances, together with—and often unfairly—a loss of reputation. Even now ringworm is the most feared problem amongst cat breeders, boarding homes, and rescue centers, but there is hope on the horizon. Research is currently being undertaken into new preparations (such as Lufenuron) that are safer and easier to apply than the more traditional methods used to control ringworm.

A cross of Persian Longhair and Norwegian Forest Cat

Viral diseases

Feline Infectious Enteritis (FIE)

Feline Infectious Enteritis (FIE), also known as feline distemper, is caused by the Panleukopenia virus, which causes an infection of the gastrointestinal tract. At the same time, a significant proportion of the cat's white blood cells die. The symptoms of FIE include a high fever, diarrhea, which often contains blood, and vomiting, resulting in rapid dehydration. FIE is notorious for the high percentage of cats that die from it.

A cat that roams outside runs a greater risk of contracting feline distemper

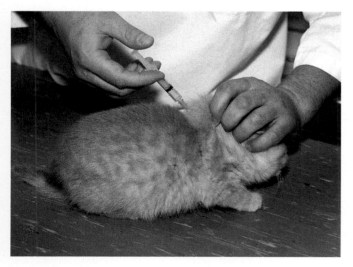

A kitten can be inoculated against feline distemper from the age of nine weeks

If the disease is allowed to run its course, nine out of ten adult animals will die, and virtually all kittens. If treatment is started promptly, however, the chance of the animal surviving does improve. Treatment for FIE is, however, lengthy and intensive. Because the cat's immune system is not functioning properly, secondary infections become likely; any random bacteria or virus, which would normally be repressed by the immune system, can attack the animal and take hold. One way of diagnosing FIE is by checking the feces for the virus. The virus is present in feces and vomit, and can live for some time on

Ocicat

surfaces from which this has subsequently disappeared. Cats that run free outside can become vulnerable to the infection simply by walking over surfaces where the virus is present and then washing themselves, thereby ingesting it. Farm cats and other cats running loose outside (particularly strays) therefore run more risk of catching the disease than cats living indoors—although in theory the virus can be carried in by people on clothing and footwear. An excellent vaccination is available against FIE. The first injection is given when a kitten is about nine weeks old, and the next at the age of about twelve weeks. After that, it is enough to give booster inoculations every two or three years, to prevent the cat becoming infected. Cats that spend a lot of time outside and so run more risk of infection may sometimes be inoculated more frequently.

Cat flu

Cat flu is caused by two different viruses, the Feline Calici virus and Feline Rhinotracheitis, and by Chlamydia, a bacterium. These cause symptoms of a serious cold in the cat: fever, sneezing, inflamed eyes, and a foul discharge from the nose. Most cats affected lose their appetite for food or drink, so that they quickly grow weak and can become dehydrated. In contrast to FIE, cat flu rarely results in death, though that can happen if it is accompanied by pneumonia. Some animals are prone to colds for

Young Maine Coons

Animals suffering chronic cat flu always display
symptoms of a cold

the rest of their life, having once suffered from cat flu. A cat can pick it up through direct contact with the virus—for example, through an infected cat sneezing. Kittens can be inoculated against cat flu at the age of nine weeks and then again at the age of twelve weeks. This inoculation offers nine to twelve months' protection, so an annual inoculation against cat flu is recommended. However, the inoculation against this disease is never one hundred percent effective, because cat flu—like human flu—can have various causes. A cat that has been inoculated will, however, have less serious symptoms than a cat that has not been. In any event, inoculation will prevent cat flu becoming chronic in your cat. Animals with chronic cat flu always have colds and may even have regular, purulent discharge from the nose; as some of them will also sneeze a lot, you will appreciate that this is not hygienic. Moreover, animals with chronic cat flu have to be given antibiotics on a regular basis whenever the disease flares up again.

Feline Infectious Peritonitis (FIP)

FIP is a dreaded disease about which there is still a great deal of uncertainty. The virus that causes it is one of the corona viruses, which are carried in the stomachs of virtually all cats, but without the animals suffering any discomfort from them. Gastroenteritis, and as a consequence diarrhea, are the more serious symptoms of infection by a corona virus. The disease arises from a combination of factors. When the corona virus undergoes a mutation, which in itself happens regularly, the cat's body can react to this by producing antibodies. In many cases, the body makes short shrift of the virus, but in others a reaction starts that leads to the animal developing FIP. Through a still unknown factor, the immune complexes (the antibodies that have enveloped the virus) get more or less entangled in the blood vessels, causing inflammation and the resultant disorder.

FIP—the symptoms and diagnosis

The symptoms of FIP vary, but the animal is always listless, has a

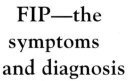
Creampoint 'Sacred' Birman kitten

fever and little appetite, and is generally in a poor condition. Two forms of the disease are known: dry FIP and wet FIP. Wet FIP shows itself in a swollen stomach and difficulty in breathing; only after an animal has died, or in the case of a live animal by a (painless) puncture of the stomach, can it be determined whether there is (or

Ailing animals are often listless and have little or no appetite

was) an inflammation of the peritoneum or pleura (thoracic membrane), with the body producing a straw-colored viscous liquid in these places. Dry FIP can cause inflammation in almost any organ. The problem with dry FIP in particular is that it is so difficult to diagnose. Blood tests that reveal antibodies against corona viruses do not distinguish between a normal and a mutated virus. Since virtually all cats have at some time been in contact with corona viruses or carry these themselves, test results are often positive; moreover, the quantity of antibodies encountered in the blood varies from one animal to another and even from time to time. Tests are therefore pointless.

Feline Immunodeficiency Virus (FIV)

FIV, also known as Feline Aids, is related to the Aids that affects people (HIV), but is not transferable to people or vice versa. A cat becomes infected with this virus when it enters its bloodstream. This usually occurs through fighting with a cat suffering from FIV, very occasionally by mating, and in rare cases is transmitted from a mother cat to her offspring. The cause of the disease is similar to that of human Aids. A cat infected with FIV can go for years without showing a single symptom, but can also suddenly fall ill. FIV attacks the immune system of the cat so that it becomes susceptible to all kinds of problems. Familiar symptoms of the disease are diarrhea, loss of weight, the formation of tumors, and a fever. All kinds of infections and inflam-

Black classic and white non-pedigree cat

FIP—no remedy or inoculation

FIP is an incurable disease that is always fatal. For the dry form a vet can prescribe corticosteroids, but these only delay the process and provide no cure. There is an inoculation against FIP, but this is only useful if the animal has never been in contact with the corona virus and it is still an open question whether this inoculation is in fact free of risk for the animal. Research is currently underway into how this disease can be halted or cured. Heredity may possibly play a role, since the effectiveness of the immune system of a cat plays an important role in the genesis of this disease. It is generally accepted that it can be prevented to some extent by excluding stress factors and unhygienic living conditions as much as possible, because these lower an animal's resistance.

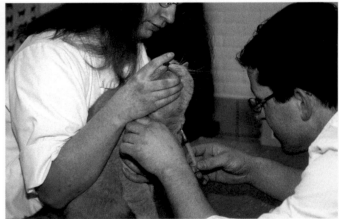

Pedigree cats used for breeding are routinely tested for Feline Aids

mations may present. FIV is incurable and always ends in death once the cat becomes ill. The symptoms can be suppressed for a time by (very expensive) medication. At the moment, unfortunately, no vaccine against FIV is available. The presence of the virus can be confirmed by a blood test. Fear of FIV is one of the reasons that breeders of pedigree cats do not let their animals run free out-of-doors; it is, after all, always possible that a neighboring cat or stray

Feline Aids may be transferred during mating

with the disease will infect their breeding stock. Before two pedigree cats are mated, breeders as a rule have their animals tested for the presence of FIV. If you buy a pedigree kitten from a serious breeder then you will know that the kitten is free of FIV at the time you take it home. That can never be said with certainty of other cats. In cat rescue centers, for instance, newly arrived animals are by no means always tested. In essence, the same goes for all cats that are allowed to roam free outside. If you have cats at home of an uncertain provenance, or if you have cats that run free outside, then it is sensible to have them checked for FIV before you acquire a kitten.

Feline Leukemia Virus (FeLV)

FeLV, usually known as cat's leukemia or cat's viral leukemia, is a fatal disease that appears in various forms. Like FIV, FeLV attacks the cat's immune system. FeLV can be passed on to other cats quite easily: for example, if an infected cat eats from the same bowl as an uninfected one, or if they groom each other's coats. It is also pos-

sible for a mother to infect her unborn kittens. The virus can only survive for a very short time in the open air, so cats have to be in close proximity to each other to pass it on. A cat that comes into contact with the virus need not, however, become ill as a result. A healthy, adult cat with sufficient resistance has a reasonable chance of escaping it. In kittens and old or weaker animals the virus can, however, multiply rapidly, and these animals will succumb to the disease. The first symptoms may appear three months, to sometimes as long as three years, after infection. There are various symptoms, but the best known is leukemia (cancer of the blood). Other common symptoms are various reproductive problems and tumors, which can cause a number of related problems (tightness of the chest, paralysis, etc.). Because the immune system is affected, the cat becomes vulnerable to all the bacteria and viruses it encounters and reacts to them violently. There is a vaccination against FeLV, but this is not widely used as there is still some risk of an inoculated cat getting the

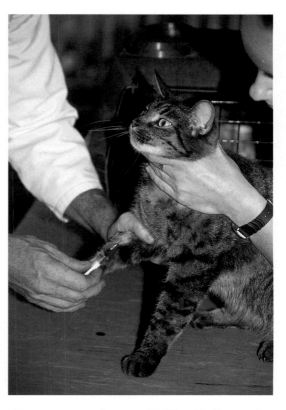

The presence or absence of FeLV antibodies can be established via a blood test

FeLV can easily be transferred to other cats

Rabies (hydrophobia)

Rabies is a dreaded viral disease that can affect all mammals, including humans. The virus attacks the nervous system and is found virtually all over the world, though in western countries it is found mainly in wild animals, such as bats and foxes. An animal can get rabies from the bite of an infected animal. The first symptoms occur from about two, to as long as eight weeks, after infection. The symptoms always start with remarkable changes in behavior, such as aggression, restlessness, and fear. Next follows a stage in which the animal makes uncontrolled movements and can often attack other animals and people. This stage can last about a week, during which time the virus can very easily be passed on due to the infected animal's aggressive behavior. After this period, the animal becomes paralyzed and finally dies. In some countries rabies never, or hardly ever, occurs, and pets are not normally inoculated against it. In other countries, inoculation against rabies is compulsory. An animal that is exported to another country almost always has to be inoculated against rabies. Often this is a legal obligation, particularly because the disease can transmit to humans.

disease. Because the first symptoms sometimes only reveal themselves after three years, with the cat appearing normal and healthy in the meantime, a blood test is the only way to determine whether a cat has FeLV or not. Serious breeders of pedigree cats have their breeding stock tested as a standard procedure for the presence of FeLV in the bloodstream. The problem here, however, is that cats that are actually at that moment infected, but hard at work killing the virus, may test positive, while the result for the same cat at a later stage will turn out negative (i.e., no FeLV infection). It may also happen that definitely positive animals, which are in fact suffering from FeLV, sometimes give a negative test result. In spite of this, a blood test is the only method available for detecting FeLV in a living animal. FeLV is always fatal for affected animals—it is incurable.

Aggression is one of the symptoms of rabies

Diseases and disorders of the eyes and ears

Squinting

Squinting is a condition that in the past mainly affected early Siamese cats. Nowadays, it is still mainly found in Siamese cats, but occasionally also in other breeds. Squinting is not a

Squinting is not a disease

disease. It is a symptom of a 'mistake' in the brain. What the cat sees, the visual stimuli, is sent by the optic nerves to the brain, where the information is interpreted. In squinting cats, a fault occurs in the last section of the brain, which causes an abnormal positioning of the eye. Squinting is an inherited problem. It used to be regarded by some people as a racial characteristic of Siamese cats, but breeders soon began to exclude cats with a squint from breeding and it is much less in evidence today.

Progressive Retinal Atrophy (PRA)

PRA, also called night blindness, is an inherited disorder. The condition also occurs among other mammals, including dogs, and starts with night blindness. The cat cannot, or can hardly, see in the dark, with the condition being revealed, for example, by the animal being afraid of going outside at night. PRA eventually ends in total blindness. Most cases of PRA are inherited through an autosomal recessive gene (rdg), which means that a cat affected by it must have inherited the gene from both its parents, without either parent having the condition themselves. The cat affected may also have

PRA is sometimes called night-blindness, which is
in fact the first symptom of this disease

are caused by a dominant autosomal gene (Rdg). PRA can be confirmed by means of an ophthalmoscope test, but only when the condition has already manifested itself. The condition may first present between the age of three months and seven years. It is therefore quite possible that a cat affected with PRA will already have had offspring before the condition is discovered. There is, alas, not a single medicine or operation that can help with PRA. PRA affects non-pedigree cats and a number of pedigree ones. Normally, breeding stock is only tested for the condition if it is known in the breed or the bloodline. Some weakness in sight need not actually indicate PRA—there are plenty of other possible causes.

already saddled his or her descendants with a single PRA gene. A smaller proportion of cases

Entropion

Entropion is a condition in which the eyelid curves inward. This causes the eyelid and the hairs on it to come into contact with the eyeball and triggers an irritation. If it is not treated this can damage the cornea, with attendant problems. Entropion can be inherited, but can also arise from a variety of other factors, such as mor-

Cinnamon spotted Oriental Shorthair

Entropion can be corrected by a surgical intervention

Conjunctivitis

The conjunctiva are the tissues on the eyeball-side of the top and bottom eyelids. Conjunctivitis is one of the secondary problems that a cat suffering from cat flu may get. It can also be caused by bacteria. Dependent on the cause, a vet will prescribe antibiotics and a special eye ointment. Conjunctivitis should always be taken seriously, because neglect can lead to chronic problems with the conjunctiva such as adhesions, which themselves can cause problems that are difficult to treat.

bid growth of tissue on the bottom eyelid—for instance, after an injury—or through conjunctivitis. A vet will therefore always look for an underlying cause that must be treated first. Entropion can only be resolved by correcting the eyelid surgically. Because this is a very precise operation it is usually carried out by a specialist or experienced vet. The operation will usually be carried out when the cat is fully grown.

A flat-faced cat runs a greater risk of developing problems with its tear ducts

Conjunctivitis may be due to a variety of causes

Tear duct problems

Cats' eyes, like human eyes, always need to be slightly moist. This moisture prevents them from drying out. Various glands ending up near the eyeball keep it almost continuously moist. Teardrops must, of course, also be carried away. On the nose-side of each eye a cat has a drainage

An ear shriveled up as the result of an
untreated hematoma

always. Ear inflammations can, among other things, be caused by ear mites, bacteria, or yeasts. An ear inflammation should never be neglected. If nothing is done, the result may be an inflammation of the middle ear, which in its turn can affect the animal's balance. There can also be a morbid growth of the affected tissues in the ear, which can block or partly block the auditory canal. This results in chronic problems, in the sense that nothing can be done to relieve them. From the symptoms and possibly a bacterial culture, a vet can discover the most appropriate treatment.

channel—a tear duct—in the bottom eyelid for this purpose. Under normal conditions the teardrops are caught in these and slip down towards the nostrils, where they can escape further. Sometimes the process is disturbed and there is an "overflow"; the tears run away across the eyelids down the cat's face. If this happens several times in succession, it will result in "tear stripes"—a dark, stripe-shaped discoloration of the hair on both sides of the bridge of the nose. Persians and other cats with a flat face are more likely to get tear-duct problems than cats with a normal shaped head. Sometimes the ducts can even become blocked, and have to be syringed out by a vet, or else relieved by a special lotion. Sometimes the tear duct can be in the wrong position and has a kink in it. If it gives the animal a great deal of trouble, surgical intervention may be necessary.

Inflammation of the ear

Ear inflammations are common among cats. Symptoms of an ear inflammation are shaking the head, excessive scratching, and expressions of pain—an inflamed ear can be exceptionally painful. The auditory canal can smell unpleasant and look reddish. Sometimes there is a discharge, but not

Ear hematoma

Ear hematoma

A hematoma in the ear can have several causes and occurs relatively often. The most common cause is a rupture of the blood vessels in the earflap caused by an injury; hematomas can also be caused by an ear inflammation. The blood collects between the thin layers of skin in the ear and cannot be dispersed fast enough, so that the ear swells up. This is extremely troublesome for the cat, which develops a heavy "floppy ear" that presses the auditory canal shut. It will try to get rid of the problem by scratching. If nothing is done, then the blood will automatically be carried away by the body, but in the time this takes the thin cartilage in the earflap can become affected and lose its firmness, such that the ear, as it were, collapses and shrivels up. This new shape is then permanent and can

Head-shaking and continual scratching may be symptoms of an ear inflammation

days, so that the blood vessels have already closed up and the ear will not "fill up" again. The vet will make an incision in the earflap, so that the blood can be drained, and clean it properly. Next the skin of the front and back of the earflap is sutured together. This gives sufficient firmness to the thin cartilage and prevents it from collapsing, thus ensuring that the ear retains its proper, erect position. The stitches will, however, irritate the cat. It will therefore need to wear a cap to prevent it scratching the stitches out. A comparable problem can occur from a bite or scratch wound, which does not cause a hematoma but a gathering of pus. The treatment is the same as for a hematoma, the difference being that, with an abscess, there is no need to wait ten days.

create problems. The shriveled ear can partly block the auditory canal, and the ear, with all its folds and wrinkles, is difficult to keep clean. The best remedy against such a hematoma is surgical intervention. This is usually only done after ten

Deafness

Deafness in cats can almost always be blamed on the single dominant inherited W-gene that is

Deafness is associated with the dominant "W" gene that is responsible for a white coat

Serious breeders have their white breeding stock tested for deafness

also responsible for a plain white coat. Deafness occurs virtually only in plain white cats, both pedigree and non-pedigree. In some cases the W-gene can alter the sensors in the inner ear, so that they can no longer, or only partly, pass auditory stimuli to the auditory nerve. The color of the eyes, and whether or not the kittens have a colored patch on their heads, is no indication of whether a white cat will be deaf or not. Deafness can be revealed by the BAER test that can confirm both bilateral (both ears) and lateral (one ear) deafness. Serious breeders of pedigree cats are aware of this problem and do not breed from or show deaf cats. Nor will they mate white animals to one another, because duplicating the W-gene gives an increased risk of deafness. They will, by researching pedigrees, try to breed white kittens from bloodlines of white cats with normal hearing. When a deaf cat lives in a protected environment, the animal can have a long and happy life and usually get on well, despite its handicap. There is a problem, however, if a deaf cat is unfortunate enough to end up in the outside world, where it will be at great risk of accidents, because it cannot hear danger (e.g., aggressive dogs or traffic) approaching.

Diseases and disorders of the skeleton and teeth

Breeding stock of breeds that are prone to hip dysplasia are tested beforehand

Hip dysplasia (HD)

Hip dysplasia can arise from a combination of inherited and environmental factors. The problem is well known and notorious among owners and breeders of large dogs, but can also affect cats. HD is a collective name for abnormal developments of the hip joints, which can result in loosening of the joint socket and swelling, and weakening, and tearing of the ligaments or parts of them. Usually the cartilage is also affected, leading to morbid growth (arthrosis—articular degeneration). Cats suffering from this condition usually have difficulty in walking and getting up, although not all cats with HD present any symptoms. Whether a cat has HD or not can only be confirmed by having the animal x-rayed, preferably by a specialist or vet who has experience of this. From photographs of the hip it is possible to tell whether the animal has HD and the extent of the problem. Cats with HD, even if it does not give them any trouble, are not usually bred from. For cats that are actually handicapped by their hip disorder there are several possibilities, ranging from an operation to correct the hip to a life-long course of muscle-strengthening medication. It depends on the degree and the nature of the HD as to which treatment is applied. HD only occurs on a very small scale in cats.

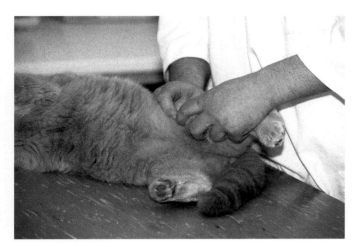

An experienced vet can feel whether a cat is suffering from PL

Patella Luxation (PL)

A free translation of Patella Luxation is "loose kneecaps." It is an inherited disorder that can occur in all cats, but also in other animals such as dogs. PL is inherited, but it is not yet known how. It is suspected that different genes are to blame for triggering it; in any event, no single gene can be blamed for its cause. A cat with PL often has difficulty running and jumping, and in extreme cases the kneecap can "shoot" out of place. In serious cases the knee can be operated on. It is a good practice of most breeders to have the knees of kittens and breeding stock looked at as a standard procedure by a vet. Vets will do this manually: that is to say, they will feel by hand how far the kneecap "gives" when pressure is applied. Some vets have more experience with this than others, and their diagnosis sometimes depends on their experience. Not all knee problems should be confused with PL; a kneecap can also be wrenched out of place by a bad fall or an accident. It is then not called Patella Luxation, but a knee injury.

Short, twisted tail of the Japanese bobtail

Crooked tails

Crooked tails and other deviations from normally shaped tails are incorrectly regarded by many people as a medical problem. Among cats, both pedigree and non-pedigree, variations in the shape of the tail occur naturally. The number of caudal vertebrae in cats is variable and can run from twenty to thirty (except for short-tailed breeds). A thickening, kink, or shorter tail can occur regularly in all parts of the world and among both pedigree and non-pedigree cats. The caudal vertebrae can also vary in thickness. The various forms of cats' tails are sometimes the result of a single gene, as in the M-gene of the Manx, but can also result from a recessive inherited gene as in most of the short-tailed Asiatic breeds. Kinks and thickenings of the caudal vertebrae in cats that do not belong to short-tailed breeds are not regarded with favor. This is because the standard of most breeds demands a full, normally shaped tail, and cats that deviate from this will not stand a chance at shows. Most breeders therefore select animals with a normally shaped tail. That in spite of this kittens are regularly born with a thickening or a kink in their tails is because the inheritance of the shape of the tail is still arbitrary and in all probability polygenetically determined.

It is still sometimes claimed

after about four days their chests begin to flatten and in extreme cases they can no longer lie on their sides. This can cause a number of problems, one of them being that there is too little room for the lungs and other organs. Some die before their third week of life, while others survive. Among this last group the chest reverts in the course of time to its normal form and usually from the age of four months there is no longer any sign of the problem and the kitten goes on to develop normally. The cause of this phenomenon is not yet known, but it is assumed that it is inherited in some way.

Cats' tails come in all shapes and sizes

that to breed from a cat with a kink in its tail can lead to kittens with problems of the dorsal vertebrae. So far, however, this has not been proven, while there are still plenty of tail deviations. A cat with a crooked tail can grow old without encountering any problems.

Flat-chested kittens

Some kittens are born with normal, rounded chests, without apparent abnormalities, but

Kurilian bobtail cat with kinks in its short tail

Flat-chested kitten

Polydactylic black and white male

Polydactylism

Polydactylism results from the single dominant gene Pd, which causes multiple toes. Normally cats have five toes on each forepaw, and four on each back one. A cat with the Pd-gene can have more toes on both fore and back paws, up to a maximum of seven. There are breeders who like to breed cats with extra toes. They will, however, never cross polydactylic cats with each other, because this increases the risk of split feet and other foot problems. Some cats have a normal number of toes, but none the less pass on polydactylism: x-rays have shown that these animals in fact have one or more extra toes, if only rudimentary, being hardly visible, if not invisible, to the naked eye.

Dental problems— the symptoms

Tartar and caries frequently occur among pedigree and non-pedigree cats from the age of about three to four years. A cat that has trouble with its teeth can often suffer in this way for some time without its owner noticing anything. Obvious symptoms that can point to a problem with teeth, such as an inflammation, include an unpleasant smell from the animal's mouth and

Polydactylic black tortoiseshell female

Dental problems are increasingly common in cats

its preference for soft, canned food as opposed to hard chunks that need to be chewed. Some cats can become rather bad-tempered and avoid being petted. This can be periodic: as with humans who have toothache, the pain is not equally bad throughout the day. A vet should always be consulted and, depending on the exact nature of the problem, he or she will anesthetize the animal and repair the teeth. Sometimes it is enough just to remove the tartar, but in other cases it might be necessary to extract some teeth.

Dental problems— prevention

One of the reasons for dental problems is that most cats these days do not catch and eat fresh prey, but to an increasing degree are given ready-to-eat chunks. The sideways movement of chewing the prey they catch apparently has a cleaning effect on the teeth. There is clear evidence supporting this—it used to be the custom to give wild felines in zoos only carcasses and fresh meat to eat. In most European zoos this is still the case, but in the United States wild felines are increasingly fed factory-prepared chunks. Since this started, dental problems have been reported much more frequently among felines in American zoos than in their European equivalents. So it can also help to give your cat solid pieces of meat that it has to "chop up" into pieces with its molars. Day-old chicks are very suitable for this. Most specialist pet shops have these in their freezer or can order them for you. It is also a useful habit to have a good look at your cat's teeth once a month, particularly the molars at the back. If your cat protests strongly against this, you can ask the vet to do it when he administers the annual cat flu injection. Deposits on the teeth soon turn into tartar, with caries, inflammation of the gums and of the cingulum, and loss of teeth possibly resulting. Of

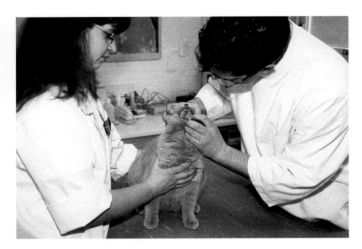

Occasionally ask your vet to check the cat's teeth

so that the tooth growing below it grows crooked or causes an inflammation. If you have any doubts, always consult your vet.

course, any disruption in the change from milk teeth can also cause problems. Cats usually change their milk teeth for permanent teeth between the fourth and sixth month of life. It is advisable to check this process. Sometimes it can happen that a milk tooth will not come out,

Adjustments to the diet can go a long way to prevent dental problems

Diseases and disorders of the urinary system and kidneys

Cystitis (inflammation of the bladder)

Normally a cat will only have the urge to pass urine when there is a certain amount of liquit in its bladder. In cases of cystitis, however, the wall of the bladder becomes inflamed, and the bladder reacts to each tiny drop of urine that comes into it by contracting. A sudden display of unsanitary behavior is therefore one of the most common symptoms of a bladder infection—the cat just cannot restrain itself any longer. Its frequent urinations are often small and the urine usually dark-colored, because there is blood in it. Inflamed bladders are relatively common in cats, both male and female. If you think your cat has a bladder inflammation, go straight to the vet. He may ask you to bring a sample of urine; you can get one by collecting the litter from the cat's litter tray and using a pipette to extract the urine. The vet will also be able to provide special, non-absorbent cat grit, or you may be able to use fine aquarium gravel. By examining the urine and also the bladder, the vet can make a diagnosis. Usually antibiotics and possibly painkillers will be prescribed; an inflamed bladder is very painful.

Manx

Red and white house cat

Bladder crystals

Crystals in the bladder are a common disorder, particularly in males. Crystals are caused by an imbalance of acid in the bladder. The crystals that are formed by this can block the urethra, which can result in a bladder inflammation, or vice versa. Cats that are troubled by bladder crystals spend a lot of time in their litter tray without actually urinating. The cat has the urge to urinate, but the urine cannot get through, because the crystals have blocked the urethra. This can often be very painful as well. If the condition is not treated quickly, the bladder will get fuller and fuller, the kidneys become swollen, the animal will suffer from shock, and ultimately will die. If it is treated too late, the animal can still die because the relevant organs (kidneys and bladder, but also the liver and heart) have been too seriously affected. If you notice that your cat keeps on going to its litter tray without producing anything, take it straight to the vet. Treatment depends on which form of crystal is found. Struvite crystals are formed in the urine when the acid level is too alkaline. If, on the other hand, the acid level is too acidic, oxalate crystals are formed. Both forms can be prevented by a special diet that

Norwegian Forest Cat

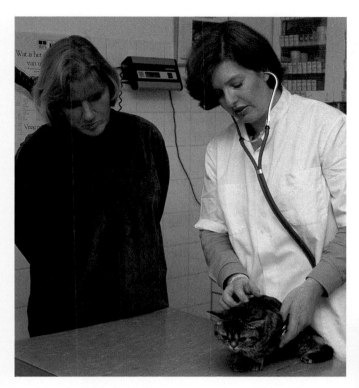

If your cat often visits its litter tray without obvious results, a visit to the vet is indicated

from it can be prescribed a special diet that puts as little load as possible on the kidneys; this does not stop the process but the cat will be able to live a little longer and more comfortably than without it. This disorder is a dominant inherited one and is based on a single gene—the disease can be prevented by simply not breeding from animals suffering from the disorder. PKD can be diagnosed by means of an ultrasound scan, but not until the age of about ten months; this has to be carried out by a vet experienced in the procedure and is often carried out at specialist clinics. Serious breeders of those breeds of cat in which PKD occurs will normally have their future breeding stock tested for kidney

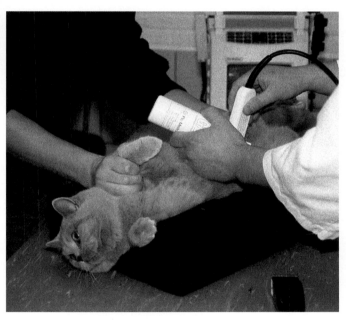

PKD can be detected by an ultrasound scan

the cat will have to be given for the rest of its life. With struvite crystals, a special diet is often enough to dissolve them. If your cat has oxalate crystals, however, the vet will usually remove them surgically, then prescribe a diet to prevent their recurrence. The actual diet is always dependent on the kind of crystals that are found.

Polycystic Kidney Disease (PKD)

PKD, also known as kidney cysts, is an inherited disorder occurring in both non-pedigree and pedigree cats, but also in other mammals, including people. A cat suffering from PKD will have several cysts in its kidneys, which will increase in number over time. These cysts increasingly prevent the kidneys from working normally. PKD is always fatal, because eventually the kidneys simply cease to function. The disease cannot be treated. The animal suffering

cysts and will exclude from the breeding program any affected animals.

Chronic Interstitial Nephritis (CIN)

CIN is sometimes known as "shrunken kidneys." This disorder causes damage to the kidney cells. Interstitial tissue replaces the damaged cells so

Male Norwegian Forest Cat, blue striped

that, over the course of time, there is more and more interstitial tissue instead of useful kidney cells, with the operation of the kidneys slowly but surely degenerating. In the early stages there are few if any symptoms. Only at a later stage does an affected cat display any symptoms, which can vary from drinking more—and so also urinating more—to loss of weight, listlessness, and diarrhea. It is generally assumed that CIN is partly inherited, but that diet also plays an important role. CIN can also be a secondary problem occurring in other diseases. Cats in which this disorder is diagnosed are given a special diet that puts as little pressure as possible on the kidneys, sometimes combined with medication.

Diseases and disorders affecting reproduction

Stud tail

On top of the tail, on the first third from its base, cats have a scent gland. Particularly among unneutered males, and to a lesser degree among unspayed females, this scent gland can be working too hard. This results in a sticky, brownish, sebaceous discharge, which not only looks ugly but can also cause the skin to suffocate and the hair in these places to fall out in tufts. This phenomenon is called "stud tail" and is relatively common. It can occur as soon as a male cat is sexually mature, but also at a later age. Neutering helps permanently. If neutering is not desirable, then the condition can in the long term be prevented or reduced by giving extra vitamin B and food with a high fat content. In addition you can treat the spot with a specific dry shampoo for cats or with cornstarch. Superfluous sebaceous matter and dirt will stick to this, so that after letting them soak in for a night, you can brush them out together with the powder. It may also help a little to dab the affected place carefully once a week with a seventy percent alcohol solution. Washing the tail with strong detergents, such as washing-up liquid or an industrial hand cleaner, gives immediate results. The gland will in most cases be activated more strongly by this, however, so that a regular bath will be necessary.

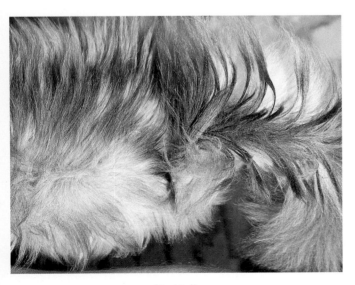

Stud tail

Blue point
British Shorthair

Black-silver classic Maine Coon kitten

Inflammation of the uterus (pyometra)

Inflammation of the uterus (pyometra) is a problem that sometimes occurs with unspayed females of a certain age. A female with this condition drinks much more than normal, may have a fever, and sometimes has a cloudy discharge from the vulva. This last will not always be noticed, because the cat herself usually cleans it up. Pyometra can lie dormant for a long time, but eventually proves fatal if nothing is done. In its very early stages the inflammation can be suppressed by antibiotics, but in most cases the vet will advise the removal of the uterus. Females that frequently come into season and are not covered during these times run a greater risk of pyometra—and all kinds of other uterine problems—than animals that are covered when they are in season (and become pregnant). Waiting too long before a female is covered can therefore also be a source of problems. This is the reason why many breeders have their females covered for the first time at an age of eleven to thirteen months, when the uterus is often still in prime condition. Waiting longer means their coming into season more frequently, each time being an assault on the regulation of their hormones and the possible cause of

Cream Persian Longhair, female

Feline Neonatal Isoerythrolysis (FNI)

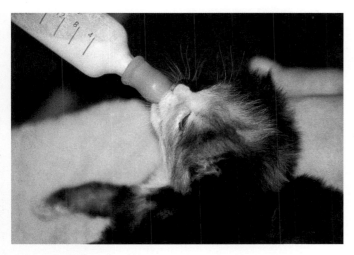

If the mother cat has blood group B and father blood group A, the kittens will need to have formula-prepared kitten milk for the first 24 hours

There are three blood groups among cats: A, B, and AB. Far and away most cats are, however, blood group A. A cat's blood plasma naturally contains antibodies against alien blood groups. In practice this can lead to problems when a female with blood group B is covered by a male with blood group A—there are no problems with other combinations. Some of the kittens from this combination will have blood group A. These kittens can in the first eighteen to twenty-four hours of their life ingest the, for them, lethal antibodies in their mother's milk. Some kittens will die immediately after birth, but most of them will have difficulty drinking or not drink at all, and suffer general weakness before they die. A reddish brown color of the kittens' urine is typical of FNI. The cause of death is then Feline Neonatal Isoerythrolysis, which freely translated means that the red blood corpuscles are destroyed. Some kittens miraculous-

problems. If you do not want to breed from her, it makes sense to have a female spayed as a preventive measure. The ovaries are then removed so that there is no hormonal stimulation of the uterus, thus preventing inflammation.

Abyssinian

Devon Rex

ly survive the antibodies to their blood group, though they are often weaker and have trouble with anemia. The problem of premature kitten death from the "wrong" blood group can be prevented by having the blood group determined before mating and not letting any females with blood group B be covered by males with blood group A. In practice this is only done with breeds that are known to have a high percentage of cats with blood group B, i.e., British Shorthairs and Devon Rex, and to a lesser degree with Persians, Abyssinians, and Somalis. If a female with blood group B is covered by a male with blood group A, it is still possible to save the kittens from an early death. If the kittens are fed in the first twenty-four hours of their lives only on artificially prepared kitten milk and not by their mother, then they have a chance of avoiding their mother's antibodies. After these twenty-four hours the kittens may drink their mother's milk normally, since the walls of the kittens' intestines will no longer absorb the antibodies. The kittens may still lie with their mother for the first twenty-four hours, but care has to be taken during this period that they only drink the replacement milk.

Other diseases and disorders

Epilepsy

Epilepsy occurs among all cats, both pedigree and non-pedigree. The disorder is characterized by uncontrolled movements of part or the whole of the body, sometimes accompanied by loss of consciousness. This means not just the familiar picture people have of epilepsy—falling down, convulsions, and foaming at the mouth. A milder manifestation of epilepsy can last just a few minutes, with a shaking of the head or a continuous tremor in a forepaw. All this is the result of an abnormal "discharge" of neurons in the brain. In a major seizure the whole brain will be entirely "discharged" in a specific rhythm, with an assault on several bodily functions. In a focal (partial) epilepsy the discharge will take place in a specific part of the brain and the attack may be restricted to, for example, a tremor in one paw. Epilepsy is actually no more than a symptom of an underlying problem. If

Red British Shorthair, tom

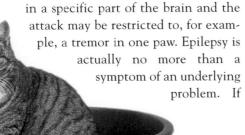

House cat

that problem is known, then we talk of secondary epilepsy. If the problem is not known, we refer to the epilepsy as primary. A vet will try to detect which underlying problem causes the epileptic seizures. This can be anything, from a tumor to meningitis or diabetes, so it is not easy to discover. Often a comprehensive blood test will be carried out first. For primary epilepsy anti-epileptic drugs are sometimes prescribed, which can make the seizures rather less severe and less frequent. Unfortunately, however, epilepsy cannot be cured.

Colorpoint American Curl, longhaired

Female Norwegian Forest Cat, black-striped tortoiseshell and white

Hypertrophic Cardiomyopathy (HCM)

HCM is an inherited cardiac disorder that can occur among all cats. The condition is characterized by a gradual thickening of the muscle wall of the left chamber of the cat's heart. This thickening increasingly prevents the heart from functioning properly and, as a consequence, a whole range of symptoms may present—heart failure, embolisms (blocking of a blood vessel), strokes, or paralysis (of the hindquarters). Cats with HCM do not necessarily reveal it. They may, for example, be quieter, get tired more quickly, breathe faster and eat less than normal, be short of breath, and/or have a cardiac murmur. It can also happen that a cat shows no symptoms at all until one day it dies of heart failure. HCM is always fatal, but the age at which the cat dies can vary. Some animals die young, others not until they are elderly. Whether or not

a cat has HCM can only be determined by an ultrasound scan, carried out by a specialist (not an ordinary vet) and with specialized apparatus: a color Doppler scan. It is not possible to test very young animals for HCM—for this, the heart must be fully grown. In respect of males, this is usually by the time they are about two years old, and for females when they are three, so there is no point in having an animal tested until or after they have reached this age. If the scan proves that the wall of the heart has not thickened, there is still a twenty percent risk that the animal has HCM. This means that one in five cats tested, which are declared free of the disease, can yet have it. All cats in which HCM is confirmed do in fact have the disease. HCM occurs occasionally in both pedigree and non-pedigree cats, and some breeds have a rather greater risk of HCM than others. Most serious breeders have their breeding stock within these breeds routinely tested. HCM is an inherited autosomal dominant disease; at least one parent of every cat in which HCM is confirmed

Burmilla

Male blue point "Sacred" Birman

substances that cause an allergic reaction in the cat. Such tests are unfortunately not always watertight, because there are a large number of substances to which a cat may be allergic, and in practice it is impossible to test all of them.

has it, and on average half the kittens born of an HCM-affected cat will also develop HCM. If HCM is confirmed, the life of the animal can be lengthened and made more pleasant by specific medication, but there is no cure.

FLEA ALLERGY

IF A CAT HAS A FLEA ALLERGY, IT IS NECESSARY TO REMOVE ALL FLEAS AND TREAT THE CAT PERIODICALLY WITH A PREPARATION THAT KILLS FLEAS INSTANTLY BEFORE THEY CAN BITE THE CAT.

Allergy—what is it?

An allergy means that the cat's immune system reacts to certain substances. Among cats the most common allergies are to fleas and food, but house mites and pollen, and countless other substances a cat may come into contact with, can cause an allergic reaction. An allergy always needs time to develop. Cats can therefore become allergic to a foodstuff that they have eaten for years, or react allergically to a fleabite for the first time when they are three or four years old. There are many different symptoms that can indicate an allergy, varying from skin complaints when the cat is obviously itching, to loss of hair, sores on the skin, ear inflammations, diarrhea, and vomiting. The most common are the symptoms on the skin. Because the allergy itself cannot be treated, all that can be done is to prevent the animal coming into contact with the substance or substances to which it is allergic. If an allergy is suspected, a vet will, first of all, try to exclude causes other than an allergy—there are, after all, plenty of problems that give the same kind of clinical picture. Next he or she will examine by skin tests and blood tests the

Food allergies

A food allergy cannot be confirmed by a simple allergy test. To see if a cat has a food allergy, it will be prescribed a special diet to eat for six weeks. This diet has to be quite different from the food the cat normally eats. Instead of dried chunks based on beef, for example, the cat will only be given chicken meat, cooked with rice. The cat will not yet have been able to build up any allergy to these new foodstuffs, different kinds of protein, and similar replacements. If there is any question of a food allergy, a "hypoal-

Baldness need not be due to a medical condition—
it is common in Rexes

lergenic elimination diet" should produce a clear reduction in the complaint. It is very important that the cat eats nothing except this diet—a very little of the substance to which the cat is allergic can, after all, produce a long-lasting reaction. Cats can be allergic to all kinds of ingredients in their food, varying from the kind of meat (chicken, beef, etc.) to the preservatives in it. As soon as a cat eats a particular food without showing any symptoms, then gradually another kind of food or another source of protein can be added to its diet, and a watch kept on which substance the cat reacts to allergically.

A single flea bite can spark off a long-lasting reaction in a cat that is allergic to it

Diabetes

Diabetes is relatively common in cats, particularly in older animals that have grown too fat. Diabetes starts because the pancreas produces too little insulin. Insulin ensures that sugar is absorbed from the blood into the body cells. If there is too little insulin in the blood, the cat will not be able to absorb sufficient sugar from its food. The cat tries to compensate for this by eating more. Bodily functions deteriorate fast from lack of sugar. The first symptoms of diabetes are an enormous increase in appetite and thirst, increased urination, and steady loss of weight. If it is not treated, the cat will continue to lose weight, then lose its appetite (through feeling nauseous); it will slowly become dehydrated (the skin loses its elasticity), its eyesight will suffer and it might go blind. If an animal gets no veterinary help, it will die. If diabetes is suspected, a vet will do both urine and blood tests to determine the blood sugar level. If diabetes is confirmed, then the cat must first be stabilized. By means of blood samples, the vet will look at what combination of insulin level and food the cat best reacts to. This will have to be repeated periodically over time to see whether the quantity of food or insulin should be adjusted. After that, the owner will have to give his or her cat an insulin injection every day at the same time.

A cat with a food allergy

This injection is given under the skin. Because insulin is administered with a very fine needle, it is easy to learn how to do this oneself, and most cats will not protest against it. The cat will also have to be given the same amount of food, of the same composition, twice daily at the same time. Normally meals will be given at an interval of eight hours. A cat that runs free outside can collect its own extras there, so that only diabetic indoor cats have the best prognosis. With proper care a cat with diabetes can have a first-class life. It does, however, demand a great deal of commitment from the owner.

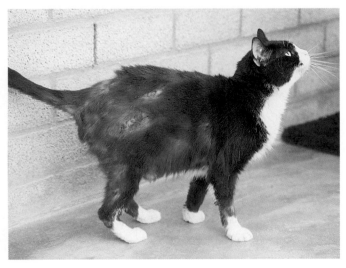

A cat with a food allergy

Male Norwegian Forest Cats

Cancer

Cancer can occur in cats as a problem in itself, or as a symptom of an underlying problem. Many forms of cancer can affect a cat, and it is impossible to cover all of them within the scope of this book. For example, in cats that have little or no pigment (white cats or cats with white patches) we sometimes see cancer cells on the edges of the ears, caused by sunlight. Also very common are small tumors on the nose leather that often

This female is suffering from diabetes

Fatty degeneration of the liver (hepatolipidosis)

A cat that for some reason does not eat for a few days can poison itself. If a cat does not eat, the body releases large quantities of stored up fat, which gets into the bloodstream. A cat's body has difficulty in processing large quantities of fat. It is stored in the liver, so that the liver function deteriorates and in the end the animal poisons itself and eventually dies. Fatty degeneration of the liver usually sets in after five days' fasting. This poisoning is irreversible if it is not treated immediately. If your cat does not eat for a day, this need not immediately point to a life-threatening problem, but it is irresponsible to wait longer—you should have the cat looked at by a vet, who will try to discover the reason and draw up a plan with you to restore the cat's appetite. In some cases this may mean force-feeding by tube.

begin with a small ulcer. Female cats commonly suffer from tumors of the mammary glands. Females that have often been in season, but have not often been covered, or who have had the cat's "pill" for a long time or irregularly, run a greater risk of forming mammary tumors. Females that have been spayed are hardly ever affected. The problem is often seen among cats of five or more years old. The only effective remedy is the removal of the whole of both mammary systems, not just the parts actually affected. Cancer can occur in any of the feline organs. Its location and nature will help to determine how it should be treated. This may mean surgery in the affected area, but radiation and chemotherapy are also available for cats.

White cats have a slightly higher risk of contracting cancer caused by sunburn

Abscesses

Abscesses are relatively common in cats. They arise from wounds (bites, scratches, etc.) triggering an inflammation under the skin that has meanwhile closed up. Some of these inflammations will not be obvious to an owner and will heal themselves. Sometimes, however, excessive pus is formed that can only be drained away to a limited extent, if at all, by the body, and a

Japanese Bobtail

tough, pus-filled lump will develop in the affected place. The cat may get a fever and become lethargic, but that is not always the case. If nothing is done, the skin will sometimes erupt and the pus run away of itself, after which a bald patch will be left on which the hair grows back slowly. Often, however, a new abscess will form in the same place. A vet will sometimes treat a small abscess by prescribing antibiotics for the animal, but here again there is a considerable risk of the abscess surfacing again after the medication ends. Recently vets have increasingly opted to open the skin under an anesthetic and clean the wound out thoroughly. An abscess is sometimes drained to prevent a new one forming. This means that a small tube is inserted into the wound, through which the liquid can be drained away.

Diarrhea

If a cat has occasional diarrhea there is no need to worry. It may, for instance, just have eaten something "bad." Diarrhea is, however, also a symptom of many kinds of illness. If your cat has diarrhea, be vigilant. If there is blood in the diarrhea or it has an abnormal color, go straight to the vet. You should also consult your vet if, in addition to the diarrhea, you notice deviations in your cat's behavior (e.g., it is listless or withdrawn) or external changes in its appearance (hollow cheeks, unkempt coat, etc.).

Sphinx, blue-cream female

Diet

Small birds make up less than ten percent of the total menu
of a cat living in the wild

no dry chunks in colorful packaging such as we know today. It usually consisted of the ground-up waste products of slaughterhouses, which was sold fresh from door to door to cat owners. Not until the 1920s and 1930s did "cat biscuits" appear in imitation of "dog biscuits"; they were a mixture of stock with ground-up meat and dough, baked into large chunks that would keep for a while. Of course, these had nothing like the quality and consistent composition of today's commercial cat food. In the 1970s and 1980s there was increasing demand for cat food of high quality and reliable composition. During this period cat food manufacturers even started keeping collections of cats on which they would

From self-caught food to ready-made meals

Most people these days feed their cats commercially compounded food. This can be seen as a relatively new development, however, when set against the seven thousand years that cats have lived with humans. For thousands of years cats were more or less self-supporting, keeping themselves alive by catching small prey, such as mice. Only when the cat increasingly attained the status of a pet could it start to count on the remains of people's food. The first commercial cat foods date from around 1900. At that time there were

Given the opportunity, an outdoor cat will also catch
and eat frogs

test their products, and experts began to research the food a cat really needed for a long and healthy life. This development is ongoing, and a cat owner today can reasonably assume that there are no bad cat foods. In most countries there are, in fact, legal regulations covering the ingredients used for pet and other animal foods, to which every manufacturer must adhere. Although there may be no bad foods, however, that does not mean that all the foods made for cats are suitable for all cats. Every cat is an individual and dietary requirements can vary considerably.

Buying cheap is expensive

Cats have more need of animal fat and animal protein than canines. In practice this means that the main ingredients in a cat food have to be fish, poultry, or meat. Manufacturers of good, premium brands know this and take care that their dry or canned foods contain high quality animal proteins and fats as their main ingredient. These types of food are usually on the pricey side, and there is a reason for this. Animal protein is, after all, more expensive than vegetable, and high-quality animal ingredients are many times more expensive than waste products such as slaughterhouse offal or bone meal. After all,

you pay more for a pound of sirloin then you do for a pound of mince, and mince in its turn is more expensive than a pound of flour. It is just the same with cat food. It is almost impossible to make a cheap cat food with sufficiently high-quality animal fats and proteins. If you want a good diet for your cat, therefore, you have to choose a high-quality cat food.

Dry chunks

Alongside canned food, dry chunks are probably the most popular food among cat owners. The advantage of dry chunks is that, of all types of food, these keep longest once opened. Moreover, they contain everything a cat needs in concentrated form. Dry chunks also have the advantage that even on warm days they can

Dried cat food contains all the nutrients a cat needs

be left standing in the food bowl, which cannot be done with canned food or fresh meat because of the risk of bacteria forming. On the other hand, a cat that is given dry food to eat needs more fresh water than a cat that eats moist food. Dry chunks contain about eight to ten percent liquid, whereas canned food contains eighty percent.

Blue point and white Cornish Rex kitten

"Semi-moist" food

A handy compromise between canned and dry food is "semi-moist" food. This is not very popular among cat owners and is not available everywhere. The advantage of this food, usually sold in sealed packages, is that it has a long shelf life and is very tasty, so cats like it, but the structure of the food is such that it gets stuck between the teeth, which encourages the formation of plaque. So it is not a good idea to give a cat this kind of food alone, but better to keep it as a treat.

Dried cat food will keep better in a food silo than when left it in an open dish

Male Ragdoll

Canned food

Together with dry food, canned food is the most popular for cats. Unopened cans often have a shelf life of years, during which time the food quality will not deteriorate. Most cats like the taste. Cans also have disadvantages, however—some cats have trouble with diarrhea as soon as

British Shorthair, lilac-cream female

they are given canned food to eat. Moreover, tinned food is relatively expensive, but the main ingredient is rarely meat or fish. Often high quality meat or fish makes up just ten percent of the contents of the tin. The main ingredient is usually water, so a cat requires relatively more canned than dry food to obtain all the nourishment it needs. Never put a can, once opened, in the refrigerator, but keep it, well covered up, in a cool place and never for longer than a day.

Frozen food

There are special frozen foods for cats that are prepared on a biological basis. Frozen foods are not often given to cats, probably because they are rather less easy to use than canned food or dry chunks, and are not available everywhere.

Ready-to-eat frozen meals for cats can often only be obtained from specialist pet food retailers or direct from the manufacturers. The great advantage of fresh-frozen foods is that very high-quality ingredients tend to be used in them and, as it is not necessary for them to be given a long shelf life; they rarely, if ever, include preservatives. Ready-to-eat frozen food comes closest to satisfying a cat's natural nutritional needs.

Preparing food yourself

It is not easy to prepare cat food yourself. Apart from the fact that a cat should get all the nutrients it needs from its food, the proportions between these nutrients are equally important. The wrong balance can sooner or later produce health problems. For instance, there are some foodstuffs that are known to counter the effect of some digestive enzymes. If in spite of this you want to take on the task, buy a good book on the subject.

Burmillas, tom and kitten

Fresh meat

Meat or fish alone?

There are people who assume that in the wild a cat only eats the prey it catches and so can best be fed just on meat or fish. This, however, often gives rise to problems, as prey does not consist only of muscular flesh, but also, for example, of bones, entrails (often with pre-digested vegetable matter in them), skin, and so on. So pure meat or fish is not a good replacement for natural prey. It is certainly unbalanced and in the long run can cause health problems. Moreover, research has shown that cats in the wild eat a very varied diet: not only mice, but also small birds, insects, and, when they can, also a little fish or frog. Precisely because of this variety, the animal takes in a large number of different nutrients that prevent it from developing problems resulting from an unbalanced diet. An exception can be made for day-old chicks (chickens that have been killed and frozen straight after being hatched). In these chicks there is virtually everything a cat needs, though variety is still advisable. Frozen day-old chicks can be bought in specialty pet shops. Be particularly wary of offal, which you should feed your cat very sparingly. For instance, liver contains a great deal of vitamin A, a vitamin that the cat cannot excrete; too much of it can cause skin and eye problems and in pregnant queens can

Eating natural food cleans the teeth automatically

Turkish Angora kitten

only occurs naturally in meat, so they soon began to suffer through this deficiency. Products have since appeared, however, that contain a synthetic form of taurine and are sold as a dietary supplement for cats. If you want to know more about them, information is available from vegetarian and vegan associations. Bear in mind, however, that not every cat can or will take to a diet without meat.

lead to abnormalities in her unborn offspring. If you want to feed fresh meat or fish, it is wise to cook it first. The best way to do this is in a small amount of water in a covered pan. Your cat might also like to drink the stock this produces.

Vegetarian cat foods

People who are themselves vegetarian or vegan may find it difficult to feed their pet a diet consisting mainly of meat. In the past, a vegetarian diet for a cat was doomed to fail. Cats have, after all, a great need for taurine, a substance that

Exotic

Good for the teeth

Feeding cats ready-to-eat, factory-made meals has the disadvantage that their teeth will not get cleaned enough, which can cause dental prob-

Male Norwegian Forest Cat, black smoke and white

lems. Cats do not chew their food— they "snip" it into pieces with their teeth. This causes the food to scrape against the enamel of their teeth and gums and cleans them naturally. Small chunks and canned food do not need to be "snipped," but can be swallowed without it, so that there is no cleaning action for the teeth. Factory-made prepared food is one of the main reasons for our domestic cats suffering with their teeth. This problem has meanwhile been recognized and various kinds of cat food in the form of dry chunks have come on the market in special shapes and compositions that encourage natural tooth cleaning. Nevertheless, it would do no harm to give your cat a piece of sheep's heart, a day-old chick, or some dried fish once a week or a little more often. It is best not to feed any bones; not only can these splinter and cause injury to the intestines, but they can also get stuck in the mouth.

Reading the label

If you want to give your cat factory-prepared food, always have a good look at the label. From this you can gain a good idea of the raw materials that have been used. The main ingredient is always at the top of this list. For the health of your cat, the main ingredient should consist of meat or fish (i.e. animal proteins). In some foods these essential food ingredients only make up a small percentage of the whole. Next look at the preservative used. Natural preservatives include Tocopherol (vitamin E). Chemical preservatives such as Ethoxyquin, BHT (E321) and BHA (E320) are best avoided. Their use is becoming less common. The disadvantage of natural preservatives is that they do not preserve the food as long as chemical preservatives. Natural preservatives can "go into reverse" and turn the food rancid, or render it poisonous. So it is better to buy small packs more often than one large pack occasionally. If you have any doubts

Black classic house cat, female

about the food, if it smells different, or if one day your cat suddenly does not want it, then it is probably past its use-by date, and you should throw it away to avoid problems.

Incidentally, there are often analyses of the food on the pack in several languages. Because the laws governing pet foods sometimes vary from country to country, it is often interesting to see whether there are any differences in the values given.

Milk?

If we look at animals in their natural state, we see that they only drink milk as young animals from their mother. They gradually get used to other foods such as grass or live prey and, once weaned, have no more need for milk. This means that humans are the only species of animal that go on drinking milk after the suckling period. Kittens no longer need milk once they have moved on to solid food. Many cats do however like milk, but if you want to give some to your cat occasionally, do not give it milk meant for human consumption, such as cow's milk. This contains lactose, to which the cat's digestive system usually reacts with diarrhea. If you want to give your cat some milk, buy the special formula prepared for cats. This kind of milk is available in small packs from supermarkets and pet shops and also in powder form, which you can mix yourself, from both specialist pet shops and vets. Another alternative is sterilized cream

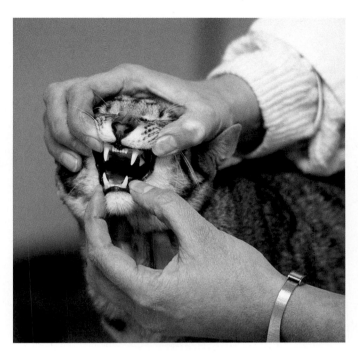

Dental problems may cause the cat to refuse its food or be choosy about it

or evaporated milk. The lactose that normally occurs in these products is rendered harmless by the heating and so rarely, if ever, leads to complaints.

Fussy eaters and food refusers

Some cats are very choosy about what they eat. Perhaps they had too monotonous a diet when they were kittens, so that they did not get used to different kinds of food, but it may also be that their food has gone rancid or that the owner spoils his or her cat too much, and that the cat has learnt that to refuse its food produces a tastier dish. In any case, a cat must eat something every day. Its digestive system is not designed for fasting; less than a week without food can cause a life-threatening, fatty degeneration of the liver. You should certainly contact your vet if your cat has eaten nothing for two days. It is, however, not a good thing to respond to all your cat's whims; your cat should normally have a good and varied diet and, if it only wants

Some cats are very choosy about their food

An active cat spending a great deal of time outside needs more food than an indoor one

hamburgers, it is undermining its own health by doing so. If your cat refuses its food from one day to the next, it may be that there is something wrong with the food itself. It may also be that your cat has a toothache or an inflammation, or a foreign object in its muzzle, esophagus, or stomach. Even stress and mental distress can result in refusal of food—you know your cat best and are best placed to judge the nature of the problem. Be vigilant and, if you are not happy, take it to the vet.

How much to eat?

It is a familiar myth that cats never eat more than they need. Boredom—which can sometimes afflict "indoor" cats—can cause a cat to eat more than is good for it. Particularly after neutering, a cat is more likely to get fat. The quantity of food a cat needs varies from one individual to another. Not every cat has the same metabolism and even litter siblings can have different food requirements. There are also a number of other factors that are important in determining how much food a cat needs. A pregnant queen, or an active tom that, especially in win-

ter, is often outside, will naturally require more food than a quiet, neutered cat that sleeps a lot and does not get much exercise. In the first instance, it is worth following the guidelines on the cat-food packet. Secondly, have a look at the cat itself. Most pet cats are given far too much to eat. You rarely see cats that are too thin. In cats, fat is first stored in the cavities of the chest and stomach; the ugly "beer belly" only appears at a later stage. If you want to know if your cat is too fat, or just the right weight, feel its rib cage. You should be able to feel the ribs easily. If you have to press down deep to be able to feel

It is a myth that cats will eat no more than they need

the ribs, then the cat is certainly too fat. In particular, neutered cats that do not move about much can sometimes get too fat. Obesity can produce serious problems that will shorten the cat's life, with diabetes being the most common

cause the fatty degeneration of the liver, already referred to, which will poison the cat. Slimming should be approached on two fronts—first, you should try to make the cat get more exercise. You can do this by playing more with it (for instance, throwing screwed up balls of paper for it to chase). Another idea is to hide its food all over the house so that it must actively hunt for it and so burn up the calories. Give less food than usual to your cat, or gradually switch it over to a lighter diet. Your vet can advise you on how to do this.

Cat treats

If a cat gets a well-balanced, complete diet, then it needs no cat treats. The extra vitamins and other ingredients (such as calcium) that are included in cat treats can disturb the nutritional balance and, if the cat eats too many of them, cause health problems. There are, for example, cat treats that contain vitamin A. This vitamin is already included in most cat foods and too much of it can be deleterious to your cat's health. If a cat, for instance, a pregnant queen, gets too many vitamin A treats, this can also have consequences for her unborn kittens. Cat treats have mainly been invented for cat owners—they look nice and colorful and you want to spoil your cat a little. If you want to give your animal cat treats, be just as critical in buying them as you are when buying cat food; if the

If a cat is too fat it is best to put it on a diet

complaint. If your cat loves its food, do not keep its bowl filled up, but feed portions at intervals throughout the day.

Slimming

If cats are too fat you should, in their own best interests, help them to slim. Remember, however, that a cat should never fast. This can

A neutered male with a "pot belly" is not a pretty sight

Cat treats are by no means
always healthy

SOME CATS PREFER WATER THAT HAS BEEN STANDING FOR A WHILE, SUCH AS WATER FROM A FISH BOWL, VASE, OR POND. USUALLY THAT DOES NO HARM, BECAUSE CLEAR WATER IS WHERE FISH AND PLANTS LIVE TOO. AFTER A TIME, HOWEVER, UNPLEASANT BACTERIA CAN ACCUMULATE IN YOUR CAT'S WATER BOWL, WHICH CAN MAKE IT ILL. SO GIVE YOUR CAT FRESH WATER EVERY DAY. INCIDENTALLY, MILK IS A FOOD, AND NOT A REPLACEMENT FOR FRESH DRINKING WATER.

manufacturer does not give full details of the ingredients, do not buy them. It is best not to give your cat more than a few treats a day. A first-class alternative to cat treats are in fact ordinary dry chunks of a type or brand of cat food that your pet does not normally find in its bowl. The extra attention paid to the cat combined with a taste and texture that is different from its normal food will appeal to it just as much, if not more, than (much more expensive) cat treats.

Many cats prefer to drink water that has been
"standing around"

House-training

18

Unsanitary behavior—a major problem

Probably the most common behavioral problem in cats is unsanitary behavior. This can have many different causes. The most obvious ones are simple to remedy; others demand solutions that require more work. Below are the most common causes of unsanitary behavior.

The cat does not recognize the smell and texture of the litter

Cats are creatures of habit. They can become very attached to a particular brand of litter. If its owner buys a different brand, it can be enough to make a choosy cat look for another corner to relieve itself. If you want to change to a different type or brand of litter, put some of the old, soiled litter on the new litter in the litter tray, so that your cat recognizes the smell and cannot make a mistake. Even so, the cat may still refuse to do its business there, perhaps because the new litter granules do not feel right under its paws or it objects to the smell of them.

Black classic shorthaired cat

Other cats

Most cats do not like to use a tray that has been used by another cat. If you have several cats, it is advisable to give each one its own litter tray. Do not put these next to each other in the same room, but distribute them through the house, to

Do not let it reach this stage—unsanitary behavior and diseases will be the result

Most cats dislike sharing a tray that is also used by other cats

prevent a dominant cat keeping the other cats' toilets "engaged."

Then there is a great risk that it will find this too "scary." It may help to take away the flap over the entrance or—for a while—put the hood beside the tray, so that the cat can gradually get used to it.

Hygiene

The most common cause of unsanitary, behavior is that the cat does not find its litter tray clean enough. A daily clean and a good scrub-out once a week is therefore essential to prevent such behavior.

Another litter tray

If you buy a new litter tray, this can cause house-training problems. Has your cat always done its business in an open litter tray and have you now acquired one with a hood and an access door?

A litter tray should be in a quiet spot

Litter tray in the wrong place

A litter tray somewhere where it is noisy, such as next to the washing machine in a main "highway" in the house, where everyone has to pass, will rarely be acceptable to a cat. In that case, putting it somewhere else will solve the problem. It can also sometimes happen that the litter tray is too close to the food bowl. Cats usually find it unsavory to do their business so near their food.

Spraying by both sexes

Tom cats become sexually mature between the ages of five and sixteen months, and can then start to spray. Toms stand to spray while they vibrate their tails. The scent signal of the strong-smelling urine does not usually go on the floor, but is sprayed onto a vertical surface. Toms spray both outdoors and indoors—in fact, spraying is quite a separate problem from unsanitary behavior. Queens in season can also spray. They do this in the same way as the males. It can also happen that a sexually mature male or a female in season does not spray, but, squatting, urinates at a place where they are not supposed to. Neutering usually remedies this problem permanently. Among males, however, spraying can become a habit, so it is advisable not to wait too long before neutering.

Stress, anxiety, and discord

Change in the make-up of the family, a move to another house, or sometimes even the acquisition of a new piece of furniture, is for some cats extremely stressful and causes them—usually only temporarily—to forget their house-training. Some cats stubbornly persist in unsanitary behavior, if, for instance, there is a new cat in the house, or a dog they do not get along with. People who own several cats will occasionally find

that one of them is always bullied by the others. Sometimes, too, this makes them so stressed that the subordinate cat starts urinating at random. It sometimes helps to spray the places it chooses

Somali

with a preparation containing pheromones. If this does not work, there is often only one solution which is to relocate the cat in question. A cat does not always express its unease or nervousness by becoming unhappy, nervous, or aggressive, but sometimes only by unsanitary behavior. Such cats may be perfectly all right in another place, where they fit in better.

Stress and quarrels with other cats can lead
to unsanitary behavior

your neighbors' cats. All you can do is to prevent your cat visiting the places where it should not be making deposits.

Underlying health problems

If a usually well-behaved cat displays unsanitary behavior without apparent reason, there is likely to be an underlying health problem. Diseases such as diabetes, bladder inflammations, or kidney problems can make it abandon its house-training. The cat cannot really help it in that case. If you suspect there may be a problem, contact your vet.

Marking out territory

If a cat defecates or urinates on the doormat, it is very likely that outside there is a— possibly new—male or female cat in the neighborhood that makes your cat feel uncomfortable and unsafe. Its urine or feces are then deposited on the doormat or in other strategic places to act as a kind of barrier to that neighboring cat. This is a difficult problem, because you cannot control

Some indoor cats regain their clean habits if they are
allowed outside again

Sudden unsanitary behavior may have a medical cause

Too little space
A small percentage of cats adopt unsanitary habits if they are unhappy with their limited freedom. Many indoor cats stop their unacceptable behavior when they are given the opportunity to enlarge their territory.

Reproduction and birth control

are more affectionate than normal. They keep nudging things, including your legs, and they demand more attention. If you stroke their back, they will press the rear part of their body upwards and their front towards the ground. Sometimes they also stamp with their back

Estrus—the symptoms

Cats have a reproductive system that works rather differently from other animals. Ovulation only occurs under the influence of stimulation, such as being covered. This is called "induced ovulation." A queen can and will only be covered, and is also only fertile, when she is in season. The degree to which she is in season varies from one female to another and is often associated with the breed. Some females are quite obvious about it and very noisy, but in others it is hardly noticeable. Usually females in season

Female cat on heat

Oriental breeds often come into season at an earlier age and more frequently

paws, and often drop to the ground and start rolling about. Females in heat are also often more vocal; the quietest animals express this by frequent soft purring, but more temperamental queens can meow very loudly. In other words, they go "calling" for a mate and, during this time, oriental breeds and cats with an oriental streak in them can in particular produce noises resembling the crying of a human baby. Obviously they are not always so active; between the peaks of emotion they sleep and rest a lot and do not look as if they were in season. The length of time they are in heat can vary; for most females it lasts about five days, but it can be anything from three days to a week. Some queens spray when they are in season; they mark objects in the house with their urine. It speaks for itself that you must be extra vigilant during this period. Queens in heat will often do anything they can to go outside, to look for potent males. These males can carry sexually transmitted and lethal diseases, such as Feline Aids (FIV) with which your female can become infected.

Estrus—when and how often?

A queen will first come into season between the ages of about four and sixteen months, but the average is nine to ten months. Temperamental animals with an oriental streak are often the earliest, while cats with more northerly origins often have their first season somewhat later. The frequency also varies from one female to another. Some come in heat virtually every month, and others every six or twelve months. The interval between two different seasons is usually two to three weeks, provided no ovulation has taken place. In cats that have ovulated, even if it did not result in pregnancy, it will be about seven weeks before the next season occurs. Coming into season can be activated by heat, an increase in the number of daylight hours, and the presence or (actually) the absence of an entire, sexually mature male. A female living indoors in a centrally heated household, who

Persian Longhair

heavy seasons and you do not want to breed from the animal, have her spayed. She will not come into season any more, cannot suffer unwanted pregnancies, and will be protected to a great extent from the health risks related to the reproductive system. If, however, you do want to breed from the animal, it is advisable not to let her go on having seasons without arranging for her to be covered. Certainly, a queen who has frequent heavy seasons is better being covered at a rather younger age. This is far preferable to her having to endure the stress of repetitive cycles or being given medication to suppress estrus, either of which can pose a risk to her fertility and/or the development of any future kittens.

never goes out, may, because of the lack of seasonal influences, spend the whole year in season. It is thought that the onset of the first time a cat comes in heat is influenced by its reaching a specific weight.

Estrus—the risks

Each time a female comes into season, it affects her resistance. During this time queens eat very little and often get excited, so that they lose weight. If they have many heavy seasons soon after each other without being covered, their health can be undermined. Their body appears to cave in, the condition of their fur deteriorates, and they become more susceptible to disease. Moreover, a queen in season has to cope with severe hormone fluctuations. These do no harm if she is actually covered, as happens in the wild, but in our living rooms it does not always reach that stage. The hormone fluctuations associated with coming into season, not being covered, and coming in heat again, can cause problems in the uterus. These problems can lead to a cat becoming infertile or developing cysts in the womb that at a later stage can obstruct the normal development of unborn kittens. If you have a female cat that has frequent and

Female Maine Coon

Cats in heat will try anything to escape

Neutering

If you do not plan on allowing your female to have a litter of kittens, it is better to have her spayed. The great disadvantage of sterilization, however, is that the operation cannot be reversed, as the vet will remove the animal's ovaries and sometimes also its uterus. Opinions differ on the age this should be done: in the United States it is quite usual for kittens, including pedigree animals, to be neutered before they go to their new owners, while in Europe the tendency is to wait until the cat is older, but preferably before they first come into season. This is because it reduces the likelihood of mammary tumors (breast cancer) developing at a later age.

The "pill" for cats

In some countries, owners who are undecided as to whether they want their queens to have a litter can temporarily suppress estrus by administering the "cat pill." To keep hormone fluctuations to a minimum, this should be given consistently at regular intervals—usually once a week or every two weeks—and not just occasionally. It is also inadvisable to give the pill to a cat that is actually in season, because of hormonal fluctuations and associated health problems. For a female that rarely comes into season and, when she does, is relatively unperturbed by it, the use of the pill is often unnecessary; you can let her come into season normally until you have her covered, the first time preferably before she is sixteen months old. Use of the cat pill over a long period is not recommended. It increases the risk of uteritis and can cause tumors of the mammary glands and diabetes at a later age. Letting a female come into season repeatedly without being covered has the same negative side effects. For the sake of her health she should

In the United States cats are neutered when they are still kittens

White Maine Coon, female

Black tortoiseshell and white longhaired female

have had her first litter well before her second birthday and preferably at a much earlier age. The risk of complications increases rapidly after that age, so do not put off spaying longer than necessary. In fact, the side effects of using the pill are one of the reasons that this form of birth control for cats is not permitted in the United States. In Europe the cat pill is generally accepted by breeders and vets, provided it is used consistently and not for too long a period.

Some entire tom cats become fidgety, restless, and noisy

The male role in reproduction

In contrast to queens, that are only interested in reproduction when they are in heat, unneutered toms do not have "seasons"—they are always fertile and ready to cover. The age at which a male develops in this way varies and is often a feature of the breed. Here, too, we see that the slim, oriental breeds and non-pedigree cats with an oriental look reach maturity earlier than the more heavily built, quieter breeds such as the Persian Longhair or Maine Coon. A tom cat can be fertile by the age of four or five months, but

Non-pedigree longhaired kittens

An "entire" male as a household pet?

A sexually mature, unneutered male is referred to as "entire." Keeping such a male as a household pet is generally not an easy job, but much depends on the disposition of the cat itself. A tom that lets itself be governed too much by its hormones will make use of every opportunity to escape and go on the prowl for females in season. This may take it much further away from home than is sensible and it could get into difficulties—each year, especially as the days grow longer, the majority of cats involved in road traffic accidents prove to be entire males less than a year old. Apart from that, an entire male can as easily as a queen in heat find a partner carrying a lethal disease such as Feline Aids. A tom governed by its hormones often does not want

may, on the other hand, not show any interest until it is more than fourteen months old. The way in which males react to their sexual maturity varies from one animal to another. Some toms can become restless, unsettled, and noisy; they might stray, lose weight, spray a lot, and forget to groom themselves. They can only think of one thing and are completely governed by their hormones. Others are quite peaceful and there is nothing to note except that, if they meet a female in season, they want to pay court to her. All types of behavior are possible between these two extremes. An unneutered male will at some point develop secondary sexual characteristics, the most noticeable being the fat cheeks of the tom, which in some are so pronounced that they influence the natural shape of the eyes—the cheeks seem to press the bottom eyelids upwards. After neutering, these typical male cheeks gradually disappear and the cat regains its normal head and eye shape.

Driven by his hormones, an entire cat may leave home

Nearly all unneutered toms put out scent flags

and be difficult to remove. For this reason, most breeders do not keep their stud cats indoors, but let them live in specially adapted accommodation outside where they can also be introduced to females in season (see also: Stud cats' accommodation). As a matter of fact, not all males spray—there are studs that have lived all their lives indoors, use the litter tray quite normally, and are very people-oriented. This is particularly the case in quiet breeds such as the Persian Longhair, and to a lesser degree in some other breeds; among these, spraying and the typical, restless tomcat behavior does not always follow. There are also toms that only spray in summer, or if there is a queen in season in the vicinity, or as a form of protest—for example, if they are not allowed out. Preparations to counter spraying are available from vets, but unfortunately do not work with all cats.

anything to do with the members of its human family and has no time for cuddles or relaxing at home, or only for a moment, after which it is off again, looking for a queen. If it is forbidden free access to the outside world, then it may get very frustrated and become even more restless. In addition, many unneutered males put out scent flags and are likely to spray indoors. The urine that they leave on vertical surfaces has a penetrating odor that can pervade the whole house

Neutering of male cats

Because a tom is quieter and more domesticated after being neutered, no longer has a tendency to roam, has a better coat, is more people-oriented, and stops spraying, male cats that are

Oriental Longhair, tom

Queens may have kittens fathered by several different toms

kept as pets are usually neutered as a matter of course. During this routine operation, the vet removes the cat's testicles. Any hormone-related behavior disappears after neutering, though very occasionally males will go on spraying afterwards if that has more or less become a habit for them. Internationally, there are differing views on the age at which a tom should be neutered. In the United States it is the custom to have kittens neutered before they go to their new owners. In Europe, it is more usual to wait until the male is about six months old, mainly because it is generally considered that the animal should have outgrown the kitten stage because of the anesthetic risk. It has been established, however, that males neutered early, i. e., at the kitten stage, actually grow larger than those neutered at a later age. This is because fusion of the epiphyses is a hormonal function. Due to the lack of these hormones, the epiphyses in neutered animals fuse later, so that they keep growing for longer. The extension of this growing period is about eight weeks. The coat of a neutered cat is often fuller, with less hair loss

during molting periods, and this—along with the size of the cheeks—is a major reason for there being separate show classes for neutered and entire cats.

Kittens from several fathers (superfetation)

The reproduction of cats is different from that of most other mammals. A queen's ovaries are activated by the action of covering. There are tiny "barbs" on the tom's penis that stimulate the wall of the vagina, so that an egg is deposited. There is then a strong probability that the female will be fertilized. If the female in question roams freely out-of-doors and is covered by several different males, there is a chance that the kittens in her litter may have several different fathers.

A litter of kittens

Preliminary considerations

Almost all cat lovers will agree that there are few things so appealing and disarming as a litter of soft and fluffy, healthy kittens, tumbling over each other. It is not unusual, therefore, for the owner of an unspayed female to feel an overwhelming desire to breed from her at some point. There are, however, disadvantages to this. Of course, if all goes well, it is a rewarding and certainly an enjoyable experience. After all, hundreds of thousands of people all over the world have become breeders. There are negative aspects to breeding, however—even if it is just one litter—and these should be considered carefully in advance.

Risks for the mother cat

Most queens are delivered quickly and without problems, but there is also the possibility that something will go wrong. A queen can reabsorb the kittens growing in her womb, so that they are never born, or it may be that she cannot deliver her kittens normally and a caesarean will be necessary. Other potential problems may include inflammation of the uterus, perhaps from a dead

A litter of healthy kittens is irresistible

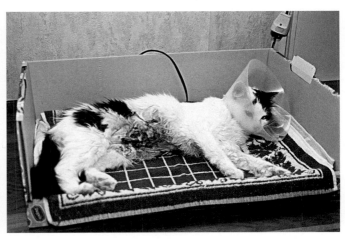

There is always a risk that something will go wrong, as has happened to this female cat

kitten or pieces of placenta left behind, eclampsia, and various difficulties during the suckling of her kittens. Pregnancy and giving birth, however natural they may be, always carry some degree of risk to the mother. It does not often happen that a mother cat dies from a problem associated with her pregnancy or period of nursing—the risk is a small one—but the possibility is there. So never think too lightly of going in for a litter; once the process has been started and the female is pregnant, you cannot turn back the clock.

Risks for the kittens

The birth and development of a litter is undoubtedly exciting. You give the kittens names, they react to your presence, and they learn to recognize your voice. The link with them grows stronger as they grow, but during that process things can also unfortunately go wrong. Congenital abnormalities such as a cleft palate, closed anus, or an open stomach are problems that can surface immediately after, or within a few days of, the birth. Other problems, if they are present, only reveal themselves as the animals grow. Viral diseases, lack of oxygen at the birth, or certain external factors can also lead to the premature loss of one or more kittens. It goes without saying that this is a distressing situation, which is felt even more deeply if ultimately abortive efforts have been made to

You and the mother cat will have your hands full looking after a litter of kittens

save an ailing kitten, for instance by hand-feeding and administering medication. Be sure in advance that you are emotionally able to cope with such a loss, because every breeder will have to face this situation at some point.

Members of your household and your living environment

A litter of kittens has to stay with its mother for thirteen weeks. During this time, the mother and her offspring impose a significant, if not dominant, stamp on the daily course of affairs in the house. For the first few weeks the kittens need peace and regularity. Too many admirers or other forms of disturbance near the litter at this time can upset the mother cat, particularly if she is still inexperienced, so that, for example, she stops giving milk or starts forcibly moving the kittens around. Afterwards, when the little ones begin to walk about and are able to find their own food and drink, everyone in the house will have to be mindful of where they tread. Still later, as the kittens grow bigger, stronger, and more capable, they will develop an irresistible urge to test everything in their path—plants, furniture, anything you put on the table, will become vulnerable to their attentions. Putting the kittens in a separate room

Three-week-old Norwegian Forest kitten

Male Chartreux

Time, space, and money

Not everyone has the temperament, time, space, and money to breed a litter of kittens and bring them up in a responsible manner. For some people, the financial aspect can be a motive to breed pedigree kittens. The value of the average pedigree kitten will easily run into hundreds and—so the reasoning goes—multiplied by five will bring in a tidy sum that will come in very handy, say, just before the holidays. Any serious breeder can tell you that it does not work quite like that. The

where they can do no harm is not the answer, as it is important to the kittens' socialization that they grow up in contact with daily life. Because all members of the household are involved in this and will have to take it into consideration, they should all agree about having a litter. It is also sensible to appoint one person who will be responsible for supervising the mother and her kittens, so that there is always someone who knows what and when the kittens have been fed, and when, for example, they have to be wormed.

Kittens are playful and inquisitive, and can leave a trail of destruction in their need to satisfy this urge

Not everyone has the inclination, time, room, and money to take on the responsibility of breeding a litter

stud fees, the extra travel costs, vaccinations, worming, replacement kitten milk, adjustments inside the house, advertising, applications for pedigrees, and tests for the mother cat can altogether make a big hole in the family budget. If all goes well and you have a litter of four or five kittens that are healthy and need no special extra care, then you may well make a small profit on your litter. Because there is also the chance that things will go wrong, however, you should always note in your calculations that your litter of kittens may in fact start costing you quite a lot of money, especially if you want to do it properly. A little extra space in the home and the heart will do no harm either if you are breeding a litter. Bear in mind that one or more of the kittens may be left with you because you have not been able to find suitable homes for all of them. It can also happen that a kitten that has left you is returned, because somehow or other it did not fit in with its new owner. Finally, there are people who were initially determined to sell their kittens, but become so attached to them that they no longer have the heart to send them away and end up keep the whole litter. There is also the time aspect—breeding kittens takes up a lot of time. Even if all goes as you wish, it means more house-work: look-

Ocicat

people who might be interested in a kitten.

Associations and clubs

If you start breeding a litter of pedigree kittens and want to apply for pedigrees, you will first have to become a member of one of the cat organizations or associations that keep a pedigree register. These only issue pedigrees to their members. Every association has its own ambience in which you may or may not feel at home. The choice of a specific association also depends on the cats you are breeding. With a widely recognized breed such as the British Shorthair, Persian, or Turkish Angora you can join almost any association. If, on the other hand, you have a breed that is still in its infancy and at the experimental stage, or a color variety that is not yet generally recognized, then it is advisable to find out first whether the organization of which your chosen association (usually) is a member, recognizes your queen as a pedigree cat, and so can issue pedigrees for your litter.

ing after the cats and their litter trays, getting their food ready, tidying up the mess the kittens make, and finally getting in touch with all the

Somali kitten, sorrel

The "cattery name"

The kittens you breed can, if you wish, be given their own "surname," which all the kittens you breed now or in the future will bear, as a prefix or suffix to the names you use for them in everyday life. To apply for a "cattery name" you should consult your association. Usually you will fill in a form suggesting names that you like and think suitable, which will then be checked to see if they are already in use or not. In practice it seems that a large number of people choose existing names so that repeatedly new names have to be thought up, with the whole procedure taking some time. If you do not apply for a cattery name your kittens will be given the year of their birth before their usual names.

Not all breeds are recognized by all organizations

and a healthy mother is the only sound basis for this. If you have a white queen, have her hearing tested; most associations insist on this and, in some countries, it is a legal obligation. The BAER test can discover if your potential mother cat is deaf, in either one or both ears.

Temperament and appearance

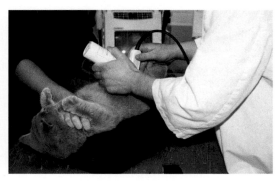

If your chosen breed is subject to an inherited problem, you should have your cat tested for it

Tests

Find out whether any inherited problems occur in the breed you have chosen and whether tests for them are available. You can ask the breeder of your queen, consult the (breed) association, or look this up on the Internet. Do not leave anything to chance on this point. If it turns out that a kitten you have bred later starts to suffer from an inherited disorder known to affect the breed and which is normally tested for, and it comes to light that you have not had the mother tested for it, you can justifiably be blamed. Certainly if the matter ends up in court the result can be expensive. Apart from this, you will want to breed a litter of healthy kittens

Oriental Longhair, white

The prospective mother cat will pass on her genes to her offspring. Therefore, not only should she be healthy, but her temperament and appearance should also be in good order. Perhaps your queen has been shown at some time and praised by one of the judges, or your cat's breeder has told you that she could make a good contribution to the breed. Even then, you should take an objective look at her temperament, as nervous, unstable, or aggressive mothers do not offer the best example to their offspring. Because such characteristics are also inherited to a significant extent, it would be better not to breed from a cat whose temperament is not friendly, stable, and open.

Siberian cat, cream-colored male

The best age

Not all breeders agree on what, precisely, is the best age to have a queen covered for the first time. Some prefer to wait until a female is grown up and has reached its full weight, or has even won a championship title, which is often not until it is two years old. There are risks attached to such a long wait, however; just as people may expect to have more problems if they have their

The expectant mother should be in prime condition both internally and in appearance

first child after the age of about thirty or even later, the same is true for cats. If a cat has her first litter after her second birthday, then the likelihood of complications during pregnancy and delivery is significantly greater than if she is a year younger; moreover, her fertility declines with the years. In general the best advice is not to wait too long. To decide on the right moment, it is important to watch the cat herself and, particularly, the frequency and intensity of her seasons. If a queen first comes into season at the age of five or six months, and then continues to do so frequently, she may be better covered for the first time at the age of ten or eleven months, because every time she comes into heat there is an increased risk of problems, particularly in connection with the uterus. For females who only come into season for the first time around their tenth or eleventh month or later, the second or third season

Turkish Van

could be regarded as the ideal time to have them covered. As far as the condition of the uterus is concerned, you would be on the safe side if you keep to an upper limit of fourteen months. Waiting longer, certainly if the queen has already been in season several times, is not wise (you will find more on this subject in the previous chapter).

The stud—ask the breeder

Have you had your queen tested for possible inherited complaints, has she been declared beautiful in terms of the breed, and is she also healthy? Does she have a friendly nature? Are you a member of an association that keeps a pedigree register? If so, it is time to start seeking a suitable partner for her. If you have no breeding experience and your cat's breeder does, then it makes sense to ask that breeder for advice.

knowledge of the cat's forebears, will usually know of a suitable male. Also, the breeder often has access to a network of well-known breeders where you can sometimes go for a stud, where without his or her intervention or approval you might not have been welcome.

The stud—finding one yourself

If for any reason you cannot approach your cat's breeder, you will have to search for a stud yourself. Keep in mind that what goes for the queen should apply equally for the tom: handsome, healthy (if necessary confirmed by test results), and a good, friendly temperament. Available studs are often listed in the journal of the breed association (if there is one) and in the journals of cat associations, but you can also find them on breeders' web sites. Sometimes breeders will state clearly that the male is available for out-

Ocicat

If he or she is experienced, they will be familiar with the breed and, taking into consideration the way the queen has developed and their

The breeder will often know a suitable stud for your queen

side mating, and can therefore cover "strange" females. Sometimes it is clearly stated that he is not available for outside mating, while other times they are listed without comment and you are free to approach the stud's owner to ask whether he or she would consider your queen for this. Of course, one place where you can meet potential studs in the flesh is at a cat show, though often only a small proportion of the active studs of the breed will be there. This does,

Chocolate tabby Persian Longhair kitten

Male Ragdoll

however, give you the opportunity to compare the animals with each other and make contact with their owners.

looking males, too, can sometimes produce beautiful and lovable kittens—it is the way the bloodlines of male and female combine that make or break a successful union. It is a good thing to research in advance the desirable characteristics of the breed you are concerned with. If, for example, you have a British Shorthair queen, a breed in which small ears are desirable, and she actually has large ears, then it would be better to avoid a stud that either has large ears itself or stems from forebears that displayed this "fault." You should rather look for a tom whose strong points are those that are weak in your queen, and that should preferably also have been present in its parents and grandparents; this applies to appearance as well as health and temperament.

Young British Shorthair, tom

The right combination

Do not be obsessed by championship titles: if a tom has been declared beautiful by the judges it does not automatically mean that he will be good at passing on the qualities of the breed or that his bloodline will be a good match for that of your queen. Conversely, it can also happen that the owner of the tom does not like showing it, but has a first-rate, healthy, and handsome cat that has fathered fine children. Less good-

Before your cat goes to the stud

Before you have your queen covered, check that the injections she has had are still valid, and for how long. In the five months during which she

Somali females, sorrel

Female British Shorthair, cream

stud. Queens have a reputation for not always treating their partners kindly. The owner of the male will not be pleased if his or her tom has to pay for his night out with an injury to his eye or a torn ear.

Contracts

Stud fees are normally about half the average price of a kitten of that breed, or a little more. Usually the money is paid to the stud cat's owner when you collect your female. Sometimes additional agreements are necessary; does the stud's owner expect extra fees if the queen does not conceive or can you come back once or twice without paying more? What if still no kittens are born? Do you get part of the stud fee back if the litter consists only of one or two kittens? It is sensible to discuss these things properly beforehand, or to put them on paper. Unless they know you very well, most stud cat owners will work with a "service contract" that states what each

will be either pregnant or nursing, you will not be able to have her inoculated, and a recent inoculation is necessary for her to pass on sufficient antibodies to her offspring. You should have her wormed well in advance of taking her to the stud and, of course, ensure that she is free of fleas. Next you should ask your vet to check by a blood test that your cat is free of infectious diseases, such as Feline Aids (FIV) and Feline Viral Leukemia (FeLV). Many, though not all, associations demand a copy of these test results and will not issue pedigrees if these tests prove positive (i.e. your cat is ill) or if you do not produce one (and so leave your female under suspicion of having one of these diseases). Do not wait for these tests until the queen is in season, because the additional stress of a visit to the vet and having a blood sample taken can affect estrus, and you would then have to wait for the next time to take your queen to stud. Of course, the same goes for the stud, which must also be recently tested for Feline Aids and Leukemia. It is, incidentally, customary to chip off the sharp points of the queen's claws before she goes to

Before you have your cat covered ask for a blood test

The stud's accommodation should be located so that the queen does not have too many distractions

party can expect of the other. In any case it is wise to have a male in reserve, as it can happen that the tom you have chosen is unavailable when your cat is in season. You can then move on to your reserve tom. It is sensible to tell the owner of the second cat that he is your second choice, as tactfully as possible. Because your queen will spend some time with her stud, it is

Persian Longhair, black tortoiseshell female

important that you are happy not only about the stud's owner, but also about the accommodation. It goes without saying that the hygiene in the stud's accommodation should be in good order and that you should feel your female will be safe there and not able to run away. The

Oriental Longhair kitten

accommodation should offer sufficient privacy to the queen and the tom. If the stud owner's other cats can come into contact with either the tom or the queen, or it is possible to see any other cats from the stud cat's accommodation, there is a considerable risk that the queen (particularly if she is still inexperienced) can be so distracted that nothing comes of the mating.

The queen is normally taken to the stud for covering

queen is not immediately covered on the first day she is with the stud, but there are exceptions. She has to get used to him and her new surroundings, and it is very likely that she will hide herself away in a corner somewhere. Normally she will not be covered until the second or sometimes third day of her stay. If the queen does not let herself be covered, then there is little you can do other than bring her back the next time she is in season. Then, because the surroundings and the stud are no longer completely new to her, there is a chance that she will feel at ease sooner and accept the cover.

To the stud

The queen is normally brought to the stud for covering and will usually stay there some three to five days. This is necessary because a tom cat will often only cover in an environment familiar to him and a female will let herself be more easily persuaded in the male's territory. This is what happens in the wild. You will, of course, have been in touch with the stud's owner and agreed on everything with him or her well beforehand. On the day the queen comes into season, you should telephone the stud's owner to make final arrangements. Normally a female is taken across on the second day of her season. On the first day, she might well be upset by a ride in a car, so that her season stops. Usually the

The stud holds the queen with a bite in the neck

The cover

Mating between cats is not so simple a procedure as it is between most other kinds of animals. Male cats often have to work very hard to make themselves acceptable to a female. Queens can also be very "catty" to the stud and it quite frequently happens that an over-precipitate tom is sharply put in his place. That is why an inexperienced female is best taken to a quiet, experienced male, and vice versa. Inexperienced studs often have difficulty in choosing the right position, and when combined with an inexperienced queen this can prevent a successful cover. As soon as the queen indicates that she wants to be covered, the stud will mount her and fix her, holding her in position by biting her in the neck.

A stud tries to make advances

When all is done, the cats are usually no longer interested in each other

If cats know each other very well this "fixing" is often omitted; the queen has so much confidence that she does not jump away and the stud realizes this. A female wanting to be covered will push the back of her body up high, keep her tail a little to one side and stamp her back paws. Queens who are still a little uncertain or even frightened, often keep their tail between their legs or roll onto their side, so that mating is impossible. As soon as the female is actually covered, no one will fail to notice it. The actual mating takes very little time, but as soon as the male withdraws, the barbs on his penis stimulate the walls of the vagina and that can, it is assumed, be painful for the queen, and cause her to scream. Some females turn round like lightning after a cover and give the male a clout. An experienced male knows that as soon as he withdraws, he must take cover at great speed. After a successful mating the female will roll vigorously on the ground. Then follows a pause for a rest, after which the whole game of courtship and mating will start again. Only when the queen is no longer in season does the tom's interest in her diminish at which point there will usually be no more activity between them. That is when the tom's owner will phone you to come and collect your queen. Of course, there are females who do not scream after being covered, and some who only let themselves be covered when there are no people around, so that the owner of the stud cannot always say with certainty that a cover has taken place.

Preventing abnormalities in kittens

It is important to give the queen a high-quality diet for the whole period of her pregnancy, but certainly no extras. Extra vitamins and minerals can adversely affect the unborn kittens. Unborn kittens can also acquire problems, such as deformities from some kinds of paint, so wait a little before painting the house. Also, do not give your pregnant cat any flea treatments or have her wormed or x-rayed.

In longhaired females the hair round the nipples may be trimmed away

Pregnancy and changes in temperament

When queens become pregnant after being covered, they are often, but not always, quieter than usual. They sleep a lot. Very occasionally a queen will display some in-season behavior as soon as

Pregnant cats are often much quieter than usual and spend a lot of time sleeping

A heavily pregnant cat

Cats can have up to twelve kittens—this cat has only one

she comes home from her mate. This has nothing to do with whether or not she is pregnant. Some females do not feel very well in the first weeks and express this by being sick. Changes in behavior can occur from about the fifth week of pregnancy. These will be particularly noticeable if the queen shares the house with other cats. A mother cat with kittens should, in fact, be highest in status and she will have to try and capture this position during her pregnancy. From about the fifth week of her pregnancy onwards she can, therefore, become rather irritable with her feline housemates, though this is certainly not the case with all female cats.

Symptoms of pregnancy

During the first three or four weeks of her pregnancy there will rarely be any noticeable changes in the appearance of the queen. After that, her nipples begin to change from a pale shade to a rosy color. The hair around the nipples starts to clear away. From the fifth week of pregnancy the cat will increase a little in girth, certainly if she is carrying several kittens and is not very large. From the sixth week she really begins to expand generally. The uterine horns lie just below and parallel to the spine, so in the first instance it is not the belly that expands, but the loins. Do not be fooled by her girth; this reveals nothing about the number of kittens she

is carrying. Large females with long bodies can produce seven kittens without really getting fat, while more thickset, smaller cats can be quite fat and yet only be carrying two kittens. Also, the amount of amniotic and body fluids that the pregnant cat holds varies from one cat to another. You will notice that a pregnant cat, in the last weeks of her pregnancy, begins to explore places in the house that held no interest for her before. With her delivery imminent, she instinctively searches for a safe and quiet place in which to bring her kittens into the world. This is the signal for her owner to organize the kittening box or kennel and familiarize the cat with it.

The kittening box

It is important that at least two weeks before the calculated date you should put a kittening box or "kitten pen" in the house and encourage your pregnant cat to become familiar with it. You can do this, for example, by giving her something tasty to eat there and putting a nice soft blanket in it. Place the box in a dimly lit, quiet spot, far from any bustle and as sheltered as possible, and there is a good chance that she will find it for herself. A good kittening box is strong and stable, large enough for the queen to lie comfortably at full length inside, and high enough to keep out draughts. Banana boxes are very popular and indeed first-rate for size, but are in fact

A kittening box has to be large enough

better avoided because of the insecticides they sometimes contain. A box of the type used to deliver a TV or microwave is more suitable. Hopefully the expectant mother will agree with your choice and with the location of the box, because it is impossible to force her—any pres-

sure can even halt the pregnancy. You could line the box with an absorbent maternity bed mat, available from drugstores. Newspapers are less suitable because they contain ink, and most cloths and towels end up with too many folds and creases in which a small kitten can get trapped or smothered, and loops in which they can catch their nails.

REQUIREMENTS FOR THE DELIVERY

- A GOOD BOX (NOT A BANANA BOX, BECAUSE OF INSECTICIDES) OR KITTEN PEN
- DIGITAL THERMOMETER
- DIGITAL KITCHEN SCALES OR LETTER SCALES ACCURATE TO ONE TENTH OF AN OUNCE
- TOWELS OR WASH FLANNELS
- ABSORBENT MATERNITY BED MATS
- HIGH-QUALITY REPLACEMENT KITTEN MILK
- INSULIN SYRINGE WITHOUT NEEDLE
- TELEPHONE NUMBERS OF VET AND STUD OWNER
- WRITING EQUIPMENT AND NOTEBOOK
- GLUCOSE

The role of the vet

If all goes well, you will not see the vet until the kittens are four weeks old, when they will need their first worming treatment. However, if anything goes wrong, a customer-friendly vet with plenty of cat experience is indispensable. Ask your vet beforehand how he or she feels about

Black tabby house cat

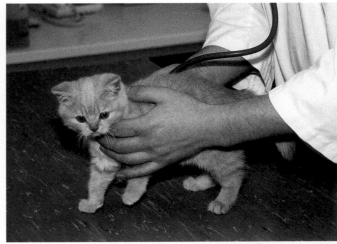

When breeding a litter a good vet is invaluable

being asked for help if your pregnant cat needs this outside the normal opening hours. After all, not all vets are anxious to interrupt their sleep for an emergency case or carry out a caesarean on a Sunday or holiday. A good, skilled vet whom you can consult at any time can, in case of need, mean the difference between life and death.

The days before the birth

A cat's pregnancy lasts about 65 days, reckoning from the first successful cover. These 65 days are an average, with some cats giving birth five days earlier, or five or six days later. Some cats have a slight show one or two days before the actual birth, in the sense that a rather dark discharge appears from their vulva, which sometimes sticks to their coat. In many—but by no means all—cats that are about to give birth, the body temperature will fall by a couple of degrees Fahrenheit from about 24 hours before the birth. Cats normally have a temperature of 101.3° F, so their temperature one day before the birth will be about 99.5° F. Other cats, however, will not show a drop in temperature until just before the birth, and there are some whose temperature will not drop at all. Almost all pregnant cats become rather

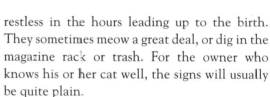
Female Ragdoll

restless in the hours leading up to the birth. They sometimes meow a great deal, or dig in the magazine rack or trash. For the owner who knows his or her cat well, the signs will usually be quite plain.

The birth— the onset of labor

Before the birth of her kittens your cat has contractions, which you can see on the outside of its flanks. They can vary in frequency, strength, and duration. From a medical point of view, however, the birth only starts when they are accompanied by the urge to push. These contractions are several degrees stronger then the earlier, dilation ones and you will certainly recognize them. Normally, the first kitten is born an hour after the first serious contractions. If it takes longer and if the queen is very restless, then it is advisable to contact your vet, because it is possible that something has gone wrong, so that the kitten cannot be born in the normal way.

Ocicat

Male Oriental Longhair

The first kitten

As soon as the kitten is in the birth canal, the mother will start turning round in circles, though there are females who remain still quite peacefully. Certainly if it is the first time the cat gives birth and it is her first kitten, it can happen that you see a piece of the bulging amniotic sac, filled with liquid, appear briefly and just as quickly slip back inside; this is just stretching the birth passage and there is no reason to panic. The kitten may be born either head first or breech presentation and, although the former is often easier, there are many breech presentations in female cats that do not cause any problems. Often the kitten has its umbilical cord still fixed to the placenta, which is sometimes born a little later. If the mother cat does not bite through the cord herself, you may, if she allows it, be able to help her by cutting off the cord at least an inch from the kitten's stomach. Because there is blood in the cord and the kitten is still only small, it is sensible first to make sure that no flow of blood is left in the cord, either by tying it up with dental floss or—and in practice this is often more convenient—by pinching the

cord hard for about ten seconds between your thumb and index finger. After that you can usually without any problem cut through the cord at the side of the placenta or fray it—always in the direction of the kitten—with your nails (which have, of course, been well scrubbed and disinfected beforehand). The kitten must be able to breathe freely and that is sometimes prevented if the membrane is still over its head, or if it has landed in a pool of amniotic fluid—

A kitten still in its amniotic sac

If the airways are blocked, dry the face

which will have come out simultaneously with its expulsion—before it takes its first breath. In such an event, dry its head and particularly its mouth and nose as well as possible with a clean flannel, so that it can breathe freely. Make a note of the time of birth of the first kitten and put a cross against it as soon as the placenta is born; pieces of placenta or whole placentas left in the womb can cause very nasty inflammations. As many placentas should be born as there are kittens. It may be that a kitten that is just born lies quite still. You can then dry it with a rough but clean flannel. Massage it on the back and sides with circling movements. If that does not help, a drop of seventy percent proof alcohol on the tongue can sometimes work wonders.

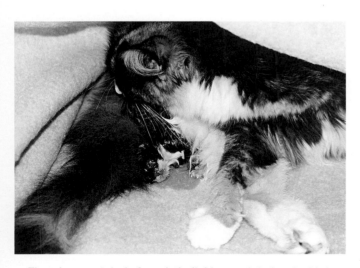

There is a great deal of amniotic fluid around during the birth

Two kittens at the same time?

The second kitten may follow straight after the first. In fact, it sometimes happens that the umbilical cord of the first kitten is still in the vulva where its placenta is, while the head of the second kitten is already born. This is clearly a case in which you should break the first kitten's cord, particularly if your cat is the type that keeps turning round, which will put unreasonably heavy pressure on the attachment of the cord to the kitten's navel, with possibly disastrous consequences. That the placenta of the first kitten can still be in the uterine horn while the second kitten is born can happen because female cats have two horns to their womb, or

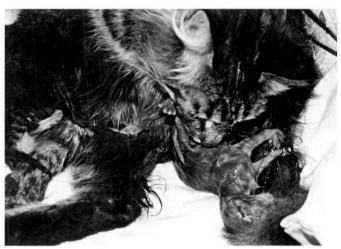

Newborn

rather two long tube-shaped horns, in which the kittens and their placentas are located in tandem. Usually the kittens are born turn and turn about, first a kitten from one uterine horn and then one from the other.

Complete—kitten, with umbilical cord and its head resting on the placenta

expel the next kitten. Because it can take several hours before the last kittens are dry, it is important to make sure that the ambient temperature does not get too low. Cats need less warmth than dogs, so that an infrared lamp (a pig lamp), a hot-water bottle, or a heated pad will hardly be necessary. Nevertheless, if your cat gives birth at a cold time of year in an unheated place, make sure that the kittens do not get too cold. Maintaining body temperature takes up a great deal of energy and a kitten will do better to expend that same energy on growing.

What does the mother cat do?

An experienced mother cat, or one with a natural gift for it, will wash her kittens clean herself, get them breathing, bite off the umbilical cord, and then eat the placentas. This latter may not seem very nice, but must always be allowed because the placenta contains substances that are particularly important for, for instance, her milk yield. The kittens will instinctively crawl to her nipples, where they start drinking almost immediately, still wet from the birth. This drinking encourages the contractions that will

Kittens instinctively crawl towards the nipples

The subsequent course of the delivery

The second kitten may be born straight away, or perhaps an hour or more later. As long as the mother cat is behaving quite calmly and does not panic, you need not immediately phone the vet if the second kitten takes a long time. Sometimes, however, the mother cat is weakened by the contractions, and then it is sensible to con-

An experienced mother cat or a "natural" one will clean up her kittens herself

sult your vet, because kittens that are already in the birth canal can die if the birth takes too long. You can sometimes see from the kitten's mucous membranes if it is all taking rather too long; these are then rather dirty looking, very pale or even blue-gray in color instead of a healthy pink. Also, if a cat pushes for a long time without result, it would be better to contact the vet.

When is it all over?

It is difficult to say when a delivery is complete. After all, the size of a litter can vary from one to twelve kittens, with an average of four. Usually a mother cat that has expelled all her kittens looks tired but satisfied and goes to sleep. Mother cats that have not yet finished can stay restless, often a sign that something has gone wrong.

When the mother goes to sleep it is an indication that her litter is complete

Even if the mother cat does go to sleep, however, that is not automatically a sign that the litter is complete; latecomers are quite often born up to twelve hours—or even more—after the litter looks as if it is complete. As soon as the mother cat is quiet and the kittens have had their drink, you can start cleaning up the kittening box. After the birth of the kittens the linings are often soaked through and very dirty. You can now give the mother cat some water in which glucose has been dissolved. This gives her extra energy that can be absorbed quickly.

Weighing and marking

As soon as everything calms down, you can weigh the kittens one by one; birth weight is often linked to breed or bloodline, but varies a great deal, between two-and-a-half and five ounces. On average a kitten weighs about three to three-and-a-half ounces at birth. It is a good idea to make a note of your results and to start some kind of growth record; in any case, the kittens should be weighed daily for the first four weeks of life, at about the same time every day. This is essential, because a kitten whose weight remains stable, or even drops, may have got hold of a nipple that is not working properly. It may then acquire an irreversible handicap, and will need to be bottle-fed. It may also be that the kitten has a congenital abnormality that hinders its

Ocicat

growth in some way or other, such as a split palate, a closed anus, or some other problem. Slight drops in weight are often not easy to perceive, so weighing, preferably with digital scales, is very important. If you have kittens that look very similar to each other, it is a good idea to mark them. The best way of doing this is with a little nail varnish on the toes of, for example, the back paws. It is not advisable to tie threads of wool round their necks: the mother cat may be inclined to

A Norwegian Forest kitten just a few hours old

remove these "foreign bodies" from the kittens and may not always do so gently. A kitten should in fact gain about ten percent a day in its first week, so that seven days into its life it should more or less have doubled its birth weight.

Bottle-feeding

If one or more kittens do not gain weight sufficiently, you should do something about it immediately. Very young kittens can stand very little and have little resistance. Each additional fraction of an ounce is a gain. So do not wait a few days if you see the kitten's weight is not increasing, but start additional bottle-feeds. For this you should get a good-quality replacement kitten milk, recommended by your vet. Experience teaches that the more expensive brands give the best results. All other kinds of milk are unsuitable for kittens. It is possible to feed kittens younger than two weeks with a bottle, but it is certainly easier to do with a needle-less insulin syringe, as you can give much more accurate dosages this way. Most vets can help you obtain such a syringe. How often you have to feed the kittens is dependent on their growth. If you feed them twice a day and they do not, or hardly, gain, you should do it more often. When feeding, it is important that the kitten sucks properly. Most kittens protest against being fed at first—they only recognize their mother's nipple. If you put slight pressure on the plunger a drop will come out, and the kitten will understand more quickly. In feeding, it is very important that the kitten itself drinks, so you should never press the plunger too far in, but leave it to the kitten. Forcing it to drink can cause the kitten to get milk in its lungs, or in its nostrils, with attendant consequences. So be patient. Meanwhile, give the mother cat water with some glu-

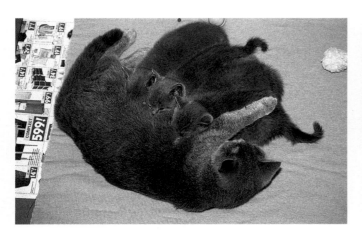

It is a good idea to put an identifying mark on kittens that strongly resemble each other

Occasionally it may be necessary to bottle-feed a kitten

Female Maine Coon

Aftercare of the mother cat

Certainly in the first few weeks after delivery you should keep a close watch on the mother cat. Her mammary glands should stay supple. If they become red or hard, consult your vet immediately. Be generally vigilant; if she looks as if she does not feel well, or her behavior is strange, contact your vet. It can, after all, happen that there is still a kitten or a placenta (or piece of one) left in the uterus, which could make her very ill. A discharge after a delivery, at first red to brownish and later increasingly lighter in color, is normal.

The first weeks of life

If the mother cat and her kittens are healthy, the mother has sufficient milk, and the litter is granted plenty of peace, the first weeks after the birth should run very smoothly and the owner need do little more than weigh the kittens at about the same time every day. Their eyes start to open between the fifth and tenth day of their lives, although this can sometimes happen later or earlier. At first, however, the kittens

cose dissolved in it, let her drink as much replacement kitten milk as she wants, and give her, in addition to her dry chunks, plenty of red meat to eat. This will stimulate her milk yield. It is important that the kittens go on drinking from their mother. Not only does she provide substances that heighten the kittens' resistance in the first few days, but as soon as they stop drinking from her, her milk production will decline.

Somali kitten, sorrel

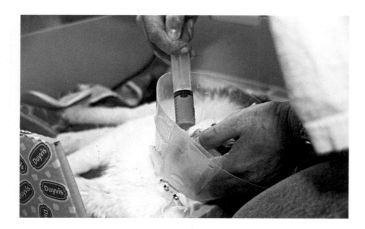

Sometimes problems develop well after the kittens have been born

Socialization

It is, incidentally, very important to ensure that the kittens and their mother in particular have peace and quiet: your mother cat would not be the first to start bullying her kittens, or giving them less milk, simply because too many different people come to look at the litter. So wait to show off your litter until the kittens are at least three or four weeks old, and restrict traffic near the kittening box (and the associated distur-

still cannot see very well—that comes later. It is sensible to replace the lining of the kittening box once every two days, for the sake of hygiene. As long as all goes well, the kittens will spend their days and nights sleeping and drinking. You will not find any excrement from them, because the mother cat cleans it up herself. She goes on doing that until the kittens start eating solid food. If the kittens squeal a lot and plaintively, crawl around as if they are looking for something or, on the other hand, withdraw to themselves, it is a sign that something is wrong. It may be too hot or too cold, perhaps the mother cat has not enough milk, or there may be a health problem. Often that can be discerned from the growth of the kittens (i.e., if their weight stays the same or drops). Consult a vet if you are concerned.

If the mother cat and kittens are healthy, the first few weeks pass by quietly

bance for the mother cat) to a minimum, but do see that the kittens get used to people very early, that is, to you and any other members of your household who are familiar to and trusted by the mother cat. Stroke the kittens gently on their backs and, if necessary, give them extra food. In this way, the kittens will learn at a very early stage that they can only expect good things from people. This is important for their socialization

It is never too early to start getting the kittens used to people

Week-old kittens—one of them has already opened its eyes

Holding and stroking the kittens a great deal encourages
them to be people-oriented

ready for it, explore your living room themselves. Bear in mind, however, that they are still very vulnerable to infections and diseases. Some caution will still have to be taken with respect to the people who come to look at your litter.

A kitten pen

You will notice that from an age of about four weeks, and sometimes even earlier, the kittens will try to climb out of the kittening box. If by then you have put it in the living room, you and the other inhabitants of the house will have to "pussy-foot" around, because there will be a potential accident in every little corner. Of course, it is not always possible to be completely on your guard: certainly in a household where there are small children or where you have many visitors; the house becomes unlivable if everyone has to watch every step. For that reason the purchase of a kitten pen is a good investment. Such a pen is not meant to shut the kitten in, but to protect it. You can buy them ready for use, but you can also make your own. The ideal size

and contributes not only to the genetic make-up of the kittens, but also to a friendly, person-oriented temperament. As soon as the kittens are a little older, from four to five weeks onwards, the kittening box can be moved to a slightly less quiet spot in the house, such as the living room. Then quietly turn the radio up a little so that they get used to all kinds of sounds, and let the kittens, if they indicate that they are

Cornish Rex kittens

The kittens go on suckling as long as their mother allows it

not the intention that the kittens should move about freely. Use only safe materials without splinters or hard edges, such as plasticized net or wood that has been planed smooth.

Additional solids

You can start giving additional solid food when the kittens are about four weeks old. If it is a small litter, and the mother has plenty of milk, then you can very well wait another week. You may choose to give them ready-prepared kitten chunks of a good brand, soaked beforehand in warm water or kitten milk, but in addition it is undoubtedly worth giving them some fresh fish and/or meat every day. This benefits the intestinal flora and a varied menu also prevents them from becoming too choosy about the types of food they will consume. To avoid the menu from becoming too one-sided, which might cause shortfalls or excesses of particular vitamins or nutrients, it is best not to give the same kind of fish or meat every day. Of course, canned food can never replace fresh meat or fish. As soon as

for a kitten pen is about five feet long, and at least two feet wide and high. Make sure there are two doors in it: one in the front of the pen for the kittens to go in and out, and one on the top where the mother cat can go in and out, if it is

Mother's milk contains important antibodies against diseases

From the age of about four weeks extra solids can be
introduced into the diet

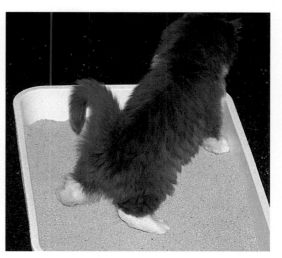

As soon as solids are introduced, a litter tray
becomes a necessity

the kittens eat solid food, it is necessary to put
a litter tray with a low step into it in the kitten
pen, because now the mother cat will stop cleaning up her kittens' excrement and they will have
to learn sanitary habits of their own. Make sure
that fresh drinking water is available to the kittens every moment of the day. It is vital for their
health that kittens have enough water at all
times.

Playing and fighting are part of growing up—they are lessons for later life

As soon as the kittens feed independently it is time to arrange their first inoculations

Inoculations and worming

As soon as the kittens are mainly feeding them-selves, it is time for their first injections. Usual-ly kittens are inoculated twice: the first time at an age of about eight weeks, and the second when they are about eleven or twelve weeks old.

Not until after the second inoculation do they have sufficient immunity to last about a year. It is, for that matter, wise to wait for at least a week after the second inoculation before you take the kittens to their new owners. The body of a newly inoculated animal is very busy making antibod-ies, and stress lowers their resistance, so that a reaction is almost bound to set in. Kittens are almost always infected with worms. As soon as they are about four or five weeks old, or weigh at least a pound, you can give them their first worming. By preference, worming preparations supplied by the vet should be used for this. Instructions for the best way to proceed with them will be on the packaging of the worming treatment. Kittens are usually wormed three times before they are thirteen weeks old.

MALE OR FEMALE?

THE DIFFERENCE BETWEEN MALES AND FEMALES IS MOST EASILY SEEN WHEN THE ANIMALS ARE A FEW DAYS OLD—IN MALES, THE DISTANCE BETWEEN THE ANUS AND THE SEXUAL ORGANS IS GREATER THAN IN FEMALES, OFTEN NO HAIR GROWS ON FEMALES BETWEEN THE TWO OPENINGS, WHILE MALES DO GROW HAIR THERE.

Left a male, right a female kitten

The origin of coat colors

21

Black and its dilutions are eumelanins

Melanins

Coat colors arise from the reflection of light on small particles of pigment, called melanins, on the hair shaft. These melanins can differ from each other in shape, size, and quantity, and also in their position on the hair shaft. They can be distributed fairly evenly over the shaft or in groups close to each other. The color we observe depends on all these factors. In cats we distinguish two basic melanins: phaeomelanin and eumelanin. Eumelanin is responsible for all the colors based on black, and phaeomelanin for those based on red.

Red is a phaeomelanin

Chocolate is a mutation of black

Mutations of black (eumelanin)

If the granules of eumelanin change shape as a result of a mutation, this reflects the light differently, so that we see a different color. Nor-mally the eumelanin particles are round in shape, and optically that produces a black coat. One mutation of the round shape is an oval, and the optical effect is a chocolate-colored coat. A second familiar mutation of the black pigment granules produces the color cinnamon. These particles are neither round nor oval, but rod-shaped. These variations from the basic shape also occur in phaeomelanin particles, but they do not produce such clear distinctions. All the various shades of red in a cat are therefore sim-ply called "red."

Dilution

A diluted color occurs when the melanins are clustered together in groups, so that there are spaces between the groups of melanins and the color is diluted optically. Black becomes blue, chocolate becomes lilac, and cinnamon becomes fawn. The red color can also be dilut-ed, and fades optically to a cream.

Blue (right) is the diluted form of black (left)

"Solid" or "self" colors (with the exception of white)

General

When a cat has no agouti (A) genes but is a "non-agouti" (aa) it is referred to as "solid" colored in the U.S. (N.B., British references are to "self" color). Without agouti genes, the tabby pattern, which is always genetically present, cannot show up in the coat, so that it is evenly colored. The solid or self colors are black, chocolate, cinnamon, and red, with the dilutions blue, lilac, fawn, and cream, and also "solid" white and all possible tortoiseshell colors (black tortoiseshell, blue-cream, chocolate tortoiseshell, lilac-cream, cinnamon tortoiseshell, and fawn-cream). In many self-colored cats, the hairs are rather more lightly colored at

The tortoiseshell pattern goes with solid colors

the root than at the tip. Among breeds of cat that are bred not only for type and coat structure and length, but also for their color, it is nonetheless very important that in solid-colored animals the coat color should be "well distributed throughout." This means that each separate hair should, as much as possible, be the

Blotched or classic ghost markings in a Nebelung kitten

same color from tip to root. In solid or self-colors (except, of course, for solid white), white hairs in the coat are neither desirable nor allowed.

Ghost markings

Every cat has a tabby pattern in its make-up. This is plainly to be seen in non-agouti kittens, which often in fact have vague, but still quite clear, tabby markings that disappear as they get older. Very occasionally the tabby marking remains visible, but only in certain lights—for instance, if the cat is lying in the full sun, and then on the tail and legs in particular. These fading tabby markings are called "ghost markings." At shows these ghost markings on fully-grown cats are not appreciated, except in breeds in which color is not important, such as the Maine

Coon. An exception is made for ghost markings on red and cream-colored cats, on which a tabby pattern is almost always visible (see "Solid" or "self" red and cream).

"Solid" or "self" black and blue

To many people, nothing is more beautiful than a cat with a glossy, deep-black coat, such as can be observed, for example, in the Bombay. Yet, in fact, there is nothing more difficult to achieve than that because, particularly in the summer, black coats—and especially their soft under-coat—can become slightly brownish to reddish in color. It is a normal phenomenon for black to show this "tarnish." It is in fact moisture (from

Black Persian Longhair

Blue Cornish Rex

keen to show a cat that is as black as possible. Occasionally a discolored coat can indicate an excess or shortage of some substance in the animal's diet, such as copper, but usually it is only an aesthetic problem. Blue is the diluted form of black. This coat color is caused by the black pigment particles clustering together, so that spaces occur between them and the color is optically bleached. Often blue hairs are softer than black hairs and this, too, results from the position of the pigment particles. This coat color, often called "gray" or "mouse" by the uninitiated, has always been very popular among cat fanciers. Several breeds are only bred in blue-colored coats, such as the Chartreux and the Korat, but blue is not an unfamiliar color among non-pedigree cats either. In blue cats, too, the coat often becomes slightly reddish in the course of time from the operation of sunlight and moisture, but among shorthaired blue cats this reddish tint is not really very noticeable. During molting, the old hairs that have turned reddish are replaced by new hairs without the red discoloration.

the cat washing itself, rain, and mist) and sunlight that cause slight bleaching and discoloration. There is usually nothing wrong with a black cat that develops brownish or reddish patches—it is just annoying for people who are

Blue is one of the most popular colors in British Shorthairs

Lilac British Shorthair

"Solid" or "self" chocolate and lilac

Chocolate is a mutation of black pigment. The shape of the black pigment particles has changed from round to a more oval shape, so that the light is reflected differently and a chocolate brown color is seen. Solid chocolate is a very popular coat color, particularly for oriental breeds. One particular breed of cats, the Havana Brown, is only bred in this color. A breed being developed, though it is not yet clear whether it will actually win a place in the cat world, the York Chocolate, is also bred only in chocolate and lilac (lilac is the diluted form of chocolate). Just as is the case with black and blue, the chocolate pigment cells are clustered together with spaces between them, so that we see a faded form of chocolate. Lilac is a soft pastel tint, very popular for oriental

Chocolate kitten

breeds in particular. Lilac is sometimes also called lavender. These colors are hardly ever seen in non-pedigree cats.

"Solid" or "self" cinnamon and fawn

Cinnamon is a comparatively new color for cats and another mutation of the black pigment cells. The pigment cells are longer and more rod-shaped, so that optically the color of the coat comes across as cinnamon. The first breed of cats with a cinnamon-colored coat is the Abyssinian, in which this color is more familiar as "sorrel." The pigment cells that cause the cinnamon color can, like black and chocolate, cluster together with spaces between the clusters, so that the color we see is optically bleached; it produces a very light pastel shade of

Cream Persian Longhair

British Shorthair, cream genetically ticked tabby

cally self-colored cat, which is by a crossing with a ticked tabby. This tabby marking is comparable to the tabby markings of a wild rabbit and lacks the clear pattern of striped, spotted, and marbled (blotched or classic) tabbies. When a ticked tabby pattern shines through the coat, it is hardly noticeable—the coat looks solid red. If you meet a virtually solid red cat, it is almost certainly genetically a ticked tabby. It works the same way with cream, since cream is a diluted version of red, and the underlying tabby pattern in cream cats is naturally less visible than in red cats. In cats that are bred, among other things, "for color," such as British Shorthairs or Persians, it is obviously ill-advised to choose a tabby partner (other than a ticked tabby) for a solid red or cream cat: at a stroke it would undo years of selection to achieve the faintest possible tabby marking in the coat. We meet red non-pedigree cats in various

fawn. Cinnamon and fawn are colors that rarely, if ever, occur in non-pedigree cats. However, we do find them in pedigree cats, obviously in the Abyssinian and Somali in particular, and in solid form (without tabby markings) in Oriental Shorthairs and Longhairs.

"Solid" or "self" red and cream

Red cats have always been very popular. It has been said of red tomcats that they grow larger than other cats, but color has no influence on growth, so this must be regarded as an old wives' tale. Breeding beautifully even-colored red cats is no simple task. This is because with phaeomelanins a tabby pattern is almost always visible and seems to "shine through," even if the cat in question is non-agouti. Many years of selection of red cats with the faintest tabby markings has made it possible to render the tabby pattern less pronounced. However, breeders have discovered a more successful possibility of breeding an opti-

Red tabby Persian Longhair

Red cats can be either female or male

shades of red, ranging from very light red (almost cream) to a beautiful warm, deep red, and we often see a beautiful, warm red color in pedigree cats, particularly, of course, those that are bred "for color." The depth of the red color is a polygenetic matter. This means that, by selection of parents always with the warmest red color, a very warm, deep red can be achieved. The cream coat color, for that matter, results from the clustering of the phaeomelanins—the red pigment particles—on the hair shaft. Consequently, there are spaces between the pigment particles and the red color is optically diluted. Cream is a very popular color and found in non-pedigree as well as in pedigree cats. In red-pigmented cats there is in fact another phenomenon, known to cat fanciers as "freckles," which are small, black flecks at the rims of the eyes, lips, ears, and nose.

Red and gender

Many people think that red (or cream) cats are always male, but that is not true. Red cats are just as likely to be female. There may, however, be more red males than females in the world. This is because the likelihood of red males is greater, since they can be born from red females (one hundred percent probability of red males) or from tortoiseshell females (fifty percent probability of red males), regardless of the coat color of the father of the litter. Red females, on the other hand, can only be conceived when a red or tortoiseshell female has a red male as partner. You can read more about this in the chapter on Genetics.

Tortoiseshell

Tortoiseshell cats are also known as "tortie," for short. They owe their name to the fact that their blended coats have a tortoiseshell pattern. In a tortoiseshell coat we see both eumelanins and phaeomelanins, so that the cat has both black and red pigment cells in its coat. Black tortoiseshell and blue-cream with or without white are both common in non-pedigree cats, but we often see this color combination in pedigree cats, too.

A blue-cream cat is sometimes called blue tortoiseshell
or blue tortie

Of course, tortoiseshell also occurs in the two colors developed from black: chocolate and cinnamon. These are called "chocolate tortoiseshell" or "chocolate tortie" and "cinnamon tortoiseshell" or "cinnamon tortie." Because these are not diluted colors, the second color of these tortoiseshell cats is red. Diluted tortoiseshell is also

quite common. The coat is then a blend of blue and cream, lilac and cream, or fawn and cream.

Tortoiseshell— the distribution of colors

The distribution of eumelanins and phaeomelanins in the coat is dependent on chance—the distribution of color is different in every tortie cat. The patches can form quite large, demarcated plates or be very small and merge into each other. They are, however, all referred to as "tortoiseshell." In tortoiseshell kittens, the eumelanins in the coat are at birth almost always the most dominant. Only as the kitten grows will the phaeomelanins become more prominent. Sometimes the amount of eumelanin continues to predominate over the phaeomelanin. Once fully grown, the cat is then almost completely black (or chocolate, cinnamon, blue, lilac, or fawn) with a little red (or cream). It has happened that a female cat that appeared to be blue proved to be a blue *tortoiseshell*; she eventually bore red and cream male kit-

Blue-cream Norwegian Forest Cat

Black tortoiseshell Turkish Angora

tens, which would be impossible for a female without red in her coat. An investigation proved that the queen in question had a small cream spot on her paw pads, which made her a tortoiseshell.

Tortoiseshells and their peculiarities

Because red and cream always denote a tabby pattern, tortoiseshell cats often give the impression of having more than just two colors. When people are asked what color their black tortoiseshell is, it is often described as red with black as well as light red or cream. The light red or cream parts refer in fact to the lighter agouti hairs of the red patches in the coat; genetically it is impossible for a cat to have cream parts while it has black (or chocolate or cinnamon) hairs in its coat, because the gene that causes dilution of the color does not discriminate. It influences all the pigment cells. Tortoiseshell

cats are almost always females, but male tortoiseshells occur sporadically; research has shown that one in every three thousand cats born is a male tortoiseshell. You will find more about this in the chapter on Genetics.

The distribution of black and red is different in every tortoiseshell cat

"Solid" or "self" white

23

White (W)

Solid white cats are far from rare. We regularly come across non-pedigree cats with a solid white coat, and solid white is also common among pedigree cats. One breed, the Foreign White, is only bred in a white coat color. The gene that causes a completely white coat is the dominant inherited W-gene. This gene ensures that the coat stays free of pigment over the whole body and is therefore white. The W-gene is inherited separately from all other genes for colors, the

White is a very common color, both in pedigree and non-pedigree cats

White lies like a kind of fitted sheet over the cat's actual coloring

tabby pattern, and other factors. So genetically, a white cat can carry all colors, patterns, and factors invisibly under its white coat, including white patches, and pass these colors on to its descendants. In these animals, white lies like a kind of fitted sheet over their actual colors. Some white cats have a slightly yellowish deposit on top of their coat. This can be caused indirectly by hormone fluctuations in the body, ingredients in their diet, or external factors such as dirt and moisture. A white cat that is shown sometimes has to be washed with a special shampoo for white cats—and sometimes powdered—so that its white coat shows to advantage. White cats are often more sensitive to sunburn than other cats.

In white kittens the colored patch on the head gradually disappears

Head markings

Young kittens often have a patch of color between their ears which fades as they grow older. This spot of color is the actual color of the cat that is under the white in that place and it can give the breeder an idea of the possible color inheritance of the cat, which will be completely white when fully grown. A white cat may display such a youthful color patch until it qualifies for the senior classes at shows.

White spotting

24

Cats with a great deal of white, such as the Turkish Van, may have blue eyes

S-gene

White spotting is one of the first "domestication" phenomena, alongside solid black. Among wild animals, such as rabbits, we often see that the first mutation of the natural wild coloration (black ticked) is black, followed immediately by white spotting. In cats, white parts of the coat are the result of the presence of the dominant inherited S-gene. This gene ensures that no pigment is produced on some parts of the coat. Cats with a lot of white in their coat can have one or two blue eyes. In cats with a great deal of white, whether or not with blue eyes, deafness is not a problem, because deafness is associated with the W-gene and white patches are caused by the S-gene.

An arbitrary inheritance

It is virtually impossible to predetermine the exact positioning and amount of white. White patches are inherited arbitrarily. If two animals with the same amount of white are mated with each other, then the kittens may have similar markings, or virtually no white, or much more white. Breeding for beautiful white markings and a specific percentage of white is therefore more often a matter of luck than of judgment. A cat with two S-genes normally has a greater amount of white then a cat with only one. The amount of white (and its location) is also dependent, however, on polygenes—"assistant" genes. The amount of white can be

Blue and white Cornish Rex kitten

Not a single white marking is the same

and in those colors that is just the place where the coat is lightest, so that it can be very hard to detect such a white mark. There are also many cats that go through life officially "without white," but in reality do have the S-gene and so can pass on white spotting to their descendants.

In the bicolor Ragdoll symmetrical markings are very important

increased by crossing animals with a great deal of white, and by carrying on breeding only between descendants with a lot of white. By applying reverse selection, i.e., mating animals with as little white as possible with each other, it is possible in the long run to eliminate the white entirely. Yet it is sometimes difficult to discover whether an animal has white spotting or not. This is, for example, the case with silver tabbies or cream tabbies, which have very light-colored bellies. Cats with a little white often have a single white spot between the back legs

British Shorthair, harlequin

Part colors

For show animals in which color and marking are important, there is a terminology for the desired amount and location of the white. Thus "bicolor," literally "two colors," is a term for a cat with about thirty-three percent of white, often with a symmetrical, reversed V-marking on its face. Among bicolor we meet cats with one, as well as two, main colors, tortoiseshell and white. These last are also known as "tricolors," literally "three colors." The term

The distribution of white always runs upward from below

Black tabby and white non-pedigree cat

"harlequin" is used for cats that have only a colored top to their heads, a colored tail, and about three colored patches on their body. A more extreme version of harlequin is "van." In this coat pattern, named after the Turkish Van, the cat has only a colored tail and one or two patches of color on its head.

Delaying cells

The process that determines where the white patches will turn up takes place while the kitten is still an embryo. The distribution of color to white always goes from the top downwards: on top (back, ears, tail) the cat still has color, but not on the underside (belly, chin, neck). Also, if the cat has only very little color, such as a cat with van markings, the patches of color are found on the top of the cat and not on its belly or legs. This is because the cells (melanocytes)

controlling, among other things, color production, make a path for themselves from the spine
of the embryo to the rest of the kitten. If there
is an S-gene in these cells, in single or double
form, then these cells have a tendency to start
slowing down. They do not progress so fast and
there is a great probability that they will not
"complete" their way to the further extremity of
the embryo. This means that only the places
they reach become pigmented, with the others
remain unpigmented and hence white. Of
course, we also come across many cats that have
a white streak on their back, or a white patch on
the top of their neck, caused by extremely
retarded cells. In practice, however, there are
very few colored cats with white on the tops of
their bodies.

Tortoiseshell and white

If a tortoiseshell cat has white patches, it is often
affectionately called a "calico cat" by non-
professionals, though officially it is a tortoiseshell and white. A notable difference between
tortoiseshell and white cats and those without
white is that the former always have large patches of color clearly distinct from each other, and
the latter have a more blended coat. This is
because the white "pushes together" the two
main colors.
White patches cover the underlying color or
colors like a kind of whitewash. In tortoiseshell
females, which have only a few black or red
patches, the crucial patches that make them
into a tortoiseshell may well lie "under the
whitewash." At first sight such a cat looks like
an ordinary black and white or red and white.
Sometimes she passes her coloring on to her offspring as if she were a tortoiseshell, from which
it appears that either the phaeomelanin or the
eumelanin lies hidden under the white. It does
not happen often, but this phenomenon crops
up from time to time, and always gives rise to
fresh speculation. Certainly in females with a lot
of white there is more likelihood of one of the
melanins being covered up by the white.

Tabby

Tabby—a camouflage pattern

A tabby marking is in essence nothing more than a camouflage pattern that enables the cat to merge more or less into its environment, so that its prey does not see it, or not until it is too late. Throughout the world we find wild felines with all kinds of different camouflage patterns. Think, for instance, of the virtually unpatterned lion that hunts on the barren savannah, or the contrasting black stripes on an orange background of the tiger that hunts in the dark jungles and forests, equally rich in contrast. The better its camouflage, the more advantage an animal will have over its prey and its competitors for food. Animals with a pattern favorable to them can therefore find food more easily and are consequently better—and sometimes also more frequently—able to reproduce than animals with a color and markings that render them too conspicuous. Because a coat pattern is inherited, any descendants will also have that pattern, and in their turn reap the benefit of it. It is not surprising that some coat patterns predominate in some regions. In a large and varied habitat there are different camouflage patterns even within the same species. In non-pedigree cats this is also historically the case, although

Male silver tabby British Shorthair

The tabby pattern provides excellent camouflage

today's pampered house cat no longer actually has to lie in wait to catch its prey and has no trouble at all with competitors for its food. That was not always so, however. This is why we see a variety of tabby patterns in cats, from the virtually unpatterned ticked tabby, which has from time immemorial been seen in cats that inhabit regions with a sandy soil such as the Middle East, to the striped and marbled classical tabby pattern in cats that originated in the forests of Europe. Among domesticated cats the black tabby is the model on which they are all based. All the other colors, factors, and patterns that we recognize in our cats today—and there are many—are mutations of the black tabby.

Tabby patterns

Cats with a tabby pattern possess the dominant inherited agouti gene (A), through which the design of the tabby pattern manifests itself. The pattern comes into being because the agouti gene to a greater or lesser extent suppresses the production of the basic color, the pigmentation, on the hair shaft in specific places, so that a set of alternating dark and light-colored bands is formed on each hair, "missing out" the hairs in some places. These retain their basic color over their whole length and form a pattern on the

Red classic house cat

agouti background. Four different tabby patterns are distinguished in cats:

a) ticked tabby (sometimes referred to as "Aby")
b) striped tabby (mackerel)
c) classic or blotched tabby, also called marbled
d) spotted tabby

Ticked tabby and white shorthaired kitten

Ticked tabby (Ta)

Ticked tabby is a pattern we are familiar with from the Abyssinian and Somali, and from, for example, wild rabbits. It is found in cats that originated in desert areas, such as the Middle East and parts of Africa. In essence, "tabby pattern" is a misnomer, because the ticked tabby is completely without pattern; ticked tabby cats have neither stripes nor any kind of coat marking on their body, but a ticking evenly distributed over it. Sometimes a ticked tabby may have rings round its tail, stripes on its legs, and a typical M-shaped outline on its forehead. In breeds such as the Abyssinian, which for generations have been selected, among other things, for a pattern without stripes, such stripes and rings rarely occur nowadays. On the other hand, in breeds that are not bred for color, we do see

Singapuras have a ticked tabby pattern

striped markings. Often striped tabbies have interrupted stripes on their body. At shows there is a preference for uninterrupted, thin stripes, an ideal that can be reached by selecting animals that have as clear a stripe pattern as possible. The opposite can, of course, also be achieved by selection; by consistently mating animals both of which have clear interruptions in the pattern of their stripes, a spotted tabby marking can be the final result. Striped tabbies are also called "mackerel," with the gene inherited dominant to blotched tabbies.

them. In some natural breeds, too, such as the Norwegian Forest Cat, we find cats that as kittens were clearly striped or blotched, but when fully grown look ticked. These are, however, not really ticked tabby cats, but cats with an "untidily" striped, spotted, or blotched tabby pattern that has become blurred. Because the Abyssinian was the first cat with this pattern, ticked tabby is also known as the Abyssinian, or Aby, tabby pattern. The ticked tabby gene lies in another location (locus) than the genes that cause striped or blotched tabbies. Nonetheless, it influences these genes—if a cat has the ticked tabby gene, that gene masks the operation of the genes that cause a blotched or striped coat.

Classic, blotched, or marbled tabby (mc)

Striped tabby non-pedigree cats

This pattern enjoys several names. The common English description is "blotched," but "marbled" is also used, and in the United States it is generally known as "classic." Cats with this pattern ideally have a butterfly marking on each side at the height of the shoulder. An obvious spot is often visible inside the "wings" of this butterfly. A broad stripe runs along the back from the butterfly to the tail, with two thinner stripes on each side parallel to it. However, the distinguishing mark of the blotched tabby is the

Striped or mackerel tabby (Mc)

Striped tabby cats are popularly known as "tiger cats." The pattern derives its name from the vertical stripes on the sides of a striped tabby. In cats that are not bred for color, such as non-pedigree cats and some originally natural breeds, these stripes are often half-way between a spotted tabby and an uninterrupted striped marking. There are also some with very vague, unclear

A short-legged, curly-haired kitten with classic tabby markings

back they have a clearly defined pattern of spots. The spotted tabby pattern may have originated in two different ways, either by selection for generations of interrupted stripe markings, or through a dominant gene that "breaks up" the underlying tabby markings into spots. This gene, called Sp, is located in a different place from the genes that cause striped or blotched tabbies and it can influence both tabby patterns. Sometimes it is still possible to see from a distance which tabby pattern the spotted animal in question has because, for example, the interrupted lines of the oyster markings on the flank of a blotched tabby can be notionally extended. The Ocicat is a breed that

"oyster mark" on both flanks, surrounded by one or more closed rings. In breeds that are bred for color, and so automatically also for pattern, we come across very pure blotched tabby markings, but in the majority of non-pedigree cats and breeds that are not bred for color, there is a wide range of blotched markings. The tail rings, and the rings on the legs and on the neck, are wider in blotched animals than in striped ones.

Spotted tabby markings on an Ocicat

Spotted tabby (Sp)

Spotted tabbies have the same markings on their head, legs, tail, chest, and belly as blotched and striped tabbies, but on the sides and

House cat with classic tabby markings

has blotched tabby markings broken up by the dominant Sp-gene. Because animals also occur in this breed in which the Sp-gene is not duplicated, animals can be born without it. These are normally blotched.

Naming

As a rule, the basic color of the cat comes first in the description, followed by its tabby pattern: for instance, blue striped tabby or blue macker-

Spotted tabby markings on a female Norwegian Forest Cat

el tabby, and lilac blotched tabby or lilac classic tabby. Because all kinds of other genetic factors may be involved, it is not always easy to see what the basic color of some cats actually is. It is then useful to know that the real color can always be found on the tips of the hairs, and in more extreme cases may only still be visible on the tip of the tail. There is, incidentally, a popular term for a black tabby, which is "brown tabby"—in actual fact an incorrect description, because brown refers to the ground color, while the description of all other tabbies indicates their basic color. A true "brown tabby" would be a

The tip of the tail (unless it is white) always shows the basic color, in this case black

Blue classic Maine Coon

Tortie tabby and white non-pedigree cat

chocolate tabby, since "chocolate" is the only brown coat color description used for cats.

may be referred to as a chocolate tortie mackerel or chocolate tortoiseshell striped.

Tortoiseshell or tortie tabby

Tortoiseshell cats with a tabby pattern are also called tortie tabbies (or sometimes torties). It is essential that the pattern in the coat is visible in both colors, and not only in the red and cream parts, because phaeomelanins almost always display a tabby pattern. A tortoiseshell cat displaying a slight tabby pattern in its cream or red colored patches is therefore not by definition a tortie tabby. We only call it a tortie tabby when the parts with a basic eumelanin color (black, chocolate, cinnamon, blue, fawn, or lilac) display a tabby pattern. A cat whose basic color is, for instance, chocolate, and whose tabby pattern in the chocolate-colored parts is striped,

Is it a tabby?

In newborn kittens it is sometimes difficult to distinguish which kitten is a tabby and which is not. This is particularly so in black or blue animals, whose backs are often still dark and unpatterned at a very young age and, with very long-haired animals, too, inexperienced breeders sometimes have particular difficulty in determining whether or not a kitten is a tabby. There are, however, some firm guidelines to follow. In such a case, look at the belly: a solid-colored kitten has a solid-colored belly with perhaps some vague ghost markings, but a tabby kitten has a light-colored belly with darker patches. Often, even in very young kittens, lighter rims round

Tabby kittens can be identified by their spotted bellies

Golden tabby

The term "golden" comes from the worlds of the Persian and British Shorthair, where selection is traditionally based on eye color. In both breeds, preference was given to tabbies with deep orange eyes, except for a few silver variants, which were also bred with green eyes. Because in these breeds eye color is so important, particularly its purity and depth, animals with different eye colors were (and still are) rarely mated with each other. Sometimes, however, black tabby animals with green eyes were born from green-eyed silver lines. They were not silver, so could not be shown as silver, but they also did not have orange-colored eyes, so neither could they be shown as ordinary tabbies. This led to green-eyed, non-silver animals being described as "golden tabby" or "golden shaded."

the eyes are already visible and the inside of the ears is lighter in color. The nose leather can also offer a clue: in solid-colored cats this is even in color, but in tabbies normally (but not always) a little lighter in shade and with a dark outline. As a kitten gets older, the tabby pattern becomes more plainly apparent and, by the time the kitten is a week old, there should be no more doubt. Apart from a few breeds that are bred for even red or cream-colored coats, red and cream-colored cats almost always have more or less of a tabby pattern in their coats, including cats that do not carry an agouti gene. These are not, however, always tabbies.

Not a tabby—this black smoke kitten has clear ghost markings

Golden Exotic

Kitten with tabby markings somewhere between striped and spotted

So golden tabby is the official term for non-silver tabbies with green eyes. Golden tabbies can have any basic color. The term "golden" is always put directly after the basic color: a Blue Brit with a blotched tabby pattern and green eyes would for instance be described as blue golden classic tabby or blue golden blotched tabby. The term "golden" is sometimes also used in breeds not bred for color, such as Maine Coons or Norwegian Forest Cats, which have a warm ground color. Since the term "golden" originated purely and simply to distinguish green and orange-eyed tabbies, and eye color in these breeds is usually not of primary importance, the use of the term golden for these breeds is in essence incorrect.

Tipped and shaded

Golden shaded and golden tipped or golden chinchilla are lighter versions of the golden tabby. Tipped and shaded tabbies are from time to time born from silver-tipped and silver-shaded animals. Breeders of silver-shaded and silver-tipped cats have for generations selected on the basis of cats with the vaguest possible tabby

markings, so that ultimately these only lie like a haze over the ground color. Although these breeders mostly specialize in silver, now and again kittens are born from these bloodlines that are not silver. Instead of a silver-white undercoat, they have a beige-colored one. The actual basic color of the cat is pushed back to the tips of the hair shafts and lies like a haze over the ground color. Non-silver-tipped and shaded cats often have green eyes, because they are descended from silver bloodlines with green eyes. They are then also called golden. Such a cat with a blue basic color is, for instance, called blue golden tipped or blue golden shaded, depending on how heavy the shading of the blue ground color is (see also silver tipped and silver shaded, in the following chapter).

Smoke and silver

26

The Inhibitor gene

Smoke and silver are caused by the same dominant gene, the "Inhibitor gene," referred to in genetics as "I" for short. This gene inhibits the formation of pigment cells, starting from the root of the hair. This means that part of each hair is unpigmented, so optically white or silver-white presents. The rest of the hair is pigmented normally, and can display all possible colors, patterns, and factors; the inhibitor gene is inherited separately. When the Inhibitor gene affects a non-agouti, or solid-colored cat, the resultant color is called "smoke." If the same gene affects a tabby cat, the result is "silver." Silver and smoke non-pedigree cats are not common, but in pedigree cats we see a relatively large number of silver tabbies, undoubtedly the result of the luxurious aura they present.

Silver tabby

The term "silver tabby" is used for cats with a silver-white undercoat overlaid with a tabby pattern in the basic color of the cat. The tabby pattern can be any color, from black and blue to red or chocolate tortie. The most fashionable, however, are silver tabbies with a black basic color, because a black tabby pattern produces the greatest contrast with the white back-

Red silver classic and white house cat

Male black silver classic British Shorthair

Polygenes

A "good" smoke or silver has a clearly silver-white undercoat. In such cases there is no doubt that the cat is a silver (or smoke) and so has the I-gene. We see really "good" smokes or silvers particularly in breeds such as the British Shorthair, American Shorthair, or Persian Longhair. These are bred and judged not only for type, but also for color. In a number of other breeds that are not bred for color, and in non-pedigree cats, there are plenty of vague smokes and also, to a lesser extent, doubtful silvers. This is because the inhibitor gene does not work alone. Various polygenes ensure that the predisposition for a silver-white undercoat is expressed more clearly. If, for example, among silvers (and therefore tabbies), cats with a clearly silver-white undercoat are consistently mated with each other, the loss of color is increased by the influence of the polygenes. This does not mean moving the borderline where the silver stops, but purely the

ground. Think here particularly of British and American Shorthairs, in which black-silver tabbies are particularly popular.

Smoke

When the Inhibitor gene affects a solid-colored cat (i.e., not a tabby), then the cat is called a "smoke." In the ideal smoke, a third to a half of each hair, starting from the root, is not colored. Smokes are encountered particularly in long-haired breeds. The longer coat also shows the smoke color to advantage, so it is not surprising that smokes are common in, for example, the Persian Longhair.

Oriental Longhair, chocolate smoke

Male black smoke and white Norwegian Forest cat

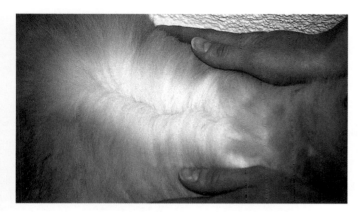

The Inhibitor gene prevents pigmentation from the root upwards

lighter colored head (the "raccoon" or "spectacle" marking) and lighter hairs on the underside of the tail and round the neck. The smoke coloring can, however, disappear temporarily in puberty and only return when the animal is adult. Often in such low-grades you will see that the coat has lost color clearly in some places and not so clearly in others. The degree of the loss of color also changes after molting—this means that a low-grade smoke in the course of its life may sometimes clearly look like a smoke and sometimes like a cat whose coat is colored normally throughout. In doubtful cases it is often better, if only for technical breeding reasons, to have a kitten registered as a "smoke." The Inhibitor gene is, after all, inherited dominant, and if a male or female not registered as a smoke produces kittens that plainly are, this can lead to additional confusion in the registration of the kittens. At shows, a fully-grown doubtful smoke can, however, become a center of discussion.

extent to which the colorless parts lose their color. By selection, the colorless part of the coat becomes "whiter" and the contrast with the overlying tabby pattern becomes greater. If there are few polygenes present, the resulting animals have a poor penetration of silver coloration. In silver tabbies this produces a "tan" color; parts of the coat are brownish instead of silver-white, or become so in the course of time. In non-tabbies, the absence of sufficient auxiliary genes produces a cat where you really have to search for the uncolored undercoat. These are called "low-grade smokes." In fact, brownish or reddish discolorations sometimes occur temporarily in silver cats; this is not a tan color, but a temporary discoloration influenced by hormones, damp, and the weather. This temporary discoloration is sometimes called "rufism."

Is it a smoke?

Uncertainty about the absence or presence of the I-gene occurs particularly among smokes in breeds that are not bred for color, such as the Maine Coon and Turkish Angora. In a kitten it is sometimes difficult to determine if it is a smoke or not. Indications are a

Female silver tabby

Low-grade smoke and blue-cream female

Silver tipped and silver shaded

Silver tipped cats are silver tabbies whom breeders have for generations selected for the vaguest tabby pattern. This selective breeding has suppressed the tabby pattern so far that the tabby markings only show as a darker haze over the silver-white background. Anyone not entirely familiar with cat colors will probably call a silver-tipped cat a "white cat." The darker pigment surrounding the eyes and the nose (the "make-up"), as well as the darker haze over the back and upper side of the tail, however, show that the animal is not white, but has, for instance, a black or blue basic color. Another name for silver tipped is chinchilla: a very desirable color type in the Persian Longhair. In the Asian group of breeds it is a popular color—the Burmilla is bred only in this color. When the darker haze over the white or silver background is heavier, it is called "shaded." Because this is a matter of polygenes, silver tipped and silver shaded kittens are usually found together, in the same litter.

The Burmilla is only bred in silver tipped coloring

The Albino Series (Siamese, Burmese, and Tonkinese factors)

Albino?

The albino series is a series of factors that belong together as a group and are mutations of the gene that produces a normal, fully colored cat, in which all the pigment cells can be given their full expression (C). The most familiar factor in this series produces a cat in which the color pigment can only be normally expressed on the extremities of the body (ears, muzzle, legs, tail, and the scrotum on males). On the rest of the body the color is lighter, to a greater or lesser extent depending on the factor the cat has inherited. Various intermediate stages are in fact possible, starting with the dark-est factor, the Burmese (cb), to the slightly lighter Tonkinese factor (cbcs), the much lighter Siamese coloring (cs), the blue-eyed albino (ca), and finally the red-eyed albino (c). We do not include the albinos here because they rarely occur, but confine ourselves to the most familiar and common factors in the series: the Siamese, Burmese, and Tonkinese factors. All these factors are inherited recessive in respect of complete coloring, so that a kitten always has to have inherited the relevant gene from both parents to be able to show one of these factors in its appearance.

Thai, seal point

Exotic, seal point

Cinnamon-point Siamese kitten

THE ALBINO SERIES
* FULLY COLORED (C)
* BURMESE FACTOR (CB)
* TONKINESE FACTOR (CBCS)
* SIAMESE MARKINGS (CS)
* BLUE-EYED ALBINO (CA)
* RED-EYED ALBINO (C)

Burmese

The Burmese factor

The Burmese factor is the darkest of the three factors. In a cat that has this factor duplicated, the extremities of the body are dark and the rest of the body a fraction—but not much—lighter. Often, too, the color of the extremities is partly suppressed, so that a genetically black cat with the Burmese factor often gives an almost chocolate brown impression. Because the Burmese factor also influences eye color, we often see rather yellowish or yellowish-green eyes in cats with Burmese coloring. A breed that is known for the Burmese factor is of course the Burmese, but this factor has recently been bred into various other breeds as well, such as the Munchkin and Devon Rex, and it also occurs in the Tonkinese.

Devon Rex, seal point

The Siamese factor—colorpoint

The Siamese factor (in genetics indicated by cs) is the best known factor in this series. It produces an animal whose actual color has been pushed to

Siberian Forest Cat, seal smoke point

The Tonkinese factor
—the intermediary

In the Tonkinese factor, indicated in genetics by cbcs, there is something special going on. This factor is in fact the intermediate form between the Siamese and Burmese factors, and occurs when the factor for Siamese coloring (cs) and Burmese coloring (cb) come together in the same cat. If, for instance, a colorpoint—Siamese factor (cs)—is mated to a cat with the Burmese factor (cb), then a litter of kittens with the Tonkinese factor (cbcs) will be the result. This factor is not inherited pure; mating two cats with the Tonkinese factor, in addition to Tonkinese kittens (cbcs) also produces kittens with the Burmese factor (cbcb) and Siamese factor (cscs), usually in the proportions 2:1:1. The eye color of cats with the Tonkinese factor is rather exceptional. It is neither so blue as that of the colorpoint, nor pigmented yellow-green as in a cat with the Burmese factor, but is somewhere between the two. It is described as "aqua," an attractive blue-green color which only occurs in cats with the Tonkinese factor. A familiar

the extremities of the body. The formation of pigment is partly suppressed over the rest of the body, which in colorpoints leads to a creamy to white color on the body. In addition this factor influences eye color—colorpoints always have blue eyes. The archetype of the Siamese factor is, of course, the Siamese. Later, by making use, directly or indirectly, of Siamese, the colorpoint was bred into a great many other breeds. Hence we are familiar with colorpoint Persian Longhairs ("Himalayan") and "Sacred" Birmans, but colorpoint is also a color variant in many other breeds, such as the Selkirk Rex, Siberian Cat, British Shorthair, and Cornish Rex. The Siamese factor is also seen in a small percentage of non-pedigree cats. Because the Siamese factor is inherited in addition to all other colors and factors, the extremities of a cat's body with the Siamese factor can be of any color, varying from ordinary black (seal point) and tortoiseshell smoke (tortie smoke point) to blue-cream silver tabby (blue-cream silver tabby point). A typical phenomenon of the Siamese factor is that the kittens are usually born very light in color, verging towards white. The color of the "points" only develops after birth. You will find more on this below under "The Burmese, Tonkinese, and Siamese factors and temperature."

Tonkinese

As the animal ages, the shading on the body becomes darker

peratures, however, the actual body color appears on those parts of the body that are the coldest and that frequently have fewer blood vessels, i.e., the extremities—ears, tail, paws, and muzzle. In cats with a darker basic color, such as black, the pigment appears more quickly than in kittens with a very light basic color, such as, for instance, lilac. Because a cat is less capable of maintaining its temperature as it gets older, in the course of time there are more places where gradually darker pigment appears. This is certainly the case with cats that spend a lot of time outside and live in a cold climate. In a warm or very warm climate, the body of a cat with the Siamese factor will often remain "purer" and free of "shading." In a cold climate, on the other hand, an average cat with the Siamese factor will display dark shadows on its body fairly soon, with these shadows becoming darker and larger as the cat grows older.

breed with the Tonkinese factor is the Tonkinese itself, though, of course, the Burmese and Siamese factors also occur in this breed—and are recognized as such. We very rarely encounter the Tonkinese factor in non-pedigree cats, except in the Far East where the partial albinism factors originated.

The Burmese, Siamese, and Tonkinese factors and temperature

Temperature has a strong influence on the formation of pigment in cats with one of the albino factors. The warmer the surface of the skin, the lighter the color there. Cats with the Siamese factor are most sensitive to temperature. That is why kittens with the Siamese factor are usually very light in color or even completely white when they are born; in the womb they are, after all, in warm surroundings with no possibility of cooling off. As soon as the kittens are born and have to acclimatize to colder tem-

Young silver tabby point British Shorthair

White spots show themselves through the colorpoint

Naming

The partial albinism factors just described are inherited separately, in addition to all other colors and factors. A cat can therefore have all possible colors and factors that may, through one of these factors, only be revealed in its bodily extremities. A black cat with the Siamese factor is a seal point, black influenced by the Burmese factor is called "Burmese brown" or "sepia," and black influenced by the Tonkinese factor—a combination of the Siamese and Burmese factors—is called "natural mink." There are also animals with one of the factors from the albino series, which at the same time have white patches. White always covers everything that lies below it, acting rather like a "whitewash" over all colors and factors. White will therefore always be in evidence if the cat has the S-gene, over the points and on light-shaded body colors.

Chocolate Burmese

The albino factors also occur among rabbits

NOT ONLY IN CATS

THE ALBINO RANGE OCCURS NOT ONLY IN CATS, BUT ALSO IN RABBITS. "MARTEN" RABBITS ARE, FOR EXAMPLE, A BREED IN WHICH THE WAY COLORS ARE INHERITED, AND THE FORMS IN WHICH THEY ARE DISPLAYED ARE VERY SIMILAR TO THE ALBINO RANGE IN CATS. FOR INSTANCE, CROSSING "MEDIUM MARTENS" ALWAYS PRODUCES FOUR DIFFERENT FACTORS IN THE LITTER: DARK MARTENS, MEDIUM MARTENS, RUSSIANS (COMPARABLE TO COLORPOINTS, WITH RED, INSTEAD OF BLUE EYES), AND ALBINOS (WHITE WITH RED EYES). THE MEDIUM MARTEN FACTOR IS BROADLY VERY SIMILAR TO THE TONKINESE FACTOR IN CATS—ONLY IN CATS THERE ARE NO ALBINOS. WHEN TWO DARK MARTEN RABBITS ARE MATED TO EACH OTHER, ONLY DARK MARTEN RABBITS ARE BORN (COMPARABLE TO THE BURMESE FACTOR), AND MATING RUSSIANS PRODUCES ONLY RUSSIANS (COMPARABLE TO THE SIAMESE FACTOR). MATING A DARK MARTEN RABBIT WITH A RUSSIAN PRODUCES A LITTER OF ONLY MEDIUM MARTENS, WHICH IS COMPARABLE TO WHAT HAPPENS IN THE CAT WORLD IF A CAT WITH THE BURMESE FACTOR IS MATED TO ONE WITH THE SIAMESE FACTOR.

Genetics

29

Chromosomes

In each cell of their body, including the nails and ears, cats accommodate nineteen pairs of chromosomes, on which genetic information is stored. The sperm cells of males and the egg cells of females are an exception to this. These cells contain nineteen *single* chromosomes; these chromosomes are the random half of a pair of chromosomes. This is logical, since in the fusion of the egg and sperm cell the nineteen single chromosomes of the male cat and the nineteen single chromosomes of the female cat together neatly form the nineteen pairs of chromosomes that between them contain all the inherited properties needed to make up a cat. A kitten will therefore always receive exactly half the genetic properties of the father and half the genetic properties of the mother.

Lilac Cornish Rex

What is inherited?

The pairs of chromosomes carry genes in which all kinds of data are stored. All these genes (and hence their data) together contain all the information necessary to compose a new life. Properties such as length of coat, color, patterns of color, length of legs, and shape of the ears are determined by these genes. But also non-external properties, such as a predisposition for a specific abnormality, the operation of the digestive system, the structure of the brain and resulting characteristics (e.g., a tendency towards a gentle or lively temperament), and even things such as the operation of the glands and the release of hormones, are determined by the genes. The genes contain only inherited material—in other words, innate properties.

Genes cannot pass on attributes that the animal has acquired in its life. For example, a cat whose tail has been docked will produce

Manx

crowded, stressful environment, then its promising features will be hindered in their development. Inheritance and environmental factors thus go hand in hand.

Dominant and recessive genes

As earlier noted, a kitten inherits half its genes from its father and half from its mother. Each gene represents a particular property, such as having or not having a tabby pattern or white patches. Each gene also has its counterpart. For instance, the counterpart of the gene that produces a tabby pattern (A) is the gene that suppresses the tabby pattern (a). The gene that prevents the formation of pigment over the whole body and so causes a cat to be completely white (W) has a counterpart (w), which ensures that the color and pattern can penetrate the entire body, so that the cat is normally pigmented. Genes do not mix in the same way as two pots of paint: if so, it would mean that, from a white cat and a red cat, a pastel pink cat would be produced, of a shade that could be bred softer and lighter by continuing to mate its descendants with a white cat. In genetics it does not work like that (with a few minor exceptions). Almost all genes are either dominant or recessive. Dominant means that this property overrides its counterpart and will always manifest itself in the appearance of the cat if it possesses that gene.

Two dominant properties
in a single cat—tabby (A)
and silver (I)

kittens with normal tails and a female that has suffered a change of temperament as a result of an accident (trauma) will be similarly unable to pass on this new character trait.

Inheritance and environmental factors

Temperament is, in fact, inherited only to a certain extent—a cat that has, for instance, a tendency for aggressive behavior, but is well cared for and never gets into situations in which its aggression can develop or might be triggered, will show little or no sign of this inherited character trait. This applies in equal measure to physical appearance. A kitten can inherit everything needed to grow into a top show champion, but if it is not given a proper diet and/or grows up in an unhygienic, and over-

Because of their poor living conditions, the genetic make-up of stray cats is not always apparent

A litter of Thai kittens

coat (b). Such an animal is not purebred for black; even though it has a black coat it carries chocolate invisibly in its genetic package and can pass that color on to its descendants. Such an animal is also called a "carrier"—it "carries" chocolate. This is useful to know because, if a carrier of chocolate is mated to another carrier of chocolate, chocolate kittens can be born as a result, even though both parents are black.

A recessive property can be carried genetically and passed on to descendants, but will never be revealed in the appearance of the cat as long as a dominant counterpart gene is present. A recessive property can only be manifest in the appearance of an animal if that recessive gene has been inherited from both the father and mother; moreover, that recessive gene need not always be evident in the appearance of either parent animal. It is usual in genetics to identify dominant genes with upper case letters and their recessive counterparts with lower case ones, so it is clear to everyone at a glance whether a gene (and its property) is inherited dominant or not.

This kitten is purebred for non-agouti and dilution

Purebred and non purebred

In genetics the terms purebred or homozygous, and non purebred or heterozygous are used. Homozygous means that the animal has two of the same genes for a particular property. An animal with no tabby markings (a "non-agouti" or solid-colored cat) has, for example, the recessive gene "a" duplicated and can only pass on an "a" to its descendants. Such an animal is said to be purebred or homozygous for non-agouti. Heterozygous means that the animal has two different genes for a given property. An animal may, for example, be black (B) but carry as its counterpart the recessive gene for a chocolate brown

Phenotype and genotype

Phenotype and genotype are two other terms frequently used in genetics. Phenotype is used in reference to the outward appearance of the animal and genotype to its genetic make-up; hence, a black cat that carries chocolate is phenotypically black, since black is dominant over chocolate and this color is therefore manifest in its appearance, but genotypically it is a carrier for both black *and* chocolate. The phenotype, the appearance of the cat, need not automatically be the same as the genotype.

White patches and tabby are dominant, blue is a dilution and inherited recessive

Solid white is caused by the dominant "W" gene

An example

To clarify this, here is a simple example. A completely white coat, indicated by an upper case W, is dominant over a normally pigmented (colored) coat (w). If we were to mate a pure-bred white male (WW) with a pure-bred normally pigmented female (ww), each kitten born would have the dominant gene for a white coat (W) from its father and the recessive gene for a normally colored coat (w) from its mother. The kitten's genotype would then be Ww. Because the gene that gives a fully white coat is dominant over its counterpart, all the kittens from this combination would be white. They have the combination Ww and in their egg and sperm cells there are as many cells with a W as there are with a w. If these sperm and egg cells meet each other in a mating, the following fusions are possible:

- WW: a solid white kitten, homozygous white;
- Ww: a solid white kitten, heterozygous—it carries the gene for normal pigmentation;

Maine Coon kittens

- ww: a normally pigmented kitten, homozygous for normal pigmentation.

Normal-colored kittens can therefore be born from two white parents, but only if both parents carry the recessive gene for normal pigmentation.

Spotted tabby lilac mother cat with a kitten of the same coloring

Calculating probabilities

In one litter you will normally find kittens in the proportions given in this example, so that more white than colored kittens can be expected, but it is possible for there to be no colored kittens at all, nor even white ones. The fusion of the egg and sperm cells is, after all, completely random. If a sperm cell containing a "w" meets an egg cell with a "w", then the whole litter will be colored. Only if an animal is purebred for a particular property and mated with another that is purebred for that particular property, can we be one hundred percent certain that no surprise packages will be born. In all other cases we can only calculate the *probability*, using the genetic code or the presumed genetic code for a particular property carried by the parent animals. This is conveniently set out in diagrammatic form— the probability of any particular property can then be seen at a glance.

Male Ww	W	w
Female Ww		
W	WW	Ww
w	Ww	ww

It is clear from this diagram that the probability of homozygous white cats (WW) is twenty-

five percent, of heterozygous white cats (Ww) fifty percent, and of normally pigmented cats (ww) twenty-five percent.

Many different properties

Once these probability calculations have been understood, simple calculations can easily be made, provided it is known which properties are dominant and which recessive in each animal. Below is a summary of the current genetic codes for a number of the colors and properties found in cats. You can see whether they are dominant or recessive from the use of upper case or lower case letters: upper case means that the property is inherited dominant, lower case that it is inherited recessive.

The location of genes on the chromosome*

Strictly speaking, a dominant gene suppresses manifestation of the recessive gene that acts as

The backward-folding ears of the American Curl are inherited dominant

B	BLACK	b/bl	CHOCOLATE/CINNAMON
A	AGOUTI (TABBY PATTERN)	a	NON-AGOUTI (NO TABBY PATTERN, SO "SOLID" OR "SELF")
W	COMPLETELY WHITE	w	NORMAL PIGMENTATION
S	WHITE PATCHES	s	NO WHITE PATCHES
I	SMOKE/SILVER UNDERCOAT	i	NO SMOKE/SILVER UNDERCOAT
C	COMPLETE PIGMENTATION	cs	ALBINO SERIES (INCL. COLORPOINT)
D	UNDILUTED COLOR (BLACK, RED, CHOCOLATE, CINNAMON)	d	DILUTED COLOR (BLUE, CREAM, LILAC, FAWN)
Mc	STRIPED TABBY	mc	BLOTCHED/CLASSIC TABBY
Sp	STRIPED AND BLOTCHED TABBY PATTERN BROKEN UP INTO SPOTS	sp	STRIPED AND BLOTCHED/CLASSIC TABBY PATTERN NOT BROKEN UP INTO SPOTS
Ta	TICKED TABBY*	Mc/mc	STRIPED/BLOTCHED OR CLASSIC TABBY
L	SHORTHAIRED COAT	l	LONGHAIRED COAT
Wh	WIRY-HAIRED COAT (AMERICAN WIREHAIR)	wh	NORMAL HAIR STRUCTURE
R	NORMAL COAT OF HAIR	R	CURLY COAT (CORNISH REX, GERMAN REX)
Se	CURLY COAT (SELKIRK REX)	se	NORMAL COAT STRUCTURE
Re	NORMAL COAT OF HAIR	re	CURLY COAT (DEVON REX)
Hr	NORMAL COAT OF HAIR	hr	HAIRLESSNESS (SPHINX)
M	SHORT-TAILED (MANX) EXPRESSED IN VARIOUS WAYS	m	NORMAL TAIL
Fd	FOLDED EARS (SCOTTISH FOLD)	fd	NORMAL EAR SHAPE
Cu	EARS BENT BACKWARDS (AMERICAN CURL)	cu	NORMAL EAR SHAPE

its counterpart. This is the case with genes that are in the same location on the chromosomes and which are, literally, counterparts of each other. There are also, however, genes that can influence the operation of genes located elsewhere. This is, for example, the case with the ticked tabby gene (Ta). For a long time this gene was thought to be located in the same place as the gene for striped tabbies (Mc) and blotched/classic tabby (mc), but more recent research has shown that this is not so. Ticked tabby is located somewhere else. If the gene is in fact present, then the phenotype of the cat is always ticked tabby. Phenotypically ticked tabby is inherited dominant over the other tabby patterns, but genotypically this dominant inheritance is rather more complicated.

Incomplete domination

Another deviant from the simple principle of dominant versus recessive is incomplete domination. We find this in the albino series, of which three are illustrated below:
- Burmese factor (cbcb)
- Tonkinese factor (cbcs)
- Siamese marking (cscs)

As can be seen, the Burmese and Siamese factor are homozygous (i.e., two of the same genes) and the Tonkinese factor is not. If the gene for the Siamese marking comes together with the gene for the Burmese marking, the competition between these two genes for the phenotypical marking remains undecided. This is one of the few forms of inheritance in which the genes are

Fawn ticked tabby Oriental Shorthair kitten

Tonkinese

mixed optically, as it were, in the appearance of the cat, like two different colored paints. A kitten with the Tonkinese factor is, in pigmentation, halfway between the Burmese and the Siamese factors. Genetically (genotypically) this cat has, however, the genes for both the Siamese and Burmese factors. If two cats with the Tonkinese factor are mated, we see the following.

MALE CBCS		
FEMALE CBCS	cb	cs
cb	cbcb	cbcs
cs	cbcs	cscs

The probability of kittens being born with the Burmese factor (cbcb) is twenty-five percent, with the Tonkinese factor (cbcs) fifty percent, and of colorpoints, i.e., the Siamese factor (cscs), twenty-five percent. We can draw a similar diagram for mating a male with the Siamese factor and a female with the Burmese factor:

MALE CSCS		
FEMALE CBCB	cs	cs
cb	cbcs	cbcs
cb	cbcs	cbcs

This shows that all the kittens of such a mating will carry the Tonkinese factor (and, of course, display it). Diagrams of mating can be similarly drawn between a cat with the Siamese factor and one with the Tonkinese, and between a cat with the Tonkinese factor and one with the Burmese.

Polygenetic inheritance

The term "polygenetic" has already appeared several times in this book. This term indicates that the inheritance is based not on one single gene, but depends on (many) more factors. A good example of polygenetic inheritance is, for instance, the depth of the ground color in tabbies. This ground color is highly variable and can run from a "cold" dull-gray shade to a dark red, very "warm" one. Such a "cold" shade can even look rather like a silver tabby. The enormous variety in this ground color comes not from one single gene, but is polygenetically determined. In virtually all breeds a very warm, almost red, ground color is desirable. Breeders strive for it by only breeding from animals that have a warm ground color, or from animals

A litter of "Sacred" Birmans—blue point, seal tortie point, and seal tortie tabby point

Maine Coon, black classic

In tabbies the ground color is very variable and determined by their polygenetic make-up

descended from a bloodline in which the ground color has tended towards warm. So there are several factors in cats that are dependent on a polygenetic base. The only way to establish a desired color, which is only one variation in a wide spectrum, is by selection based on the optically desirable quality—the selection can always be brought to naught by one single cross with a cat in which the desirable quantity lies on the other side of that spectrum.

Inheritance of red and black

The principal colors of cats—red, black, and derivations of these—are not inherited dominant or recessive, but linked to the sex chromosomes. To explain how this inheritance works, the first fact to remember is that females have two X chromosomes (XX) and males, one X and one Y chromosome (XY). The Y chromosome ensures that the prospective kitten is of the male

sex. The genes determining whether the pigment cells in the coat are eumelanin (black and all the colors derived from it) or phaeomelanin (red) are located only on the X chromosomes. Y chromosomes are "empty" so far as color is concerned. This means that male cats have only one gene that carries information relevant to the type of melanin and are therefore either red or black (or chocolate/cinnamon). For the inheritance of red and black it is, therefore, only necessary to look at the X chromosomes.

Shorthaired kittens: red, and blue and white

Red and black in male cats

The two kinds of melanin cannot occur next to each other on an X chromosome. The gene contains data for either eumelanin or phaeomelanin. Male cats can only derive their color from their mother, from whom they inherit the X-gene, while from their father they inherit the "colorless" Y-gene that renders them male. The black or red color of a male is consequently of no influence at all on the color of his sons. If we want to know what color male kittens might be,

Red and black in females

The color of the male does have an influence on his female descendants. After all, females have two X chromosomes, one from their mother and one from their father. Between them, therefore, father and mother together determine what color their daughters will be. The two types of melanin are not dominant or recessive in respect of each other, but nor do they mix; they simply both manifest themselves in the appearance of the female kittens. If the mother cat is black (XoXo) and the father red (XOY) then the mother cat can only pass on her black (Xo) and the father only his red (XO) color to their daughters. A female from this combination has the genetic code XoXO. The result is a tortoiseshell or "calico" cat. These calico females (XoXO), if mated to a black male (XoY), can produce both female calico kittens (XoXO) and female black kittens (XoXo). Mating to a red male (XOY) produces two possible combinations, XOXO and XoXO, i.e., either red and/or calico females. This also explains why two black cats can never produce red or tortoiseshell kittens, nor two red cats ever produce black kittens.

Red Exotic

all we have to do is to look at the mother cat. The genetic symbol for phaeomelanins (red with its diluted version cream) is O, and that for eumelanin (black with the derived versions blue, chocolate, lilac, cinnamon, fawn) is o. If the mother cat is black (XoXo) then all the males she bears will be XoY, and black. If the mother cat is red (XOXO) then all her male offspring will be XOY, and therefore red. If the mother cat is tortoiseshell (XoXO) then her sons can be either black (XoY) or red (XOY). The probability of black or red males being born to a tortoiseshell queen is random, but in theory it is fifty percent.

Black tortoiseshell classic and white female house cat

Tortoiseshell Exotic

WHAT IS BORN OF WHAT?

- **RED MALE X RED FEMALE:** RED MALES AND FEMALES
- **RED MALE X TORTOISESHELL FEMALE:** RED AND BLACK MALES, RED AND TORTOISESHELL FEMALES
- **RED MALE X BLACK FEMALE:** BLACK MALES AND TORTOISESHELL FEMALES
- **BLACK MALE X RED FEMALE:** RED MALES AND TORTOISESHELL FEMALES
- **BLACK MALE X TORTOISESHELL FEMALE:** BLACK AND RED MALES, BLACK AND TORTOISESHELL FEMALES
- **BLACK MALE X BLACK FEMALE:** BLACK MALES AND FEMALES

A red male and a black tortoiseshell female

Tortoiseshell males

A tortoiseshell male is consequently a genetic impossibility, since that would require him to carry two X chromosomes, just like a female, whereas his genetic code is XY (it is the Y chromosome that makes him a male). Yet, very occasionally, a tortoiseshell male *is* born. This can have several different causes:

• XXY

The male cat has an incorrect code: XXY instead of XY. This happens very occasionally. The male involved is then sterile.

• "Chimera"

It happens occasionally that two clusters of cells fuse at a very early embryonic stage. These two clusters would normally develop into two kittens, but through their early fusion only one kitten is born of them. This phenomenon is called "chimera." If a male is born from such a fusion, he is normally fertile. He can, however, have different DNA in different parts of his body.

Around 1900 "Samson" caused quite a stir—he was a tortoiseshell tom

• Pigmentation disturbance

In some breeds, such as the Norwegian Forest Cat, but also in non-pedigree cats, red males occur with small black spots in their coat. The males then resemble tortoiseshells, although they are often not so colorfully blended as "real" tortoiseshell males and in fact are not torties, even if they look like them. These cats pass on their genes as a normal black male. This phenomenon results from a disturbance in the pigmentation that produces black spots in some places in the coat. Although the male does not pass on "tortoiseshell," the disturbance of the pigmentation itself runs in families, with such false "tortoiseshell males" occurring from time to time in some bloodlines.

Tortoiseshell female

Part 2: Breeds
Classification

No classification by exterior characteristics?

Though many kinds of domestic pets are classified into groups, this has so far not been done for pedigree cats. They are often simply subdivided into "longhair," "medium longhair," and "shorthair." There is, however, only one gene that causes long hair in cats, so that it is actually wrong to classify "longhair" and "medium longhair" separately. Moreover, there are an increasing number of breeds with varying hair structures, such as the Rex breeds, which can be both longhaired and shorthaired. Also, smoothhaired breeds, which traditionally occur and are bred in both short and longhaired versions, are difficult to classify separately: they belong to one and the same breed, with a shared ancestry and the same breed type and temperament, in which the hair length of each individual specimen can vary. It would not be logical to classify kittens from the same litter, which only differ from each other in the length of their hair, into two completely different groups of breeds. Sometimes other exterior characteristics are taken as the criteria for classifying cats, such as the "breed type" (body structure and shape of head, i.e., the overall appearance). There are breeds, for instance, with a very oriental type, by which is meant a very slim, elegant cat, and cats with a stocky, compact structure, such as the Persian, and all kinds of shapes in between. Classification by external appearance, however, actually says very little about the breed itself. One of the things we know about dogs is that, if a breed is classified as terrier, the dog will be active and energetic, with a will of their own and a lively character. This breed was originally used for hunting small game. These are characteristics common to all breeds in the terrier group. Only the name of the breed gives more information about the breed itself, and puts it

Abyssinian kittens

Persian Longhair, chinchilla

Bobtail, Exotic, and Siamese differ so enormously from each other, both in temperament and in their origins, that this classification is far from adequate.

Classification by origin

It is possible, however, to make a classification for cats that gives more information about the breed than just its external characteristics. If we look at the history of the development of the various breeds, a certain picture emerges that provides a base on which to start a classification into groups. After all, the history of the breed in particular determines its characteristics today, and whether or not it is desirable to cross with other breeds, introduce new colors, or "modernize" the breed type. The history of a breed of cats is therefore more than just an interesting story. Some breeds are in a sense "self-created." They already existed in some region before anyone took an interest in breeding pedigree cats. Other breeds have been deliberately created out of existing breeds and/or non-pedigree cats by breeders with a specific end in view—the creation of a new breed. Again, other breeds began as barely homogenous breeds that occurred naturally in a particular region, but in the course of time have been changed, or "modernized," sometimes involving a cross with other breeds. Then there is another

into perspective with relation to the whole population of pedigree dogs. If a cat is classified as one of a shorthaired breed, however, that says little more about the breed than the length of its hair. Shorthaired breeds such as the Japanese

Norwegian Forest Cat, marbled kitten

Somali kitten, silver

In this encyclopedia, breeds are classified as follows:

• Established breeds

Established breeds are, without exception, breeds of cat that have been in existence for a long time. Generally they existed by the start of the twentieth century, if not before. Many breeds that come under this group originated from a natural breed or a population of cats with a common characteristic, which was not deliberately bred into them, but which already existed before anyone became interested in breeding and showing cats. The difference between today's natural breeds and the established breeds is, however, that the appearance of the established breeds has changed in the course of time—the appearance of today's representatives of the breed is different from that of those animals that used to live or still live today in the region where they were first found. The change in appearance is partly the result of selective breeding for specific characteristics, but is sometimes also influenced by crossing with other breeds or non-pedigree cats. For many (but certainly not all) established breeds, it is the case that crossing with other breeds or non-pedigree

group of breeds, which have in common that one or more of their forebears possessed some unusual exterior characteristic on which the resulting breed is based. Because the origin of a breed—its rationale—is affected by the consequences of rules on whether or not it should be crossed with other breeds, or new colors or types of coat introduced, it has been decided in this encyclopedia to make a classification that takes account of the background of the breed. There are, however, some breeds that are difficult to classify, whose origins lie somewhere between two groups of breeds. These cases have therefore been classified within the group with which they have most in common and this, together with the description of each breed's origin, will hopefully provide a platform for further research.

White Persian Longhair

Japanese Bobtail

cats is allowed subject to strict conditions, or has at some time been allowed, perhaps to introduce new colors or improve the breed type. Familiar examples of established breeds are the Siamese, British Shorthair, and Persian Longhair.

• Original breeds

The term "original breed" refers to breeds that have not been deliberately created or altered by mankind, but already existed in a specific region as domestic or farm cats. Apart from the fact that these breeds, also called natural breeds, already existed before people became interested in breeding true-bred pedigree cats (and are sometimes hundreds of years old), it is also the case that they can still be found in their countries or regions of origin in more or less unaltered form. The introduction of new color varieties and crossing with other breeds is generally not

allowed in this group. Breeders of these breeds are more interested in maintaining the breed than in "modernizing" it. For many but not all breeds in this group, it is permissible for cats found in their region of origin to be entered in pedigree registers. In this group, we might, therefore, find cats that have some unknown ancestors in their pedigrees, because animals are regularly imported from their regions of origin by current breeders for inclusion in their breeding programs. Familiar representatives of this group are the Turkish Van, Japanese Bobtail, and Norwegian Forest Cat.

• Combination breeds

The term "combination breed" indicates a breed that has not been bred for very long. They have no region of origin, as do the established or natural breeds, and are not based on a single deviant

Main Coon kittens

external characteristic, like the mutation breeds. Combination breeds, as the name suggests, have been developed from a combination of one or more existing breeds (and/or non-pedigree cats) with the deliberate intention of creating a new breed. Familiar representatives of this group are the Ocicat and the Exotic.

Sphinx kittens

• Mutation breeds

The term "mutation breeds" refers to breeds that have not been bred for very long and are based on a single striking, unusual, hereditary external characteristic. Sometimes one single cat has formed the basis of a new breed, but more usually it is several cats with the same external characteristic of this kind. In each case, the characteristic that distinguished them from other cats has become the hallmark of that breed. Familiar representatives of this group are the Cornish Rex, Sphinx, and the Scottish Fold. Use is frequently made of other breeds or of non-pedigree cats, partly because most of the mutation breeds themselves are still in the early development stage.

Young blue-cream British Shorthair, female

Established Breeds

Blue British Shorthair in the early days of the breed

BRITISH SHORTHAIR

ORIGIN

EARLY ORIGIN

The British Shorthair originated in England in the late nineteenth century. At that time shows were dominated by "exotic" breeds, such as the Siamese from the Far East and the longhaired Persian. Because only wealthy people with connections in the colonies could afford these luxury cats, breeding and showing them was an elitist practice. Some people deplored this and felt that cat fancying should be accessible to everyone. Moreover, they considered their own British farm cats to be just as beautiful as the exotics, at least if they were seriously bred to a specific type. With the creation of their own authentic British breed from British farm cats, the less well-off were now also given the opportunity of showing their own household cats, which they did. The breed was developed from good-looking British house cats with a stocky, or "cobby," build, and with round heads. There were occasional crosses with Persians. This was done to achieve the desirable "chubby" cat more quickly; to make the shorthaired, often still smooth-lying, coat thicker and softer; and, finally, to introduce new colors into the authentic English breed. The very first breed club for shorthaired breeds, the Short-Haired Cat Society and Manx Club, was started in 1901. This club aimed to promote the national shorthair cat. At first the British Shorthair was just called

Black silver classic tabby British Shorthair
around 1900

"Samson," a black tortoiseshell British Shorthair
male, around 1900

"Shorthair," and sometimes the "English" or "British" cat. The original British Shorthair cats were mainly bred in the following colors: solid blue; black and white; black, red, and silver tabby; tortoiseshell; tortoiseshell and white; and tabby and white.

RECENT HISTORY

Only later, partly as a result of the crosses with Persians mentioned earlier, other new colors were added. The aim of the British breeders was to create a breed that, while it was still as robust as a farm cat, was clearly distinguishable from the average farm cat by its lovely, intense colors and color distribution, and by a uniform, attractive appearance—its "type." At the same time, cat fanciers on the continent were also engaged in breeding a uniform breed from their own existing stock of farm cats and household cats. These, originally called "European Shorthair," were much the same type as the cats which were meanwhile being bred in Britain under the name of "British Shorthair." The British breed standard was adopted

Lilac-cream British
Shorthair, female

by the continental pedigree cat organizations, and animals were regularly imported from Britain to bring in new blood. This blend of cats from Britain and from the continent, and the observance of the same breed standard, eventually led to a more or less uniform breed, in spite of being bred under a different breed name on each side of the North Sea. In the late 1970s the breed name "British Shorthair" was standardized and the term "European Shorthair" was retained only for pedigree cats originating from European house cats which had no Persian in their bloodlines (see "European Shorthair"). Today the British Shorthair is one of the most popular breeds all over the world; only in the United States is the breed relatively rare, as the Americans have their own comparable shorthaired breed, the American Shorthair.

TEMPERAMENT

British Shorthairs have a friendly, even-tempered and quiet disposition. They are tolerant of other cats and can also get on very well with dogs and other domestic pets. They are very human-friendly, but rarely force themselves on their owners. They are also very adaptable. Up to an age of about one or two years they are as playful as any other breed, but after that their level of activity declines. It is not in their nature to demand attention, as some other breeds do. British Shorthairs can, on the whole, find their own amusements quite well. Sometimes they will lie for hours sleeping somewhere, but they also like being cuddled and stroked, so they should certainly not be denied plenty of contact with members of the household. In spite of their gentle nature, a British Shorthair cat has a character of its own, and will certainly react if anything upsets it.

British Shorthair cats have an easy-going social disposition

Black silver classic tabby British Shorthair, male

CARE AND MAINTENANCE

British Shorthairs do not in general need a great deal of care. A brush once a week with a bristle brush is enough to keep their coat in good con- dition. At molting times—spring and autumn— a small rubber brush is an ideal accessory for removing dead and loose hair effectively and quickly from the coat. If a British Shorthair is shown regularly, it is altogether wrong to brush the coat too hard; this may pull out whole tufts of the undercoat, so that the coat ends up look- ing rather moth-eaten. If you want to show your cat it would be better to brush the molting coat with a very coarse comb, so that no "gaps" can

Black spotted British Shorthair, male

Black tipped British Shorthair, male

BODY

The British Shorthair is a compact, well-balanced, and powerful cat with a cobby, muscular body. The chest is broad and deep and the line of the back straight. The firm, short, straight legs give the impression that it stands low on its legs. The paws are round. The tail has an average length, thick at the base and round at the tip. The body is medium to large—males are appreciably larger and more imposing than the females.

HEAD

The head is carried on a short, thick neck and is round, with full cheeks and a broad skull with rounded bone structure. The chin is firm. The large, round eyes are far apart and set horizontally, so they do not slant. Seen in profile, the

develop in it. Because British Shorthairs should have small ears with rounded tips, exhibitors usually pluck out any longer hairs at the tips, to make the ears look smaller and rounder. Special eye care is hardly ever needed for these cats. If it is necessary, then a visit to the vet is essential. Because British Shorthairs, by their nature, like to eat, are not terribly active, and have a tendency to get fat, their diet has to be carefully supervised.

A British Shorthair's build gives a round and compact impression

British Shorthairs have full cheeks and a round head

Young white British Shorthair, female with orange eyes

British Shorthair has a rounded forehead, going down to a short, straight nose with a not-too-pronounced nose-break and a slight curve, but without a "stop" (an abrupt nose-break, or indentation). The small ears are wide at the base, rounded at the tip, and far enough apart not to spoil the outline of the head. There is plenty of space between the ears.

COAT

The coat is short and feels crisp, dense, and springy.

COLORS AND PATTERNS—GENERAL

The British Shorthair is one of the breeds encountered in virtually all colors, patterns, and markings. In the early days of the breed, solid blue coats were the most popular. In past decades there has been a steady demand for blue British Shorthairs, but silver tabbies have also enjoyed great popularity.

"SOLID" OR "SELF" COLORS

British Shorthairs have been bred in all the normal "solid" or "self" colors—white, black, blue, red, cream, chocolate, lilac, cinnamon, fawn—and in all the tortoiseshell varieties of these colors—(black) tortoiseshell, blue-cream, choco-

Young lilac British Shorthair, male

Young white British Shorthair, female with blue eyes

white, are possible in a tabby pattern. The dark hairs that form the tabby pattern are then black, blue, red, cream, chocolate, lilac, cinnamon, or fawn, or tortoiseshell in one of these colors. These last, which are both tortoiseshell and tabby, are called "tortie tabbies." If the tabby pattern is over a silver-white background, it is called a "silver tabby." Silver tabbies were traditionally mainly bred with deep green eyes, while "normal" tabbies should have orange eyes. They are rarely, if ever, crossed with each other, because the mixture of orange and green eyes results in kittens whose eyes are neither a good

late-cream, lilac-cream, cinnamon-cream, and fawn-cream. The most common solid colors, however, are blue, cream, lilac, and blue-cream. The popular blue color was at one point sometimes wrongly described as Carthusian or Chartreux, but this is a different French breed (see "Chartreux"), similar to the Blue British Shorthair. Self-colored cats of this breed should also have uniformly colored orange eyes, without green spots or green rims. White British Shorthairs can have both orange and blue eyes; odd-eyed white cats (with one blue and one orange eye) also occur and are recognized.

TABBIES

Tabbies are rather less popular than self-colored British Shorthairs, apart from the silver tabby that enjoys great popularity. All four tabby patterns occur in British Shorthairs: blotched or classic, striped or mackerel, spotted, and ticked (also known as the Abyssinian pattern), with the most common being the blotched/classic and the spotted tabby. In theory all the colors listed under the heading of "solid" or "self" colors, with the exception of solid

Red classic tabby British Shorthair, male

orange nor a good green. Hence it is usual in this breed to choose cats with the same eye color to breed from. In the past, and still occasionally, silver tabbies have non-silver kittens with green eyes. These green-eyed, non-silver tabbies are called "golden" or "golden tabbies." They only differ from other tabbies in their eye color (green instead of orange).

PARTICOLORS

Particolor is the collective name for British Shorthairs with white markings. The main color can be either self-colored or within a tabby pattern. Four varieties are distinguished in particolors: bicolors,

Black golden tabby
British Shorthair, male

Black tortoiseshell and white British Shorthair, female (tricolor)

tricolors, harlequins, and vans. For bicolors, the cat has to be one-third to one-half white, preferably with an inverted V on its face and forehead. The same goes for tricolors except that, in addition to white and main color, they must also have cream or red patches in their coat (tortoiseshell and white), preferably large and clearly separated from each other. Harlequins have about two-thirds to nine-tenths white in their coat—the precise proportion of colors may vary from one cat organization to another, because there are various standards current for this color. In any event, the color should only be found on the head, tail, and a few patches on the body. The van marking is even whiter than the harlequin; these animals usually have only a colored tail and one or two patches on the head. Opinions on the markings desirable in a van also differ. White patches are inherited randomly and it is virtually impossible to breed these true. In a litter of particolors there are often kittens that satisfy the requirements for specific markings

(they are either bi or tricolor, or harlequin or van), but also kittens with too much or too little white, or a distribution of white that does not

Young blue and white British Shorthair, (bicolor)

A blue and white British Shorthair with
too little white

meet the standard. Such kittens can often not be shown, but as they are otherwise good-looking and healthy and their coat color and eye color are right, they can still be used for breeding. Often, however, British Shorthairs that do not have the right distribution or amount of white are sold as pets at a reduced price.

SILVER AND SMOKE

Silver and smoke are caused by the same gene, the Inhibitor gene, that causes a silver-white undercoat. The term "silver" is used for tabbies with a silver-white undercoat, and "smoke" for self-colored cats, also with a silver-white undercoat. In smokes, each hair is without color from the root up to one-third or one-half of its length. Smokes are always self-colored and should also have orange eyes. It is not easy to breed a good smoke, which may be why this variety is only occasionally bred. Silver tabbies are much more popular than smokes, particularly the black silver spotted and black silver blotched/classic ones—partly as a result of being featured in cat food promotions. In silver tabbies about half of each hair, from the root upward, is colorless. Their eyes can be either green or orange, but green has always been the most common color. Animals with eyes of one color are, of course, not mated to those with the other. Tipped and shaded British Shorthairs are in fact tabbies whose tabby pat-

Black tipped British Shorthair

tern has been suppressed by generations of selection into a "veil" over the lighter colored undercoat. The lightest ones are called "tipped," "chinchilla," or "shell;" cats with a darker shadow pattern are called "shaded." Because this is a polygenetic issue, tipped and shaded kittens often occur in the same litter. Tipped and shaded British Shorthairs should have green eyes. Normally they are only crossed with each other, but sometimes a silver tabby, also with green eyes, is included in the breeding program to introduce new blood.

COLORPOINTS

In the recently developed colorpoint the actual color of the cat is suppressed to the animal's extremities—the ears, muzzle, paws, and tail—and the scrotum in males, as these are the colder parts of the body. The color cannot come through to the rest of the body, so it has a very pale shade. Colorpoints are always white at birth, and the points appear gradually. A pointed animal gains color throughout its life, and will always end up a fraction darker. Colorpoints come in many colors, from the classic seal point to the latest varieties of silver tabby point. The eyes should be a deep blue.

Black silver classic tabby, male with orange eyes

The coats of colorpoints become darker as the years go by
(here a tortie point)

Red point British Shorthair, male

REMARKS

- Until 1973 it was possible in Great Britain to have a non-pedigree cat registered as a (British) Shorthair, provided it met the breed standard.
- Very occasionally longhaired kittens are born. They are normally sold as non-pedigree cats at a reduced price. Some breeders want them recognized as a British Longhair breed.
- If you visit a litter of British Shorthairs, study the pedigrees of the parents closely. Scottish Straights (Scottish Folds with upright ears) are sometimes wrongly registered as British Shorthairs.
- Occasionally British Shorthair breeders cross them with an Exotic or a Persian Longhair.

Young blue point British Shorthair, male

Young female Abyssinian, wild color

ABYSSINIAN

ORIGIN

Abyssinians are thought to be one of the oldest breeds of cat, although their exact origin is still uncertain. The breed resembles the pictures and images of cats from Ancient Egypt, but no direct links with them have ever been discovered. The name of the breed is taken from Abyssinia (the present Ethiopia) from which a female, named "Zula," was brought to Britain in 1868. The unusual aspect of that female was its tabby pattern, the ticked tabby, which had not been seen before in Britain and the rest of Northern Europe. Today this pattern occurs in several breeds, but it is the "trade-

mark" of the Abyssinian and therefore sometimes called the "Aby" pattern. There are conflicting accounts of who actually imported the cat: either Captain Sir Robert Napier or Mrs. Barrett-Lennard. Be that as it may, it is often thought that Zula was the ancestor of all Abyssinians. This is not so. Zula certainly displayed the typical "ticking" in her coat, but in no other respects did she resemble the modern Abyssinian as a type. It is more likely that the breed is the result of a mixture of British and Oriental cats. In 1882 the Abyssinian was recognized in the original wild color (black ticked tabby), but the breed had already been described in *Cats, Their Points and Classifications*, published

Late nineteenth-century photograph—an Abyssinian and two Manx cats

in 1877. The first official breed standard dates from 1889 and was drawn up by Harrison Weir, the famous cat fancier. From the early twentieth century Abyssinians have regularly appeared at cat shows, if in small numbers. In 1907 the first

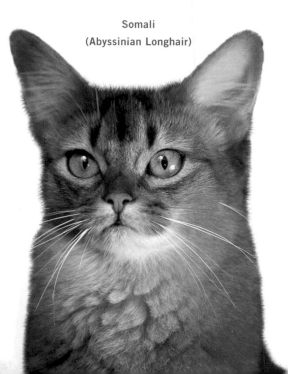

Somali
(Abyssinian Longhair)

Abyssinian kitten, sorrel

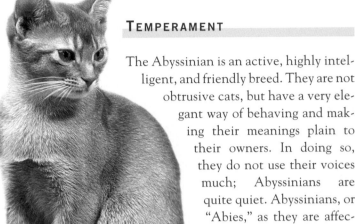

TEMPERAMENT

The Abyssinian is an active, highly intelligent, and friendly breed. They are not obtrusive cats, but have a very elegant way of behaving and making their meanings plain to their owners. In doing so, they do not use their voices much; Abyssinians are quite quiet. Abyssinians, or "Abies," as they are affectionately called by their owners, are real personalities with a strong character of their own. They need a great deal of contact with other members of the household if they are to feel happy, and pine away or certainly

Abyssinian was exported to the United States from Britain, a male called Aluminium II, and more followed him. The first breed association, the Abyssinian Cat Club (A.C.C.), was set up in 1929 in Britain. The driving force behind this association was Sydney Woodiweiss, one of the better known breeders of Abyssinians of the time. From the start the Abyssinian was a breed that attracted a firm host of supporters, but never actually made the break through to the "top five" breeds in popularity. The breed is usually kept by people who like its ticked tabby pattern and elegant build, combined with the special temperament of these cats.

protest if this is denied them. Abyssinians are fastidious, sensitive animals and they demand a great deal of attention from their owners. They are not obvious lap cats, but they are people-oriented; they go everywhere their owner goes and are interested in everything. An Abyssinian is certainly not a cat to leave to look after itself all through the day, not even if it has another cat as a playmate. They must be treated as a member of the family and they like to be involved in everything. Usually they get on well with other cats and they can also make friends for life of dogs. The males are in general rather more easygoing about this than the females, who can sometimes stand on their dignity when meet-

Abyssinians have a distinctive temperament

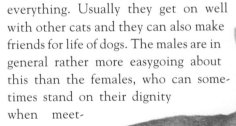

Abyssinian kitten, sorrel

ing their fellows. You will come across very few Abyssinians in overcrowded, small catteries, as they do not usually feel comfortable in a large group of cats. They are known for their intelligence and cleverness, but also for their curiosity. In effect, anything new in the house has to be thoroughly investigated and approved. Cats of this breed are playful and enterprising; a good scratching post or safe access to a balcony or garden is to be recommended.

CARE AND MAINTENANCE

An Abyssinian's coat is quite easy to keep in good condition. At molting times you can easily remove the dead and loose hair from the coat with a rubber massage glove. Outside these peri-

Abyssinian, wild color

Black silver Abyssinian

ods the coat needs to be brushed occasionally with a bristle brush, then combed with a fine-toothed comb and wiped with a damp chamois leather to bring out the sheen. Some bloodlines are rather susceptible to the formation of tartar on the teeth, which in the long run can lead to their loss, so it is worth inspecting them regularly and having the deposit removed in good time by a vet.

APPEARANCE

BODY
Abyssinians are of medium size and give the impression of standing high on their legs. The muscular, sturdy, and elegant body of the Abyssinian is of medium length. The build of an Abyssinian lies between the two extremes of compact (such as the British Shorthair or Persian) and the very graceful (Siamese). Its body should look well balanced. The legs, proportionately slim, have small, elegant, oval-shaped paws. The fairly long tail is firm at the base and tapers gradually to a point.

Two Abyssinian kittens, wild color

HEAD

The head is broad and moderately wedge-shaped. The line of the nose is slightly curved and the chin is very firm. The front of the muzzle is neither pointed nor square. In the most ideal case the chin and the nose, seen in profile, form a straight vertical line. The almond-shaped eyes are large, brilliant, and full of expression. Regardless of the color of the coat, the color of the eyes can be amber, green, or yellow, but

The "boots" typical of the breed

Abyssinian, male in profile

should always be as pure as possible. The eyes are rimmed by a fine dark line surrounded by an area of lighter color. The relatively large ears are set low, wide at the base and running to a point. They point slightly forward. There is plenty of space between the ears. The inside of the ear is hairless, but small wisps of hair on the top of the ears are highly desirable.

COAT

The springy coat of the Abyssinian is fairly short and fine, but firm in structure, and lies close against the body.

COLORS AND PATTERNS—GENERAL

Abyssinians have the Ta-gene that causes the ticked tabby pattern. In this the basic color of the coat is alternated on each separate hair with two or three more lightly pigmented bands, as

also occurs in wild rabbits. The ticking (the darker color that is the cat's actual color and in the wild is actually black) should be distributed evenly over the body. The darker bands of ticking on the tips of the hairs contrast with the lighter colored sections. The color of the undercoat should be clear and the same color down to the roots. A deep warm ground color (in silvers a brilliant silver-white) is preferred, but should not be at the cost of the ticking. Some darker shading along the line of the back is allowed. All color varieties may show some white on the chin and the whisker pads, but the white must not extend too far. Color faults are a white medallion, stripes on the legs, closed rings round the neck or rings on the tail, a cold color, or a gray undercoat. The tip of the nose is always brick-

Abyssinian, wild color

red with a darker surround. The "boots" on the back paws are typical. In Abyssinians without silver-colored undercoats there is often a grayish undertone to the coat, for which the cause must be sought in the gray-colored roots of the hairs. Like too much white, this gray undertone wins no prizes at shows. The original coat color of the Abyssinian is the wild color, "ruddy." In the course of time various other attractive coat colors have emerged from this original color, but the ticked tabby pattern has always remained the characteristic mark of the breed.

RUDDY

The wild color, better known as "ruddy" in this breed, is the original, most familiar, and most common coat color of the Abyssinian, and with the color "sorrel" is one of the classic colors of the breed. A ruddy coat has a warm reddish-brown base with black ticking— genetically, the cat is black. The paw pads and the back of the hind legs (the "boots") are always black in wild-colored Abyssinians.

SORREL

Sorrel is also a well-known color. It was recognized in England in 1963 by the G.C.C.F. (Governing Council of the Cat Fancy). Here the undercoat is again a warm, reddish-brown wild color,

Blue Abyssinian

BLUE

Blue Abyssinians have been seen more frequently in recent years. The basic color of their coat is oatmeal, and the ticking, paw pads, and "boots" are steel-blue in color. Blue Abyssinians were recognized in England in 1984.

FAWN

Abyssinians with a fawn-colored coat are still relatively rare. The basic color of the coat is light cream with dark cream-colored ticking. The "boots" and paw pads are a warm dark cream. Fawn Abyssinians were recognized in Britain in 1992.

SILVER

The silver factor was "borrowed" some thirty years ago from the silver shaded Persian and the silver tabby British Shorthair. Although silvers have existed for a considerable time and look very attractive, they are not recognized by the American Cat Fanciers Association (C.F.A.), the largest cat organization in the United States.

Sorrel-colored
variant kitten

but the ticking and paw pads, together with the backs of the hind legs, are not black, but cinnamon.

Black silver Abyssinian

In Europe, however, they have a growing host of supporters. In silvers the undercoat is always a clear silver-white color. The markings can include black (black silver), blue (blue silver), warm dark cream (fawn silver), and cinnamon colored (sorrel silver). Silver Abyssinians were recognized in Britain in 1979.

OTHER COLORS

Apart from the colors mentioned above, Abyssinians are currently bred on a small scale with other colors, such as red, cream, tortoiseshell, chocolate, and lilac, both with and without a silver undercoat.

REMARKS

- Kittens of this breed have a dark coat at birth, which gradually turns lighter as they grow up. The eventual coat color usually takes several months to appear.
- Because Abyssinians can carry the gene for long hair, it is possible for a litter of Abyssinians also to contain Somalis (long-haired Abyssinians)—the reverse is not possible.
- Abyssinians carrying the gene for long hair are called "variants." Often the hair in parts of their coat is rather longer and silkier than in the non-variants.

Abyssinian and Somali, both wild color

Somali, sorrel kitten

SOMALI

ORIGIN

The Somali arose by accident. In the early days of breeding Abyssinians, the breeders were occasionally surprised to find one or more kittens with a longhaired coat in a litter of Abyssinians. Here it should be remembered that long hair is inherited recessive in relation to short hair, and that the genes for long hair can for generations "move along" without necessarily having to show themselves in the appearance of the cat. Only if two carriers come together is there a chance of longhaired kittens being born. Research into the origin of the Somali always came up with the same name, that of a male cat,

"Raby Chuffa of Selene," born in Britain in 1952 and exported to the United States a year later. The mother of this cat was a female of unknown origin, so that the "suspicion" of carrying the gene for long hair fell on her. But longhaired Abyssinians had occasionally been born before—and it is also known that some Persians were crossed in around 1900. In any event, the longhaired kittens that were born every now and

American-bred young black silver Somali

then were regarded as undesirable by most breeders of Abyssinians. They were passed on to friends and acquaintances and not used for breeding. Only in the 1960s was a serious attempt made to breed and gain recognition for longhaired Abyssinians. The pioneer was the American breeder of Abyssinians, Evelyn Magua, who bred longhairs several times from Abyssinians in her cattery. In 1972 she set up

Somali, wild color male

the Somali Cat Club of America (S.C.C.A.) and seven years later, in 1979, the Somali was recognized by the C.F.A. Since then the breed has become well known in all cat-loving countries and can boast a firm army of supporters.

TEMPERAMENT

The temperament of the Somali is similar to that of the Abyssinian. The Somali, too, is a friendly, active, and intelligent cat, which is also very sensitive to the moods of the household.

Somali, wild color female

Somali, wild color kitten

CARE AND MAINTENANCE

The Somali needs relatively little care. The structure of its coat is such that it rarely tangles. All the coat needs is to be combed through once a week. It may need rather more care during molting to prevent the cat swallowing too much loose hair when it is grooming itself.

They certainly need the full attention and approval of their owner if they are to feel happy. Although they generally get on well with their fellow cats, Somalis are not comfortable in a large group of cats. Both mentally and physically they need space. They like going outside, but that is not necessary if they have sufficient opportunity to play indoors. The Somali is not a cat that will lie for hours in your lap, but it does want plenty of interaction with its owner. The animals are interested in everything that goes on in the house and like to keep close to their owner. Little escapes them. Somalis stay playful to a very great age.

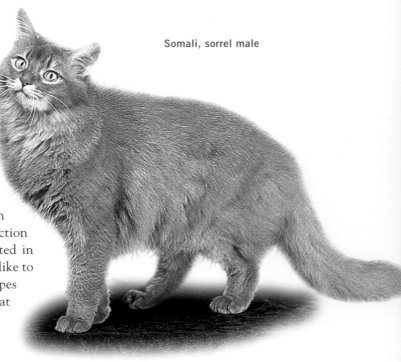

Somali, sorrel male

APPEARANCE

BODY

The body is medium-sized, fairly slim, well-muscled, and supple, with a straight, horizontal back. The slim, elegant legs are well proportioned in relation to the body. The paws are small and oval-shaped. The fairly long tail is broad at the base and tapers gradually. If the tail is held against the body, the tip of the tail reaches to just behind the shoulders.

Somali, wild color male

HEAD

The head is medium and wedge-shaped. The skull is broad at the top and the muzzle rounded. Altogether the outline of the head is round. Seen in profile the line of the nose should show a slight curve, but any upward trend is undesirable. The chin should be firm. The large ears are set wide apart from each other and seen from the front they extend the lines of the wedge-shaped head. The ears point slightly forward. Tufts on the ears are desirable. The large, slightly almond-shaped eyes are slanting and spaced wide apart.

COAT

The coat is soft and fine in structure. It is dense, but in spite of this lies smoothly along the body. The coat may be shorter on the shoulders. There should preferably be a full ruff and "breeches," and the same goes for tufts in and on top of the ears, and between the toes. Somalis have a full, bushy tail.

COLORS AND PATTERN—GENERAL

Somalis come only in the ticked tabby pattern, caused by the Ta-gene. In fact this has no pattern, which means that all the hairs in the coat show alternate light and dark bands of color, as in a wild rabbit. The ticking (the dark color) is the cat's real coat color, which is shown most clearly on the top of the tail and the back. This should be evenly distributed over the body. The color of the undercoat should be bright and uniform to the roots. A deep, warm ground color (in silvers, a bright silver-white) is preferred. The chest, belly, underside of the tail, and inside of the legs and breeches have no tabby pattern, but show the warm, solid ground color. All color varieties may show a little white on the chin and whisker pads, but the white should not extend too far. Somalis without these white markings are, however, very rare. Color faults include a small white medallion on the chest, stripes on the legs, closed bands of color round the neck, rings round the tail, or a "cold-colored" or gray undercoat. The original color of Somalis was the wild color (ruddy), but new attractive coat colors were quickly developed. The eyes may be amber-colored, hazel, or green, as long as the shade is clear and deep.

Black silver Somali, female

Somali, wild color male

COLORS

WILD COLOR (RUDDY)

The wild color is the best known and most common of coat colors in Somalis. The ticking is black and the ground color a warm apricot; in combination, these colors give a warm brown impression.

SORREL

The color "sorrel" is in fact called "cinnamon" in other cats. The ticking has a warm cinnamon color, and the ground color is a warm apricot.

CHOCOLATE

In "chocolate," the ticking is chocolate-colored and the background dark apricot. Altogether, the coat has a deep warm-brown appearance, softer than the wild color.

BLUE

The color "blue" is a dilution of black (wild color), characterized by steel-blue ticking with an oatmeal ground color; together this produces a soft blue-gray shade.

FAWN

Fawn is the dilution of cinnamon. The ticking is sand-colored and the ground color light beige. Together they give the appearance of a warm, sand-colored cat.

Somali, chocolate female

Somali, fawn male

Black silver Somali, female

SILVER

All colors may occur with a silver-white undercoat. In silvers the ground color is not apricot or sand-colored, but preferably a brilliant white. This brings the ticking pattern very plainly into prominence.

OTHER COLORS

There are breeders engaged in the development of new colors, including red, cream, and tortoiseshell, with or without a silver undercoat.

REMARKS

- Kittens of this breed have a dark coat at birth, which gradually becomes lighter as they grow up. The ticking develops slowly. The final coat color usually only appears after several months.
- The name of the breed is derived from Somalia in Africa, but that country has nothing to do with its origins; the first Somalis were born in the United States.

Silver Somali, female

Red Burmese kitten

brown extremities (muzzle, ears, tail, and legs). Seen from a distance her contrasting colors were rather reminiscent of the Siamese but her markings were not as sharply defined and her body color was darker. Wong Mau's type was also different from that of a Siamese: she was more compact in body, had a shorter tail, and her head and eyes were rounder in shape. Together with several other people, Dr. Thompson decided to develop a breeding program to perpetuate Wong Mau's special features. He had her covered by a Siamese male (Tai Mau) and went on breeding from the resulting kittens. Their progeny proved to have three possible colors—the point pattern

Burmese with kitten

BURMESE EUROPEAN TYPE

EARLY ORIGIN

The Burmese owe their origin to the female "Wong Mau." In 1930, this cat was taken to New Orleans from the Far East (Burma). Wong Mau became the property of Dr. Joseph Thompson of San Francisco. At that time Wong Mau's color was exceptional: she had a walnut-brown body with darker

Brown Burmese

like the Siamese, the Tonkinese factor like Wong Mau, and the third group being rather darker than Wong Mau. These last had a brown-colored body, with extremities of an even darker brown—the Burmese factor. It seemed that Wong Mau was of an "intermediate" color, somewhere between the Siamese and Burmese factors. Wong May's color pattern has since then become known as "Tonkinese," on which yet another breed is based (see: Tonkinese). It was later discovered that, if the darkest shaded cats

Lilac Burmese

(Burmese factor) were mated to each other, only the same, dark-colored kittens were born. This was in contrast to the colors the kittens could have if two Tonkinese-colored cats were mated to each other, when Siamese and Burmese, as well as Tonkinese, kittens could be born. Because the Burmese coloring was inherited true, and because this color was greatly admired, it was decided to go on breeding with cats that had this Burmese color. The Burmese breed was developed from descendants of Wong Mau, with Burmese coloring and Burmese-colored cats imported at a later stage from Burma. The results of the experimental breeding program were published in April 1943 in the *Journal of Heredity*. In 1934 the Burmese was proposed as a new breed to the C.F.A. and was recognized by them as a breed in 1939. At this time Burmese were still regularly crossed with Siamese to prevent inbreeding. In 1947, eight years after recognition of the breed, the C.F.A. asked breeders of Burmese to reduce these outcrossings. The ultimate intention was that the breed should stand alone, without further "help" from Siamese blood. Ten years later, in 1957, this stage was reached and the pedigree register was closed, since which time Burmese crossed with Burmese has been the only permitted mating.

RECENT HISTORY

In the early years of the breed the Burmese were mainly an American hobby. Only later did the Burmese find their way to other countries, particularly to Britain, where it was recognized by the G.C.C.F. in 1952. Until 1955, Burmese cats were only bred in their original brown color

(genetic black). In that year, however, a blue Burmese was born, and was given the striking name of "(Sealcoat) Blue Surprise," to be followed soon afterward by more blue Burmese.

Blue Burmese kitten

The blue color was recognized by the G.C.C.F. in 1960. Later breeders began again to devote themselves to the introduction of further colors. With the help of red non-pedigree cats and red point Siamese, the colors red, cream, and tortoiseshell were developed and recognized in 1972. Meanwhile breeders in the U.S. had not been idle; a new color had emerged called

Chocolate Burmese

"champagne." A number of these animals were exported in the late 1960s to Britain, where the color was re-christened "chocolate." In combination with the blue Burmese this produced a further new color, "lilac," the dilution of chocolate, called "platinum" in the U.S. Chocolate and lilac Burmese were recognized by the G.C.C.F. in 1975. In the 1990s two new colors came along—cinnamon and its dilution, fawn. These colors were developed in The Netherlands.

Burmese are very sociable

Burmese need a great deal of attention

TEMPERAMENT

Burmese make very affectionate and sociable pets. They enjoy human company and little escapes their notice. In spite of their small size (six to eleven pounds) they are cats that make their presence felt; visitors are extensively examined, as are the contents of their handbags. If their owner does not take sufficient notice of them, they will demand this through noisy meowing and mischievous behavior. They require a great deal of attention, but will give a great deal of love in return. Burmese become very attached to "their" people, and often particularly to one specific person in the family. These cats are well known for readily jumping on to their owner's shoulders and "riding" along with them round the house. They can also be taught to walk on a leash. Burmese are playful and intelligent, a combination that can

sometimes produce surprises. There are numerous Burmese who know how to open a door, a lever tap, a kitchen cupboard, or a cookie jar. Periods of high activity, when they use the whole house as a gym, are interspersed with cuddling sessions, so that the Burmese is really for people who enjoy plenty of interaction with their cat and playing with it; there are, for example, many Burmese that enjoy retrieving scrunched-up balls of paper. Their tolerance threshold for children and dogs is on the whole high, although this depends, of course, on their socialization. Most Burmese also get on well with other cats, although it cannot be denied that they have some domineering traits. For this reason they are not often seen in catteries where large groups of cats are kept together; they usually require a

Burmese love to be cuddled and enjoy company

great deal of individual attention and do not always appreciate having to share attention (or space) with too many of their own kind. In spite of this a Burmese is not the best breed to be the only cat in a house where people are not at home much. In such cases, it is best to give it a playmate. This may be another Burmese, but not necessarily so, provided the other cat has a stable and good-natured temperament.

CARE AND MAINTENANCE

Looking after a Burmese's coat is not difficult. Plenty of stroking keeps it glossy and gives the cat the attention it needs. Weekly grooming with a soft brush is enough to keep the coat in good condition. The gloss can be heightened by wiping the coat down with a damp chamois leather after brushing it. Burmese mature early; sometimes queens come into season for the first time at the age of five to six months.

APPEARANCE

Brown Burmese

BODY

The Burmese is graceful, lively, and alert; it is a well-muscled cat. The breed has its own unique oriental type that should neither verge toward the slimmer Siamese type, nor toward the compact appearance of the British Shorthair. The medium-sized body feels hard and muscular, and is heavier than it looks. The chest is rounded and powerful and the medium-length back is straight. The legs are proportionate to the body, but slim, and the hind legs are a little longer than the front ones. The paws are oval in shape. The tail is of medium length.

HEAD

The head is moderately wedge-shaped, with wide cheekbones. The chin is firm. The skull should be clearly rounded between the medium-sized ears. A "pinch" (a constriction behind the whisker pads) is classed as a fault. The ears are set wide apart from each other and, seen from the side, point a little forward. They have a wide base and slightly rounded tips. The outside line of the ears follows the wedge shape of the head. The bridge of the nose has a clear stop. Their eyes are large and bright, set wide apart, and should be neither round nor Siamese in shape. The top edges of the eyes slant toward the nose, and the lower edges are rounded.

Chocolate Burmese

253

COAT

The coat is short and fine, silky in texture, and lies smooth. Its glossy coat is an important feature of the Burmese.

Burmese

COLORS AND PATTERNS— GENERAL

The Burmese coloring is typical of the breed. The color of the extremities (muzzle, ears, tail, paws, and scrotum (in males) is a shade darker than that of the rest of the body. The back, too, is often darker. The underside of the body is rather lighter in shade. Burmese kittens are, in general, a lighter shade at birth, becoming darker as they grow up. White patches or obvious white hairs in the coat are classed as faults. The eyes can be any yellow color, but preferably golden yellow—the deeper the color, the better. The eye color of a Burmese is very sensitive to the degree of color dilution, so that the dilute colors (lilac, blue, fawn) often go with rather lighter colored eyes.

BROWN

The brown coat color is a combination of black and the effects of the Burmese factor, so that the black appears as a warm, dark brown. This dark-brown shade is a little lighter on the underside of the body. Apart from this and the rather darker ears and face, no other markings are allowed. The nose leather and paw pads are brown. Too dark a brown color, verging toward black, is a fault.

BLUE

Blue is a dilution of Burmese brown, which in essence is genetic black. Burmese blue is a soft silver-gray with a darker shaded back and tail.

Brown Burmese

Blue Burmese

Chocolate Burmese

The ears, face, and paws should show a clear, silver gloss. The nose leather is dark gray.

CHOCOLATE

This color is called "champagne" in the United States. The body is a warm milk-chocolate color with darker ears and face. The legs, tail, and lower jaw should be the same color as the back. The nose leather is a warm chocolate-brown.

LILAC

This color is called "platinum" in the United States. Lilac is a dilution of chocolate and is a soft dove-gray color with a light-pinkish glow. The ears and the face should be darker in color. The nose leather is lavender pink.

CINNAMON

This color, which originated in The Netherlands, is a light cinnamon color with a warm glow. The ears and face may be rather darker in color. The nose leather is salmon pink.

Cinnamon Burmese

FAWN

Fawn is a dilution of cinnamon. The color is described as broken white with a hint of pink. The ears and face may be rather darker in color and the nose leather is pale pink.

RED AND CREAM

Red Burmese have a pale-orange coat. In otherwise outstanding cats vague tabby markings are allowed (except on the sides and belly). A few dark pigment freckles on the ears, eyelids, lips, and paw pads are also allowed. The ears are clearly darker than the back. Cream is a dilution of red and the same requirements apply as for red, bearing in mind that the coat color of a cream cat is a pale cream.

Tortie kitten, Burmese

TORTOISESHELL OR TORTIE

With the introduction of red and cream, it was possible to breed tortoiseshell Burmese. Tortie Burmese can come in all colors: brown tortie, champagne or chocolate tortie, blue tortie, platinum or lilac tortie, cinnamon tortie, and fawn tortie. In a Burmese, the distribution of the patches is not important.

REMARKS

- Although both European and American breeders started with the same basic material, the differences between Burmese bred in

Chocolate tortie kitten, Burmese

Europe and America have become so great that a distinction is made between the American and the British (European) Burmese (see: Burmese, American type).

- In an old Thai book on cats, *Smud Khoi*, there is an illustration of a cat with Burmese coloring. This cat is called "Thong Daeng." The breed is described as follows: "A cat of brilliant appearance with a superbly shaped body. Copper-brown in color, this cat is beautiful to behold. The golden light of her eyes is like a clear radiance. She protects you against all danger and saves you from all evil and brings you good fortune."

no flat parts anywhere, whether seen in profile or from the front. The muzzle had to be short and well developed, with large, round eyes that should not protrude. In essence the breed should make a "rounded' impression from every aspect and this is what American breeders were aiming for. This eventually resulted in a completely different type of Burmese from the type that was (and still is) bred in other countries. In the 1970s the breed reached its peak of popularity in the United States; during that time the Burmese was the third most popular breed of cat directly after the Persian and the Siamese. The Burmese is still popular today, and is frequently seen at cat shows in the United States.

TEMPERAMENT

The American-type Burmese does not differ fundamentally from the European type in temperament. These Burmese, too, are very affectionate, need a great deal of interaction and contact to feel happy and have a friendly, accommodating

Burmese, American type

Brown Burmese. American type

BURMESE, AMERICAN TYPE

ORIGIN

Although all Burmese are descended from the original American descendants of Wong Mau, and at the time of the first imports into Britain they were all of the same type, differences emerged in the course of time. The Burmese type bred in the United States gradually differed from the type that is in demand at shows in Europe (and in Australia, New Zealand, and South Africa). This resulted from the breed standard drawn up in the United States in 1958 by the United Burmese Cat Fanciers. This standard demanded a cat with a well-rounded head and

nature. American fanciers, in fact, sometimes call their Burmese "velcro cats," because they like to attach themselves to their owner and follow them all over the house. This does not mean that they are pliant and docile—they know just what they want and can be very persistent in getting it. Like many other breeds that originated in

Burmese, American type

the Far East, the Burmese also mature early. The queens usually come into season more strongly and more frequently than those of other breeds.

CARE AND MAINTENANCE

It is fairly simple to keep a Burmese in good condition. It is enough to stroke it frequently and brush the coat once a week. If you wipe the coat over with a damp chamois leather, it will keep the already natural gloss of the coat looking its best. If you show a Burmese, you should wash it a few days beforehand. The coat should not be blow-dried, but be left to dry naturally in a warm place to prevent it from looking dull.

APPEARANCE

BODY
The Burmese has a medium-large body with good muscles and makes a compact impression. The cat should feel heavier than it looks at first sight. The chest is rounded and the legs proportionate to the body. The tail is straight and of average length.

HEAD
The head is round in shape without any flat surfaces; it should look round from all directions. The face is well filled with a substantial width between the eyes and gradually runs down to a well-developed short muzzle that conforms to the round outlines of the head. The chin is well-rounded and the teeth close well. The medium-sized ears are broad at the base and rounded at

Burmese

Brown Burmese

Burmese, American type

the tip. They tend to point slightly forward. The large round eyes are set wide apart.

COAT

The short coat, lying very close to the body, is fine and glossy and has a satiny texture.

COLORS AND PATTERN—GENERAL

The American-type Burmese comes in four different colors— sable (brown), champagne (chocolate), blue, and platinum (lilac). The color of the eyes can run from gold to yellow, preferably as deep and bright as possible. Green eyes are not acceptable.

REMARKS

Solid black Burmese of the American type are regarded as a separate breed. They are called "Bombay." They are different in type from the British Black Asians, of which the black specimens are also known as Bombay (see also: Asian).

Burmese, American type

EGYPTIAN MAU

Bronze Egyptian Mau

ORIGIN

One of the most striking features of the Egyptian Mau is its spotted tabby pattern. This pattern is not the result of deliberate selective breeding, but has been a feature of the breed from its very beginning. Many fanciers regard the Egyptian Mau as one of the oldest breeds of cats, which probably existed in Ancient Egypt. Pictures and images of cats have been discovered that demonstrate many similarities to the breed. The only fact known

with certainty is that in the 1950s the forebears of the breed came from Egypt (Cairo) to the United States via Italy. The owner of these three cats was a Russian lady, Nathalie Troubetskoy, who lived in Italy. She acquired her cats from an Egyptian ambassador to Italy, who told her that they came from Cairo. In 1955 she showed her Egyptian cats at a cat show in Rome. When she emigrated to the United States in 1956, she took her cats with her and began to breed under the cattery name "Fatima." Three cats were, of course, too narrow a base on which to build a sound breed, so that breeders later introduced spotted tabby cats from the streets of Cairo, to bring in new blood. Recognition by the C.F.A. followed in 1977. Recognition of the breed by a number of European breed institutions only followed much later, in 1993. Even today, the Egyptian Mau is quite a rare breed, although its breeding is no longer restricted only to the U.S.A., but has extended to Europe.

TEMPERAMENT

Cats of this breed are lively and active; not only young, but also fully-grown Egyptian Maus enjoy playing and running about. Sufficient opportunities for exercise and climbing in the house are, therefore, essential if you want to make your Egyptian Mau happy. Cats of this breed are not only playful, they also need a great deal of attention and do not like to be left alone for too long. They like being stroked and cuddled, and are very affectionate. They do not make friends with everybody, however;

Smoke Egyptian Mau

Egyptian Maus have a sociable disposition

very well, not only with other cats, but also with dogs and children.

CARE AND MAINTENANCE

A weekly brush is sufficient for an Egyptian Mau's short-haired coat. Preferably a bristle brush should be used, after which you can, if necessary, go over the coat with a fine-toothed comb. To bring out the gloss of the coat you can rub it over with a wet chamois leather after brushing it.

APPEARANCE

BODY

The body structure of the Egyptian Mau is in many respects similar to that of the Abyssinian. Its body gives an oriental and graceful impression, but should be more muscular and rather coarser in build than the Oriental Shorthair. The fine and elegant legs are long in proportion to the body. The paws are small and compact. The hind legs are longer than the front ones, so

with people they do not know they cautiously wait to see which way the proverbial cat jumps before they let themselves be stroked. The Egyptian Mau's voice is soft and melodious. Altogether they are very sociable and can get on

Egyptian Maus do not need a great deal of coat care

Silver Egyptian Mau

that the line of the back slopes up toward the rear. The tail is of average length and has a rounded tip.

HEAD

The Egyptian Mau has a slightly wedge-shaped head. The relatively large ears are broad at the base and rounded at the tip. The line of the nose is straight and joins the forehead smoothly without any indentation. The large eyes are almond-shaped at the top and round at the bottom.

COAT

The short, thick coat feels silky and shines.

COLORS AND PATTERN—GENERAL

The Egyptian Mau is bred as a spotted tabby. The round spots should be marked in the coat as clearly and distinctly as possible. Stripes formed by the spots running into each other are regarded as a fault at shows. The Egyptian Mau is bred in the colors bronze, silver, and smoke (black smoke). The color of the eyes is described as "gooseberry green" and may not be fully developed in young animals; the eventual color of the eyes should be reached, however, by the age of two years. Very occasionally solid black animals are born. These are not recognized, but are still sometimes involved in breeding programs.

Silver Egyptian Mau

REMARKS

"Mau" is an Egyptian word meaning "cat." The Egyptian Mau has sometimes been confused with a breed developed in Britain from Oriental Shorthairs and Siamese, which for a long time was known by the same name. The British breed has nothing to do with the "real" Egyptian Mau—they were black-silver spotted Oriental Shorthairs.

Bronze Egyptian Mau

Blue point "Sacred" Birman, male

"SACRED" BIRMAN

ORIGIN

There is not a single breed of cat that can boast of a history that appeals so much to the imagination as the "Sacred" Birman. It is claimed that a long time ago white cats lived in a temple in Burma and enjoyed special protection. One day the temple was attacked and many of the worshippers were killed. One of the priests was by the statue of the blue-eyed goddess Tsun-Kyan-Kse at the moment when he was struck down. While he breathed his last, a white cat jumped on to his body and looked at the image of the goddess. Its eyes became blue, and its ears, muzzle, legs, and tail took on a dark shade. Only its paws stayed white. All the cats in the temple underwent the same transformation at that moment. That is only one of the stories and versions that circulate about the supposed origins of the breed. The literature has it that the first

"Sacred" Birman came to France from Burma in about 1900, which in itself seems quite plausible. Some people hotly dispute this, however, and suspect that French breeders started the breed by means of crosses. Naturally there would be nothing "mystical" about that, so the breeders would have had to think up a good story to create a certain aura round the breed—and drive up the price of kittens. This, too, is plausible and is supported by old pedigrees, featuring long-haired, colorpoint cats

Young tabby Point
"Sacred" Birman, female

Seal point "Sacred" Birman, female

TEMPERAMENT

"Sacred" Birmans have a predominantly quiet and tolerant disposition. Their voices are unobtrusive and soft. If they set their heart on something, they use mainly body language and eye contact to make their wishes known. They enjoy the companionship of their family, but are usually not real lap cats, although they like to be near their people and will lie close to them on the sofa. Many Birmans tend to forge a special link with one individual in the household. Birmans are subtle in their behavior, and sensitive—they certainly do not appreciate the humor in being teased or chased. Such rough treatment can thoroughly upset them, although they rarely show their claws in such cases. Aggressive behavior is foreign to a Birman. A Birman does not like too much bustle and should therefore always be given the opportunity to find a quiet spot in the house to which it can retreat. They usually get on well with other cats, just as the presence of a quiet dog should present few problems. They also get on excellently with children, as long as the children treat

with an unknown provenance. It is generally accepted that the breed originated in France, by means of crossing breeds. It was also in France, in 1925, that the breed was first recognized. Only later did the "Sacred" Birman reach other countries in Europe and the United States. Today it is one of the most common and popular breeds in the world.

Litter of "Sacred" Birman kittens

them equably. Although they are essentially quiet, they are certainly not phlegmatic, and enjoy games and fun at appropriate times.

CARE AND MAINTENANCE

One of the advantages of the "Sacred" Birman is that its luxuriant coat rarely tangles and needs little care. Normally a metal comb is not used

Blue tortie tabby point "Sacred" Birman, female

Tabby point "Sacred" Birman, male

on a Birman's coat because it can damage the undercoat. A good quality, hard-bristled brush is more suitable. Nevertheless, a brush with plastic-covered metal bristles can prove useful when the hair is molting. Because shows tend to concentrate on the quality of the coat, Birmans that are shown regularly need rather more grooming than animals kept purely as pets. It is recommended that the cat is washed about five days before the show, and the coat powdered occasionally in the intervening days. For this you should use a fat-free powder, which you distribute well through the coat and then brush out thoroughly with a bristle brush. After this treatment the coat "lies" much better on the day of the show, and the cat looks well-groomed. Any tufts of hair on the tips of the ears spoil the shape of the ears and should be carefully trimmed off.

APPEARANCE

BODY
The "Sacred" Birman is a medium-sized cat with a slightly elongated and well-proportioned body. The legs are firm and relatively short, with round paws. The tail is of medium length, full, bushy, and dense. Males are more robustly built than females.

HEAD
The skull is powerful and the forehead slightly domed. The cheeks are full and slightly rounded. The nose is of medium length and has no "stop," but a slight "dip." The chin is firm and well-developed. The ears are quite small and

Young tabby point "Sacred" Birman female

Blue point "Sacred" Birman, male

have rounded tips. They are reasonably wide apart and should not be set too high. The eyes are not completely round, but preferably slightly oval-shaped. Very occasionally we see "Sacred"

Blue point "Sacred" Birman kitten

Birmans that have a slight cast or squint. This is classed as a fault.

COAT

The coat is long to semi-long, with a full ruff round the neck in cold climates. On the muzzle, the coat is short. The fur is silky in texture and

Seal tortie point "Sacred" Birman, female in summer coat

lies over the cat like a luxurious veil. Birmans have a short undercoat.

COLOR AND PATTERNS—GENERAL

The Birman is recognized in the Siamese pattern and only comes in that pattern. The Siamese factor ensures that the true color of the coat is only manifest at the extremities or "points." These are the ears, muzzle, paws, tail, and the scrotum (in males). The other parts of the body have a very pale shade. In the case of the "sacred" Birman the hairs on the back and sides should preferably have a light to warm golden-beige shade. The rest of the body has a pale eggshell color. White patches on the body are classed as faults. Ideally the "Sacred" Birman has no dark shadows or other color irregularities on its body, but in practice this is an unattainable ideal, certainly in older cats and those with dark points. Dark shadows are produced over the

"Sacred" Birman, cream point kitten

years by climatic influences, hormone fluctuations, and injuries, so that often only young animals display the desirable pale body color. The color on all the points should be the same. They should have no white or lighter colored parts or even individual hairs (brindling). "Spectacles," lighter colored hairs round the eyes, which occasionally occur, are also undesirable. The whole of the nose leather should be pigmented on self-colored animals. The desired color for the eyes is deep blue.

GLOVES

An important breed feature of the "Sacred" Birman is its paws, among fanciers also called "gloves." There is only one other breed where the breed standard requires white paws, and that is the shorthaired Snowshoe, an American breed. Because white patches are inherited at random, it is difficult to define these markings, and deviations from the ideal image are allowed at shows. There are, however, basic requirements with which the markings must comply. They must be pure white without spots of another color. The white marking must be nicely symmetrical and should not extend too far up on the back of the forelegs (a "runner-up" in cat fancy circles). On the back of the hind legs the white should run up in an inverted V shape ("spurs") but not past the heel. In an ideal case, both V-shaped markings should run parallel on the hind legs.

COLORS

The original colors of the "Sacred" Birman are seal (genetic black) and blue point (genetic blue), colors that are considered to be the only true ones by a number of purists among Birman breeders. Occasionally, in the early days of the breed, chocolate and lilac points were born, but only a very small percentage. Only later were these colors cultivated further, and also accepted. In the course of time, other no less attractive colors, including red and cream points, were produced by crossing in. This made breeding tortie points (genetic tortoiseshell) possible. In addition, there are now also

"Sacred" Birmans are known for their white "mittens"

"Sacred" Birman, red point male

REMARKS

- A typical phenomenon in point cats is that the kittens are born white. Their dark points only color up later. It can be a year before a Birman reaches its ultimate color, with its "mask" also only fully developing over time.
- The requirements set for cat shows are high. Not only must breeders aim at the right body structure, coat length and structure, and shape of head, but the white paws, points, and body color are also important. In practice it is not easy, perhaps even impossible, to breed a Birman that is satisfactory on all fronts. There are Birmans with too light an eye color, asymmetric markings on their paws, a white chin, a face mask not clearly marked, or animals with white hairs in the dark-colored points—and this summary is far from complete. If you are interested in a Birman just as a pet, then these imperfections are usually unimportant, but if you want to show them you would do well to immerse yourself in the breed standard first and, if possible, visit several shows and breeders before you make your choice.

tabby points. The complete range of colors of the non-agouti (hence solid-colored) "Sacred" Birman is seal point, seal tortie point, blue point, blue tortie point, chocolate point, chocolate tortie point, lilac point, lilac tortie point, red point, and cream point. Agoutis (hence tabbies) come in seal tabby point, seal tortie tabby point, blue tabby point, blue tortie tabby point, chocolate tabby point, chocolate tortie tabby point, lilac tabby point, lilac tortie tabby point, red tabby point, and cream tabby point. Moreover, black "freckles" are allowed in red and cream-colored animals. It is a requirement that both colors should be present in the torties at all the points.

"Sacred" Birmans are born white; this kitten's ears are beginning to show color

SIAMESE

ORIGIN

EARLY ORIGIN

Siamese cats come from the Far East and derive their name from Siam, the present Thailand. From 1871 onwards, cats were regularly imported into Britain from the East. Among them were slender cats with blue eyes, a cream-colored body, and with a dark brown to almost black muzzle, ears, tail, and feet—the Siamese. These cats created great interest in nineteenth-century England, because its color pattern and blue eyes were still completely unknown in Europe. Siamese cats, therefore, became a special attraction, and keeping them at that time was largely the preserve of the wealthy. These shorthaired "exotics" were very pampered. Because they had a slender build and thin, short coats, their owners were afraid that they would not stand up to the cold, wet, Eng-

Blue point Siamese

lish climate, so they tended to be kept in heated conservatories, in which luxurious trees and shrubs from the Far East were also protected against the elements. A few Siamese were kept in zoos, including those in Berlin and in Paris. Of course, the animals were not only kept as a hobby; Siamese were soon

being bred and shown. In the earliest cat shows these Orientals with their blue eyes were very striking among the British Shorthairs, Persians, Manx, and Abyssinians. The first Siamese were shown in 1884, at the famous Crystal Palace in London; these were two cats that had been imported from Siam the previous year. The breed was officially recognized in 1900. Siamese soon became popular, but keeping these cats—as was the case with other exotic breeds—was still largely restricted to the British (and to a lesser degree the French) aristocracy, who had the time, money, and other resources to keep and breed them. In the early days Siamese did not have the build of the present-day Siamese. They were more robust and their skull was slightly more wedge-shaped, rather than tri-angular. There was also only one color—seal point (genetic black).

A photograph of 1900—Mrs Roberts Locke with her Siamese cats "Calif," "Siam," and "Bangkok"

"Champion Wankee," a Siamese of around 1900

"Ah Choo," one of the first Siamese in England

RECENT HISTORY

Cats with colors other than seal point, such as blue point and chocolate point, were sometimes born, but in the early days these colors attracted little success. They were regarded virtually as "color faults." Only later did breeders start to apply themselves more to other colors than the original seal point. Some of these other colors were possibly already present in the genetic make-up of the Siamese from Siam. Other colors were deliberately created by crossing in other breeds and also non-pedigree cats. As early as 1894 there was mention of a blue point Siamese, although this color was not recognized until 1936. The chocolate points that were probably also occasionally born from seal point parents from the early days were only recognized in the 1950s. The lilac point, recognized in the 1960s, could emerge from combining the dilution factor of blue point and chocolate. Seal point, chocolate point, blue point, and lilac point became regarded throughout the world as the "classic" Siamese colors. In the 1960s new colors were added rapidly. By resorting to crosses that included Abyssinians and non-pedigree cats, colors such as red point, cream point, and tortie point were produced. The basis for tabby points was also laid in this period. Slowly but surely, not only were new colors introduced into the breed, but the type of the cat also underwent changes. In the course of time, by selective breeding, a new type of Siamese was developed. This Siamese is more graceful, with a longer head and ears which are set differently from the original Siamese.

TEMPERAMENT

Siamese are known throughout the world for their temperament, which is particularly pronounced. Siamese generally have a vocal disposition. They "chatter" a lot and have a noisy,

Chocolate is one of the four traditional Siamese colors

Seal point Siamese

harsh voice that they use a great deal, even if there is no one to talk to. Your neighbors, and other residents of your street, will not be left unaware when your Siamese queen is in season. At home the presence of a Siamese is always emphatically clear and they need companionship and attention if they are to feel happy. This means that they are not a suitable cat for people who only want to get one "because it is pretty." They want interaction; to be involved; and to

Siamese have a distinctive, people-oriented character

one feline playmate. Siamese normally get on very well with other cats—although they can sometimes display dominant traits—and also with dogs. Siamese are also playful; scrunched-up paper, little balls, toy mice, a scratching post—all will be appreciated and found interesting. The more intelligent of the breed can be taught to retrieve paper balls, and you can even

Chocolate point Siamese

meddle with everything. They like to be the center of attention. They appreciate being stroked and cuddled, and can spend hours on your lap, but may also choose to ride on your shoulder all day. If you do not give them enough attention, they demand it, and can do so very persistently. If you are regularly away from home, then it is advisable to give them at least

Siamese love company

take a Siamese for a walk on a leash, providing you accustom the animal to it at a young age.

CARE AND MAINTENANCE

A Siamese cat's coat needs very little grooming. It is very short and has little undercoat, so that under normal circumstances it will not be necessary to brush it more than once a week. A damp wash leather can remove dead and loose hair easily and quickly during molting times. If you want to show your Siamese, it is sometimes necessary to wash the animal a few days before the show. Always do this with a shampoo designed for cats and at least three days beforehand, as the coat needs time to recover after being washed. Siamese can have sensitive teeth, and some lose them before they are ten years old. Try to prevent this disaster by regularly giving the animal pieces of cooked meat to chew, and check its teeth regularly. Tartar can result in tooth decay, which in turn can lead to inflammation and loss of teeth, so it is best to get your vet to remove any tartar as soon as it occurs.

Chocolate tabby point Siamese,
eight month old male

APPEARANCE

BODY

The Siamese is a medium-large cat with a long, slim, supple body. Its long legs are relatively thin and the paws are oval-shaped. The hind legs are longer than the forelegs. The tail is long and thin and runs to a point, like a whip, without a kink. The neck is long and graceful.

HEAD

The head is long and well proportioned, with eyes placed wide apart and a long bridge to the nose. The head and the fine muzzle are in a perfectly straight line. The ears are large and upright, broad at the base, and set wide apart from each other. The chin is firm. The clear, bright, deep-blue eyes have an Oriental shape and are set slantwise towards the nose. A Siamese should not show any tendency to squint.

COAT

The coat of a Siamese is very short and fine in texture, glossy, and lies smoothly against the body. Hairs that are too long, too much undercoat, or a coarse hair structure are classed as faults.

COLORS AND PATTERNS

PATTERN

Siamese kittens are born completely white. Only later do they get their colored "points" on the face, ears, tail, and legs, and the scrotum (in males). This pattern is known by a variety of different names: colorpoint, Siamese pattern, Himalayan pattern or simply "points." By the time a Siamese is about three years old, the color of the coat should be well-developed. The fully colored mask should be linked with a line to the ears in an ideal case. Under the influence of moisture (grooming, rain), hormonal influences, and a cold environment, however, it is normal for darker shadows to form on the lighter colored parts over time. Also in places where the skin has been damaged, the new coat may come back darker. Siamese are mostly at their best for color between the second and fourth year of their lives. If they go out very little or never, or live in a warm, dry climate, they are usually purer in color. Cats displaying too much dark shadow are put in a lower classification at shows.

CLASSIC COLORS

The first imports from Thailand were seal points. Later these cats produced kittens in other colors spontaneously, such as blue, chocolate, and lilac point. These four colors, all solid, have come to be regarded as the "classic" Siamese colors. Colors that were developed later

Siamese have an elongated head and slanted eyes

Seal point male—over time, the development
of lightly colored patches leads to the appearance
of shadows

TABBY POINTS

Tabby points do not have a single-colored mask,
legs, ears, and tail, but tabby markings on these
places. The markings can be in any of the usual
colors from seal tabby point to fawn tortie tabby
point. Tabby points have been recorded as early as
1902 and, in 1924, a publication on tabby point
Siamese appeared in Switzerland. In spite of this,
it was not until the 1960s that serious work began
on the creation of the tabby point Siamese.

Seal point Siamese

came from crossing in, which is why in the U.S.,
and some other countries, colors other than the
classic ones are not recognized as Siamese.
There tabby and tortie points, as well as red,
cream, and cinnamon points, are treated as a
separate breed under the name "Colorpoint
Shorthair." The undesirable darker shadowing
on the body occurs most often on the seal points

Because cats other than Siamese were crossed in
to produce tabby points, the American C.F.A.,
among others, decided not to call these colors
within the breed Siamese, but "Colorpoint Shorthair." In spite of this, they are today, apart from
the color, no different from the Siamese with classic colors.

Blue point Siamese

and blue points. White hairs in the darker
points, or bringing, is not allowed.

Lilac tabby point kitten

RED POINT, CREAM POINT, AND TORTIE POINT

The red points, cream points, and tortie points emerged in Britain. In the late 1940s, with the help of a red non-pedigree cat, a breeding program was set up with the object of breeding red point, cream point, and tortie point Siamese. They come both with and without tabby markings. The breed standard requires a solid-colored face mask without stripes in non-tabbies, and also rejects stripes on the tail and legs. In red and cream, however, that is, in practice, virtually impossible. Red, and its dilution, cream, do not take any notice of the non-agouti gene, which is why a tabby marking will always filter through. Often red tabby points and cream tabby points

Cream point, male

cannot be distinguished visually from red points and cream points. Surprisingly, within these colors we meet the "freckles," small dark spots of pigment on the skin of the eyelids, ears, nose, and edge of the lips, which we often see in all red cats, and also in Siamese. For tortie tabbies the distribution of the spots is not important, however, both colors must be represented at all the points.

FOREIGN WHITE

The Foreign White has a status apart. This Siamese is solid white with blue eyes. In contrast to some other white cats with blue eyes, Foreign Whites are hardly ever deaf. The blue color of the Foreign Whites' eyes comes from the (pointed) Siamese, which it is, underneath its white coat, and not from the W-gene that causes blue eyes and the deafness associated with it in other white cats. The coat of the Foreign White should be a solid white color, and there should be no trace of yellow or other color in it. Nor

Foreign White

may Foreign Whites have any darker pigment. Their paw pads, the inside of the ears, and the nose are always a pink color. The color of the eyes is blue, preferably a deep, lively dark blue. Foreign Whites have a small but devoted circle of fanciers and breeders across the world. The variety was developed in the 1970s by crossing Siamese with white non-pedigree cats.

SIAMESE WITH WHITE PATCHES

From a late nineteenth-century photograph of a litter of Siamese we learn that, in those early days, there were Siamese with white markings. These markings, however, were suppressed by selective breeding. For years one of the spearheads of Siamese breeding was the ban on white patches. When in the 1970s and 1980s breeders in various countries began to be interested, independently of one another, in crossing in white markings in Orientals, it was ignored by most

Foreign White

Seal point Siamese with white patches

Siamese breeders. Nevertheless, the Siamese with white patches seem to have won a place for themselves within the breeds of pedigree cat, and the circle of their fans is growing. For the (re)introduction of white patches in Siamese (and also in Oriental Shorthair, Oriental Longhair, and Balinese), non-pedigree cats with white patches, tortoiseshell and white Persians, and White Spotted Cornish Rex were used. Recently a number of organizations have granted recog-

nition, so that these cats, too, can be shown, but there are also organizations that reject Siamese with white patches. Siamese and Balinese with white patches are referred to as "Seychelles."

OTHER COLORS

Various new colors and factors have been recently created. So we now have a cinnamon point and fawn point (fawn is the dilution of cinnamon), colors "borrowed" from the Abyssinian and, through the introduction of the silver factor, the smokes and silver tabby points.

REMARKS

- You may come across a Siamese whose owner says that it is a "variant." This means that this (shorthaired) cat carries the gene for long hair. Variants are not used for breeding Siamese, but only for breeding longhaired Balinese and Oriental Longhairs.
- A feature of the breed, which around 1900 was regarded as the height of ideal beauty and proof of being true-bred, was a Siamese with a squint and an obvious kink in the tail. It is striking, however, that Siamese kept in the temples in Siam did not display either of these abnormalities.

Siamese, cinnamon point kitten

Seal tortie point Siamese with white patches and heavy shading

BALINESE

ORIGIN

The Balinese is really a longhaired Siamese. The first longhaired Siamese were registered in the United States in 1928. From time to time, however, longhaired kittens were born to Siamese cats and nobody felt sufficiently interested to breed from them. There are various ways in which the recessive gene for long hair can get into a Siamese, varying from "accidents" with a longhaired cat that were not publicized to a spontaneous mutation of the gene that controls the length of hair. In any case, Siamese breeders regarded these longhairs as a "by-product" of their Siamese and sold them as pets. Only in the 1950s, when the Siamese breed was at the peak of its popularity, did some breeders in the United States decide to campaign for the recognition of longhaired Siamese. The breeders who led the movement were Marion Dorsey of California and Helen Smith of New York. The name "longhaired Siamese" came up against opposition among Siamese breeders, however. It was final-

Blue point Balinese kitten

ly decided to give this breed (in reality a variety of coat) another name—Balinese. Slowly but surely more breeders became interested. A breed association was set up—the Balinese Breeders and Fans of America (B.B.F.A.)—and the first breed standard was put on paper in 1965. Five years later, the Balinese was recognized by virtually all organizations in the United States and was also recognized in Europe very soon after. At that time, the breed only occurred in the classic Siamese colors of seal point, blue point, chocolate point, and lilac point. In the United States only these colors were considered

Blue tabby point Balinese

to be "real Siamese colors" and cats of other colors were regarded as hybrids. In the U.S. these have another breed name: Colorpoint Shorthair. Some Balinese breeders wanted to broaden their bloodlines with the colors of the Colorpoint Shorthairs, but this met opposition, even among the group of Balinese breeders and fanciers. Many people thought that the Balinese was a "pure"

Seal point Balinese

Blue point Balinese

Siamese with long hair and that this was destroyed by crossing them with "the hybrids." A solution to this dilemma was found by dreaming up another name for Balinese with non-classical colors—in 1979, longhaired Siamese that did not have one of the classical Siamese colors were recognized by the largest coordinating organization in the U.S.A. as "Javanese." This is not the case in Europe, where all Balinese, whether or not they have the classic colors, are called Balinese.

TEMPERAMENT

The temperament of the Balinese is similar to that of the Siamese. Like the Siamese, they are highly intelligent and lively cats with a character very much of their own. Balinese are playful and remain so up to an advanced age. They can amuse themselves for days with all kinds of cat toys, and the scratching post is also generally put to good use. Above all, however, these cats are designed for human companionship. They are

true cuddle-cats that enjoy being with their owner and want to be involved in the daily routine. A Balinese is always emphatically present and needs a great deal of attention and companionship—so much so that most breeders will not sell a single kitten if it transpires that its new

Balinese cats

A Balinese is just as talkative as a Siamese

owner has no other cats and/or is away a lot. A lonely Balinese can develop behavioral disturbances out of frustration. A Balinese will come and ask to be played with or cuddled and does not let itself be turned away; like other cats in the Oriental group, they can be very persistent. Their relationship with other cats is excellent, particularly with those of a similar temperament, such as other Orientals. These animals can also get on well with dogs and children.

They are not usually clingy, although they often show a preference for one specific person. They look slender and fragile, but are not so in the least and in fact feel much heavier than they look at first sight. Like other Oriental breeds, the Balinese are also talkative: they "chatter" non-stop and their voices are loud and harsh. Because of their human-oriented disposition and intelligence, it is easy to teach kittens of this breed to walk on a leash and to retrieve things.

CARE

The Balinese is longhaired, but its coat has a silky structure with little undercoat, so that a weekly brushing session is normally enough. Preferably use a bristle brush, after which you can run over the coat with a comb. Before you show a Balinese, it has to be washed. Do this at least two or three days before the show, so that the coat has a chance to recover, and always use a special cat shampoo.

Red point Balinese

Balinese have a slender build

hairs on the tail are long, silky and not too thick in structure.

COLORS AND PATTERNS

Since the Balinese is a longhaired Siamese, all the colors that we see in the Siamese, and in the U.S.A. in the Colorpoint Shorthair, are allowed in the Balinese, including solid white (Foreign White). The eyes, regardless of the colors of the coat, should be a very dark blue.

APPEARANCE

BODY
The Balinese has the same body build as a Siamese. The muscular body should be long and slim, and should display no coarseness anywhere. The hindquarters stand higher than the fore, and the legs are long and slim, with oval-shaped paws. The tail is long and thin and should have no kinks or other abnormalities.

HEAD
The head is wedge-shaped and, seen from the front, forms a perfect triangle with the large ears. Highly developed cheek muscles spoil the line of the head and are not desirable. The chin is firm, but not too pronounced, and a weak reversing chin is considered a bad fault at shows. The line of the nose displays no stop, but flows without interruption into the forehead. The eyes of the Balinese are almond-shaped and slanted, and their color should be as pure as possible.

COAT

The semi-longhaired coat of the Balinese feels silky and fine and should lie close to the skin. The Balinese has little undercoat. In no circumstances should the coat stand out, be coarse in structure, or have too much undercoat. The

Blue tabby point Balinese kitten

White Balinese (Foreign White, longhaired)

tens carrying the gene for long hair are called "variants." They are not used for breeding Siamese, but only to breed Balinese or Oriental Longhairs. Sometimes, but not always, variants can be recognized by their short-haired coat being just a little longer than that of "true-bred" Siamese.

- Balinese with white patches have recently turned up, a breed type called "Seychelles Longhair." This variety first appeared in England from crossing Siamese with (tortoise-shell and white) Persians and other Oriental cats. Seychelles were shown for the first time in 1989.

Blue point Balinese

REMARKS

- The breed standard for the Balinese is the same as for the Siamese, apart from the length of the coat. In practice, however, Siamese often conform better to the breed standard and therefore a Siamese is occasionally crossed in to improve the Balinese type. The kittens born from such a combination are always shorthaired. They do, however, carry the gene for long hair in their genetic package and with the right partners (a longhair or a longhair carrier) they can, in their turn, produce longhaired kittens. Shorthaired kit-

ORIENTAL SHORTHAIR

ORIGIN

The Oriental Shorthair has only recently become known as a breed. A number of breeders decided to breed a fully colored Siamese In the 1950s. Britain, which can undoubtedly be regarded as the nursery of the cat fancy, was in the forefront. At first only solid chocolate-colored Orientals were bred. These were called Havanas and, apart from their color, had the same breed standard as the Siamese. These chocolate-colored animals were recognized by the G.C.C.F. in 1958 under the breed name "Chestnut Brown Foreign."
Later the dilute form of chocolate appeared—lilac, also called lavender—and people also started to breed solid white Siamese with blue eyes (Foreign White). More colors were gradually added. In Britain, a new breed name was thought up for each new color, although the criteria laid down for the type were the same as those for the Siamese. The fully colored Siamese could be crossed with one another and each individual animal was given a pedigree with a breed name appropriate to the color of its coat. So it could happen that there might be three different colors in one and the same litter, with three different breed names. Outside Britain, too, in the United States, breeders began to be interested in breeding solid-colored Siamese. They started with Havanas (chocolate brown), imported from Britain, but were soon also breeding black (ebony) and blue. In the course of time, so many colors were being bred both in England and America that it no longer made sense to give each color a separate breed name, and all colors were lumped together in a single new breed, the Oriental Shorthair. The Oriental Shorthair range of colors has expanded enormously and today it

Black silver spotted Oriental Shorthair, female

Cinnamon ticked tabby Oriental
Shorthair kitten

Chocolate tortie ticked tabby Oriental Shorthair,
female

Young blue Oriental Shorthair, male

is one of the breeds in which virtually all possible colors can be found. In spite of this, not all the colors that occur are generally recognized globally.

TEMPERAMENT

It not surprising that the temperament of the Oriental Shorthair is essentially the same as that of the Siamese. They are talkative cats that like a great deal of attention from their owners and certainly do not stay quietly in the background. Oriental Shorthairs are very affectionate and physical. They like sleeping in their owner's lap—or draped round his or her neck—and enjoy being pet and cuddled. Some people class this behavior simply as intrusive, while others enjoy their cat showing so plainly that it values its people's company. Oriental Shorthairs are extremely inquisitive and little escapes them. Your visitors do not have to look for the cat; it will come running to make their acquaintance as soon as they come in and to investigate the contents of their pockets and handbags. Another striking trait these Orientals have in common with their ancestors is their very sociable temperament toward other cats. Oriental Shorthairs can often get along with each other extremely well, so well that they are not always at their best when they are on their own. Behavioral problems, such as unsanitary behavior, destroying furniture, and extremely noisy demands for attention, are some of the problems owners of a solitary Oriental Shorthair may have to cope with. Therefore, people who work full-time are urged by most breeders to take two kittens, rather than just one. A well socialized kitten can usually get on very well with dogs. Moreover, these slim Orientals are remarkably playful and active, and continue to be so to an advanced age. Often nothing can be wild enough for them. They can stand rough treatment and are not quick to take offence, which is one of the reasons that children and Oriental Shorthairs often get on so well together. Oriental Shorthairs are, in general, intelligent cats. Their intelligence, together with their sociable, people-oriented disposition, means that they are very quick to learn tricks and often greatly enjoy performing them. Teaching an Oriental Shorthair kitten to walk on a leash should, therefore, present no

Black tabby Oriental Shorthair, male

insuperable problems. There is, however, also a downside to this intelligence, spirit of adventure, and inquisitiveness—they will know how to open a door, a kitchen cupboard, and even a refrigerator within a very short time, and operating a lever tap is rarely an insoluble problem for them. So Oriental Shorthairs are not everyone's ideal pet. People with little spare time or people who want a quiet, peaceful cat, will do better with a different breed.

CARE AND MAINTENANCE

A good Oriental Shorthair's coat molts very little and, therefore, needs very little attention of any kind. It is usually enough to brush the coat once a week with a soft bristle brush, and often just stroking it is sufficient. When it does molt, the loose hair can be removed from the coat with a damp chamois leather. Be warned that these cats often mature sexually very early. Males are often fertile by the age of five months and females can come into season for the first time when they are about six months old.

Chocolate silver ticked Oriental Shorthair, female

APPEARANCE

BODY

The Oriental Shorthair is a medium-sized cat with a long, supple body and a slim build. The cat should make a lithe, graceful, and elegant impression, without any coarseness. The hindquarters are higher than the forequarters. The legs are relatively thin, and have a fine bone structure. The small paws are oval-shaped.

The Oriental Shorthair has an elegant build

The thin tail is long and narrows at the tip. The neck is slim and graceful. Although a typical Oriental Shorthair gives the impression of being very slight, it weighs much more than you would expect at first sight. It is in fact well-muscled and far from fragile.

HEAD

The head is long and wedge-shaped, and runs in perfect lines that meet at the fine muzzle. The large ears are set wide apart and are broad at the base. The bridge of the nose is long and displays no dip (stop). The chin is firm. The eyes are really

Black tabby Oriental Shorthair, male

The head of an Oriental Shorthair is elongated
and wedge-shaped

"Oriental," almond-shaped and slanting. They
look lively and expressive.

COAT

The glossy coat of the Oriental Shorthair is very
short, has a fine structure, and lies smoothly
against the body.

COLORS AND PATTERNS—GENERAL

The Oriental Shorthair cat may be bred in
numerous colors and color patterns except for
the Siamese pattern. The most popular coat colors include ebony (black), Havana (chocolate
brown), lavender (lilac), cinnamon, fawn, and
blue. In the solid colors, care must be taken that
there are no ghost markings (vague tabby markings). Each separate hair should as far as possible have the same fine, deep color down to the
root. The most popular solid color is Havana.
Tabbies, in particular, have gained in popularity in recent years. All four tabby patterns
(ticked, blotched/classic, striped, and spotted)
occur in the breed and in virtually all colors,
with or without a silver undercoat. This silver

Young black classic tabby and white Oriental Shorthair, male

Black silver classic tabby Oriental Shorthair

- It is typical that some countries have chosen to class the Foreign Whites, the white Orientals with blue eyes, among the Oriental Shorthairs; while others, because of its blue eyes, class this breed among the Siamese.

SYNONYMS

THE GROUP OF BREEDS STEMMING FROM THE SIAMESE IS KNOWN BY DIFFERENT NAMES ACROSS THE WORLD:

- JAVANESE: THE SYNONYM OF ORIENTAL LONGHAIR, BUT USED IN THE UNITED STATES TO INDICATE BALINESE WITH STRIPES OR RED IN THE POINTS
- MANDARIN: SYNONYM FOR ORIENTAL LONGHAIR
- SEYCHELLES: SYNONYM FOR BALINESE OR SIAMESE WITH WHITE PATCHES
- ANGORA: THE NAME USED ONLY IN BRITAIN FOR THE ORIENTAL LONGHAIR (NOT TO BE CONFUSED WITH THE TURKISH ANGORA)
- POINTED ORIENTAL LONGHAIR: BALINESE BORN TO TWO ORIENTAL SHORT OR LONGHAIRED CATS (UNITED STATES)
- POINTED ANGORA: BALINESE BORN TO TWO ORIENTAL SHORTHAIRS OR LONGHAIRS (GREAT BRITAIN)

undercoat is in any case "borrowed" from the Chinchilla Persian. Some years ago a start was made with Oriental Shorthair cats with white markings—bicolor. These are not recognized everywhere yet. The color of the eyes is preferably a pure deep green, without a trace of another color such as yellow or brown.

REMARKS

- Oriental Shorthair cats may be crossed with Siamese, Oriental Longhairs, and Balinese. In reality they are all the same cats, of the same type, except for their color and the length of their fur.
- Oriental Shorthair cats carrying the longhair factor are called "variants." These sometimes, but certainly not always, have slightly longer shorthaired coats than their fellows. Because the difference between a "true" Oriental Shorthair and a variant can usually not be seen, variants are shown as Oriental Shorthairs.

Oriental Longhair, profile

Oriental Longhair

ORIENTAL LONGHAIR (SYN. MANDARIN, JAVANESE, ANGORA)

ORIGIN

The Oriental Longhair is an Oriental Shorthair with a silky, semi-long coat. The long hair gene was already there in the 1950s when the Oriental Shorthair (a fully colored Siamese) was developed. Longhaired kittens were, therefore, sometimes born to Oriental Shorthair cats. In addition, breeders, particularly in Britain, were working on crossing Oriental Shorthair cats with Balinese (longhaired Siamese) and in the course of time this, too, resulted in longhaired animals. Although nowadays the breed is encountered all over the world, there is no unanimity in its naming. The most obvious name for a longhaired Oriental Shorthair would be

Oriental Longhair, but the breed was given different names in different countries. In the United States it is now also called "Oriental Longhair," but it was formerly known as "Mandarin." In Britain they are called "Angoras" (not to be confused with the Turkish Angora, a totally different breed). FIFé, the coordinating cat organization, which has many members particularly in Europe, called the breed "Javanese," and sometimes, too, "Oriental Semi-Longhair." The breed name "Javanese" was already in use in the United States for Balinese with non-classical point colors.

TEMPERAMENT

The temperament of the Oriental Longhair is identical to that of the Siamese, Balinese, and Oriental Shorthair.

CARE AND MAINTENANCE

The Oriental Longhair requires little care for its coat. It can look after its sleek coat very well itself. A weekly brushing session is sufficient.

Odd-eyed white Oriental Longhair

Lilac Oriental Longhair

APPEARANCE

The Oriental Longhair should be identical to the Siamese in type. At the moment, this has not yet been achieved; development is continuing. Breeders are, of course, aiming for the Siamese type.

COAT

The Oriental Longhair has a sleek, longhaired coat that feels silky, but does not get tangled or matted. In summer, the ruff and "breeches" are often not really clearly present, but a cat in its winter coat certainly has them. Neutered cats of both sexes gener-

Chocolate smoke Oriental Longhair

ally have a longer and fuller coat than their unneutered fellows.

COLORS, PATTERNS, AND MARKINGS

Oriental Longhairs are bred in almost all possible colors, patterns, and markings, like the Oriental Shorthair.

REMARKS

Oriental Longhair cats are occasionally crossed with Siamese, Oriental Shorthairs, and Balinese. In reality these are all the same cats, of the same type, except for their color and the length of their coat. Kittens of all these different breeds can occur together in the same litter.

Havana Brown

HAVANA BROWN

ORIGIN

The history of the Havana Brown in its early days is linked to that of the Oriental Shorthair. When British breeders decided to start breeding fully colored Siamese in the 1950s, they concentrated on the chocolate brown color. This color, which quickly gained popularity, was called "Havana." In 1956, the American Elsie Quinn from El Monte, California had a Havana imported from Great Britain. This was a female named "Roofspringer Mahogany Quinn," which was later mated to a male, also imported from Britain, "Laurentide Brown Pilgrim of Norwood." The kittens born from this union laid the foundations of the Havana Brown in the United States. Many imports and litters followed, and in 1964 the breed was given the name Havana Brown in the United States and awarded championship status by the C.F.A. This marked a parting of the ways for the Oriental Shorthair and the Havana Brown since, whereas British breeders continued to select animals that resembled the Siamese as much as possible in body structure and type, the Americans wanted to keep their Havanas the same as they were when they were first imported. Over the course of time, the British and American Havanas have grown so far apart that they can be regarded as two separate breeds. Whereas the Oriental Shorthairs in Britain and the rest of Europe have a body structure the same as the Siamese, the Havana Browns have a more moderately Oriental body structure, rather like that of the Russian Blue. The Havana Brown is a relatively uncommon breed in the U.S.A. and very rarely seen outside it.

Havana Brown kittens

TEMPERAMENT

The Havana Brown is a pleasant, highly people-oriented and social member of the household. Cats of this breed need real companionship, preferably from their owners, but if that is impossible they may be satisfied with one of their own kind. Unlike most Orientals, these cats have fairly subdued voices. Fanciers claim that their Havana Browns have a

Havana Brown

Young Havana Brown

CARE AND MAINTENANCE

Care of the Havana Brown's coat is very little trouble. It is enough to comb the coat once a week with a fine-toothed comb and then to wipe it over with a damp chamois leather to bring out the gloss.

BODY

The Havana Brown is a medium-sized, muscular cat with a medium long neck, and its body structure should be halfway between that of the Siamese and the European breeds. It stands high on its elegant legs, the hind legs being slightly longer than the forelegs. Its compact paws are oval-shaped. The tail is middling long and thick. It should not be too wide at the base, and should taper to a point.

special way of indicating that they want attention; they pat their owners with their claws sheathed, to draw their attention to something. Havana Browns can get on very well with other cats, and also with dogs and children.

Havana Browns

Havana Browns have oval eyes
with an expressive look

Coat

The coat is short, lies flat, and is glossy.

Colors

Havana Browns are bred in two colors—chocolate and its dilution, lilac. Lilac, called Oriental Lilac, is actually not recognized by all cat organizations. The eyes should be green in both coat colors; the deeper the green the better. Kittens may show ghost markings which disappear as they grow older.

Head

The head is longer than it is wide and, seen from above, gradually narrows into a rounded, rather narrow muzzle, with a definite indentation behind the whisker pads. Seen from the front, the muzzle section is almost square, an impression that is emphasized by the well-developed chin. The ears are large and have rounded tips. The medium-sized eyes are oval in shape and expressive.

Kittens often still have ghost markings

PERSIAN LONGHAIR

ORIGIN

EARLY ORIGIN

In the history of the origins of the Persian Longhair an important role was played by the (Turkish) Angora. These longhaired Angora cats,
almost without exception with white coats,
were introduced into Europe around the seventeenth century by seafaring traders. Because of
their rarity and luxurious appearance, these elegant, longhaired cats very quickly became popular in circles that could afford to keep expensive, unusual cats. It is known, for example, that
Marie Antoinette, Louis XVI's queen, had sev-

Two Persians of around 1900

Black tortoiseshell Persian Longhair, female

Predecessor of the chinchilla Persian from the early days
of breeding Persians

eral of these Angoras. For years the status of
Angoras as luxury cats remained unassailable. In
Britain some of the non-pedigree cat population
had longhaired coats, so it is not impossible that
Angoras and longhaired British cats were
crossed, if not deliberately. Moreover, Britain
had many colonies from which longhaired cats
came. It is known that unusual looking cats from
these colonies were regularly brought back to
Britain; one example is the forefather of all
chinchilla Persians, a tom cat brought back from
India. These longhaired cats from the colonies,
Turkish Angoras, and longhaired, British, non-
pedigree cats together made up a group of longhaired cats from which sprang the Persian Longhair.

"Brown tabby" (black tabby) Persian
Longhair of around 1900

A Persian cattery in the early twentieth century
(left the cattery attendant, right the owner)

RECENT HISTORY

In the late nineteenth century, people in Britain began to breed and show cats seriously. A standard was drawn up for longhaired cats—"Longhairs"—that were later re-christened "Persians." The "Longhairs" were selected for the beauty of their color and patterns, with as luxurious a coat as possible, and an imposing, sturdy type. The Persian cat soon found its way to fanciers in continental Europe, and also to the United States, where it was bred from animals imported from Britain. In the first decades of the twentieth century there were no great changes in their appearance. Coats may have become rather longer and also denser

The Persian Longhair in early days was
different from the current one

as a result of selective breeding, but body structure and the shape of the head remained similar to that of sturdily built, shorthaired, non-pedigree cats. Only from the 1950s onwards, some fifty years after the emergence of the first Persians, was there any striking alteration in the type. At that time, by coincidence, the first Persians were born with a very brachycephalic type of head, combined with a very short nose and a deep "stop." It was a type of head familiar at that time amongst dogs, and found in such breeds as the Pekinese, pug, and bulldog. Persians of this type were mainly bred by American fanciers. Hence the Persian Longhair acquired a very individual type in the United States, different in appearance from European Persians. Increasing international contacts between pedigree cat fanciers brought the American type of animal to fanciers in Europe from the 1960s onwards. Through the import of these American animals, the ideal of European breeders shifted in the direction of a more short-headed animal. This "new" type of head is unique to the modern Persian, and occurs in no other breed of cat except for its shorthaired peer, the Exotic. Persians have always been a very popular breed and today the breed is still one of the five most popular breeds in all cat-loving countries.

TEMPERAMENT

Persians are known for their peaceful, almost phlegmatic temperament. They are very unassuming, friendly, sociable, and sympathetic. They like being pet and stroked, and enjoy being pampered. They rarely show their claws; obviously a Persian can get angry, but their tolerance threshold is substantially higher than that of the average cat. This means that they can often get on very well with other cats, and sharing their

Cream Persian Longhair female

pered. This does not apply to kittens, which are as playful and tireless as any other kittens. Most Persians have a soft voice, but they do not let you hear it much. Compared with the average cat, a Persian Longhair can be left on its own. If, however, you are out a great deal, because you work away from home, then it would be nice to provide your Persian with a feline friend. Persians find life indoors much to their taste and most of them do not pine for the outdoor life. Here, too, what they are used to is important; Persians that from a young age have been used to going outside will want to do so later on. Animals that are not familiar with outdoor life will not miss it.

CARE AND MAINTENANCE

Chinchilla

environment with dogs and other household pets raises no problems. They are not easily upset in a menage with young children, but need a hideaway to which they can withdraw when things get too busy. In spite of their peaceful nature, Persians love to play. The level of their activity depends to some extent on you—Persians that have been played with from a young age are in general, when adult, more active than animals that have only been stroked and pam-

A Persian Longhair can never be considered separately from the care needed by the breed. The luxurious, thick, soft coat tangles very easily and, if it is not regularly groomed, matting and felting lie in wait. Whether you keep your Persian as a pet or regularly show it, the care of its coat will never be a task you can fit in at odd

Cream Persian Longhair

moments and certainly not one you can put off for a week or longer. So you should really only get a Persian Longhair if you enjoy looking after your cat every day. Fortunately, most Persians enjoy this daily grooming, but there are some who have a profound dislike for it. This does not depend only on the temperament of the cat. A responsible breeder will accustom his kittens early to a daily brushing session, so that later they will find it a normal, and even enjoyable, interruption to their everyday concerns. Persians are at their most beautiful in the winter months. In the spring and early summer they shed much of their coat and you will have to be careful that the cat does not swallow too much hair whilst washing itself.

Black tortoiseshell smoke Persian Longhair, female

CARE OF THE COAT

If you just keep a Persian for company and do not show it, it should be enough to brush through the coat each day with a wire brush, and about once a week gently comb out any tangles with a coarse comb. In particular, the parts between the fore and hind legs, the hairs below the tail, chest, and the chin need extra attention. Never pull too hard on the coat, but work carefully and patiently. If the coat has become rather dirty, then you can dust an unscented and fat-free powder into it that will absorb the dirt and any excess oil from the coat. This will make the

Red Persian Longhair

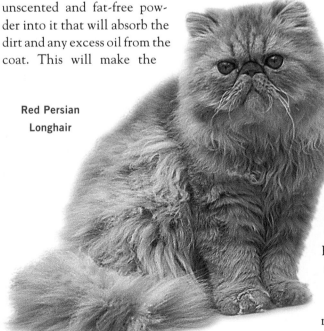

coat cleaner and looser, so that it tangles less quickly. This powder is usually available at larger pet shops, and you can also get it at shows. After rubbing it in, brush the coat until no trace of the powder is left. About every three months you can give the animal a bath. Always use a good quality cat shampoo for this; there are special ones that will enhance the color of your cat. After a bath, the dead loose hairs that cause tangles in the coat are easier to brush out.

COAT CARE FOR SHOWS

The care of the coat for show specimens is broadly comparable to that for Persians kept as household pets. Cats that are shown regularly should, however, be bathed more often. They should be brushed as well and as thoroughly as their domestic fellows, but their owners more often decide to pick the dead hair out with their thumb and forefinger. This is an intensive task, but prevents the coat from starting to look "bitty." The ears of a Persian Longhair, according to the breed standard, should be small. Exhibitors will sometimes carefully cut off, or gently pull out, the small hairs growing on the rims of the ears (but not those inside the ear), because they make the ears look larger. Finally, a show cat must be brushed and powdered much

Chinchilla

CARE OF THE EYES

Persian Longhair cats sometimes have weeping eyes, with unsightly dark tear stripes running down the creases in their face. Light-colored Persians seem to have more trouble with this, but this is simply because it shows up more clearly on them. Try to prevent the dark discoloration of the creases in the face as much as possible, since neglected tear stripes will in most cases become permanently visible. A daily check on the eyes and creases of the face can prevent this. You can clean them with a Kleenex dipped in cooled, boiled water or use a special eye lotion for cats.

more regularly to prevent tangles and to keep the coat nicely loose, clean, and as full as possible.

Chinchilla

APPEARANCE

BODY

The Persian Longhair is a cat of medium-large to large size, with a robust bone structure. The body is compact, with a broad chest, muscular shoulders and back, and a short, powerful neck. The legs are short and sturdy, and the paws large and round. Tufts of hair between the toes are desirable. The tail is short, in good proportion to the body, and has a slightly rounded tip.

HEAD

The head is round, massive, and well-proportioned with a broad skull and full cheeks. The forehead is nicely domed, and the short, very broad nose has a clear stop. The top of the

Silver point

Black tortoiseshell and white ("tricolor") and red Persian Longhair

rhinal mirror should lie in a horizontal line with the lowest eyelids. The stop (the indent in the bridge of the nose) should be at the height of the middle of the eyes. The Persian Longhair has firm, broad jaws and a firm chin. The teeth should have a scissor-like action and preferably be complete. Seen from the side, the chin, the top of the nose, and the forehead should lie in a straight vertical line. The small ears are broad at the base and rounded with a full ear tuft in each ear. They are wide apart and set low on the skull.

Black Persian Longhair

The large round eyes are wide apart and should be brilliant and full of expression. Depending on the color of the coat, the color of the eyes is copper or dark orange, green, or blue, and sometimes odd-eyed; the color should be as pure as possible. Faults include: too large ears, too long a nose, or the bridge of the nose pushed in, and almond-shaped eyes.

COAT

The coat of the Persian Longhair is long and abundant, with a dense, fine, silky structure. The coat forms a substantial ruff, and the tail, too, should be fully haired. Persians look their

Persian Longhair kittens

best in autumn and winter, since most of them shed a substantial proportion of their coat in spring and early summer.

COLORS AND PATTERNS—GENERAL

In the early days of registered Persian breeding, around 1900, particularly popular colors and color combinations were black, white, blue, red, cream, smoke, silver tabby, brown tabby, red tabby, chinchilla, tortoiseshell, and bicolor. Because of the great diversity of longhaired cats that reached Britain from all quarters of the globe, in theory virtually all basic colors and

Blue Persian Longhair

patterns were present when breeding began. Later on other breeds were very rarely "borrowed" for breeding-in other colors. For instance, the colorpoint pattern was not one that occurred traditionally in Persians; it was bred into Persian Longhairs later by crossing in Siamese. Today almost every color or combination of them occurs in Persian Longhairs and, at shows, high requirements are set for depth of color and patterns, including the color of the eyes.

"SOLID" OR "SELF" COLORS

"Solid" or "self" colors are white, black, blue, red, cream, chocolate, lilac, cinnamon, fawn, and tortoiseshell. Persians with these coat colors have copper-colored to orange eyes, except for white Persians, which may either have two blue eyes or be odd-eyed. A Persian with a solid color (except, of course, white ones) should show no white hairs or markings, and each hair should as far as possible be the same color from its tip to its root. This is called "well-colored throughout." "Ghost markings" often occur in kittens and sometimes these vague tabby mark-

ings are still visible in the coat when the animal is older. These ghost markings win no prizes at shows. Because it is very difficult to achieve a self-colored coat in red Persians, a blind eye is sometimes turned to this color at shows. Nor is it a simple matter to keep a beautiful black Persian black—sunlight and moisture can discolor it in some places to red or brown. A solid-colored cat with a silver-white undercoat is called a smoke (see: Silver and smoke). In recent years black, blue, cream, red, and (black) tor-

Odd-eyed, white Persian Longhair

toiseshell have been the most popular and usual solid colors in Persians.

TABBIES

Tabbies occur in four different tabby patterns, the Abyssinian (ticked), striped (mackerel), spotted, and blotched or classic. The tabby markings should be as clear as possible. Because tabby is a color pattern that is inherited independent of the basic color, a tabby cat can be bred in any color. The most popular are black and red tabbies. With the exception of silver tabbies (see: Silver and smoke), Persian Long-

Chocolate tabby Persian Longhair

hair tabbies should have copper-colored to orange eyes.

Blue-cream and white female (a "tricolor")

PARTICOLORS

Particolors are that group of Persians with white markings. The exact term used depends on the amount of white in the coat. Cats in which the white covers about a third of the body are called "Bicolor." They should have one basic color with as symmetrical as possible white markings. The tricolor is, in essence, a bicolor with two basic colors (such as a tortoiseshell and white). Persians with a few patches of color on their (white) bodies and a colored tail, and one or more patches on the head, are called "harlequin" and cats with only one or two head patches and a colored tail are called "van." Some cat

Black and white Persian Longhair, harlequin markings

organizations allow one or two additional patches on the body for the van marking. It is not easy to breed a good particolor Persian, because mating two particolored Persians often produces kittens with a different quantity of white—in other words, mating two bicolor Persians can produce a litter with bicolor kittens, but also vans or harlequins and kittens with an amount or distribution of white that does not meet a single standard. Particolors should have copper-colored to orange eyes.

SILVER AND SMOKE

Persians with a silver-white undercoat, such as chinchillas, cameos, and smokes, are very fashionable. The silver-white undercoat that typifies these animals is caused by the operation of the dominant Inhibitor gene, which inhibits pigment formation at the root of the hair. This

Chinchilla

Left a chinchilla, right a smoke

means that color can only occur further up the hair shaft, but part of the hair remains without color, and so becomes silver-white. The Inhibitor gene can work on a self-colored cat, which is then called a "smoke." In smokes, the hairs usually lack color up to about half their length and the eyes should be colored orange. If a tabby has the same gene, it is called a silver tabby and its eyes should be green. There are, however, degrees of silver tabby that have been given special names. The term "shaded" is used for black, blue, chocolate, lilac, cinnamon, or fawn Persians with hair that lacks color for about two-thirds of its length. The same degree of lack of color in cream or red Persians is often called "cameo." Red and cream-colored Persians lacking color for seven-eighths of the hair shaft are more often called "shell" and the same degree of colorlessness in black, blue, chocolate,

lilac, cinnamon, and fawn Persians is called "chinchilla." Because there is still so little color left in their coat, chinchillas and shells are often mistaken for white cats by the inexperienced. There is, however, pigment on the tips of the hairs (particularly on the back and top of the tail) and it is also clearly present round the eyes and nose—chinchillas can look as if they are wearing make-up. There are breeders who devote themselves to breeding silver Persians with orange eyes, but by far most silver blood-

Silver tabby kitten, about one week old

Golden Persian Longhair kitten

lines have green eyes. Because eye color should be as deep and even as possible, animals with green and orange eyes are not normally mated to each other.

GOLDEN

Because the Inhibitor gene is inherited dominant, non-silver kittens can sometimes be born to silver Persians. These have still inherited their parents' green eyes, but not their silver-white undercoat. These cats, called "goldens," are judged in a separate class.

COLORPOINT (HIMALAYAN)

In Europe, the Persian Longhair colorpoint does not form a separate breed; it is seen as a color variant of the Persian Longhair. In the United States, these cats are called "Himalayan" and judged separately from other Persians. The first colorpoint Persians saw the light of day in the

Persian Longhair colorpoint kittens

United States in the 1930s. To introduce the colorpoint pattern into Persian Longhairs, use was in the first instance made of seal point Siamese. Because the bodily structure of the Siamese is quite different from that of the Persian Longhair, the earliest generations of colorpoints did not conform to the standard for the Persian type. Its fanciers had a clear goal before them, however, and slowly but surely the Persian Longhair colorpoint began to acquire more of the correct shape in appearance and coat length. The first Persian Longhair colorpoints were seal points, but by careful back-crosses with Siamese, breeders were able to add red, cream,

age will later, influenced by the weather, small injuries, and by licking their coat (saliva), end up by getting dark shadows. The colorpoint will keep a purer body color if the animal is not exposed too much to cold temperatures, and is not allowed out in wet weather, both of which can cause the coat to become darker. At present, most colorpoint Persians have light-blue eyes, but breeders are trying to achieve darker blue eyes. Persian Longhair colorpoint kittens are always born white, and the point color appears sometimes after only a few days, but in most cases takes rather longer to show up.

Cream point Persian Longhair in its summer coat

blue, chocolate, lilac, tortie, and tabby points to their range of colors, and also these colors combined with silver or smoke. In spite of many successive generations of Persian Longhair colorpoints being bred without a single Siamese assisting in the process, a Siamese influence is still noticeable in the colorpoint temperament. Usually colorpoint Persians are rather more lively and more extroverted in temperament than other Persian Longhairs. The queens often come into season for the first time at the age of eight months, earlier than other Persians. The contrast between the body color and the colored points (also called the "Himalayan" pattern) should be as clear as possible. Dark shadows on the body are not looked up on favorably at shows, but particularly in seal point and blue point colorpoints it is virtually impossible to breed cats without shadow markings. Kittens which display a nice light body color at a young

Seal tortie point Persian Longhair kitten

Russian Blue mother and kittens

RUSSIAN BLUE

ORIGIN

Russian Blue male

EARLY HISTORY

The Russian Blue, sometimes called Blue Russian, is one of the oldest breeds of cat we know. Russian Blues were already being shown at cat shows by around 1900. It is known that about two hundred years ago shorthaired blue cats with a slim build were encountered in Archangel, a Russian port on the White Sea. Over time, a number of these cats were taken home with them by British seamen and shown in England as Archangel Cats. An English woman, Mrs. C. Carew Cox, was one of the first people to own a Russian Blue

"Bayard"

Cat. From 1889 onwards she possessed several blue cats, most of them of unknown, but in any case not of Russian descent. From 1893 onwards she started buying blue cats imported from Archangel more frequently, such as the queens "Lingpopo" and "Olga," and a tom, "Moscow." Olga was the mother of one of the most famous Blue Russians of this early period—"Bayard," born in 1898. His father was "King Vladimir," a name that makes one suspect he also came from Russia, but this point is not certain. In the period around the turn of the century, Russian Blues were not regarded as a separate breed. All shorthaired blue cats were more or less crossed with each other, and everyone had his or her own opinion about what such a cat should look like. What is certain is that Mrs. Carew in later years imported more cats from Archangel, Russia, and also bred from them. The blue, semi-Oriental type of cat from Archangel was not really con-

Russian Blue

sidered as true-bred in this early period. Only in 1912 was a separate class for foreign breeds created in Great Britain, and the Russian short-haired type began to be bred more or less true. At that time the breed did not yet have its present name, as a consequence of the Russian revolution, which made things Russian unpopular in England. Until 1939 the breed was known in Britain by the name "Blue Foreign," showing that it was a foreign, but not an Oriental, breed.

RECENT HISTORY

The Second World War proved a watershed in the evolution of this breed. After the war, there were so few breed-typical Russian Blue cats left that problems of inbreeding loomed and breeders were forced to "borrow" genes from other breeds. Blue point Siamese were sometimes crossed in during this period. They helped to widen the gene

Russian Blue

pool and so produce greater vitality, but also brought an unwanted color pattern—points—into the breed, something that present-day breeders sometimes still come up against because of the recessive inheritance of points. Influenced by the Siamese factor, the Russian Blue became slimmer and more elegant than they originally were, until in the 1960s a group of breeders was formed who together tried to breed back to the "old" Russian type, at which they were successful. Breeding Russian Blues is not actually an exclusively British affair. They were also bred quite early on in Scandinavia, particularly in Sweden, and breeders have set themselves the goal of maintaining the short-haired Russian breed. The first C.F.A. registered Russian Blue cats in the United States were recorded in 1949 and it is known that, decades before that, Russian Blue cats were exported to America. Yet it was not until 1964 that the breed was given official championship status in the U.S. Today, the Russian Blue is familiar in all countries where cats are bred. The breed has a loyal, if not very large, band of supporters who are seriously involved in maintaining and, where possible, improving the breed. Russian Whites and Russian Blacks are also now bred on a small scale.

TEMPERAMENT

The Russian Blue has its own temperament typical of the breed. The animals are good-tempered and well balanced, and are fond of a peaceful life and harmony at home. Above all, they become very attached to their owner. Statements such as "There is no cat as true as a Russian Blue" are not totally unfounded. There are even tales of Russian Blue cats who refuse to eat if their owner is away. They

Russian White

Russian Blue kitten

dote on their owners, like sitting on their lap, and forge close links with them, but, even so, never for a moment lose the sense of their own worth—they are anything but intrusive. They are in no hurry to make up their minds about people they do not know. A typical Russian Blue reaction to a stranger is to walk away and watch him or her from a distance, a reaction

Russian Blue

that should not be confused with fear—they decide for themselves when it is time to see how the land lies. Russian Blue cats are not exactly little friends of all the world, eager to climb into the laps of visitors—that privilege is reserved for

Russian Blue

their owner. Their fanciers particularly appreciate this trait. Russian Blue cats can get on very well with other cats and raise no objections to the presence of dogs or children. This breed is less suited to a noisy home with small children, however, because they like peace and quiet. They are active and restful in turn; they enjoy playing, but not excessively. It is also a very intelligent breed; Russian Blues soon learn, for example, how to open doors. All in all they are very owner-oriented. If you are away from home a great deal this is not the breed for you.

CARE AND MAINTENANCE

Keeping Russian Blues is not hard work. Their coat is short and resilient and needs requires a minimal amount of care. It is enough to brush through the coat once a week with a bristle brush. Do not brush or comb a Russian Blue too fiercely, because you may pull out some of the fur.

APPEARANCE

BODY
The body is relatively long, muscular, and graceful. It should not look massive (like the British Shorthair) or too delicate (like a Siamese), but should be somewhere between the two. The legs are long, and the paws oval in shape. The tail is long and tapers at the tip.

HEAD
Seen from the front, the head forms a short wedge and should not be too long. The ears stand

Russian Blue

305

Russian Blue

COLORS

Originally, Russian Blues were only bred with blue colored coats. This blue color (a dilution of black) is preferably medium blue, as even as possible, with a soft, silvery gloss over the tips of the hair. White hairs in the coat are a fault. Also ghost markings (a hint of tabby pattern) are not allowed. The color of the eyes is a beautiful deep green. A hint of yellow in the eye is classed as a fault, but it can sometimes be several years before the eyes have their final deep green color. There are also white and black Russians; in their case, the white must be really pure white and the black a deep black. For these color types, the eyes should also be deep green.

up vertically, far apart, are broad at the base, reasonably large, and have a rounded tip. The bridge of the nose should have as straight a profile as possible, be of medium length, and run without a stop into the flat crown of the skull. The almond-shaped eyes are set wide apart (about one-and-a-half eye's length from each other). The chin is firm and the whisker pads should be pronounced. The neck is long and strong.

COAT

One of the unique aspects of this breed is the combination of a double, densely set coat and an elegant body structure. At shows, the emphasis is heavily on the coat, for which almost half the total number of points is given. The double coat is short, silky, and fine in structure and feels very soft. The coat should never lie too flat, but should stand away from the body a little. Together with its dense setting, this gives a velvety effect. The structure of the Russian Blue's coat is unlike that of any other breed.

The white variety of the Russian Blue should have green eyes; this one is odd-eyed

Original breeds

EUROPEAN SHORTHAIR

ORIGIN

From the late nineteenth century onwards, people began to take an interest in showing and breeding pedigree cats. At first it was particularly exotic-looking cats "from foreign parts," such as Siamese and Persian Longhairs, which were exhibited at shows. The desire soon developed, however, to perfect the shorthaired farm cats indigenous to Northern Europe into a local breed with a uniform appearance. What was wanted was a shorthaired, robustly built cat with a round head. Both in Great Britain and on the continent of Europe, the most beautiful domes-

Red silver classic tabby European Shorthair, a three-month-old kitten

Black silver tortoiseshell classic tabby
European Shorthair female

tic cats were introduced into this breeding process, with the occasional inclusion of a Persian Longhair to speed things up. These shorthaired cats were bred on the mainland of Northern Europe, in Scandinavia, and in Great Britain. There was, however, one great difference—the Scandinavian breeders rejected crossing in Persians and other breeds. They

Blue European Shorthair, male

Although the European Shorthair originated from the selection of domestic cats with many different temperaments, breeders have usually concentrated on animals with a stable and pleasant disposition. Today's European Shorthair cats are friendly, sociable, and highly adaptable. They like human company and can also get on well with cats and other pets. They enjoy playing, but are certainly not overactive; their activity level is average.

Blue and white European Shorthair

CARE AND MAINTENANCE

This breed needs very little care. It is enough to brush the coat once a week with a bristle brush. You can occasionally comb the coat through. During molting periods a rubber brush can be helpful in removing any dead hairs from the coat. In general the European Shorthair is a healthy and strong breed that can live to a relatively advanced age.

APPEARANCE

BODY

European Shorthairs are medium large to large in size, strongly built and muscled, but should certainly not look "cobby," like the British Shorthairs. The animals have a round, muscular chest. The sturdy legs are medium length and

wanted to keep the breed as pure as possible, so they only crossed in household cats of the type they wanted. The Scandinavians called their shorthaired breed "European Shorthair," which was, and still is, a description that covers it extremely well. In the rest of Europe (except Great Britain), however, cats were also being bred under the European Shorthair name, with the same genetic basis and background as the British Shorthair from Great Britain, which meant that, as well as that of domestic cats, they also carried Persian Longhair blood. At international shows, "European Shorthair" cats from all European countries came together and those from Scandinavia always proved to look different. In the long run the same breed name for two different cat types was no longer practical and very confusing. In the 1980s the Scandinavian breeders therefore applied to FIFé, the coordinating cat organization, for a separation, which was granted. From 1982 onwards only Scandinavian European Shorthairs could be described as such, and they acquired their own breed standard. "European Shorthair" cats from the rest of Europe were equated with British Shorthair cats—they counted as the same breed and complied with the same breed standard. So the European Shorthair is an original breed with a pure descent from European domestic cats; it is mainly bred in Scandinavia. Particularly in Finland, it is one of the most popular shorthaired breeds.

Blue European Shorthair

the paws are round in shape. The tail is quite thick at the base and tapers to a rounded tip.

HEAD

The relatively large head has a rather round shape with well-developed cheeks, but is certainly not as round as that of the British Shorthair. The ears are middling large, as high as they are broad at the base, set reasonably far apart, and held erect. The tips of the ears are slightly rounded. The eyes are round in shape and can be any color.

COAT

The dense coat of the European Shorthair is short, soft, and glossy, and should lie close to the body. A coat standing out is a fault.

COLORS AND PATTERNS—GENERAL

Unlike the British Shorthair, the European Shorthair comes only in the "natural" colors (i.e., colors historically associated with North-European domestic cats). These are black, red, blue, cream, tortoiseshell, and blue-cream, with or without white markings or tabby markings in the coat, and also solid white. Smoke and silver are allowed, too, and are in fact very popular. Colors such as chocolate and lilac, but also points as in the Siamese, are not allowed in this breed. Eye color corresponds to the color of the coat and can be yellow, green, or orange. In white cats, blue eyes or odd-eyes are also allowed.

Black silver classic tabby
European Shorthair kitten

REMARKS

- It is still possible to enter European Shorthairs without pedigrees in the novice class and to breed from them. It is rare for non-pedigree cats to satisfy the standard for European Shorthairs in color, build, and type, however.
- "European Shorthair" is a term widely used outside Scandinavia by lay people when they speak of an ordinary, non-pedigree cat. However, they are wrong to do so, because the European Shorthair is an officially recognized breed, with its own pedigree.

Black silver spotted tabby
European Shorthair

309

AMERICAN SHORTHAIR

ORIGIN

The American Shorthair is considered to be the national original shorthair cat of the United States. Historically speaking, there were no indigenous domestic cats in America—short-haired cats with a sturdy build arrived by sea with explorers and colonists. In the early days, people used to take cats on long sea voyages to control rats and mice. Once on the North-American continent, the animals could continue their work in settlements and on farms. The American Shorthair developed from these tough, sturdily built, shorthaired farm cats without the admixture of other breeds. Although towards the end of the nineteenth century these cats had populated the North-American conti-

Red silver classic tabby American Shorthair

Black silver classic tabby American Shorthair

nent for some centuries, the first registered American Shorthair came from Great Britain, a red tabby male called "Bell of Bradford." The name "American Shorthair" was only adopted in the 1960s—before then, these cats were called "Shorthair" or "Domestic Shorthair." Until the early 1960s, the national shorthairs were not really taken seriously at shows, which were dominated by Persians, Siamese, and other exotic-looking breeds. After the name of the breed was altered to "American Shorthair," the fashion for these animals grew, and appreciation of them increased. In 1964, a silver tabby American Shorthair was declared "best kitten of the year" by the C.F.A.; this can be regarded as a milestone and probably the start of the advance of the breed, which is by now one of the most popular in the United States. Particularly in the early days of breeding British Shorthairs, this was done mainly for silver tabbies, possibly because the color looked special and more "purebred" than the ordinary red, black, and tortoiseshell coats. Silver tabby remains one of the most popular colors today.

TEMPERAMENT

The American Shorthair is a friendly, pleasant, and tough cat, which does well in the most diverse of living conditions. They feel as much at home in a town flat as they do in the country. Their relationships with other cats are excellent

Black and white (bicolor) American Shorthair

Black silver classic tabby and white American Shorthair kitten

and the same goes for their reaction to dogs. They also get on very well with children. They are straightforward, uncomplicated, stable, and intelligent. They enjoy playing, but are also very pleased to curl up on their owner's lap in the evening. If you keep your American Shorthair indoors, make sure

Black silver classic tabby American Shorthair

there is plenty of opportunity for it to play, such as a sturdy climbing post, preferably the full height of the room, where the animal can exercise and enjoy itself whenever it wants to. In general, cats of this breed are healthy animals, who can live to a relatively advanced age.

CARE AND MAINTENANCE

The coat of an American Shorthair is very easy to look after. A weekly brushing session is sufficient. When it molts, the undercoat in particular will fall out profusely. A helpful accessory is therefore a small, rubber brush with which you can easily and quickly remove the loose hair from the coat. Do not be too vigorous, however—too violent use of a rubber brush can harm the coat.

APPEARANCE

BODY
The American Shorthair is a strongly built, powerful cat of a medium to large size. The shoulders, chest, and hindquarters are well-developed. The back is broad and straight—seen from above, the outside lines of the body run parallel. The females are less massive than the males. The body is somewhat longer than it is high.

Black silver classic tabby American Shorthairs

The length of the tail is the same as the distance from the shoulder blades to the root of the tail. The neck is middling long, muscular, and strong. The legs are medium length and well-muscled. The sturdy, round paws point forwards. The cat should not appear compact, like a Persian.

HEAD

The head is large with well-filled cheeks and a little longer than it is wide. The bridge of the nose is of average length and the same width all the way up, with a slight arch. The muzzle is square. The firm chin is well-developed and,

Black silver classic tabby American Shorthair

seen from the side, forms a straight line with the upper lip. The ears are medium-sized and have a slightly rounded tip; they are set two eye-lengths apart. The large eyes have an alert and clear expression. The top eyelids are almond-shaped and the lower ones round. The outside corners of the eyes are set slightly higher than the inside corners. There should be at least one eye-length between the eyes.

COAT

The coat is short and thick, and has quite a hard texture. In the winter the coat may be rather dense and heavier than in the summer months.

Black silver classic tabby American Shorthair

COLORS AND PATTERNS—GENERAL

The American Shorthair may only be shown in the "natural" colors and patterns that traditionally occur in a Western breed of cat. These are black, white, red, blue, cream, tortoiseshell, and blue-cream, with or without white patches; spotted, blotched (classic), or striped tabby patterns; and a smoke or silver undercoat. Colors and patterns that traditionally occurred in cats from the East or Far East, such as ticked tabby, the Burmese, Tonkinese and Siamese patterns, and the colors lilac, chocolate, cinnamon, and fawn, are not recognized, because they would indicate that Oriental breeds had been crossed in. Depending on the color of the skin, the color of the eyes is copper or green, but in white cats can also be blue or odd-eyed (with two different colored eyes).

CHARTREUX

ORIGIN

There are various theories about the origin of the Chartreux, none of which can be proven. One known fact is that there is mention in the sixteenth century of sturdy, shorthaired cats with a blue coat encountered both in Rome and in France. The breed name "Chartreux" surfaced for the first time in the eighteenth century as the name for the blue shorthaired cats that were often seen in Paris, but which came originally from an isolated mountainous region of France, the Grande Chartreuse. During the eleventh century the Carthusian order established itself in the area, with the monks being reported as keeping these cats. Although this is plausible, no proof has been found that it was actually the case. The more recent history of the breed is better documented. The Chartreux surfaces again

Young Chartreux, female

in the nineteenth century as a popular breed seen at the earliest cat shows. Blue cats were very popular at that time because they looked so luxurious. It is known, however, that these animals were rarely bred true—breeders often crossed blue cats with each other, without worrying about where they came from. This in fact happened with virtually all the shorthaired, blue breeds of cat. Only later did the breeders become more aware of their different provenances and shorthaired blue cats kept more or less true-bred. This actually happened relatively late with the Chartreux which were only recognized as a separate breed in the 1980s. In France, where the Chartreux originated, the breed is a familiar sight at shows. They are not seen so much in other countries.

TEMPERAMENT

Chartreux, male

The Chartreux is an easygoing, well-balanced, and friendly cat. The breed is fairly quiet; it is sweet-tempered, with a positive disposition. The Chartreux gets on very well with other cats and the same can be said of its relationship with dogs and children. They are calm and not easily provoked. Aggression is foreign to the average Chartreux cat. Taken as a whole, this makes the breed suitable for almost every household. The animals do not need free access to the outside world and can very well be

The Chartreux is an easygoing, friendly cat

CARE AND MAINTENANCE

The Chartreux's shorthaired coat can be kept in good condition with a minimum of care. Weekly grooming with a bristle brush should be enough. At molting times a small rubber brush will help in removing loose and dead hairs from the coat quickly and easily. Take care not to use it too vigorously, as this could damage the coat.

APPEARANCE

BODY

The Chartreux is a medium to large sized cat, well-muscled and sturdily built. It stands fairly high on its legs and has relatively large paws. The medium-length tail is broad at the base and tapers to a fine, rounded tip. If held along the back, it reaches to the hollow between the shoulder blades. The males are noticeably more imposing and larger than the females.

kept in a flat; although, like all other cats, they obviously appreciate an opportunity to go outside. The Chartreux cat does not need excessive attention, but in the evening it is quite happy to look for a spot near its owner or on his or her lap. The voice is soft and fairly unassuming; as a breed, the Chartreux rarely uses it.

The Chartreux is a muscular, robust cat

HEAD

The head is shaped like a reversed trapezium and is rather longer than wide. The bridge of the nose is straight, wide, and long, and has no stop. The ears are medium large and set high on the head, giving the cat an alert expression. The eyes are large and should not be too round, and the outside corners of the eyes should curve slightly upwards. Adult males have pronounced jowls.

Young Chartreux, female

Chartreux, male

COAT

The Chartreux has a double, glossy coat with a rather woolly undercoat. The coat should not lie flat, but its density should make it stand away a little from the body, and it should feel soft.

Young Chartreux, female

pads, back of the ears, and edges of the paws, the coat is more silver-colored. The eyes are a yellow-gold copper to amber color (clearly lighter in color than the deep-orange eyes of the blue British Shorthair). The eyes should show no flecks of green, but as the cat gets older the colors will get rather lighter.

REMARKS

- Most Chartreux kittens have a light tabby pattern in the coat at birth—"ghost marking"—but this gradually disappears over time. It should have completely gone by the time the cat is about two-and-a-half years old.
- There are still people outside France who confuse the Chartreux with the British Shorthair. The breed standard of these animals differs, however, in essential points— they are two separate breeds. Two outstanding specimens, one from each breed, will clearly display a difference if shown together.

Chartreux, female

COLOR

The Chartreux is only bred in a blue coat color. All shades of blue from pale to deeper blue-gray are allowed, but the preference is for cats with a very pale blue-gray coat. On the nose, whisker

Seal point Thai

THAI (TRADITIONAL SIAMESE)

ORIGIN

EARLY ORIGIN

The history of the Thai, also called the Traditional or Classic Siamese, runs parallel to that of the Siamese. As with several breeds, the Siamese, in the course of time, also underwent a change in type. The animals became slimmer and more elegant, and the head, ears, and eyes also changed. This was achieved over a relatively short period; only in 1980 were several alterations to the breed standard of the Siamese carried through, after which the slimmer, more modern Siamese started to dominate the shows. Yet there were breeders who preferred the "older" type of Siamese and saw no benefit in starting to select for extra elegant cats. They remained faithful to the "old" type. It soon proved that they could not win prizes at shows any more with this type, however; they were reserved for the slimmer, "new" Siamese. A number of breeders of the old-type Siamese consequently withdrew from the show circuit. They

quietly went on breeding their beloved, old-type Siamese. They were not alone, for a growing number of Siamese owners could also find little to please them in the modern Siamese. When their old pet died, they wanted to replace it in their household with the same kind of stocky built Siamese and not with the new sleeker version. Moreover, there were also countries where the change to a new type of Siamese had not yet penetrated, where breeders were still breeding and showing the old type. So the latter type of Siamese never really disappeared, but was overshadowed by the modern Siamese that does so well at shows.

Seal point Thai kitten

Lilac point and blue point Thais

RECENT HISTORY

A number of people thought this a pity, the more so since there were breeders of the old type who no longer took the trouble to apply for pedigrees for their animals. Because the old type no longer complied with the modern breed standard for Siamese, it was decided to give a new breed name, "Thai," and to a lesser extent also "Traditional Siamese." It was agreed that Thais should be judged on the basis of the breed standard published in 1934. So the Thai is not a new breed. It has the same genes as the modern Siamese, but its breeders have devoted themselves to maintaining the old Siamese type. Internationally, the Thai can rejoice in a growing band of supporters and breeders. Because it is mainly the modern Siamese cats that are officially registered as Siamese, Thai breeders sometimes have to have recourse to animals without a pedigree which satisfy the requirements for the old type but have a known pure Siamese background. They also bring in Siamese from countries where the "new" type has not yet established

Seal point
Thai female

itself, and some breeders import "street Siamese" from the Far East to include them in their breeding program. Thais are not yet recognized everywhere, but, considering the interest there is in the breed and the enthusiasm of breeders and fanciers, this can only be a matter of time.

TEMPERAMENT

The Thai is a friendly, companionable cat that needs plenty of interaction with its owners to feel happy. They are on the whole rather less "busy" than the average Siamese. Thai cats can get on very well with dogs and their relationship with other cats is excellent.

The Thai is a friendly and sociable cat

CARE AND MAINTENANCE

Looking after a Thai is little trouble. It is often enough just to stroke the cat regularly. At molting times their coat can be brushed occasionally.

APPEARANCE

BODY

Ideally, the Thai is a medium-large cat with a robust, but elegant appearance, and a slightly arched back. Its muscular neck is medium in

Seal point Thai, male

rest of the head. The chin is firm and, seen in profile, the nose leather and chin form a single, straight line. The medium large ears are broad at the base and set more at the side of the head than on top of it. Very small ear tufts are allowed.

COAT

The coat is soft and springy. An undercoat is not desirable.

length. The length of its muscular legs is in proportion to its body and the paws are slightly rounded. The tail suits the rest of the body, in length and thickness being rather broad at the base and then tapering towards a pointed tip.

HEAD

The head is of medium length and medium width. The eyes are medium-large. The upper eyelids are almond-shaped and the lower eyelids somewhat rounder. The shape of the eye should neither be round nor narrow, and preferably the eyes should not be set too slanting. The bridge of the nose should show a slight dip at the height of the eyes, but certainly no stop. The round, well-developed muzzle is in proportion to the

Thai female with kitten

COLORS AND PATTERNS—GENERAL

The Thai comes in all the classic Siamese colors—seal point, blue point, chocolate point, and lilac point, and also these colors in tabby. The eyes are clear, bright blue. Just as in the Siamese, in the Traditional Siamese or Thai the formation of dark shadows on the bodies of older animals (particularly seal and blue points) is almost inevitable.

REMARKS

The name of the breed, "Thai," is derived from Thailand, which was formerly called "Siam" and is the country where Siamese cats were first discovered.

Seal point
Thai, male

JAPANESE BOBTAIL

The Japanese Bobtail has been known for centuries
and is very popular in Japan

ORIGIN

The Japanese Bobtail is probably one of the oldest breeds of cat. Cats with a very short tail have
been around for more than a thousand years in
the Far East and there is plenty of ancient doc-

Red and white Japanese Bobtail

umentation of them. In many old Japanese and
Chinese drawings we find pictures of cats resembling today's Japanese Bobtail and it is clear that
these cats were once quite highly esteemed. It is
known that in the early twentieth century the
occasional Japanese Bobtail reached the United
States. In spite of this, it was not until well into
the twentieth century that the Western cat
fancy more or less discovered the breed. In 1968
the American Judy Crawford imported the first
official Japanese Bobtails to the United States
and more were imported soon afterwards. Three
years later, in 1971, the breed was granted pro-

Red tabby and white Japanese Bobtail, male

visional recognition by the C.F.A. In 1976 they
gained championship status in the United
States. FIFé, based in Europe, only followed in
1989, but there are still organizations (including the G.C.C.F. in Great Britain) that do not
recognize the breed. In the early days of the
Japanese Bobtail there were still no longhaired
Japanese Bobtails in the United States, but

these had been around in Japan for centuries. Proof of this comes from a fifteenth-century painting exhibited in Washington D.C., in which two longhaired Japanese Bobtails are portrayed. Yet the longhaired variety only gained official recognition in 1993. Meanwhile, the breed has begun to venture into the outside world, though it is still rarely encountered outside its country of origin. All the bloodlines of Japanese Bobtails, regardless of which country they live in, in fact go back to imports from Japan—no other breeds have been or are crossed in with them.

Japanese Bobtails with a great deal of white often have one or two blue eyes

live to an advanced age. Because of their great adaptability, cats of this breed can feel at home in the most diverse family situations.

CARE AND MAINTENANCE

The coat of both the shorthaired and longhaired Japanese Bobtail has little tendency to tangle, molts surprisingly little, and can therefore be kept in good condition with a minimal amount of effort. Many Japanese Bobtails have a predominantly white coat and muzzle, so cats of this breed will sometimes need a bath

TEMPERAMENT

Japanese Bobtails are friendly, sociable, very stable, and companionable pets. They are inquisitive, intelligent, and compliant. With a little patience they can be taught all kinds of tricks, such as retrieving balls of scrunched-up paper or walking on a leash. They get on excellently with other cats and the same goes for their relationship with dogs and children. They are keen on company, but are not intrusive—with their soft, melodious voice they can make their wishes quite clear to their owners. The breed is known for its strong constitution and the animals can

Odd-eyed Japanese Bobtail

Red and white Japanese Bobtail

before a show. Only wash them with a special shampoo intended for cats and at least three days before the actual show. This gives the coat time to recover.

Japanese Bobtail, white with black patches

APPEARANCE

BODY

The Japanese Bobtail has a medium-large body and stands high on its legs. It has a slim, elegant build and is well-muscled. It should not be cobby in build, but nicely balanced. The neck is in proportion to the body. The legs are long and slim, but strong, with the hind legs being longer than the forelegs, yet angled in such a way that the back remains relatively horizontal and does not run up towards the hindquarters. The paws are oval in shape. The tail is an important feature of the Japanese Bobtail breed. It is different in

every cat. The tail is quite short and usually has one or more bends, kinks, or angles. The last phalanx of the tail should not be more than three inches from the body. It is unimportant how the cat carries its tail; this can vary from one individual to another. In any case, the tail must harmonize with the rest of the body. In longhaired cats the tail can form a "pompom." Males are noticeably larger than females.

HEAD

Seen from the front, the head has a triangular shape (ignoring the ears). Particularly striking are the prominent cheekbones, the constriction behind the whisker pads (the "pinch" or "whisker break"), and the large, oval-shaped eyes. The muzzle is quite broad and well rounded, and should not be pointed or stubby. The bridge of the nose is long and has a slight dip at the level of the eyes or just below. The large ears are held erect and set wide apart.

COAT

The coat has a silky structure, without any undercoat to speak of. In the longhaired Japanese Bobtail the coat is, of course, longer, but should still lie close and not be too dense. Tufts

Red and white Japanese Bobtail

Blue odd-eyed Japanese Bobtail, longhaired

in the ears and between the toes are good points in this longhaired variety.

COLORS AND PATTERNS—GENERAL

In essence all coat colors (except Siamese, Burmese, and Tonkinese coloring and ticked tabby) are allowed, but in practice breeding is mainly for animals that are predominantly white with a colored tail and patches on the head, and possibly patches on the body (patterns which in other breeds are called "van" and "harlequin.") The most common colors are solid black, red, and tortoiseshell (red and black) with plenty of white, often with one or two blue eyes. Japanese Bobtails in these colors are called "Mi-Ke" in Japan and thought to bring good luck.

Japanese Bobtail

REMARKS

The gene that causes the shortened tail of the Japanese Bobtail is inherited recessive, so that when two Japanese Bobtails are mated to each other, all the kittens have short tails. In contrast to some other short-tailed breeds, Japanese Bobtail kittens are never born without tails, or with complete ones.

Japanese Bobtail

KURILIAN BOBTAIL

ORIGIN

The Kurilian Bobtail is a natural breed of cat that developed in the Kurile Islands, between Japan and Russia. The cats have been on these rather isolated islands for at least a hundred years. In the 1950s, scientists and members of the armed forces stationed on the islands sometimes brought Kurilian Bobtails back to the continent. These cats were not regarded as pedigree cats, but as popular pets. It was only much later that the Russians began to breed Kurilian Bobtails seriously. The first two breeders were Lilia Ivanova and Tatiana Botcharova (Renaissance Cattery), the second of which in particular regularly imported new blood from the islands. Other breeders soon followed their example and today the breed is firmly established as one of the top five in popularity in Russia. Most breeders of Kurilian Bobtails are to be found in Moscow, but there are also catteries concentrating on this breed in other parts of the country.

Kurilian Bobtail

The W.C.F. (World Cat Federation) recognized the breed in 1995. At present, several Russian breeders are pressing for the recognition of the Kurilian Bobtail by non-Russian organizations, such as the American C.F.A. and FIFé, primarily established in mainland Europe. But this is a laborious process because of the distance, language problems, and the fact that the breed is still relatively unknown, both to the general

Kurilian Bobtail

Kurilian Bobtail

public and to breeders outside its country of origin. In spite of this, these animals are now being bred outside Russia on a small scale and there is hope that this will continue.

TEMPERAMENT

Kurilian Bobtails are friendly, well-balanced cats with a peaceful temperament. They are not easily perturbed and adapt themselves to all kinds of circumstances. They can get on very well with other cats and their relationship with dogs and children is excellent on the whole.

CARE AND MAINTENANCE

Looking after the coat of both longhaired and shorthaired Kurilian Bobtails is little trouble. The coat structure of the longhaired variety is such that it does not tend to get tangled, so that the coat needs little more care than that of a shorthaired cat.

APPEARANCE

BODY

The Kurilian Bobtail has a medium-large body with long, strong, muscular legs in proportion to its body. The hind legs are slightly longer than the forelegs. The strong paws are oval in shape. The tail is short, but in proportion to the body.

HEAD

The head should form an equilateral triangle with a broad, but not flat, forehead and strong, rounded cheeks. The bridge of the nose is medium length and has no stop. The chin should be firm. The medium large ears are set neither too high on the head, nor too far apart, and point a little forward. The tips of the ears are lightly rounded. The large eyes are slightly oval-shaped and give the animal an alert expression.

Kurilian Bobtail

Kurilian Bobtail kittens

COAT

Kurilian Bobtails are bred both as longhairs and shorthairs. The longhairs have a semi-long-haired coat that feels soft and silky, with a soft undercoat. The hair on the head, shoulders, and forelegs is shorter than that on the rest of the body. Longhairs have a ruff and well-developed "breeches." The shorthaired Kurilian Bobtail has a close-lying, soft, and shiny coat.

COLORS

All colors are allowed except colorpoint. Tabbies, particularly silver tabbies, are very popular. The color of the eyes depends on the color of the coat, but is preferably yellow, green, or yellow-green.

REMARKS

- The gene that causes the shortness of the Kurilian Bobtail's tail is inherited dominant and causes no defects or problems. Nor is there any question of a lethal factor in homozygous animals (those that have two of the genes causing short tails).
- The Kurilian Bobtail is sometimes confused with the Karilian Bobtail, the more so because this breed, too, is of Russian origin. The Karelian Bobtail comes from western Russia (whereas the Kurilian is from the extreme east) and the Karelian Bobtail's lack of tail results from a recessive inherited gene. They also look different—the Karelian Bobtail is in all respects rather less compact in build and type.
- Because the Kurilian Bobtail is a natural breed of cat that developed on its own, no crossing with other breeds is allowed.

Young blue silver classic tabby Maine Coon, male

MAINE COON

ORIGIN

Maine Coons were already being shown at shows in the United States by the early 1900s. In all probability these "Maine Cats" were animals descended from the first longhaired cats imported into the colonies and, later, from Britain. These included both longhaired domestic cats and Persians, although it must be said that these were at that time not so compact in body and shape as they are now. It is assumed that, in the state of Maine, an authentic breed developed from these animals that combined

the vitality and strength of farm cats with the long coat of the (early) Persian. In the early nineteenth century the Maine Coon was a familiar sight in and around farms in the state of Maine. Moreover, there were people who were deliberately breeding them. The animals were shown in the same classes as Persians, but a distinction was made between animals imported from Britain (Persians) and those of American origin (Maine Coons or Maine Cats). It is known that in 1895 a black tabby longhair of American descent, called "Cosey," took first prize in an important cat show in Madison Square Garden, New York. The C.F.A. was set up in 1908 and Maine Coons were also added to the pedigree register. From 1915 onward, however, Maine Coons were no longer bred as a separate breed. At that time, American cats that were registered for breeding and shown were more or less classified as Persians. In spite of this there were still many Maine Coons that, regardless of cat breeders and pedigrees, continued to exist in the state of Maine and were kept as domestic pets. Not until the 1950s were these

"Tobey," a Maine Coon of around 1900

"Leo," a black classic tabby Maine Coon male of around 1900

Black silver tabby Maine Coon, female

animals rediscovered, at which time the Central Maine Cat Club was set up with the object of maintaining and promoting the indigenous American breed. A breed standard was drawn up and cats from Maine that complied with the prescribed appearance could be involved in the breeding program. It was, nevertheless, 1976 before the breed again gained official recognition from the C.F.A., although before that date it was registered by some smaller organizations. A few years later the first specimens found their way to Europe and in 1983 the breed was also recognized by FIFé, the overall coordinating cat organization based in Europe. Meanwhile, the breed has become one of the best-known and most popular type of pedigree cat across the world.

Maine Coons always look rather cross,
but they are in fact friendly

TEMPERAMENT

The facial expression of the Maine Coon is often rather bad-tempered, but that is only its appearance. It is a friendly, good-humored, and sociable cat with a stable temperament. A well-socialized Maine Coone gets on excellently with children and the same goes for other cats and dogs. A Maine Coon likes to romp about, climb, and play, but can, when it feels like it, also be a very peaceful and even lazy cat, preferring to spend the evening lying in its owner's lap, or just being near him or her. Most of them like being stroked and pet, and will think a weekly brushing a pleasant change from their everyday routine. It is sometimes said that a Maine Coon needs free access to the outside world, but that is not true. Cats that are kept indoors from a young age and have enough to keep them interested and freedom of movement, will be quite content. Because of their great adaptability,

Blue and black silver tabby Maine Coon kittens

they feel at home both in the country and in a flat in town. Maine Coons are not noisy, but they do use their voice

A red silver tabby Maine Coon kitten

when they want to make something clear. Surprisingly, most Maine Coons have soft, small voices that do not seem appropriate for such large cats.

CARE AND MAINTENANCE

Looking after a Maine Coon's coat is little trouble. The structure of the coat is such that it hardly ever gets tangled, an appropriate feature in a breed with a farming ancestry. Some cats do have softer coats, particularly those with dilute colors and silver/smokes, which require rather more work, but the effort required of a Maine Coon owner is nothing like that required of the owner of a Persian. Whatever their color, Maine Coons usually need only a weekly brushing, preferably with a brush with plastic-coated bristles, a bristle brush, or a "shepherd's rake" (a brush originally developed for German Shepherd dogs). A Maine Coon should usually be washed a few days before being shown. The way the texture of the coat reflects the light is affected by its color, so that the type of shampoo you

use and how you prepare your Maine Coon for a show must depend on the cat's coat color. Because the males of this breed can be quite large, an extra large travel carrier and litter tray are no superfluous luxuries. The average scratching post also soon gets too small and unstable for a Maine Coon. Most fanciers end up with a scratching post the height of the room, preferably one that can be fixed with a ceiling fitment.

APPEARANCE

BODY

The Maine Coon is a large cat with a broad chest and muscular body. Seen in profile, the body presents a rectangular, harmonious picture. The sturdy legs are of medium length on average. The paws are large, round, and have tufts of hair between the toes. The tail is long. The neck is medium in length. The males are, in general, appreciably larger and more imposing that the females, although in some bloodlines the females are just as large. These cats develop slowly—they can be four years old before they are fully grown.

HEAD

The Maine Coon has a medium-large, broad head with a square, medium-length muzzle. The cheekbones are prominent. The firm chin, seen

Blue classic tabby Maine Coon, male

The Maine Coon has a square muzzle

COAT

The Maine Coon's coat is shaggy and heavy in structure, but falls sleekly. It is shorter on the shoulders than on the hindquarters or the belly. A good ruff round the neck is desirable.

COLORS

Maine Coons are only bred in "natural" colors.

Black tortoiseshell and white Maine Coon, female

from the side, should form a straight line with the nose and upper lip. The bridge of the nose is medium long. The large ears are broad at the base and taper to a point. They are set about an ear's breadth from each other. Lynx tufts on the tip of the ears are a desirable feature. The large eyes are set far apart and have an expressive look. They are set slightly slanting, so that the outside corner points toward the ear.

Blue-cream and white Maine Coon kitten

These are black, blue, red, cream, tortoiseshell, and blue-cream, with or without tabby markings, white patches, or a silver-white undercoat. Tabby patterns encountered are striped (mackerel), spotted, and blotched (classic). Any quantity of white is allowed, as is a solid white cat. The eyes may have any color—in white cats and those with a lot of white there are animals with blue eyes, as well as with two different colors (odd-eyed). Not allowed in Maine Coons are colors and factors originating in Far Eastern

Red tabby and white Maine Coon, male

breeds, such as colorpoint, Burmese, or Tonkinese coloring, cinnamon, fawn, chocolate, and lilac.

REMARKS

- Various stories are in circulation about the origin of the Maine Coon. It has, for instance, been suggested that the first Maine Coons originated from crossing cats with raccoons and that this explains the thick, ringed tail of the tabby animals. Such crosses, however, are genetically impossible. Another well-known story is of the English sea captain, Coon, who brought longhaired cats with him over from England to the United States.
- The Maine Coon is considered to be a natural breed of cats, so crosses with other breeds are not allowed.
- Maine Coons should have five toes on their fore paws and four on their hind paws. More toes lead to disqualification at most cat organizations' shows. In spite of this, a relatively large number of Maine Coons are bred with extra toes, and there are breeders who aim especially at producing this phenomenon within the breed.
- At present, Maine Coons without a pedigree can still be involved in Maine Coon breeding programs. This is only possible with cats from the American state of Maine, which must be declared at shows as "U" (outstanding). Such cats can be entered in the pedigree register of the A.C.A. in Maine.

Litter of white Maine Coons

"Pans Truls," the prototype of the Norwegian Forest Cat

NORWEGIAN FOREST CAT

ORIGIN

EARLY HISTORY
There have been longhaired cats in Norway for centuries, as traditional farm cats and also roaming in the surrounding forests. Traditionally people called them "forest cats." They were not wild cats, but had actually been domesticated for a long time. The existence of the forest cat population with its long hair was so normal that nobody thought of labeling the animals as a special breed—they were just longhaired farm cats. Some forest cats were entered at shows in the 1930s, but there was still no question of a distinct breed. The animals were mostly entered as "domestic cats." Only in the 1950s did people in

Male blue striped tabby Norwegian Forest Cat

Norway begin to take serious steps to gain recognition for their native breed. One of the most important reasons for this was that longhaired forest cats were by now rarely seen and some fanciers feared that this breed of cat would become extinct if no dedicated breeding program was started. In 1963 the N.R.R. (Norske Rasekattklubbers Riksforbund—Norwegian Pedigree Cat Club) was founded. A breed standard was drawn up based on a male cat that, in the eyes of fanciers, embodied the ideal image of a Norwegian Forest Cat—this was "Pans Truls," a black and white striped tomcat, owned and bred by Egil and Else Nylund of the Pans Cattery in Oslo. Pans Truls was the prototype of the breed. Next, people throughout the country were invited to contact the association if they had a cat that met the description of a Norwegian Forest Cat (i.e., looked like Pans Truls). Each cat owner was visited by members of the association who assessed—point for point, on the basis of the breed standard—whether their

"Truls av Bolke," one of the best known
Norwegian Forest Cats of the early period

Norwegian Forest kittens

White Norwegian Forest Cat, male

animal could be registered or not as a Norwegian Forest Cat. The response was so great that a call went out to meet at a single venue. Here some hundred as yet unregistered Norwegian Forest cats were brought in and listed in a single day. Since then, the group of cat fanciers and enthusiasts has slowly but surely increased.

RECENT HISTORY

In December of 1975 the Norsk Skogkattring (Norwegian Forest Cat Club) was founded with the object of preserving the breed, developing it further, and promoting it as the Norwegian national breed of cats. A year later the breed gained provisional recognition from FIFé, the European coordinating organization for pedigree cats, and by 1977 official recognition of the Norwegian Forest Cat had been achieved. This recognition was treated as "hot news" by the Norwegian media, which gave it full, national coverage. Until the late 1970s, breeding Norwegian Forest Cats remained a purely Norwegian affair. Later, Norwegian Forest Cats were

exported for the first time to neighboring Sweden. In 1979 the first Norwegian Forest Cats made the significant crossing from Norway to the United States. At that time it was still possible to have longhaired cats from Norway of unknown origin registered as Norwegian Forest Cats and included in the breeding program. Such cats were called "novices." In 1987 Sverak (the Swedish pedigree cat association) stopped the acceptance of novices and the Norwegian N.R.R. followed suit in 1990. By this time there were so many registered Norwegian Forest Cats that the gene pool was large enough to sustain a healthy breed. Other countries followed this lead, but later. Today it is no longer possible to register novices with the regulated organizations; the pedigree register for the Norwegian Forest Cat is closed. In a reasonably short time, the Norwegian Forest Cat has developed throughout the world into one of the most popular cat breeds. In almost every country where people breed cats as a hobby, there are one or more clubs concentrating on Norwegian For-

Cream and white, young Norwegian Forest Cat, male

gian Forest Cats have a strong tendency to attach themselves to one person in particular. They are not pronounced "lap cats." They like being with their people, but prefer lying beside their owners rather than on them. Norwegian Forest Cats are on the whole friendly and good-humored. They regard a visitor with some caution at first, before they decide to make friends, but always in a self-confident manner. They usually communicate with humans by means of subtle body language and eye contact, and are less obviously "present" in the house than, say, Turkish Angoras, which have an Oriental type of temperament and can be demanding of their owners. Although several more sedate bloodlines are known in the breed, most Norwegian Forest Cats are playful—certainly the young ones. Chasing after twists of paper and sparring with small balls is considered fine sport, and most of them also like climbing. It is often said that a Norwegian Forest Cat should have free access to the outside world, but this is not essential for their welfare. "Indoor" Norwegians must, of course, have the opportunity to enjoy themselves, so that one or more strong climbing posts should form part of their standard play equipment.

est Cats. The breed is particularly popular in Europe. Outside the Scandinavian countries this is one of the best-loved breeds; in Germany, The Netherlands, and France it is particularly highly valued.

TEMPERAMENT

"Rough diamond" aptly describes the Norwegian Forest Cat. A well-socialized and carefully bred Norwegian has a tolerant and stable temperament; they are not easily thrown off balance by anything and aggression and anxiety are foreign to them. Most can get on extremely well with other cats, and also with dogs and children. Norwe-

Litter of Norwegian Forest kittens

CARE AND MAINTENANCE

A Norwegian Forest Cat with a well-structured coat, typical of the breed, needs scarcely any grooming. Cats with silver undercoats and dilute colors sometimes need rather more care because their coat is, by nature, much softer. In spring, the coat undergoes a heavy, but short-lasting molt, losing a high proportion of the undercoat. A daily comb and brush session is then, of course, welcome in cats endowed with a good coat structure, to prevent tangles forming. Many breeders do not brush or comb their animals, but pick loose dead hairs from the coat with thumb and forefinger, since too much brushing can cause "gaps" in the coat. There is usually an appreciable difference between the appearance of a Norwegian Forest Cat in winter and in summer. In winter the coat is luxurious, very dense, and often with a large ruff, while in summer the cat can look almost shorthaired. Neutered cats usually lose less hair than their entire fellows.

Blue spotted and white Norwegian Forest Cat, female

APPEARANCE

BODY
The Norwegian Forest Cat is a large, powerfully built cat, with a massive skeletal structure and a long body. Males weigh on average twelve to seventeen pounds, whilst females are in general lighter in build and smaller, although in some bloodlines there are exceptions. The cat stands

Blue striped tabby and white Norwegian Forest Cat

**Black classic tabby and white
Norwegian Forest Cat, male**

The structure of the coat is usually slightly softer in the dilute colors (blue, cream, and blue-cream) and in cats with a silver or smoke undercoat. Norwegian Forest Cats develop slowly—it can be two years before the perfect coat structure is fully developed. Norwegian Forest Cats living indoors will develop a less luxuriant coat than those accustomed to going outside.

COLORS AND PATTERNS—GENERAL

Traditionally, Norwegian Forest Cats come in the natural farm-cat colors, which are familiar in Europe from non-pedigree cats, such as red, black, blue, and cream, with or without a tabby pattern, white patches, or a silver or smoke undercoat. All four tabby patterns are recognized in Norwegian Forest Cats. The breed standard explicitly states that Norwegians should

high on its legs and has large, round paws. The hind legs are longer than the front ones. The tail is bushy and when held along the back should reach at least as far as the shoulder blades. It can take three years before the cat is fully grown.

HEAD

The head is triangular with a long, straight profile (no stop) and a strong chin. Seen from the side, the chin and the nose should lie in a straight line. The large ears have pointed tips with lynx-like tufts and long tufts of hair coming out of the ears. The outermost line of the ears follows the triangular line of the head. The eyes are large and oval, set slightly slanting, and have an alert expression.

COAT

The half-length double coat consists of a woolly undercoat covered by a smooth, water-repellent topcoat of coarse, glossy, guard hairs.

Black smoke and white Norwegian Forest Cat, male

only be judged on the quality of the coat, not on the depth of its color, distribution of color, or the contrast of the tabby markings. Colors and factors not allowed are colorpoint (Siamese factor), Burmese and Tonkinese factors, chocolate, lilac, cinnamon, and fawn.

Black tortoiseshell striped tabby and white Norwegian Forest Cat, female

REMARKS

- The size of a litter fluctuates between three and six kittens, but there may be exceptions—the largest litter of kittens ever produced was by the Norwegian Forest queen "Trollfjell's Goldi," then living in Germany. In 1992 she bore twelve healthy kittens, all of which grew to adulthood. This won her a place in the Guinness Book of Records.
- One "color" occurs in the breed that is not yet universally recognized—the "X" color. This is a factor—not more closely specified—which over time changes the coat color of what at birth look like black or blue tabby kittens into a more reddish to very light cinnamon-colored shade. Often only the tip of the tail in otherwise completely colorless cats with this "X" factor remains black or blue. What causes this change of color is still not known. A lively discussion amongst fanciers is ongoing across the globe as to whether or not these colors should be generally recognized.

Litter of Norwegian Forest kittens

TURKISH ANGORA

ORIGIN

EARLY HISTORY

The Turkish Angora is one of the oldest breeds of cat in the world, but in spite of this has only been recognized for a relatively short time. Tradition has it that the first Turkish Angora cats were brought to Europe from Turkey, their home country, in the seventeenth century by Italian merchants. The cats, usually with white coats and blue eyes, were adored by European aristocrats. They feature regularly in old paintings, beside highly placed ladies of the period. Because the animals were particularly fashionable at the French court, they were also known as "French cats." Serious breeding of them started in the late nineteenth century. Turkish Angoras

Red and white Turkish Angora male

were crossed with other cats, resulting in the forerunners of the Persian Longhairs, which had a more luxurious appearance than the less lushly haired and more slimly built Turkish Angoras. As the crosses became more popular, the original Turkish Angoras tended to be pushed into the background. The breed reached its lowest point in the 1920s. Not only in Europe, but in their home country of Turkey, the original Turkish Angora had become a rarity. Fortunate-

Black tortoiseshell Turkish Angora, female

ly the Turks became aware of this threat to their cultural heritage in time. They set up a breeding program to save the breed from extinction. As many specimens as possible were collected for this purpose into Turkish zoos including the Ankara zoo, and a stringent ban on export was imposed.

RECENT HISTORY

The Turks regarded only the solid white Turkish Angoras as special, and then only those cats with at least one blue eye. Colored specimens that were also often born were "selected out." As a consequence of this, a high proportion of the cats in Turkish zoos were stone deaf—which the Turks did not regard as a problem, since deafness only enhanced the purity of the breed and with it, the status of the Turkish Angora. Obviously it was a problem for those fanciers who, after the export ban was lifted, took some animals out of Turkey with them. Because colored animals were almost never obtainable from Turkey, at

Young white Turkish Angora with blue eyes

Blue classic tabby and white Turkish Angora, male

first virtually only white animals were exhibited at shows in the West and, of course, most of the kittens born to them were also white. So it is hardly surprising that the various American and European cat organizations only recognized a pure white coat. Yet colored kittens went on being born, and it was precisely with these col-

ored specimens that breeders could challenge the deafness in the breed. These breeders had to devote great efforts to convince the cat fancy organizations that recognition of colored Turkish Angoras was highly desirable from a health point of view. Eventually they were successful. White animals were recognized in the United States in 1970, and recognition of colored ones followed two years later. FIFé only recognized white Turkish Angoras in 1988 and colored animals were granted the same recognition five years later—a fortunate development, since there is virtually no incidence of deafness in today's Turkish Angoras. Serious breeders in Europe never mate two white animals with each other because that increases the likelihood of deafness, and they always have their white animals checked by an official B.A.E.R. test. Deaf animals are not used for breeding in Europe, though they still are in the U.S.A. and Canada. Meanwhile, the Turkish Angora has become a familiar sight in almost all cat-loving countries, including Germany, the U.S.A., Finland, the Czech Republic, and The Netherlands. On a smaller scale it is also bred in Spain, France, Portugal, Italy, and Canada.

TEMPERAMENT

Although the Turks thought the world of their white, odd-eyed/blue-eyed cats, most of these animals did not really enjoy tender loving care. The colored ones in particular, which had to hunt for their own food, could count on little support from the majority of the population, so that only the most cunning and lively cats would have the opportunity to reproduce. This toughness and cleverness is still visible in the modern Turkish Angora. Turkish Angoras are extremely inquisitive, temperamental, and confident cats. They are the first to welcome visitors, at once comprehensively examining and assessing them, including the contents of their pockets and handbags. What a Turkish Angora wants most, however, is the attention and love of its owner. They do not just ask for attention, they usually demand it and can be very persistent. Their owners will have to accept that their cats

Red tabby Turkish Angora, female

Litter of Turkish Angoras

expect to ride on their shoulders, spend the evenings in the lap or round the neck of their favorite household member, get involved in all household activities, and only with difficulty be restrained from pinching tidbits off their plates. Turkish Angoras are particularly suitable for people who want a great deal of interaction with their cat and appreciate one with a pronounced character. Turkish Angoras are not suited to

being left at home alone all day; they will certainly get up to mischief out of frustration, so if you are out most of the time you would be well advised to get two. Survival of the fittest has, however, given them a dominant character that does not permit other cats to take the best bits of food. Most Turkish Angora breeders therefore keep the groups small, to ensure harmony. The average Turkish Angora has a strongly developed predatory instinct. They love playing and are excellent hunters. Anything that is small and moves, buzzes, or flies is competently and efficiently helped into the next world. They also enjoy all kinds of toys and make full use of them—often bringing them to you. These cats will usually get along very well with dogs. If they grow up together, they often become friends for life. In general, they also get on excellently with children. Because of their high intelligence and human orientation, these cats can easily be trained to do things such as retrieving scrunched-up balls of paper or walking on a leash. Turkish Angoras enjoy good health. No congenital abnormalities are known in this breed, although some bloodlines may display too high a level of activity and domination—the breed is still very

Black tortoiseshell striped tabby and white Turkish Angora kitten

close to the wild. Serious breeders therefore select not only for appearance, but also for temperament.

CARE AND MAINTENANCE

Turkish Angoras are excellent climbers and hunters

In the summer Turkish Angoras have an almost shorthaired coat

Care of their coat is little trouble. They molt about twice a year like other cats, but the structure of the coat has little tendency to tangle. A weekly brushing session should be enough to keep the coat in good condition.

APPEARANCE

BODY
Turkish Angoras are lithe and elegant cats, with good musculature and a strong constitution. They are small to medium-large in size with a relatively long body. The hind legs are longer than the forelegs, so that the line of the back runs slightly upwards to the rear. The paws are small and round, with small tufts of hair between the toes. The bushy tail is thick at the base and tapers to a narrower end. If the tail is laid along the back, the last segment of it should reach at least to between the shoulder blades. It may take two years before these cats are fully grown.

White Turkish Angora, male

Black tortoiseshell and white Turkish Angora, female (harlequin markings)

HEAD

The proportionately small head is moderately wedge-shaped. The almond-shaped eyes are set slightly slanted. The large, pointed ears are set high on the head and show small tufts of hair. The bridge of the nose is medium long and has a slight arch, but no stop. The slightly rounded chin is perpendicular to the nose.

COAT

The half-length coat has a fine, silky structure and should lie close. The undercoat is shorter than the topcoat. The ruff and breeches, as well as the tail, are bushy. In warm climates, however, the cat looks almost shorthaired, except for the bushy tail and ear tufts.

COLORS AND PATTERNS—GENERAL

The coat color in which the Turkish Angora became known is brilliant white, often with blue

Female blue-cream and white Turkish Angora in full winter coat

White Turkish Angora kittens: the kitten on the right
is odd-eyed

- Over the course of time, various types of Turkish Angora have emerged. The type bred in Germany is rather coarser in build, whereas the American type is finer and more elegant. In most countries, breeders prefer a type that is somewhere between the two.
- It happens occasionally that kittens are born from this natural breed that have a color not natural to farm cats, such as lilac, chocolate, or colorpoint. Pedigree research has shown that far back in the bloodline of these kittens there was a lilac Balinese, which should not happen in a natural breed such as the Turkish Angora in which crosses with other breeds are not allowed.

eyes, but the breed is bred in all the "natural" colors, i.e., colors occurring in farm cats, such as black, white, red, cream, blue, and, of course, tortoiseshell. All four tabby patterns (classic/blotched, spotted, striped, and ticked) occur in this breed, as do a smoke undercoat (in solid-colored animals) and a silver undercoat (in tabbies). A Turkish Angora may also display any quantity of white in its coat, from a small medallion to predominantly white. The depth of color of the coat, the symmetry of the markings, and the contrast in the tabby pattern are of no importance in this breed. Nor are they selected for eye color, so that all shades of green and yellow, and also blue eyes or odd-eyes (two different colored eyes) can occur.

REMARKS
- A breed called Angora is bred in Britain, but these should not be confused with Turkish Angoras; they are Oriental semi-longhairs (Mandarins).

Red Turkish Angora kitten

Auburn Turkish Van, male

TURKISH VAN

ORIGIN

The Turkish Van owes its name to Lake Van at the foot of Mount Ararat in southeast Turkey, formerly part of Armenia. The summers there are very hot and the winters are cold, and the Turkish Van's coat and patterns are well adapted to this. The breed has been there for centuries, developing largely on its own. No one knows where the animals originally came from. Some think they may be descendants of longhaired Chinese

Auburn Turkish Van, male

cats that reached Lake Van along the busy Silk Road, but there is no certainty. The breed was discovered in 1955 by two English ladies, Lushington and Halliday, who were visiting the area. They are reported to have encountered white, spotted, and colored specimens, but the type that Lushington and Halliday considered the most beautiful were the predominantly white cats with deep red-brown patches on their heads and tails. They brought several cats of this color back with them to Britain. Breeding started there from these and other animals imported later from the region, whose specific markings became a mark of the breed. It is not certain, because no records are available, though very probable, that in the early days of breeding Vans in Britain, other breeds of cat were crossed in. It is known that Van breeders in other countries, including The Netherlands, kept their bloodlines pure and only used cats from Turkey to introduce new blood. This is in fact still done today—Turkish Van breeders travel regularly to the country of their cat's origin. Turkish

343

Auburn Turkish Van kittens

Vans were accorded official recognition in Britain in 1969, and FIFé recognition for the continent of Europe followed two years later. Meanwhile, Turkish Vans have spread throughout the world.

TEMPERAMENT

Turkish Vans are trusting and affectionate and often attach themselves to one person in particular. All the Turkish Van's expressions of love, affection, and its softer side in general are projected at this person. The rest of the family is, of course, accepted, but these smothering expressions of affection are usually reserved for one or, at the most, two individuals to experience. Turkish Vans are playful, high-spirited, and active, and with their large size this may sometimes produce wild, impetuous maneuvers. People with little understanding of cat behavior may possibly label them "unpredictable," so the breed is best placed with people who can under-

stand and appreciate their original character. They are not cats that take anything lying down, and have a strong individual personality. It is characteristic of them that most Vans can get on very well with dogs, and the presence of other cats shouldn't raise any problems. They are tough cats that are not easily upset; loud noises, for example,

Auburn Turkish Van, male

do not worry them. When hunting, they are fanatical and tenacious, and they are one of the best mousers. Virtually all Turkish Vans can be taught to retrieve very easily. They are rarely afraid of water. They will not, as has often been described, go swimming for fun, but if they want to catch a fish they are not afraid of a dip in the water. Most owners label their Vans as talkative cats, which very much want to be heard, but their voice is not harsh or loud. Turkish Vans need space. They can be very much at home in

Female auburn Turkish Van with blue eyes

Black tortoiseshell Turkish Van, female

a flat, as long as there is a balcony that is well enclosed—Turkish Vans can get so engrossed in chasing insects or birds that they "forget" how high up they are and accidents can easily follow. Because many of these cats still have their primeval instincts, mother cats may sometimes be over-protective of their litters and not tolerate any visitors looking at the litter at first. There is no doubt that owning a Turkish Van is a special experience, but only for those who can really appreciate this exceptional cat with all the typical attributes of the breed.

CARE

The Turkish Van's coat has no undercoat and its structure means it needs very little care. The coat does not tangle much. If a cat has gotten used to it as a kind of game while still a young kitten, brushing should not cause any problems later on. In spring, the coat molts and becomes a shorter, summer one, after being a luxuriant, thick winter coat. A daily brush is not wasted effort, tt this time, if only to prevent the cat swallowing too much hair when grooming itself. The Turkish Van keeps its predominantly white coat very clean itself. Nevertheless, it certainly makes sense to treat the cat with a dry shampoo before a show.

APPEARANCE

BODY

The Turkish Van is a large, muscular, long, and strong cat with a broad, deep chest and a strong, skeletal structure. Its legs are medium-long and

Black tortoiseshell Turkish Van, female

Young auburn Turkish Van, male

well-muscled, with round paws. The tail is bushy and in good proportion to the body.

HEAD
One of the features of the breed is the sturdy, broad, wedge-shaped head with rounded outlines, prominent cheekbones, and rounded muzzle. The chin is firm. The line of the nose, seen in profile, is straight with an almost invisible dip at the bridge. The fairly large ears are well haired, and set fairly erect and very close to each other. The backs of the ears are quite hairy. The large eyes are oval in shape, set rather slanted, and have an alert look.

COAT
The coat is long, soft, and silky, with no undercoat. The ruff starts right at the base of the ears and has a bib. The tail is full and bushy.

COLOR AND PATTERNS—GENERAL
The Turkish Van is famous for its typical "van" pattern, a term also used in descriptions of many other breeds of cat. The amount and location of the white cannot be firmly predetermined, so that many Turkish Vans are born which, although outstanding in type and coat structure, do not comply with the breed standard in the distribution of their colors.

Auburn Turkish Van, male

Litter of Turkish Vans

PATTERN

The Turkish Van has a single colored patch on its head, which should not reach the eyes and also not past the back of the ears. This patch is split in two by a vertical white blaze. The tail is colored throughout. A few small random spots are allowed on the back of an outstanding animal. An odd patch on the head or a less symmetrical marking is also allowed. Usually cats of a good type, but with less clear markings, are more appreciated at shows than cats with perfect markings, but of a less perfect type.

Turkish Van kittens

COLOR

The white of a Turkish Van should be chalky white, with no trace of yellow. The colored parts could formerly only be red, but recently more colors have been allowed. So, in addition to Vans with red (auburn) markings, we now also meet animals with cream, black, blue, and tortoiseshell markings, with or without a tabby pattern. Most Turkish Vans have light to medium amber-colored eyes, but two blue eyes or odd eyes (two different colors) are allowed.

REMARKS

- Turkish Vans with typical markings are now a familiar sight at shows, but in Turkey itself solid white, odd-eyed Turkish Vans are preferred. Great efforts are currently being made to gain recognition for solid white Turkish Vans, and this recognition is expected within the foreseeable future.
- Turkish Vans can take three to five years to become fully grown. The long coat can also take some time to develop fully.

Black tortoiseshell Turkish Van, female

SIBERIAN FOREST CAT

Black tortoiseshell striped tabby Siberian Forest Cat, female

ORIGIN

EARLY HISTORY

In Russia, the name "Siberian cat" has for centuries been in popular use for a sturdily built, longhaired cat, but little is known of the early origins of the Siberian Forest Cat. It is known that these cats traditionally occurred in all parts of the former Soviet Union and certainly not

Drawing of a Russian longhaired cat around 1900

only in Siberia. Animals resembling Siberian Cats were already known in the Late Middle Ages—there are several popular superstitions from that period involving longhaired Russian cats that watch over their owners. In this, the Siberian Forest Cat reveals similarities with the Norwegian Forest Cat, which—like the Siberian—occurred in one region for centuries without the cat population being regarded as a breed. A proportion of the domesticated cats in the former Soviet Union was longhaired and, if the owners of these longhaired cats were asked what kind of cat they had, would usually answer: "a Siberian cat." As a result of the Communist regime, after 1917 Russian cat fanciers were not able to engage seriously in breeding and show-

Smoke Siberian Forest Cat, young male

ing pedigree cats until the 1980s, with the first Russian cat show being held in 1986, in Riga. Lack of money, little knowledge of foreign languages, and limits on contacts with cat fanciers abroad (there was no Internet in these days), meant that mainly "novices" were shown. These were cats without a pedigree, which looked like some specific breed and which, after official approval, could be used to start a breeding program for that breed in the former Soviet Union. The Russians concentrated mainly on breeds recognized by FIFé and invited mostly Czech judges to officiate at these "novice" shows. Owners presented their cats as, for instance,

Norwegian Forest Cats, Turkish Angoras, or Maine Coons. However, many of these cats proved not to resemble these breeds enough. They had a type all of their own, compact in build, with a red head and unique coat structure; these were the "ordinary" Russian household cats that, if longhaired, had for centuries been known as "Siberian cats." Hence the idea emerged to register and start breeding Russia's own authentic longhaired farm cat, as the Norwegians had done with the Norwegian Forest Cat. This was the genesis of the Siberian Forest Cat as a breed.

RECENT HISTORY

In the early days, breeding Siberian Cats was concentrated in St. Petersburg (formerly Leningrad) and centered on the Kotofey Dog and Cat Association. St. Petersburg, located in the cold North, was severely hit by a plague of rats in the postwar period. During the Second World War there was starvation in the city, to the extent that no cats were left there. To call a halt to this plague of rats, the cat population had to be replenished by cats imported from the remotest parts of Russia. Consequently, cats of every kind, color, and type, from all corners of

Black striped tabby and white Siberian Forest Cat, female

the former Soviet Union, could be found in St. Petersburg and it was here that the first "novices" were recruited for the breed from strays and house cats. It is hardly surprising that longhaired colorpoints, too, coming from the extreme south of Russia, also made their appearance there. Registration of these novices took place from 1987 onwards and was done on the basis of the first breed standard. This was written by the president of Kotofey, Mrs. Olga Mironova, who took a tom called "Roman" as her model. The breed was recognized in 1989 by the S.F.F. (the first Russian cat federation) and recognition by the W.C.F. followed two years later, in 1991. Interest in the Siberian Cat was soon aroused in Western Europe and the breed is now bred and shown, not only in various countries of Europe, but also in the U.S., Japan, Australia, and South Africa, and is recognized by most organizations—although, understandably, it is still in the development stage.

Red tabby Siberian Forest kitten

Red Siberian Forest kitten

Black tortoiseshell striped tabby Siberian
Forest Cat, female

TEMPERAMENT

The temperament of the Siberian Forest Cat is very similar to that of the Norwegian Forest Cat, although people who own both of these breeds generally describe the Siberian Cat as being rather more affectionate and on the whole more peaceful. Although Siberian Cats appreciate attention and like to be stroked and cared for, most of them do not welcome too much petting from strangers. In all circumstances, they retain their dignity among other cats, and they usually get on well with dogs. Their relationship with children is also excellent. Siberian Cats enjoy climbing and are very good at it. A good scratching and climbing post is therefore by no means a bad investment if you are thinking of acquiring a Siberian Cat. Above all, however, the Siberian needs sufficient attention and wants to play an active part in the family's activities. Many representatives of the breed are intelligent cats that can very easily be taught tricks, such as retrieving scrunched-up balls of paper. The Moscow State Circus has several Siberian Cats in its program, proving that the animals have more to offer than is often realized by their owners. As the only cat in a family which is out most of the time, a cat of this breed is not at its best.

CARE AND MAINTENANCE

The care of a Siberian Cat's coat takes up little time. The coat is water and dirt repellent. Brushing can encourage loss of hair and it is best only to groom the animal when the undercoat starts to come loose (i.e., in molting periods). In cats with a coat structure typical of the breed, brushing is not really necessary and it is enough to pull out the coat as it comes loose between your fingers and thumb. The Siberian Cat has a short, but heavy molting period in early spring, followed by a milder molt in the autumn. It may sometimes be necessary to give the cat a daily brush during molting times, if only to prevent it from swallowing too much loose hair when it grooms itself. You are advised against washing the animal before a show, because this might affect the water-and-dirt repellent layer, typical

Black striped tabby Siberian Forest Cat, female

of the breed, which lies over the coat. It is better to use a dry shampoo for cats, which you can find at the better-equipped pet shops and also at cat shows.

APPEARANCE

BODY

The Siberian Cat is a medium-large and muscular cat (males weigh between eleven and twenty pounds, and females between nine and thirteen pounds) with a body rather longer than it is high. The neck is short and well-muscled, and the powerful legs are medium-long. There should be tufts of hair between the toes. The tail is broad and powerful at its base and it tapers to a rather rounded

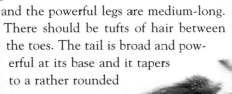

Black classic tabby
Siberian Forest Cat,
female

tip. The tail should reach the shoulder blades when laid back along the body. At shows, cats with hind legs clearly longer than the forelegs, and those that are as long as they are high (squarely and too compactly built), are penalized. Delicately built cats, or those with a long, narrow neck, or no tufts of hair between the toes, do not get far at shows either.

HEAD

The ideal image is that of a short, stumpy, wedge-shaped head with well-developed cheeks extending outside the outline of the wedge. The

Cream Siberian Forest Cat, male

head should be as broad as it is long. The line of the nose from its point to between the eyes is the same width all along and lightly arched; it may under no circumstances show a stop. The chin should follow the circumference of the head and not be as pronounced as that of the Norwegian Forest Cat or Maine Coon. The front of the muzzle should have well-developed whisker pads, which look rounded and have no pinch behind them. The large eyes have a slightly oval, rounded shape. They are set quite far apart from each other. The ears are medium-

Blue tabby point Siberian Forest kitten

large and set about the width of an ear apart. The tips of the ears are rounded and display lynx tufts, and tufts of hair are clearly visible in the ears. All shapes of the head should give a rather rounded impression.

COAT

The Siberian Cat has a medium to longhaired coat with a dense undercoat and longer, water-repellent, rather oily topcoat. The coat is usually rather shorter on the shoulder blades. The breed displays a full coat with lavish undercoat in the wintertime. In summer, Siberian Forest Cats are virtually shorthaired.

COLORS AND PATTERNS—GENERAL

Colors encountered are red, cream, black, blue, tortoiseshell, and blue-cream with or without a tabby pattern, a silver-white undercoat (smoke or silver), and white markings. The three tabby patterns allowed are classic/blotched, spotted, and striped.

In addition, the Siamese factor ("Neva Masquerade") also occurs, which pushes the colors to the extremities (ears, legs, tail, and muzzle), with, of course, the blue eyes associated with this factor. The Neva Masquerade is also bred with white patches, but these must not be located in a way that would lead to confusion with the "Sacred" Birman. Siberian Forest Cats with a van pattern and solid white cats are very scarce. Siberian cats have amber-colored or green eyes. In contrast to most other breeds, blue or partly blue eyes are not desirable in colors other than the Neva Masquerade—not even in white animals or those with a high proportion of white.

REMARKS

- Because there is no general agreement on the various breed standards applied in different countries, aspects such as the distribution of

Seal smoke point Siberian Forest Cat, female

white can be a matter of debate at shows. One organization may reject small white markings and only accept clearly bicolor cats, while others consider any amount of white that conforms to comparable natural breeds acceptable.

- There are still differences in the breed standards applied in different countries and organizations today. In essence, only the original W.C.F. breed standard, drawn up in 1987,

Siberian Forest Cats, mother with kittens

Siberian Forest kitten

should be considered as authentic because this was drawn up by the first breeders of the breed, in the country where it originated.

- The colors that appeared in litters up to 1990 inclusive were regarded by the Russians as the colors of the breed. From catalogs dating from its early years, it appears that the following coat colors were exhibited: black, blue, red, and tortoiseshell with or without white markings, and striped or blotched/classic tabby patterns. From this it can be concluded that blue-cream and cream also belong in the range of colors, since blue is a dilution factor that is inherited separately and affects red as well as black. It can only be accidental that no cream or blue-cream animals appeared at shows in those early years. Animals with a silver-white undercoat (smoke and silver) were also shown in those days, and those with points (like the Siamese). In this connection it is important to know that before 1990 pedigree cats were hardly ever imported into Russia. Such imports only took place later. Therefore, colors, factors and tabby patterns, which differ from the "foundations," are seen as nontypical of the breed and possibly indicative of the influence of other breeds. These unrecognized colors and factors include the Burmese and Tonkinese factors, the colors cinnamon, chocolate, fawn, and lilac, and the ticked tabby pattern.

Siberian Forest kitten

Black striped tabby Manx, female

MANX AND CYMRIC

ORIGIN

ORIGIN OF THE SHORTHAIRED MANX

The Manx and its longhaired cousin, the Cymric, are centuries-old breeds that evolved naturally. The roots of the breed are in the British Isle of Man, in the Irish Sea between England and Ireland. It is not clear exactly how these animals evolved, but what is certain is that cats without tails and those with a very short tail have been in the Isle of Man as farm cats for centuries (probably for more than four hundred years) to the extent that these cats predominated over those with a long tail. The Manx was one of the first pedigree cats to be shown in the late nineteenth century, both in Britain and on the continent of Europe and in the United States. It was also one of the first breeds to be officially recognized and standardized. For instance, the first pedigree cat club was founded in 1901—the Short Haired Cat Society and Manx Club. The great interest amongst breeders throughout the world in tailless cats from the Isle of Man forced the government of the island to set up a state cattery in the 1950s. This cattery could prevent too many tailless cats living on farms with their owners from being taken to other countries as pets. They feared that part of the gene pool could be lost. In the 1990s this

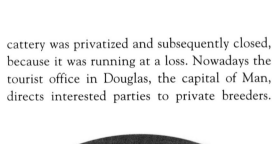

Black classic tabby Manx male of around 1900

cattery was privatized and subsequently closed, because it was running at a loss. Nowadays the tourist office in Douglas, the capital of Man, directs interested parties to private breeders.

Black spotted Manx of around 1900

The Manx was one of the first breeds to be given a pedigree standard

Longhaired Manx, also known as a Cymric

Even now a visitor to the Isle of Man can still find Manx cats without a pedigree on farms and with private individuals, although their numbers are not so great as they used to be; in the last hundred years the island's stock has been thoroughly "creamed off."

ORIGIN OF THE LONGHAIRED MANX

The longhaired Manx—also sometimes called "Cymric"—was in the early days not so well known outside Man itself. Although in the 1950s longhaired Manx kittens were born outside the island, these were not at first thought to be "right." In the 1960s, first of all in Canada, a deliberate breeding program for this longhaired version was started. In 1963 the first Cymric was shown. It was then found that longhairs were actually occasionally born to all shorthaired bloodlines, so the name Manx Longhair was preferred. At the same time the breed standards in America accepted that the cats could be longhaired as well as shorthaired. The present-day population of Manx includes many cats carrying the gene for long hair, and most Manx breeders have a litter with one or more longhaired kittens from time to time.

TEMPERAMENT

Manx have great social intelligence. They are very trusting, pleasant, and stable cats that can get on well with other cats and dogs, but also with adults and children. Some of them tend to attach themselves particularly to one individual. They are well balanced and gentle-mannered, and often are still playful at an advanced age. Accommodating as they are, they can easily be taught to walk on a leash or to retrieve paper balls. Cats of this breed are healthy and strong, and with good care can reach a great age—fifteen to twenty years is not an exceptional age for a Manx.

Manx are very friendly and stable cats

CARE AND MAINTENANCE

Caring for a Manx's coat is little trouble, being comparable to that of an ordinary, non-pedigree cat. It is enough to brush the cat regularly with a soft bristle brush and afterwards to comb through the coat lightly with a coarse comb. During molting periods a rubber brush or massage glove can be helpful in removing dead and loose hairs easily from the coat, but these should be used carefully as it is easy to damage the coat. The longhaired coat of the Cymric needs a little more looking after, although a coat typical of the breed has little tendency to tangle. It is, therefore, enough to brush the cat regularly with

Black tortoiseshell and white Manx, female

APPEARANCE

BODY

The Manx is a compactly built, medium-large cat, with a strong skeletal structure that makes it look round and cobby. The hind legs are clearly longer than the forelegs, so that the line of the back rises toward the rear. The legs are muscular. Five different lengths of tail are recorded: a cat that is completely tailless, with no caudal or sacral vertebrae, is called "rumpy;" the "rumpy riser" is a cat with no more than three sacral vertebrae and no caudal vertebrae; the "stumpy" has a short stump tail; the "longy" is a cat with an incomplete (short) tail; and finally the "taily" is a Manx cat with a complete tail. The first three can be shown in a class for tailless and stumptailed cats, whilst the last two can be used for breeding if they are otherwise suitable in type.

HEAD

The head is round with a sloping nose line. The ears are not set too high, are wide and open at the base, and are set turning slightly outwards. The eyes are large and round.

a wire brush and then to comb it through lightly with a coarse comb. If the animal is being shown, then the coat should be powdered a few days before the show with warmed bran or a special dry shampoo for cats. If this is distributed well through the coat, dirt and surplus sebaceous matter will stick to it. After about half an hour the powder or bran can be brushed out of the coat, which will look clean and fresh again.

Red classic tabby Manx, male

White Manx, female

cream, with or without white markings and a silver undercoat. Tabby patterns are classic/blotched, spotted, and striped. Any amount of white is allowed, so that there are Manx and Cymric animals with a van pattern, sometimes with one or two blue eyes. Any eye color is allowed and they vary mainly from green to gold. Colors and factors that traditionally occur in the Far East, such as ticked tabby, lilac, chocolate, cinnamon, fawn, points, and Burmese and Tonkinese albino factors are not acceptable in this breed. If Manx kittens are born with such colors, it always involves cats without a true-bred ancestry.

COAT

There are shorthaired and longhaired Manx cats. A feature of the Manx is its double coat, which feels very soft and thick. The dense undercoat seems to push up the topcoat, so that the coat stands slightly more away from the body than in the European Shorthair, though not as much as the British Shorthair. The Cymric has a half-length double coat that feels soft, dense, and resilient.

COLORS AND PATTERNS—GENERAL

COLORS

Manx are only bred in the natural farm-cat colors that traditionally occur in the north and west of Europe, and the tabby patterns and markings associated with them. These are solid white, black, red, cream, blue, tortoiseshell, and blue-

Blue and white Manx, female

Black tortoiseshell and white Manx, female

tery closed, the British pedigree register, which otherwise was complete and closed, keeps the opportunity open for registration to residents of the Isle of Man who breed Manx cats.

- In spite of its early recognition, the breed has never been very popular. There is a small, but dedicated, group of breeders, scattered across the world, who regard the breed in terms of cultural heritage and are doing their best to preserve and, where possible, improve it.

REMARKS

- Cymric is Welsh, meaning "coming from Wales."
- Manx cats, like humans (and other animals without tails) run a slightly increased risk of having descendants with spina bifida. In the past, scientific inbreeding crosses were made with Manx cats in an attempt to find out how this condition was inherited, in the hopes of being able to prevent it in humans. These laboratory crossings have sometimes unintentionally given the breed a bad name. Manx breeders select against this syndrome, and do not breed with bloodlines where it has occurred. For centuries, both in the Isle of Man and among breeders elsewhere, Manx cats have been crossed with each other without any problems.
- The lack of a tail in the Manx is not inherited consistently, so that various tail lengths can occur in the same litter.
- Manx cats lack a tail, which is thought of as a "rudder" when jumping. Manx cats, however, can climb and jump very well—the absence of a tail in no way hinders them. In the wild there are felines without a tail or with a very short tail (such as the lynx) and it cannot reasonably be claimed that their short tails limit the activities of these animals.
- Tens of thousands of Manx cats still live in the Isle of Man. Because the government cat-

Black and white Manx, female

PIXIE-BOB

Polydactyl Pixie-Bob

ORIGIN

The history of the Pixie-Bob is veiled in mystery. Some fanciers believe that the animals originated in the wild, possibly by voluntary mating between lynxes and farm cats. Blood tests, however, have shown that the breed carries no "wild" genes. Be that as it may, the breed has an undeniable aura of wildness combined with a friendly and even temperament, which taken together encapsulate the great attraction of the Pixie-Bob. The breed owes the first half of its name to a queen—"Pixie." This cat was born to two cats, found by the American cat fancier Carol Ann Brewer, which reminded her of lynxes. The second half of the name comes from the American Bobcat, another name for the lynx. Pixie was a beautiful large female, looking like a wild lynx, and Carol Ann Brewer wanted to capture the features of this queen in a breed of cats. She found support for her plan and several breeders, among them Bernida Flynn, Gail Chaney, and Pam Richcreek, participated in the breeding program, which involved almost exclusively cats found semi-wild with attributes resembling those of Pixie. The development of the breed was taken seri-

ously from the start, and those involved were—and are—extremely dedicated to the breed. In 1968 the breed gained championship status with T.I.C.A., a major coordinating cat organization. The breed is best known in the United States, but is beginning to gain an increasing number of fanciers outside America.

TEMPERAMENT

Pixie-Bobs are friendly, well-balanced pets with an easy temperament. Fanciers sometimes call them "dogs in disguise" because they behave so much like canines. They like being pet and can in general get on well with other cats, along with dogs and children. Although they are devoted to their own people, the breed is known for being rather reserved towards strangers in general.

Pixie-Bob

CARE AND MAINTENANCE

Looking after the Pixie-Bob's coat is no trouble. A weekly brushing session is sufficient for both the longhaired and shorthaired varieties. Because the males in particular can get very large and heavy (fifteen to a good twenty pounds or more, often a third heavier than the average female of the breed) a sturdy scratching post, large-size litter tray, and an extra-large travel

Pixie-Bob

carrier must be considered essential pieces of equipment for a Pixie-Bob.

APPEARANCE

BODY

Pixie-Bobs have a medium-large to large, muscular body. The prominent shoulder blades give the cat a typically rolling gait. The hips are somewhat higher than the shoulders. The breed has deep, powerful flanks (no pulled-in belly line) and a broad, well-developed chest. The skeletal structure is round and heavy. Males are a third heavier and more muscular than females. The tail is short and flexible. Kinks and knots are allowed, but the tail should not reach further than the heel. The legs are long and have heavy bones with large, almost round paws. Polydactylism (extra toes) is allowed, with up to seven toes per paw.

HEAD

Half the points awarded at shows go to the head and the "face," with breeders of the Pixie-Bob claiming that the head, which resembles that of

Pixie-Bob female with kitten

Pixie-Bob

COAT

Pixie-Bobs can be either longhaired or short-haired. Both types of coat are water repellent. The coats of shorthairs should stand slightly away from the body. The hair on the belly is longer than on the rest of the body. The long-haired Pixie-Bob has a half-length coat. The hair is longer on the back, belly, and tip of the tail than it is on the rest of the body. The hair on the face is long but does not form a ruff around the neck.

COLOR AND PATTERN—GENERAL

The Pixie-Bob is only recognized in spotted tabby, with a dark gray base at the roots. The ground color is warm, with black or brown ticking and white tips to the hairs. The eyes can be gold-colored to brown, and green is allowed. Copper-colored (orange) and blue eyes are not allowed.

a lynx, is a particularly important feature of the breed. Seen from in front, the head is shaped like a broad, upside-down pear. The forehead is slightly rounded. The nose is large, and the muzzle is broad and long. Pixie-Bobs have fleshy whisker pads. The cheeks are well developed and the chin is large, rounded, and fleshy. The animals have prominent, arched eyebrows. The eyes are medium-large, deep set, and about an eye's width from each other. The upper eyelids are straight, and the lower ones slightly curved. The corners of the eyes are at the same level as the base of the ears. The large ears are set low on the back of the head and preferably should have lynx tufts.

REMARKS

- Because Pixie's father was a polydactylic cat, with more toes than normal, and poly-dactylism is inherited dominant, a proportion of Pixie-Bobs have extra toes. This is the only breed in which extra toes are allowed, although they do occur occasionally in other breeds, including the Maine Coon.
- The breed develops slowly and can continue growing and gaining weight up to the age of about four years.

Pixie-Bob

Korat

mals have been passed on to foreigners. The first Korat outside its country of origin was shown in London in 1896 by someone who had brought the animal back from Thailand. At the time, it was entered as a Blue Siamese, but it is now accepted that it must have been a Korat. Later there is further mention of such cats that had found their way from Thailand to the West, but it was not until 1959 that they were bred seriously outside their country of origin. In that year, Jean Johnson from Oregon was sent two Korats ("Nara" and "Dara") by the American ambassador to Thailand, and there was more interest in starting a breeding program in the West. Later, more Korats from Thailand followed. A breed association was set up, the Korat Cat Fanciers Association, which forbade crossing in from other breeds and laid down that the pedigree of a Korat must always go back to its ancestors in Thailand. In the 1970s, Korats reached Britain and The Netherlands. By now the Korat was no longer unknown, and the breed has been recognized by nearly every organization. In spite of this, it is still a relatively unusual breed, with its few breeders being scattered over the whole world.

KORAT

ORIGIN

The Korat is a breed that has evolved naturally. It owes its name to the province of Cao Nguyen Khorat in Thailand where it originated. There have been slender, solid blue cats with green eyes in this province for centuries. An old papyrus book of poems about cats (*Smud Khoi*) in the Bangkok museum describes the Korat as follows: "with a color like Dok Lao (a silvery flower) and smooth hair, with a color like the clouds and tips like silver. Her eyes shine like dew drops on a lotus leaf." The cats are sometimes given as wedding presents to bring luck. It is plain that this cat has been established in Thailand for centuries and that only a few ani-

Korat

TEMPERAMENT

Korats are affectionate cats that often select one individual in the family with whom they form a special bond. They sometimes find it difficult if their owner has to divide his or her attention amongst several different animals. They need real attention if they are to be happy. In spite of

Korats are playful, intelligent cats

this, they get on well with other cats of the same kind and their relationship with dogs is first-class. The same goes for children—the combination of a Korat and a child on average works very well, although they are less suited to a busy household with young children. Korats are intelligent and learn fast: both the things that you teach them (i.e., walking on a leash or retrieving) and the things that they learn for themselves (i.e., opening doors and taps). They are active and enjoy climbing and playing, about which they can be very enthusiastic. Korat owners claim that the cats do not tend to break anything when doing this. It is claimed that the Korat is a silent cat, but this is certainly not true of all representatives of the breed. There are plenty of Korats that chatter non-stop. Their voice is melodious and gentle.

CARE AND MAINTENANCE

Caring for a Korat's coat is very simple. If you groom the coat about once a week with a soft bristle brush, this should be quite sufficient.

APPEARANCE

BODY

Korats are medium-large, muscular cats (i.e., seven to nine pounds in weight). The hind legs are slightly longer than the forelegs, with small paws that are oval in shape. The tail is medium-long with a rounded tip.

HEAD

The Korat's head is heart-shaped, with not too long a muzzle and a firm chin. The forehead is broad and flat. The nose is very short and has a slight stop. The medium-large ears are broad at

Korat, female

Korat, female

COLORS

The breed is only recognized in a silver-gray (blue) coat color. A feature is the silver tips at the top of the hair shafts that give the coat its silver appearance. The Korat should have no white hairs or white patches. The eyes are a clear green. Most Korats take some time to develop their full eye color; it can be four years before the eyes reach their final color—before then they are a greenish yellow.

REMARKS

- In Thailand, the breed is called "Si-Sawat" (the sawat is a purplish nut or seed) and also "Koraj." Freely translated, "Si-Sawat" means "bringer of luck."
- As with most other natural breeds, in-crosses between the Korat and other breeds are not allowed.
- Occasionally, the birth of a colorpoint Korat is reported. Although very beautiful, these animals do not comply with the breed standard requirement for a solid blue coat color.

the base and set very high on the skull. The eyes are large and bright and set slightly slanted. When the cat is alert they have a good, round shape.

COAT

The coat is fine, glossy, and smooth, and feels like satin. Because there is no undercoat, it lies close against the skin.

Korats

SINGAPURA

ORIGIN

EARLY ORIGIN

The Singapura owes its name to the place where the first cats of this breed were found—Singapore. In the 1970s an American couple, Hal and Tommy Meadow, were living there. Before the couple went to Singapore, Tommy had bred Burmese, Abyssinians, and Siamese and was struck by the color of some of the street cats they came across in Singapore. These animals combined the ticked tabby pattern of the Abyssinian with the Burmese factor, which produced a remarkable combination. When in 1974 they returned to the United States, they took three of these exceptionally colored cats with them. These animals, "Tes," "Ticle," and "Puss," are

Singapura

Singapuras

the ancestors of the present-day Singapura. The couple started breeding with these cats and exhibited their offspring at cat shows throughout the country to promote their new breed. In 1978 other breeders also took an interest in the breed and slowly but surely a small but tight-knit group of breeders emerged, who started pressing for recognition of the Singapura as a pedigree cat. Of course, the whole breed was not based on just the first three cats; in 1980 a fancier brought over a Singapura from Singapore, a cat that still features in many pedigrees and was called "Chiko." Six years later, in 1987, Gerry Mayes, a breeder, traveled to Singapore and collected several cats there off the streets. So the gene pool was gradually widened, although it is still narrow in comparison with most other breeds of cat. In 1981 the breed gained provisional recognition from the C.F.A. as a natural breed, with the condition that it should not be crossed with other breeds. The first Singapura breed association, the Singapura Fanciers' Society, was founded the same year.

RECENT HISTORY

When it later appeared that occasionally kittens without the ticked tabby pattern were born to two Singapuras, it caused quite a commotion.

Singapura

coloring (like that of the brown Burmese) and ticked tabby (like that of the Abyssinian), could have arisen from crosses of Abyssinians with Burmese, and some people accused Hal and Tommy of dreaming up a good story, but in reality of simply having crossed Abyssinians and Burmese to create a new breed. In fact, both the Burmese coloring and the ticked tabby pattern were originally very common in the Far East, so that it is in itself not surprising that local street cats should display combinations of both properties. Several people later traveled to Singapore to check whether Tommy and Hal's cats were really running about the streets there. This proved to be the case, and subsequent imports confirmed it. The Singapura is, in fact, a breed that has raised a great deal of controversy and emotion among cat breeders—three breed associations in a single country for a breed that is so small in numbers is sufficient proof of this. Be that as it may, the Singapura is slowly but surely becoming better known in countries outside the United States and is now being bred on a small scale in Europe, amongst other places.

There was one group of breeders who thought that test crosses should be made to find out which Singapuras did not inherit the combination of the Burmese factor and the ticked tabby pattern true, so that they could be excluded from the breeding program. Other breeders thought that the breed was too young and the gene pool still too small to exclude cats from it—they were afraid (with some reason) that exclusion of some genes would lead to too high a degree of inbreeding. Things led to a schism and resulted in the founding of a second breed association, the International Singapura Alliance. Despite the arguments, the Singapura continued in existence, and in 1988 was given championship status by the C.F.A. But rumbles continued, and in 1995 a third breed association, the United Singapura Society, was founded. All three breed associations were affiliated with the C.F.A. In the course of time, increasing doubts arose concerning the origins of the Singapura. The coat color, in essence a combination of Burmese

Singapura kitten

Singapura

Singapura

TEMPERAMENT

Singapuras are very sociable, lively, stable, and companionable cats. They are very people-oriented and fond of their owners, but certainly not intrusive. They have a positive attitude about life and can get on extremely well with anyone. Their adaptability is great and it makes no difference to them whether they have to live in a town flat or a country farm, in a busy family or a quiet one, as long as they may take their part in the daily run of affairs in the household. They are lively, energetic, and enjoy playing, something they often continue doing at an advanced age. Nevertheless, they can also enjoy snoozing for hours on a scratching post or window seat. Singapuras rarely quarrel among themselves or with other cats. In this respect, they are remarkably stable and sociable, and would rather avoid a confrontation than seek one. Some breeders even keep studs together, which would be unthinkable with most breeds. Singapuras have an unusual appearance, not only because of their color, but also because of their very small size—they are certainly one of the smallest breeds of cat known. In general, Singapuras are very inquisitive and little escapes them. Because of their large, mischievous eyes and enterprising nature they are sometimes labeled the "monkeys" of the cat world.

Singapura

Singapuras are very sociable and people-oriented

COAT

The Singapura has a shorthaired, soft, and close-lying coat.

COLOR AND PATTERN

The only color in which the Singapura is recognized is Burmese brown in combination with the ticked tabby pattern. That looks like a dark brown ticking over a warm, ivory-colored ground. Stripes on the inside of the fore and hind legs are allowed, but stripes on the tail are not. At shows, great importance is attached to the proper coat color and ticking. The eyes are green.

CARE AND MAINTENANCE

Singapuras need very little looking after. All the smooth, close-lying coat needs is a weekly comb with a fine-toothed comb, after which the coat can be rubbed down with a dampened chamois leather to bring out the gloss. They do not molt much.

APPEARANCE

BODY

The Singapura is a small to medium-sized cat. It has muscular legs and small, oval paws. The body is a compact shape, but should not be too "cobby." The slender tail is medium-long and slightly rounded at the tip.

HEAD

The head is round in shape and rests on a very short, muscular neck. The ears are surprisingly large; they are erect and set medium-far apart from each other, giving the cat an alert expression. The large, almond-shaped eyes have dark brown rims. The nose also has a dark brown outline.

Singapuras

SOKOKE

Sokoke

ORIGIN

The Sokoke is a domesticated breed of cat that has its roots in the Arabuko Sokoke Forest in Kenya, on the east coast of Africa. The Arabuko Sokoke Forest covers some 150 square miles and lies close to the coastal towns of Malindi and Kilifi. In the 1980s, Jeni Slater and her husband David lived in the small town of Watamu, close to the Sokoke Forest. Jeni was born and raised in Kenya, but was of English

Sokoke

origin. One day, Jeni's gardener found a litter of kittens in the garden. The mother had abandoned them—she seems to have been a small, wild cat. Jeni decided to take two kittens home; the two little cats, a male and a female, successfully grew up and fit in as household cats without a problem. Jeni discovered that her cats did not hunt birds, but ate only insects. A vet who was passing one day and saw the cats told Jeni that he had often come across that type of cat in the Arabuko Sokoke Forest and that he had several times tried in vain to catch some of them. He said that the local population called them "Khadzonzo," whereas the usual word for domestic cats in Kenya was "Paka." Her type of cats, said the vet, lived mostly in trees. Jeni decided to start breeding with her cats and soon expanded her group of cats with those found by local Kenyans and acquaintances. A friend of Jeni's, Gloria Moldrup, a Canadian living in Denmark, visited Jeni and took two kittens ("Mzuri" and "Jenny") from different litters back to Denmark with her. There, Moldrup started to try and gain official recognition of the Sokoke as a breed. She started a breeding program with several other enthusiastic would-be breeders. Sokoke cats were shown for the first time in 1984 in Copenhagen. The first litter was born a year later. Subsequently, and from time to time, Sokokes were imported from Kenya to prevent inbreeding, a practice that is still going on. In

Sokoke

Sokoke

1983 the breed was recognized as an "experimental breed of cats" under the name "African Shorthair Cat." In 1992, the breed was eventually recognized officially by FIFé and given the name we know now, Sokoke. The Sokoke is still not a familiar sight. One of the problems Sokoke breeders come up against is that by no means do all the animals appear to be fertile. There is a small but very committed group of breeders working to preserve the breed for posterity, most of them in Denmark, but a handful in other European countries and the United States. New cats are still regularly brought in from Kenya to prevent any problems of inbreeding arising.

TEMPERAMENT

Although the impression may have been given that the Sokoke is a wild cat, on average they adapt extremely well to being household cats. It is true that they are not as accommodating and cuddly as most other breeds, and they are certainly not explicit "lap cats." They always keep their dignity and independence. They are intelligent, playful, and active, with a love of the outdoors, and do not mind if it rains or not. Some fanciers claim that their Sokokes are not afraid of a dip in the pond. Sokokes are not solitary animals, however; they like company. In the first instance, they like the company of their own people and enjoy being near them, but they can also get on very well with dogs and other cats. Overall, Sokokes are not suitable for people who are looking for a quiet lap cat. Although they can become accustomed to living indoors, it is recommended that they be given the opportunity to go out.

CARE AND MAINTENANCE

A Sokoke's coat needs the minimum of care. It is enough to brush it once a week with a bristle brush and then rub it over with a damp chamois leather to bring up the gloss.

APPEARANCE

BODY

The Sokoke is a medium-large cat, and has an elegant and very muscular body with a well-developed chest. The legs are long and slim with small, oval paws. The hind legs are longer than the forelegs. The tail is medium length and narrows towards the tip. With its heavy skeletal structure, the cat is surprisingly weighty in relation to its size.

HEAD

The wedge-shaped head of the Sokoke is small in proportion to the body; it has a virtually straight nose and a firm chin. The ears are medium-large with rounded

Sokoke

tips. They are set high on the head so that the cat always gives an impression of alertness. The oval- to almond-shaped eyes are very expressive and set wide apart.

COAT

The very short, glossy coat of the Sokoke lies flat against the body. There is little or no undercoat.

COLORS AND PATTERN—GENERAL

The Sokoke comes only in the classic/blotched tabby pattern. The pattern is always black with a gray to warm golden-brown ground. In other black tabby cats the hairs forming the tabby pattern are black from root to tip. In Sokokes, however, the black hairs of the pattern too are more or less "ticked tabby," giving an unusual effect. The color of the eyes can run from yellow to gold to green.

REMARKS

Very occasionally, snow-Sokokes are born. These animals have a lighter body color, rather reminiscent of the color of a Siamese, the more so because they have blue eyes. This color is not (yet) recognized, however.

371

Combination breeds

Red tabby Exotic

Young black Exotic, male

ORIGIN

EARLY ORIGINS

The Exotic has its roots in the United States. In the 1950s and 1960s, several American Shorthair breeders wanted to improve the coat and eye color (green) of their silver cats. They sought to achieve this by crossing in silver Persians. At the same time, there were other American Shorthair breeders who campaigned against this in-crossing, because they considered the American Shorthair an authentic, farm-cat breed that should have no Persian blood in it. They had a case, the more so as the coats of American Shorthairs became too soft with the Persian input and the type gradually started shifting towards the Persian. In 1996, Jane Martinke, a C.F.A. judge, suggested making these "Persian-American Shorthairs" into a new breed. At first, people wanted to call the new

Black tortoiseshell classic tabby Exotic, female

RECENT DEVELOPMENT HISTORY

Although in the beginning the crosses were, of course, with American Shorthairs, it was permissible for other shorthaired breeds to be involved in the breeding program, too. So the American type of Burmese was crossed in for its lovely round head shape and compactly built body, and the Russian Blue for its double plush coat. Breeders became involved in the program not only in the United States, but also in Europe. Because there were very few American Shorthairs in Europe, but the British Shorthair was very popular there, the Europeans elected to

breed "Sterling," after their silver coat, but it was soon decided that all Persian colors should be allowed, and the breed name "Exotic Shorthair" was created. The intention was to breed cats that looked like Persians, but with a shorthaired, plush coat. Therefore, the breed standard was the same as for the Persian Longhair, with the understanding that the Exotic Shorthair of the time need not have a stop in the line of the nose. This clause was only removed from the breed standard in 1973, because the Exotic type was increasingly approaching that of the Persian and this concession was no longer necessary.

Black tortoiseshell Exotic, female

borrow the Shorthair factor from the British Shorthair. There were very few of these crosses, however. It was also hardly necessary to involve breeds other than Persian in the breeding program. Short hair is inherited dominant over long hair. That made it possible from the beginning to cross the shorthaired animals almost exclusively with Persians and to continue consistently with the shorthaired kittens born from these combinations. In spite of this, many Persian breeders of the time did not wish to cooperate in the production of a shorthaired Persian, and Exotic breeders could not always get access to the stud they wanted for their queen. This opposition declined in time, however, and today there are many Persian breeders who also breed Exotics. From 1975 onwards, crossing Exotics

Black Exotic

Black classic tabby Exotic

Black tortoiseshell Exotic, female

with breeds other than Persian and American Shorthair was no longer allowed. From 1980 onwards, crosses with American Shorthairs were also forbidden, although by then these were very rare. In most countries, Exotics and Persians are now regarded as one and the same breed and may be crossed with each other. Long and shorthaired cats can be found in the same litter. They are, however, judged and entered in pedigrees under different breed names—shorthaired Persians are "Exotics" and the longhaired are "Persian Longhairs," but this is not the same in all countries and organizations. Most organizations in the U.S. and Canada distinguish between longhaired Persians born from the Exotic breeding program and from purebred Persian lines. The former are registered as "Exotic Longhair."

TEMPERAMENT

The temperament of the Exotic is similar to that of the Persian, although there are breeders and fanciers who credit it with a higher level of activity. Exotics are sweet-tempered, gentle, friendly, sociable, and relatively quiet cats. They mix well and get on excellently with other cats, dogs, and children. They rarely display jealous traits, and keeping them in a group of cats usually presents no problems. They are not easily upset by a noisy household, although they do need a quiet spot to which they can withdraw. The average Exotic is very affectionate and likes lying in its owner's lap, but will not be intrusive and will find its own place to rest if its owner is not available. They usually have a quiet voice.

CARE AND MAINTENANCE

The Exotic is sometimes called "the lazy man's Persian." This is partly true: its shorthaired coat is much less liable to tangle, and caring for its coat is much easier work than that of a Persian. On the other hand, the coat does need some care. The dead hairs have to be picked out of the coat by hand in show animals so that it gives a beautiful even impression and does not get

Seal point Exotic kitten

Profile of a blue point Exotic, male

"bitty." The ears should be nicely small and rounded, so the longer hairs on the tips of the ears are usually pulled out in show animals. If you have an Exotic as a pet, a weekly grooming session, preferably with a bristle brush, is usually enough. Because the shape of the Exotic's head is the same as that of the Persian, care of an Exotic's eyes are also a daily recurring task; it is done with a special eye lotion or with cooled, boiled water and a Kleenex (see also: Persian Longhair—Care and maintenance).

APPEARANCE

BODY
The Exotic should be the same type as the Persian, but with a shorthaired coat. The body is compact and cobby, with rela-

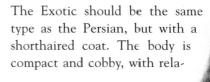

Golden Exotic,
female

tively short, strong, thick legs. The chest is broad and deep and the shoulders are as wide as the back. The width of the back should result from good musculature and not from overfeeding. The paws are large, round, and strong. The tail is fairly short, appropriate to the body, with dense hair and a rounded tip. The skeletal structure is rounded and the head is supported by a short, thick neck.

HEAD

Exotics have a round, massive head with a wide skull. The nose is short and has a pronounced stop (a dip in the bridge) between the eyes. The cheeks are full with wide, strong jaws, and the teeth close well. The ears are small and rounded, and set wide apart and low on the head. The large, full, round eyes are brightly colored. They are set square in the head and far apart, giving the head a sweet expression.

Litter brothers: left a Persian Longhair, right an Exotic

COAT

The coat accentuates the image of roundness. It is dense and firm, but feels soft and luxurious. Because the undercoat is well-developed, the coat stands slightly away from the body.

COLORS AND PATTERNS—GENERAL

Exotics are bred in all the colors encountered in Persians and the requirements for color are the same as for the Persian Longhair. Because the tabby pattern can come out better on a shorthaired than on a longhaired (Persian) coat, tabbies tend to be fairly popular in this breed, but solid black, red, and tortoiseshell Exotics are also seen quite frequently, as are colorpoints.

REMARKS

In several countries, Persians and Exotics are regarded as one and the same breed that only differ in coat length; they have the same breed association. Some associations do, however, distinguish between Persians and Exotic Longhairs—they do not allow Exotics and longhaired Exotics to be crossed with Persians.

Red tabby Exotic

ASIAN

ORIGIN

The history of the Asian does not go back very far. In 1981, four kittens were born to a lilac Burmese queen, "Bambino Lilac Fabergé," and a Persian chinchilla tom, "Jemari Sanquist." This litter was not planned by the breeder, Baroness Miranda von Kirchberg, but the kittens, all shorthaired and black-shaded, were so attractive that she came up with the idea of creating a new

Bombay

breed. The aim was to breed a black-tipped (chinchilla) Burmese. This breed became the Burmilla, a name contrived by combining "Burmese" and "chinchilla." Because silver is inherited dominant, this could best be done by crossing the best types of the kittens, by now adult, with Burmese. All kinds of colors proved to result from these crossings, giving her the idea of continuing to breed these cats under the collective name of "Asian." The Asian is a cat of Burmese type, but of colors other than those recognized for the Burmese. This group of cats does not have the Burmese coloring—in other words, a color very slightly darker in specific parts of the body. The Asian group is split into five subgroups: Asian Selfs (solid colors); Asian Burmilla (chinchilla/shaded); Asian Tabby (all tabbies including silver tabby); Asian Tiffany (long hair, all colors); and Asian Smoke (solid-colored cats with a silver undercoat). The Asian Burmillas, in particular, soon reached the con-

tinent of Europe, including Denmark. This resulted in recognition of the Burmilla as a separate breed by FIFé in 1994. The English cat organization also gave recognition in 1997, regarding the Burmilla (correctly) as not being a separate breed, and accepting this variety as a color type within the Asian group.

TEMPERAMENT

Asians are described as friendly, extroverted, intelligent, and having a sense of humor. They are moderately active—playing and romping alternates with hours of snoozing and they like lying in their owner's lap. They are affectionate and like to receive attention. Their owners must certainly be prepared to give it to them, and should have sufficient time to play and cuddle their pet. Asians are extremely adaptable, can get on with other cats and dogs, like children, and fit into almost any family situation. For an Asian to be the only pet of people who are away

Burmilla

Male Burmilla and kitten

from home a lot, however, is unacceptable from the animal's point of view. In such a case, you are advised to have two kittens, or in any case a second cat, so that they can keep each other company.

CARE AND MAINTENANCE

The care of an Asian's coat is little trouble. It is enough to comb the coat once a week and then rub it with a damp cloth to bring out the gloss. Of course, the longhaired Asians need rather more coat care.

APPEARANCE

BODY

The Asian's body should be similar to that of the Burmese (European type). It is medium-long and well-muscled, with a straight back and sturdy, but not overely wide, chest. The legs are medium-long and the paws slightly oval in

Burmillas

shape. The tail is medium to long and gradually tapers to a rounded tip.

HEAD

The head has a short, wedge shape. The chin is firm. The ears are medium-large to large, set well apart, and have rounded tips. The expressive eyes are set well apart, slightly slanted, and are somewhere between almond-shaped and round.

COAT

The coat is short, fine in texture, and lies flat against the body. The long-haired Asian (Tiffany) has a semi-long, silky coat.

Burmilla kittens

Burmilla

extend so far towards the tips of the hairs that the cat looks white. The tipping may be any color, but the most common is black.

ASIAN SMOKE
These are solid-colored (self) Asians with a silver-white undercoat. The hairs are in this case without color from the root to about half-way, and colored from half-way up to their tips.

ASIAN TABBY
Asian Tabbies come in all four tabby patterns—striped (mackerel), blotched/classic, spotted, and ticked. Silver tabbies, too, fall into this group. The most commonly bred are ticked tabbies. The tabby pattern may be in any color.

TIFFANY
Tiffany is the collective name for all semi-longhaired and long-haired Asians. They may have any of the colors that occur in Asians.

COLORS

In the Asian group, we meet all the Burmese that have one of the variant Burmese colors. About six hundred different combinations of color are possible. Depending on the color of the coat, the color of the eyes may be yellow to green. Green eyes are acceptable, but not desirable, in silvers.

ASIAN SELF
This group offers a place to all solid-colored Asians—in other words, all Asians with a coat of one color. These can include black (Bombay, European type), chocolate, cinnamon, blue, lilac, fawn, red, tortoiseshell, blue-cream, cinnamon tortie, fawn tortie, and cream.

ASIAN BURMILLA
The Burmilla has a white-silver or pale cream (non-silver) undercoat with a colored tipping or shading. This tipping/shading should not

Bombay

379

Burmilla

REMARKS

- There are various breed associations for the Asian in Great Britain. Baroness Miranda von Kirchberg herself founded the Asian Cat Association in England in 1997.
- Because of the recessive inheritance of the Burmese markings (cb), it can happen from time to time that animals with Burmese markings are born to Asians. In Britain these animals are called "Asian with Burmese color restriction" and may not be crossed with Burmese, in order to keep the Burmese breed true.
- Cats of the Burmese type without Burmese markings were previously bred in New Zealand, where the breed, which in all respects shows similarity to the Asian, is called "Mandalay." The Mandalay is a cat of Burmese type that lacks the factor for Burmese coloring. In essence, the Mandalay's relation to the Burmese is the same as the Oriental Shorthair's to the Siamese. Burmese and Mandalays can therefore be mated with each other and, depending on the color of individual kittens, these can be entered in the pedigree register as either Burmese or Mandalay. The Mandalays come from initial crossings with solid black, non-pedigree cats, subsequently combined with Burmese. The Mandalay was recognized as a breed in New Zealand in 1990.

- In New Zealand, new color types were developed in the Burmese breed (i.e. animals that did have the Burmese factor); in the late 1970s, Burmese breeders began to breed silver (silver tabby ticked) and smoke Burmese. These new color types were developed by making use of a non-pedigree cat and a Siamese-Abyssinian hybrid. After the first two crossings, they were combined only with Burmese. In 1986, the new color types in the Burmese gained full recognition from the New Zealand Cat Fancy. Four descendants of these new Burmese colors came to Europe and were accepted in pedigree registers as Burmese types in Germany and The Netherlands. The introduction of the "Asian" concept from Britain caused confusion, however— were these new Burmese color types from New Zealand really Burmese or Asians? The development in New Zealand of new color types in Burmese cats runs parallel to the introduction of new, already recognized color types in the breed, and so has nothing to do with the British Asian. The discussion continues.

This red silver Burmese was one of four Burmese with new colors imported into Europe from New Zealand

Nebelung, female

Nebelung kitten

NEBELUNG

ORIGIN

EARLY ORIGINS

It is said that in the early days of cat shows, towards the end of the nineteenth century, long-haired Blue Russians from Russia were much admired. These have, however, quietly disappeared from the stage. Although longhaired kittens are now and then born to shorthaired Blue Russians, breeders have never seriously tried to make a separate breed of them. Often the existence of these kittens was kept quiet, and they were disposed of as household pets—the gener-

al assumption was that the Blue Russian is, after all, a shorthaired breed. When in the 1990s the founder of the Nebelung breed, Mrs. Cora Cobb, pressed for its recognition on the grounds of it being a longhaired Blue Russian, she came up against strong opposition from a number of Blue Russian breeders. The longhaired Blue Russian as we know it today did not originally come from Blue Russian cats. In August 1984, in Denver, Colorado, a male kitten was born to a black, shorthaired, non-pedigree mother and a father that resembled a Blue Russian. This kitten was the only one with long hair out of a litter of six. Cora Cobb saw this kitten at her son's house, and adopted it. She called it "Siegfried," after the hero of Wagner's epic Nibelungen. Five months later another litter was born, fathered by the same cat with the Blue Russian look, and this time it contained a longhaired female with a lovely silver gloss on her soft coat. Cora took this kitten home, too, and christened her "Brunhilde," again out of the Ring. In May, Siegfried and Brunhilde had their first litter. The kittens were like Siegfried in type and had Brunhilde's coat.

RECENT HISTORY

Together with a genetics specialist from T.I.C.A. and some others, Cora started a breeding program and wrote the first breed standard. On the advice of the genetics expert, Cora called the new breed the longhaired variant of Blue Russian and adopted the Blue Russian breed standard. The only difference in the specification was, of course, the length of the coat. Later two more points were added, because the T.I.C.A. management thought that the Nebelung should not be just a longhaired copy of the Blue Russian. The changes covered size and eye color—the

Nebelung kitten

Nebelung should be just a little larger than its shorthaired counterpart and its eye color should be a little less critical. In 1987, T.I.C.A. was the first large organization of cat associations to recognize the Nebelung. After ten years in the "New Breeds and Colors" class (N.B.C.), the Nebelung was granted championship status on 1 May 1997. Recognition by various other institutions keeping pedigree registers, including the W.C.F., followed later. At the time of publication, the Nebelung, as far as is known, is bred in several American states, Russia, and in several European countries. Nebelungs are still relatively scarce.

Nebelung, female

TEMPERAMENT

The Nebelung is a playful, gentle, active, and clever cat that likes being cuddled and forms a close bond with its humans conterparts. The shyness that generally characterizes the cat, particularly towards strangers and young children, is quite striking.

CARE AND MAINTENANCE

The coat is easy to look after—an occasional combing to remove loose hair is enough.

The Nebelung is a gentle, active cat

APPEARANCE

BODY

The Nebelung is a medium-large cat of a moderately Oriental type. The breed should give an impression of elegance, but it is stronger than it appears at first sight. The body is long and muscular. The legs are long and slender, with paws that are oval with tufts of hair between the toes. The tail, when laid back along the body, should certainly reach the shoulder blades. The target weight for females is seven to nine pounds; for males, nine to eleven pounds. The neck is long and slender, although its longer hair can make the neck look shorter than it really is.

Nebelung, male

Nebelung kitten

HEAD

The head is wedge-shaped with strikingly large ears that follow the shape of the head. The profile of the cat shows a sloping transition from the forehead to the nose—no stop, no "Roman" nose (with a bulge), and no absolutely straight profile, though it may appear straight. Seen from the side, the tip of the nose forms a straight line running down to the point of the strong chin. The whisker pads may "bulge out," giving the cat a mischievous look. The eyes are slightly oval-shaped, medium-large, and set far apart.

COAT

The Nebelung has a long, soft, smooth coat consisting of a water-repellent guard coat and a full, woolly undercoat. The length of the coat can vary from one individual to another, but the tail hairs should always be the longest. The undercoat is, of course, thinner in summer than in winter. The Nebelung has breeches and a long-haired, bushy tail. Males have a ruff, whilst females usually do not.

Nebelung kitten with classic tabby ghost marking

COLOR

The coat is blue (the dilution of black) with a silvery shine. Because of the longer topcoat, however, the silver tips of the hairs often disappear so that the Nebelung looks darker than the Blue Russian. White hairs or white patches are not allowed. Kittens can display a clear tabby pattern, although this ghost marking will disappear as the cat grows up. The eyes of the Nebelung contain rather more yellow than those of the Blue Russian. The green color of the eyes develops from an intermediate yellowish color, but by around eight months a kitten should have a green edge to the pupil, which expands to the rest of the iris. The deeper the green, the better. The eyes can take up to two years to develop their full color. The nose leather is slate gray.

REMARKS

- The word "Nibelung" was changed to "Nebelung" to avoid being mispronounced in English. In hindsight, this name, with its connection with the German word "nebel" ("mist"), is even more appropriate.

- Most organizations allow Nebelungs to be crossed with Blue Russians. The first generation born from such crossings is usually shorthaired and is then called "Nebelung variant." Such cats may only be used for breeding Nebelungs and not for Blue Russians. Sometimes longhaired kittens are born to shorthaired Blue Russians and these cats can, of course, also be used for breeding Nebelungs. In addition, in Russia itself, there are also some breeders aiming at breeding longhaired Blue Russians.

Nebelung kitten

BENGAL

ORIGIN

The Bengal owes its breed name to a small wild cat, the Bengali tiger cat *Prionailurus bengalensis*, formerly *Felis bengalensis*. In the 1950s, crosses were made in the United States between these small wild cats and domestic cats. It was not initially the intention to create a new breed—the crosses were arranged by researchers, because it had been discovered that *Prionailurus bengalensis* was immune to the leukemia virus. As is perhaps known, leukemia

Prionailurus bengalensis, **the wild Bengal tiger cat**

Bengal, spotted female

has claimed many victims among both pedigree and non-pedigree cats and continues to do so, because no vaccine giving one hundred percent protection is available against this fatal virus. The researchers wanted to see how susceptibility to the disease was inherited. Later on in the research it was shown that the descendants of

the wild and domesticated cats were, in fact, normally susceptible to the dreaded virus. Moreover, it was found that many of the descendants of these crosses were not all equally fertile. In particular, some of the males that otherwise enjoyed good health proved incapable of reproduction. The hybrids came into the limelight after one of the researchers disposed of a number of cats to Mrs. Jean Mill. Mill wanted to breed cats that had, to as great an extent as possible, the external features of wild felines, but combined with the friendly temperament of domesticated cats. After Mill, many people in subsequent years crossed Bengali tiger cats with domestic cats, including ordinary household cats, but also with Abyssinians, Ocicats, Egyptian Maus, and Burmese. This eventually led to a new breed of cats, the Bengal. Although the breed is most popular in the United States, it is not recognized there by the American C.F.A., although it is by T.I.C.A., the G.C.C.F. in Britain, and by FIFé, who recognized the breed in 1999.

Two Bengal kittens

Bengal

Classic tabby Bengal

TEMPERAMENT

The Bengal is a very active and enterprising breed. What a Bengal needs more than anything else is to be occupied. Although Bengals, like other cats, sleep for many hours of the day, it is not a cat that likes to "lie around looking beautiful" all day on the sofa. It loves climbing and playing—the crazier the activity, the better. Bengals that are bored will get up to mischief and devise occupations for themselves of which their owners would certainly not approve. They do not need free access to the outside world, but if kept indoors there should be sufficient opportunities inside for them to run, climb, and jump. One or more ceiling-high, stable climbing poles are no superfluous luxury. Bengals also like company; there is nothing worse for a Bengal than being the only cat in the house, particularly if you are out regularly yourself. In spite of this, they are not lap cats or "cuddly" cats. As a rule they get on well with other felines, but because they can be very busy, with almost fanatical behavior at play,

Inquisitive Bengal kitten

they do better with like-minded, active, and tough cats. The company of an active Bengal is soon too much of a good thing for very quiet or shy cats; its challenges to play can in that case be perceived as "bullying." Unneutered Bengals can be very domineering in their attitude towards other cats, but neutered animals are much less aggressive. Queens of this breed may spray when they are in heat. It is a well-known fact, too, that some Bengals are not afraid of water and will accompany their owner into the shower or bath if given the opportunity.

CARE AND MAINTENANCE

The Bengal needs relatively little coat care; a weekly brush is enough and sometimes not even necessary.

Bengals are active, alert cats

APPEARANCE

BODY

The Bengal has quite a long body, which is muscular and well-developed with heavy bones. The hind legs are a little longer than the forelegs. The paws are relatively large and round in shape. A loose fold of skin between the hind legs is a very good feature. The tail is of medium length, feels firm, and has a rounded tip.

HEAD

The wedge-shaped head is small in proportion to the body and more long than wide. The fairly small ears point slightly forward, are set wide apart, and should have no tufts. The tips of the ears should be rounded. The long, wide nose displays a slight arching where the nose runs into the crown of the skull. The eyes are large, and almond-shaped to fairly round. Thick whisker pads are very desirable.

COAT

The coat is short to medium in length and lies smooth against the body Its structure is soft and silky. Kittens may have a somewhat longer coat than full-grown animals. Really longhaired animals occur occasionally, but are not approved

Classic Tabby snow Bengal

for shows or for breeding because the longer hair prevents the shape of the head and the contrasting tabby markings from appearing to their best advantage.

Spotted Bengal

Left, a Siamese snow Bengal; right, a spotted tabby

COLORS AND PATTERNS—GENERAL

GENETICALLY BLACK

The basic color of the Bengal is black, regardless of the factor or tabby pattern it has. Yet in fully grown animals the tabby pattern often does not look as black as it does in other breeds. The ground color in the course of time often becomes redder or browner, and the tabby pattern, which in kittens is still black, can fade to brown, so that the contrast is partly lost. Many Bengals only reach their final color when they are about eighteen months old. As in all other cats, the actual basic color of the cat can always be found at the tip of the tail, and in a Bengal this should be

The Bengal is genetically black, but because its coat fades over time, its color is sometimes only visible on the tip of the tail

jet black. Occasionally a completely black kitten will turn up in a litter of Bengals. Although such kittens can be very attractive and the solid black color also occurs in the wild in black panthers, these solid-colored Bengals are not as yet recognized by a single cat organization. Thus, most breeders will not breed from this color. That is because great value is placed precisely on the Bengal's pattern with its many contrasts; of course, in black animals it is not possible to see how sharp and contrasting their tabby pattern (genetically always present) is.

PATTERNS

Two tabby patterns occur in the Bengal—spotted and blotched/classic. In the spotted pattern it is important that the spots contrast clearly with the color of the background. If there is a third color in the spots that is plainly warmer than the ground color, or if this warm color is within a circle of spots, these markings are called "rosettes." They are highly desirable. The blotched/classic markings are broadly comparable to the blotched markings of other breeds, but instead of round patterns should form oblong ones, either horizontally or diagonally. The blotched/classic pattern should preferably also have more than two colors—the ground color, the markings, and one "extra" warm color in the markings. Classic tabbies can also have four or even more colors, because more warm colors "fit" in the broader markings, particularly on the shoulders. A striped marking (mackerel) or even a vague hint of mackerel (by which is meant vertical stripes or spot markings tending towards the vertical) is regarded as a serious fault. The contrast in a black tabby should be quite clear. It is highly desirable that the whisker pads, chin, chest, belly, and insides of the legs have as light a background color as possible with black markings. This marking includes patches on the belly, rings around the neck and chest, and freckles on the whisker pads. The rims of the eyes, lips, and nose should be outlined in black. The paw pads and the tip of the tail are always black. The eyes are green to copper-colored.

SEAL LYNX (POINT) OR SIAMESE SNOW BENGAL

The muzzle, ears, tail, and legs of the Siamese Snow Bengal are rather darker in color than the rest of the body. Whereas in Siamese—and most other breeds with points—a strong contrast between the color of the body and that of the extremities (head, tail, legs, and ears) is desirable, in the Siamese Snow Bengal the intention is that the points should not contrast too much. There should be as little contrast as possible between the color of the points and the rest of the body. The Siamese Snow Bengal has an ivory to cream ground color, and its tabby pattern can vary in color from seal (genetically black), through dark to light brown, to yellow-

Two Siamese Snow Bengals—left, classic tabby; right, spotted

Classic tabby Bengal, female

ish. The tail is dark brown to black in color, the tip of the tail black, and the eye color always blue. The paw pads are dark brown, sometimes with a pinkish undertone, but never actually pink. In contrast to most other breeds, the tabby pattern is visible from birth in many Siamese Snow Bengal kittens. They are also rarely born white, unlike most cats with points. Kittens of this color type, which display little or no tabby pattern by the age of six weeks, often do not develop one in later life either. The more obvious the pattern is at a young age, the better the animal usually develops its color at a later age. In any case, the light background grows darker over the course of time.

SEAL SEPIA OR BURMESE SNOW BENGAL

Seal alludes to the black (seal) tabby pattern and sepia to the Burmese factor. Seal sepia is, therefore, a combination of tabby and the Burmese factor (see also: Burmese). The ground color is ivory, cream, or a light tan color. The color of the markings varies from reddish to dark brown. As with the Siamese Snow Bengal, it is not desirable in these animals to have too strong a contrast in color between the points and the rest of the body. The tip of the tail can be dark brown to black. The paw pads are dark brown, possibly with a pinkish undertone, but never pink. Just as with the Siamese Snow Bengal, the color of the body grows darker with age.

SEAL MINK OR TONKINESE SNOW BENGAL

Seal mink is a combination of tabby and the Tonkinese factor (see also: Tonkinese). Seal alludes to the black (seal) tabby pattern and mink to the Tonkinese factor. Tonkinese Snow Bengals can be born to Siamese and Burmese Snow Bengals. Tonkinese Snow Bengals are rather lighter in color than Burmese Snow Bengals, but in practice it is very difficult to distinguish the two colors. Just as in other Snow

Bengal kittens

Bengals, in this color type the body color also darkens with age.

REMARKS

- Precisely because of its sometimes rather lively temperament, it is important that you look at the temperament of the parents when you choose a kitten. It is also important to choose a breeder who takes his or her responsibilities seriously and socializes the kittens well.
- If the wild appearance and associated dramatic contrast in the markings of this breed attract you, choose your breeder carefully. It is not easy to breed kittens with good, appealing tabby markings and a warm ground color.

In a Bengal it is difficult to determine whether the Burmese or Tonkinese factor is involved

"F1" Bengal, male

BENGAL: EARLY GENERATIONS

ANOTHER "BREED"

The Bengal just described, as we meet it today in shows across virtually the whole world, may well have originated from crossings with wild cats, but in

"F1" Bengal, male

most bloodlines its wild-cat features have, meanwhile, been largely or wholly "selected out" by selective breeding. Most fanciers actually only talk of the Bengal as a domesticated pedigree cat if its wild ancestors are some four generations back in its pedigree. Within this margin we find animals that in appearance, and particularly in instinct and temperament, are rather closer to their origins. These wild crosses, sometimes called hybrids or "foundations" in respect of their temperament and suitability as pets, cannot be compared with an ordinary house cat or pedigree cat. In spite of this, they are still sometimes offered to private owners, particularly in countries where keeping wild or semi-wild cats, with or without a special license, is allowed by law. In this way hybrids are often encountered in, for instance, France, Belgium, and the U.S.A. They

Early generation Bengal, classic tabby female

may be labeled as F1, F2, or F3. F1 means that the animal is a first line cross with a wild cat (i.e., his or her father is a Bengal tiger cat). F2 refers to cats that have a Bengal tiger cat as a grandparent and F3 to those whose great-grandparent came from the wild. Males in F1, F2, and sometimes F3 generations are usually sterile. Females sometimes suffer from reduced fertility. It proves in practice that these wild crossings are best brought up by hand. Most breeders take the kittens away from their mother early and raise them on a bottle, so that from a young age they get accustomed to humans as their surrogate mothers.

Classic tabby female, early generation

TEMPERAMENT

These early generations sometimes react in an unstable manner, instinctively and/or fearfully (e.g., spitting, running away, uncontrolled urination), to new or unfamiliar impressions and/or stressful situations. Mother cats can sometimes have unstable reactions while they are still suckling their kittens, which causes them to abandon their kittens or transfer them to "their people"—although this could possibly have something to do with the fact that the mother cat was herself brought up by hand. Sometimes nursing mothers will accept no other pets near them, even if they know them quite well and in other circumstances get on well with them. Although there are examples of F2 and F3 animals that behave like any other domesticated cat, this does not apply to all of them. Therefore, it is sensible to think hard about the disadvantages before you acquire one. It is sometimes thought that these hybrids will be very aggressive towards fully domesticated cats, but experience teaches that the opposite is the case—often they prove to be less on the defensive at the sight of any domesticated cats that may be present. They are generally sociable in their behavior, particularly after they have been neutered (females as well as males). They need the company of at least one other like-minded cat. The early generations often attach themselves to one person in particular and most of them have no interest in anyone else—but here again there are exceptions to the rule.

First generation ("F1"), male

Chocolate spotted Ocicat, female

the breed originated only in domesticated breeds of cat. The first Ocicat was a small male called "Tonga." Tonga was born in the 1960s in the establishment of a well-known breeder of Siamese cats, Mrs. Virginia Daly of Michigan. Tonga's father was a chocolate point Siamese and his mother a cross between a Siamese and an Abyssinian. Mrs. Daly was not aiming for a new breed with this cross. She wanted to breed the ticked tabby pattern, also known as the Abyssinian pattern, into the points of the Siamese, so

OCICAT

ORIGIN

EARLY HISTORY

The Ocicat owes its name to the ocelot, a wild feline with a dramatic pattern of markings. That is all they have in common with the wild cat—

Lilac spotted Ocicat, female

Fawn spotted Ocicat, male

she crossed Abyssinians with her Siamese bloodlines. In one of the litters born of this combination, there was a most beautifully spotted tabby kitten in addition to striped, classic, solid black, and the desired "Aby-point" kittens. Virginia Daly's daughter thought the kitten looked like an ocelot, and nicknamed it "Ocicat." Tonga with his spotted tabby coat did not meet Virginia Daly's objective, however, so he was sold for ten dollars to a medical student, Thomas Brown, with the condition that he should have him neutered when the time was right. A little later, Daly met Dr. Clyde Keeler of the University of Georgia, who had for some time been entertaining the idea of breeding a cat that looked like the extinct Egyptian fishing cat and wanted to enthuse some breeders with this project. Because of Tonga's beautiful, unusual pattern of spots, he saw possibilities for him. He asked Virginia Daly to think about using Tonga as the patriarch in a breeding program. Virginia Daly did not like the idea at all. She was a Siamese breeder and had no interest in starting a new breed. However, the idea had taken root, and when in a later litter from the same combination that had produced Tonga another beautifully marked, spotted male kitten was born, she kept it. She called it "Dotson" and decided not to have it neutered, but to register it with the C.F.A.

Lilac spotted Ocicat kitten

RECENT HISTORY

Several other breeders became interested in establishing the new breed and slowly but surely the outlines of today's Ocicat began to take shape. Until the early 1980s there were few breeders involved with the experimental breed. This is reflected in the number of C.F.A. registrations—only

Chocolate spotted Ocicat, female

ninety-nine Ocicats were registered between 1966 and 1980. Some breeders crossed in American Shorthairs. This gave the Ocicat a less slender appearance and introduced the silver gene into the new breed. From the early 1980s interest gradually increased, resulting in the establishment of a breed club in 1984. In 1987 the breed gained championship status and it was decided that no more Siamese or American Shorthairs should be crossed in. Crossing in Abyssinians was still allowed until the year 2005. In recent years the Ocicat has become very popular in the United States. The breed rates quite high in the top twenty breeds of cat. Meanwhile, the Ocicat is being exported to many other countries, including Australia and New Zealand, Japan, South Africa, Italy, Scandinavia, Germany and The Netherlands, and is also bred there.

TEMPERAMENT

The Ocicat is a friendly, sociable, and companionable cat. It is extremely inquisitive and little will escape it. People-oriented as it is, it likes to make contact with "its" humans and interact with them. It is not intrusive, however, and can amuse itself well, although it is not a cat to leave for days on end to its fate. Therefore, it is better to give it a feline companion to play with. This usually produces no problems as Ocicats have a sociable disposition and can generally get on well with other cats. Because of their great adaptability they can also get on well with dogs, provided they have become used to them at a young age. In addition to all this, Ocicats are very intelligent. They can teach themselves certain

Chocolate spotted Ocicat, female

tricks, such as opening kitchen cabinets and doors, but can also learn things from their owners, such as retrieving scraps of paper, sitting up,

Tawny spotted Ocicat, male

Tawny spotted Ocicat, male

and walking on a leash. They are very adaptable and feel just as much at home in a small flat as in a large house with a well fenced-in garden or run. It is not a problem if an Ocicat has to be kept in all the time, provided it is given sufficient opportunity to expend its energy. A good climbing post would, therefore, be very welcome.

CARE AND MAINTENANCE

Because it is short and close-lying, the care of an Ocicat's coat gives little trouble. It rarely needs brushing or combing. If an Ocicat is entered for a show, then the glossy coat can be enhanced by wiping it with a soft cloth in the direction of the hairs.

BODY

The Ocicat is a medium-sized to large cat, which looks athletic and elegant. It is well-muscled and has a solid, powerfully built body. The cat should feel heavier than it looks. It has a long body with a deep chest and lightly arched ribs. The hindquarters are higher than the forequarters. The powerful legs are medium-long and should, in all respects, be in proportion to the

Chocolate spotted Ocicat, female

body. The compact paws are oval-shaped. The tail is relatively long, medium thick, and tapers to a small point. In this breed, as in many others, the females are smaller than the males.

HEAD

The head is moderately wedge-shaped. The broad muzzle gives a rather square impression and is of good length, with a firm chin. The whisker pads are not too pronounced. The ears are medium large, set on the corners of the head. They are at an angle of 45 degrees to an imaginary horizontal line above the eyebrows. The large, almond-

Cinnamon spotted Ocicat

shaped eyes are set slightly slanted, with the outermost corners pointing in the direction of the ears. There should be an eye's length of space between the eyes.

COAT

An Ocicat's coat is short and smooth, and lies close against the skin. It has a high gloss and silky structure. The characteristic tabby pattern shows at its best on the typical coat of this breed.

COLORS AND PATTERN—GENERAL

PATTERN

Ocicats should have a spotted tabby pattern in which the many spots take the shape of thumbprints—including on the belly. In essence this spotted pattern is an interrupted, blotched or classic tabby pattern. It is important that the pattern should contrast well with the ground color, although it comes out less clearly in the dilute colors (fawn, blue, and lilac). The number of points given for them at shows reveals how important the coat, color, and pattern are for this breed. They make up nearly half the total points that can be awarded to an Ocicat. Because the gene responsible for breaking up the classic pattern into spots is inherited dominant, classic kittens are also sometimes born, but their pattern of markings is not desirable. The agouti gene that allows the underlying tabby pattern to show itself is also inherited dominant. It can occasionally happen that a kitten is born without any tabby markings. A "solid," as these are called by Ocicat fanciers, does not, however, comply with the breed standard. The same goes for point markings, which can appear in a litter through the recessive inheritance of this gene.

Chocolate spotted
Ocicat

COLORS

Ocicats come in twelve different combinations of colors—tawny spotted (black spotted), chocolate spotted, cinnamon spotted, blue spotted, lilac spotted, and fawn spotted. These colors are also recognized with a silver-white ground where the tabby pattern is very clearly expressed in one of the six recognized colors (tawny silver spotted, chocolate silver spotted, cinnamon silver spotted, blue silver spotted, lilac silver spotted, and fawn silver spotted). White markings are not allowed and the same goes for colors other than the six recognized ones. Some cinnamon or fawn-colored animals look as if they are red or cream. It is not always easy to determine the right color. Sometimes the markings on the body are a little lighter than on the head, tail, and legs. In such cases, the tip of the tail usually reveals the answer. All eye colors are allowed, except blue. The preference is for deep, intense eye color.

Lilac spotted
Ocicat

Ocicat, chocolate "solid"

Tawny silver spotted Ocicat, young female

RAGDOLL

ORIGIN

EARLY HISTORY

The Ragdoll is a relatively new breed, which has its roots in the United States. It was developed in the early 1960s by Ann Baker, a cat breeder from Riverside, California. The matriarch of the breed was a white Persian-type queen called "Josephine" that was owned by Mrs. Pennels, Ann Baker's neighbor. Josephine is purported to have been covered by a "Sacred" Birman. She had free access out-of-doors and during her pregnancy was hit by a car, but miraculously survived. According to Baker, Josephine suddenly became extremely gentle after this traumatic experience, went limp like a rag doll if she was picked up, and endured everything without spitting or scratching. The kittens she subsequently bore all inherited Josephine's "new" temperament, and Ann Baker focused on this temperament in particular in developing her new breed. From a logical perspective, it is generally acknowledged that any attribute acquired as a result of an environmental factor (e.g., a traffic accident) cannot be inherited. It does occasionally happen, however, that cats undergo a change in temperament after a bad fall or an accident, so that the reported change in Josephine is quite plausible. Josephine's off-

Seal point Ragdoll, mitted female

spring could simply have been naturally friendly and quiet. Such character traits can be reasonably well established by selection, but only up to a point. It is difficult to ascertain which cats or breeds were subsequently used in the breeding program, but in any event, it is certain that, in addition to full and semi-Persians and "Sacred" Birmans, Burmese were also involved.

"OLD WIVES' TALES"

Ann Baker, who has since died, promoted her breed intensively, but did this in a way that upset a number of people. For instance, she would "hurl" her cats across the living room in front of the television cameras to show that they had an

Ragdoll kittens

Ragdoll kittens

extremely high pain threshold and that you could do anything to them, so it is hardly surprising that many cat fanciers took an aversion to the lady and her cats; such an extremely phlegmatic cat without any sense of self-preservation would, of course, be a danger to itself and is at variance with everything a cat should be. The handful of breeders who did show interest were bound by contract to Ann Baker, to whom they had to pay a percentage of the price of every kitten they sold—Ann Baker had, as it were, a "copyright" on the breed. In the course of time she began to spread increasingly strange stories about her cats, claiming that Ragdolls carried

Ragdoll kitten

Lilac point Ragdoll, bicolor male

human genes and could even make contact with alien, non-terrestrial life. She eventually lost her credibility amongst most of the breeders under contract to her. They breached their contracts and jointly decided to carry on developing the breed further without the input or involvement of Ann Baker. This meant that they were faced with the difficult task of relegating all the odd stories with which Ann Baker had saddled the breed to the realm of fiction. The breeder Denny Dayton was one of the most important supporters of the breed in this period. He made great efforts to have the Ragdoll recognized by contemporary cat organizations in the U.S. In 1967 his efforts, and those of other dedicated breeders, began to bear fruit. Today

the breed is recognized in almost all countries and by almost all cat organizations. Although the breed itself is generally recognized, however, this does not apply to all the colors and markings in which it is bred. In 1971, Ann Baker founded her own Ragdoll society, the I.R.C.A. (International Ragdoll Cat Association), in which a small number of Ragdolls are still registered today. Ragdolls registered with the I.R.C.A. can, however, only be entered for I.R.C.A. shows and are not accepted by any other organizations.

Ragdoll kitten, bicolor

Ragdoll mother with kittens

Caring for a Ragdoll's coat is little trouble

TEMPERAMENT

It is now clear that the most peculiar stories doing the rounds about the Ragdoll have either been plucked completely out of the air or originate from the reports spread by Ann Baker. The Ragdoll is not a "slapstick" cat and *can* suffer pain. It is, however, one of the most lovable and gentle breeds we know. Ragdolls often have an excellent disposition. They are

The Ragdoll is one of the largest breeds of cat

open and full of trust, even toward strangers. That is why most Ragdoll owners do not let their cats roam free outside since, if anyone is nice to them, they easily let themselves be picked up and taken away. Ragdolls can let themselves go limp when they are picked up. This is not an automatic reflex, but an expression of the trust the animals have in their humans. They only do it when they feel comfortable and are completely relaxed. Ragdolls are very people-oriented, but they can also get on well with other cats, dogs, and children. Because of their even and stable temperament they also do well in busy families. Their voice is subdued, like their nature; they do not push themselves forward and are predominantly peaceful and quiet, though they can be quite active and playful when it suits them. These cats can easily be taught to walk on a leash.

CARE AND MAINTENANCE

The care of a Ragdoll's coat does not normally give much trouble, as it is silky and does not tend to tangle. It is enough to groom the cat once a week although, at molting periods, a daily brush and comb session may be needed.

APPEARANCE

BODY

The Ragdoll is a large, elegant, muscular cat with a long body. It is one of the largest breeds of cat we know. The animals often mature late and do not reach their full weight until they are four years old. The chest is full and the neck short and powerful. The plainly more

Seal point Ragdoll, mitted male

COAT

The semi-long, silky coat lies close to the body. The hair is longer around the neck, breeches, and tail.

COLORS AND PATTERN—GENERAL

Ragdolls only come in the colorpoint pattern, as we know it in the Siamese. Blue eyes go with that pattern, and in this breed should preferably be as dark a blue as possible. Ragdolls occur in three different varieties—colorpoint, mitted, and bicolor. The colorpoints have the same markings as a Siamese (i.e., a light-colored body with a colored tail, legs, mask, and ears); the actual color of the cat is restricted to these bodily extremities. The mitted variety is a colorpoint with white paws and a white chin, the white on the chin running uninterrupted all the way along the underside of the body to the root of the tail. The bicolor is the most familiar and popular color for Ragdolls. Bicolors have a completely white belly, chest, legs, and paws, and a characteristic, reversed white "V" on their faces. In bicolor, white markings on the back are allowed. The different varieties are bred in various colors. The "classic" colors for the Ragdoll are seal point (black), blue point, chocolate point, and lilac point. Recently, other colors have also been developed, including tabby points, cream points, red points, tortie points,

heavily built hindquarters are set higher than the forequarters. The legs are medium-long with heavy bones, and the large paws are round in shape with tufts between the toes. The length of the bushy tail should be proportionate to the body.

HEAD

The head is wedge-shaped and medium-large. The cheeks are well-developed and the chin is firm. The medium-large ears are set reasonably far apart and have rounded tips. The nose displays a slight arch. The eyes are large and oval.

Blue point Ragdoll, mitted female

Lilac bicolor Ragdoll with mitted kitten

Blue point Ragdoll, mitted female

and smokes and silvers. These "new" colors have as yet only limited recognition and are still only bred on a restricted scale.

REMARKS

- Ragdoll kittens are always born white. Only later—usually after ten days at least—do the markings and colors gradually become visible.
- It is virtually impossible to predetermine the white markings, and this frequently results in kittens being born with faulty markings, such as cats that are halfway between a mitted and a colorpoint. Because of the high requirements set on their markings at shows, mitted and bicolor Ragdolls are not easy varieties to breed. Animals that satisfy the standard for markings—particularly bicolor—are often more expensive to acquire than animals that have minor shortcomings with regards to their beauty.

SNOWSHOE

ORIGIN

The Snowshoe was developed in the 1960s. Dorothy Hinds-Daugherty, a breeder of Siamese living in Philadelphia, had the idea of breeding Siamese with white paws. The breed was developed from Siamese and household cats with the white markings she wanted. When Hinds-Daugherty retired from breeding, Vikki Olander took over her work and started to develop the new breed. Under Olander's auspices the breed, named "Snowshoe" by Hinds, gained provisional recognition. She also drew up a breed standard. From the late 1970s onward, more breeders became interested in the Snowshoe, resulting in official recognition in 1982 that also meant the breed had championship status from that year—only, however, with the Canadian C.C.F. Recognition by the A.C.F.A. followed in 1990. Today the breed is still not recognized globally. It is bred mainly in Great Britain and the U.S., but it is probably only a question of time before fanciers in other countries also take the breed under their wings. By now the appearance of the Snowshoe is no longer comparable to that of the (modern)

Blue point Snowshoe, male

Toward the end of the nineteenth century, Siamese with white markings were often seen

Siamese—the animals have a much more compact build and head shape.

Blue point Snowshoe, female with kittens

TEMPERAMENT

Snowshoes are bred from Siamese cats and cats of the household type. Their temperament, therefore, is made up of an average of these extremes. Snowshoes are friendly, sociable cats that like company. They can get on very well with other cats, and the presence of dogs or children rarely produces any problems. They enjoy playing and continue to do so into advanced age. Because of their adaptability, they feel just as much at home in a busy family with young children as they do as the only pet in quiet surroundings. What they need most, however, is their owner's attention.

Four-month-old blue point Snowshoe

Blue point Snowshoe kitten

CARE AND MAINTENANCE

The Snowshoe's shorthaired coat needs little maintenance. It is enough to comb through the coat once a week and then to wipe it with a damp cloth to bring out the gloss. As with all colorpoints, it is normal, particularly in seal and blue points, for the body to show darker shades over the course of time.

APPEARANCE

BODY

Snowshoes have a rectangular and muscular body of a medium size. Their bone structure is medium-heavy. Their neck is medium-long. The length of the legs is proportionate to the body. The paws are also medium-large and have a compact, oval shape. The

Eight-month-old seal point Snow-shoe, female

tail is medium-long to long (at least as long as the body itself), broad at the base, and gradually tapering toward the tip.

HEAD

The head should be in proportion to the body, as broad as it is long, slightly rounded, and of medium size. The cheekbones are set high. The line of the nose is medium-long and proportionate in width to the rest of the head. The ears are medium-large, broad at the base, and have rounded tips. The large eyes are walnut-shaped.

COAT

The coat is of short to medium length.

COLORS AND PATTERNS

PATTERNS

The Snowshoe combines the Siamese factor, which ensures that the actual color of the cat can only develop at the extremities of the body, with white markings. In the most ideal case, the Snowshoe has a white muzzle in the shape of an inverted "V" with the point reaching to above the eyes. It is not easy to breed this pattern because neither the distribution of white nor its location can be predetermined. For that reason, deviations from the ideal picture are allowed, but only to a limited extent. In addition, the

Seal point Snowshoe, male with almost perfect pattern

Snowshoe should have white paws as symmetrically marked as possible. By preference, the white should extend to the ankle joint on the fore paws, and a little below the heel on the hind paws. This ideal, too, is difficult to achieve in practice. In any event, the white must be solid white, without any other color in the white parts.

COLORS

The most common colors are seal point (genetic black) and blue point (genetic blue). There are, however, also chocolate, red, cream, lilac, and tortie points, although these are not yet recognized by every organization. The eyes are bright blue. The point markings should all be the same shade. The mask should cover the whole face (except, of course, the white parts) and may run up in a narrow line to the ears. The body is always light-colored and has the same shade all over, except for the shoulders, back, and hips, which are a little darker, while the belly and chest are a little lighter in shade. White on the underside of the head, the belly, and the insides of the hind legs is not penalized.

REMARKS

- Because of the requirements set for the build of the body, the shape of the head, and the color and markings, etc., the Snowshoe is one of the most difficult breeds to achieve—in Snowshoe litters you might see kittens with no white markings or with far too much white.

Snowshoe kittens

- These days Snowshoes are mated almost only with Snowshoes, but the breed is still allowed to be crossed with Oriental Shorthairs, Siamese, and American Shorthairs, although there have been hardly any crosses with this last breed.

Snowshoe kittens

American Tonkinese

TONKINESE

ORIGIN

The first authenticated Tonkinese was "Wong Mau," a female who was in fact the founding matriarch of another breed, the Burmese. Wong Mau was found in Rangoon in 1930 and taken to the U.S. where she became the property of Dr. Joseph C. Thompson. He had her covered by a Siamese male, being convinced that Wong Mau's walnut-brown body and darker extremities (legs, muzzle, ears, and tail) were a slightly darker form of the Siamese factor. Her litter contained kittens of two different colors—Siamese—and kittens that were the same color as their mother, the color later known as Tonkinese. Wong Mau was covered again by one of her sons, which, like her, had the Tonkinese factor. The resulting litter contained kittens of three differ-

ent colors—Siamese, Tonkinese, and much darker kittens of the color we now call Burmese. At that time, selection was for that particular color, and this resulted in the emergence of the Burmese breed. From later breeding programs it was found that, when the darker colored animals (Burmese factor) were mated to each other, only kittens with the Burmese factor were born. The same applied (and still does) when animals with the Siamese factor are mated to each other. With Wong Mau's Tonkinese factor, however, a shade somewhere between the dark Burmese and the

Tonkinese kittens can have any of the three partial albinism factors: top, the Siamese factor; left, the Burmese factor; right, the Tonkinese factor (all in seal)

lighter Siamese, something odd happened—this factor did not seem to be inherited true. If two Tonkinese were mated to each other, then their offspring consisted of kittens that could have

European Tonkinese, champagne tabby mink

Tonkinese, Burmese, and Siamese factors, usually in the proportions 2:1:1. Despite this "handicap," some American breeders in the 1950s thought the Tonkinese factor looked too attractive not to establish it as a breed. The breed was recognized in Canada in 1965 by the C.C.A. (Canadian Cat Association). Not until the late 1970s did pedigree cat organizations in the United States recognize the breed. The English G.C.C.F. recognized it in 2003, but FIFé has not yet done so. Meanwhile, Tonkinese are being bred not only in the U.S., but also in Europe and other countries, albeit not on a large scale. There is a striking difference between the type bred in the U.S. and the rest of the world. In the U.S., the type is much stronger and rounder than the more Oriental, elegant type that is fashionable in Europe.

TEMPERAMENT

Like its color and build, the temperament of a Tonkinese lies somewhere between that of the Siamese and the Burmese. Tonkinese are very people-oriented (their own people) and they really enjoy being the center of attention. Because of their curiosity and intelligence, these cats can be taught a great deal, such as retrieving balls of paper and walking on a leash. These same capabilities mean that cats of this breed can teach themselves things, such as opening doors and lever taps. Tonkinese can in general get on with children, and their relations with

American Tonkinese kittens

American Tonkinese

other cats and dogs are also good. Tonkinese need a great deal of love and attention to feel happy and should not have to pass their days in a closed room or outdoor run, but always in the midst of the family. If it is the only cat in a family that is not at home much, a Tonkinese is in the wrong place. Tonkinese may not be as talkative as Siamese, but their voices are still regularly heard.

CARE AND MAINTENANCE

Looking after the coat of a Tonkinese is very little trouble. It is enough to groom it once a week with a soft bristle brush, followed by a wipe with a wash leather to bring out the shine.

Tonkinese kittens—left, champagne tabby mink; right, natural tabby mink

APPEARANCE

BODY

The body type of the Tonkinese is somewhere between that of the Siamese and the Burmese. The cat is medium-large and of medium length. It should feel surprisingly heavy when you pick it up. The body should be firm and muscular, with the head, body, legs, paws, and tail all in proportion, making a well-balanced whole. The chest should be slightly rounded, the flanks flat, and the back gradually

European Tonkinese, natural mink

muzzle of the European type conforming more to a triangular type of head. In both types, a slight pinch behind the whisker pads is a good point. The ears are medium-large, broad at the base, and have rounded tips. They are set rather at the corners of the head, neither too erect nor too much to the side. In the European type, the outermost outlines of the ears seen from the front follow the triangular shape of the face. The eyes are almond-shaped.

COAT

The coat is short, lies close to the body, and feels soft and silky.

sloping down from the shoulders to the rump. The legs are long and muscular and the paws a good oval shape. The tail is semi-long and tapers to a point. Tonkinese can be late developers; they are fully grown by about two years old.

HEAD

The head of a Tonkinese is slightly wedge-shaped, with round outlines. The American Tonkinese have a blunter, fuller muzzle, with the

European Tonkinese, natural mink

American Tonkinese

European Tonkinese,
natural mink

COLORS AND PATTERNS—GENERAL

Generally occurring colors are "natural" (seal or genetic black), blue, champagne (chocolate), and platinum (lilac). In addition, other colors are bred on a small scale, such as red, cream, cinnamon, fawn, and tortoiseshell, with and without a tabby pattern. Tonkinese are not only bred with the Tonkinese factor ("mink") with its aquamarine-colored eyes, unique in the cat world, but also with the Siamese factor ("pointed") with blue eyes, and the Burmese factor ("sepia") with yellow-green eyes. Because the three factors are inherited independently of other factors, such as color and tabby patterns, all kinds of combinations are possible in each.

American Tonkinese kittens

REMARKS

- Kittens are a light color at birth and begin to grow darker after a few days. This process is ongoing; the older a Tonkinese, the darker its coat becomes.
- Longhaired Tonkinese are also bred on a small scale, under the breed name Tibetan.
- Tonkinese-colored cats were recorded in southeast Asia well before 1930. They were called Tonkinese after the Bay of Tonkin, on the same latitude as Burma and Siam (now Thailand).
- There is still no agreement on the correct spelling of the breed name. Some organizations write "Tonkinese," while others spell it "Tonkanese."
- There are people who claim that Tonkinese are not true-bred because Tonkinese litters always contain all three partial albinism factors (Burmese, Siamese, and Tonkinese). It is true that the first generation of Tonkinese resulted from crossings between Burmese and Siamese, which together produced a homogenous litter of Tonkinese-colored kittens; as a breed, however, the Tonkinese has a completely unique type of its own, with a unique appearance quite independent of its coat color, and is therefore clearly a separate breed.

Mutation breeds

CORNISH REX

Blue point Cornish Rex, female

ORIGIN

EARLY ORIGIN

The gene that is responsible for the curly coat of the Cornish Rex was first spotted in the county of Cornwall in England. There in 1950 a kitten with a curly-haired coat was born to a farm-cat mother, owned by Nina Ennismore, and an unknown father. A striking feature was that the "mutant," a red male called "Kallibunker," had no guard hairs—his coat consisted purely of a soft, wavy undercoat. Kallibunker continued to live on the farm, but when he was about two years old, two cat fanciers, Brian Stirling-Webb and Dr. A. C. Jude, persuaded Ennismore to mate this tom to his mother, "Serena." They were very curious to know whether Kallibunker's unusual coat resulted from an inherited property. This indeed proved to be the case—two of the four kittens from this coupling had a curly coat. Others encouraged Mrs. Ennismore to go on breeding these curly-haired cats, with the aim of establishing the feature in a breed. She did so, but certainly in the early days had little support from the world of cat fancy and, to a large extent, was out on her own. It is almost impossible for a single individual to start up a breeding program. The high cost involved, the intensive care of the

Red and white, and red point Cornish Rex kittens

many cats, the high degree of inbreeding with constant vet fees and kittens dying young, eventually led Ennismore to give up breeding and have a number of cats, including Kallibunker, put to sleep. That was in 1956.

RECENT HISTORY

Some of Kallibunker's descendants, including a pregnant female, were imported into the United States in 1957 by Frances Blancheri, an American fancier from California. Later, more American breeders came along who saw a future for the breed, and more Cornish Rexes from the earlier breeding program were brought from England. To prevent problems of inbreeding, there was plenty of out-crossing in the U.S. Non-pedigree cats were involved in the program, but also British and American Shorthairs, Havana Browns, Siamese, Burmese, and Russian Blues. As a result, and by selection of rather slimmer cats, the Cornish Rex type in the U.S. eventually became somewhat slimmer and coarser in build. Later on, curly-haired cats of unknown provenance were also included in the program. In spite of the lack of enthusiasm experienced by Ennismore in its early days, the breed has also been preserved in Great Britain. After 1957, breeding continued there of Cornish Rexes which in type remained rather firmer in build than their cousins on the other side of the ocean. In the early 1970s, American-bred lines of Cornish Rex came back to Europe and there was a merger of the "European" and "American" types. The Cornish Rex had been officially recognized both in Britain and the United States by the late 1960s; today it is recognized by all coordinating organizations and the

Blue and white Cornish Rex kitten

breed can be found in virtually all cat-fancying countries. The stock of Cornish Rexes is now large enough to guarantee a healthy population of cats, but occasional outcross programs still take place with this breed.

TEMPERAMENT

Cornish Rexes are extrovered friendly, and affectionate cats. They need a great deal of attention to feel happy, and therefore are most unsuitable pets for people who are out of the house a great deal. They love being pet and stroked, and are very attached to their "own" people. In addition they are active, playful, and enjoy clowning. Cornish Rex owners could fill a large volume with the peculiar and comical tricks their pets get up to. These cats can usually also get on very well with children and dogs. If you visit them, they will certainly be interested—they are not shy. Cornish Rexes have a pronounced character of their own, are often self-

Black Cornish Rex, male

confident, and can be somewhat domineering. These character traits make the breed less suitable for living in a large group of cats. Jealousy can then soon raise its ugly head and the cat with the strongest character will win the battle. This is also one of the reasons why many Cornish Rex breeders have relatively few animals: they want each cat to feel happy at home. If you work away from home, however, you are advised to have two Rexes, so that they can "talk" to each other. These cats are more suitable for people who like company and who enjoy plenty of interaction with their cat. The familiar saying among breeders and fanciers: "If you want a hex, take a Rex," is not just an empty phrase.

Two Cornish Rex kittens, a few weeks old

CARE AND MAINTENANCE

The Cornish Rex needs relatively little coat care. Most of the time, simply stroking is enough

White Cornish Rex kitten

to keep the coat in good condition. As this breed has no guard coat, it obviously molts less than most other cats. Because of this property these cats are sometimes recommended for people

Blue point and white Cornish Rex kitten

who are allergic to cat hairs, but it is risky to accept this blindly; there are individual cats that do molt heavily, just as there are people who are allergic not only to cat's hairs, but also to the flakes that come off their skin. The coat can be brushed once a week with a soft brush. At molting times, any excess loose hairs can easily be wiped from the coat with a damp chamois leather. The advantage of dampening the coat is that it then curls better again. Because the Cornish Rex only has an undercoat, it can be some time before any damage to the coat grows out, so you are advised against brushing too vigorously and certainly a rubber brush should not be used. One thing owners of Cornish Rexes have to watch is the weight of their cats—Cornish Rexes are very greedy and can easily get too fat, particularly neutered ones.

APPEARANCE

BODY

Cornish Rexes are graceful cats of medium size and have a fine bone structure. They have good musculature. The legs are long and the paws oval. The long, thin tail runs to a point.

HEAD

The skull is longer than it is wide. The line of the nose has no stop and may be straight or slightly curved. Seen from the side, the chin and the nose should be in the same line. The large ears are set high on the head. They have a wide base and rounded tips. The eyes are oval.

Lilac Cornish Rex, male

Blue Cornish Rex, male

COAT

Because the breed has no guard hairs, the coat feels very soft. In an ideal case the curls (or, rather, waves) should together form an evenly waved, dense coat. The back of a Cornish Rex with a good coat typical of the breed is a little like an old-fashioned washboard. Whiskers and eyebrows are always curled.

COLORS AND PATTERNS—GENERAL

One of the attractions of the Cornish Rex is that the breed can be bred in all possible colors, patterns, and combinations, so that we see all the colors familiar to us in farm cats, such as black, white, red, cream, blue, and, of course, tortoiseshell, with or without tabby markings, a smoke or silver undercoat, and white. The amount of white can vary from a very small medallion to an almost completely white cat. In addition, we

Lilac-cream Cornish Rex, female

Blue point and white Cornish Rex kitten

also see chocolate and lilac Cornish Rexes. Finally, Siamese markings also occur in this breed. These are sometimes called "Si-Rex" and like all colorpoint cats they have blue eyes. On a small scale, Si-Rexes are also bred with white markings (Si-Rex bicolor).

REMARKS

- Although both American and European breeders started their programs with much the same breeding material—the Ennismore cats—the Americans selected a more refined, slimmer type for their Cornish Rexes than the European breeders. As a result of this selection, a number of differences have arisen between European-bred and American-bred animals over the course of time. The latter are more elegant in build, stand noticeably higher on their legs, and have a curved nose line— the "Roman" profile. The European Cornish Rex stands a little less high on its legs, has a straighter nose, slightly less rounded eyes, and a rather long head.
- Very occasionally, longhaired Cornish Rexes are born. They are not, of course, recognized, but as household pets they are in no way inferior to their shorthaired cousins.
- The coat of the Cornish Rex feels softer than that of the Devon Rex because the Cornish Rex lacks the tougher guard hairs.
- In contrast to what many people think, the Cornish Rex is not troubled by cold weather.
- A familiar problem with Cornish Rexes is that of baldness or partial baldness. It occurs in some bloodlines more than others. This localized baldness may be caused by hormone fluctuations. Cats with a bald back often develop a better coat after neutering.

Blue-cream and white young
Cornish Rex, female

Cream point Cornish Rex, young male

Seal point Devon Rex

DEVON REX

ORIGIN

EARLY ORIGIN

The history of the Devon Rex starts in 1960 in the English county of Devon. Beryl Cox lived there beside an abandoned tin mine. A stray tomcat with an unusual appearance—it had a curly coat—kept turning up at her home. Beryl tried to entice it in, but without success—it was afraid of people—although she was able to catch a tortoiseshell and white female that had returned to the wild and was obviously pregnant. This cat had her litter and one of the kittens, a male, turned out to have the same curly coat as the stray tom. Beryl kept this kitten herself and called it "Kirlee." It grew up into a cat that not only had an unusually structured coat, but also a very peculiar small head with large ears and eyes. A little later, Beryl read about a curly-haired cat that had been found in Cornwall. Various people were involved in creating a new breed of cats with a curly coat, with this cat as the founding

father. Beryl contacted some of the breeders of the new breed, which was called Rex, and they persuaded her to let them have her tom be included in this breeding program. Kirlee went to live in Derby, with Agnes and Susan Watts. To everyone's amazement, however, Kirlee and curly-haired females between them produced only smooth-haired kittens. This showed that Kirlee's curly coat was based on a different gene than the curly coats of the Cornish cats. Kirlee was then crossed with a number of his female descendants and with various other cats, including British Shorthairs. This eventually, after several generations, resulted in the birth of curly-haired kittens.

RECENT HISTORY

Because Kirlee looked quite different than the curly-haired cats from Cornwall, it was decided to set up two separate breeding programs. The cats from Cornwall were called Cornish Rex and Kirlee's descendants Devon Rex. The organization sponsoring both Rex breeds was the Colorpoint and A.O.V. (Any Other Variety) Club. This club laid down the breed standards for both breeds, and gradually more people showed interest in them and wanted to breed them. In 1964 the Rex Cat Club was founded, and the Colorpoint and A.O.V. Club made a slight change to its name, henceforth being known as the Color-

Devon Rex

Black tortoiseshell and white Devon Rex, female

Black tabby Devon Rex

Devon Rex kittens

point Rex-coated and A.O.V. Club. The clubs worked together and their various activities resulted in official G.C.C.F. recognition of both breeds in 1967. The Devon Rex found its way to other countries, including the United States, where the first Devon Rex arrived in 1968 and became the property of Marian and Anita White. In 1972 the breed was recognized by the A.C.F.A., and in 1979 the first Devon Rex breed club was set up in the U.S. Not until 1983 was the breed recognized by the C.F.A. By now, the Devon Rex has become a familiar sight at shows worldwide, but it has never been a popular breed with general appeal. It is mainly bred by really devoted fanciers for this reason. Very occasionally, new blood is still crossed into its bloodlines.

TEMPERAMENT

Although the appearance of the Devon Rex is in itself something worth seeing, to most of its supporters its temperament is the most attractive feature of this breed. They are cheerful, sociable, lovable, and active animals. They can get on very well with other cats, but their relationship with dogs and children is particularly good. They are not intrusive, but like to be involved in what is going on and will poke their noses into everything. Whatever you are doing at home, your Devon Rex sits and watches, or joins in. They love being stroked and cuddled,

Devon Rex females—left a seal point, right a tabby point

but are just as happy playing. Because of their people-oriented nature, openness, and high tolerance threshold, they can be taught all kinds of things, and they often can develop almost dog-like behavior. Many Devons can go for walks on a leash, retrieve objects, and sit when told to.

Lilac Devon Rex

CARE AND MAINTENANCE

The coat of a Devon Rex requires little care. A weekly grooming session, preferably with a bristle brush, is enough. Although the Rex breeds are sometimes recommended for people with an allergy to cats, this should be viewed with some caution. People who are allergic to cat hair can equally have an allergic reaction to a Devon Rex's curly-haired coat. A particular feature of this breed is its relatively high production of sebaceous matter, something we also see in the Sphinx. An excess of this deposit can lead to a greasy coat or a greasy-feeling coat, making a bath necessary. Their ears, too, generate more wax than most other breeds, so they should be inspected regularly and excess wax removed when necessary.

APPEARANCE

BODY

The Devon Rex has a robust, muscular, graceful, and medium-long body with a broad chest. The elegant legs are sturdy, fairly long, and have

Seal point Devon Rex

small oval paws. The tail is medium-long and runs gradually to a point. The neck is slim.

The head of a Devon Rex is heart-shaped

HEAD

The head type is a major characteristic of the breed; owners often describe it as a broad, heart-shaped face. The head is full and broad, and forms a short wedge, with the outline of the ears, cheekbones, and whisker pads clearly sloping. The line of the nose gives the impression of having a stop and the rounded forehead runs on into a flat skull. The short front of the muzzle is well-developed with obvious whisker pads; the whiskers are curly, as are the eyebrows. The chin is firm. The oval eyes are large, clear, and brightly colored, set wide apart with the outer corners pointing in the direction of the ears. These latter are large, set low, and wide at the base, ending in rounded tips and covered with fine hair. Tufts of hair on the ears and extra hairs at the backs of the ears are allowed.

COAT

The coat is densely planted. The hair is most dense on the sides, back and tail, legs, face and ears, and

The Devon Rex comes in all colors

As with Cornish Rexes, temporary and local baldness can affect the Devon Rex

rather less so on the top of the head, neck, chest, and belly. Bald patches are a fault. The texture is fine, soft, and full, and wavy or curly in structure.

COLORS AND PATTERNS—GENERAL

All colors, patterns, and combinations are allowed. We, therefore, meet Devon Rexes in all colors and combinations of colors, including Si-Rexes (Siamese markings), spotted animals, tabbies, solid whites, smokes, and silvers.

REMARKS

- The coat of the Devon Rex does not only differ genetically from the Cornish Rex. Devon Rexes have guard hairs, an undercoat, and downy hair, all of which are wavy. Cornish Rexes have no guard hairs,

so that their coat feels softer and looks less "untidy" than that of the Devon Rex.

- Its unusual appearance, odd-shaped head, and the setting of its eyes, have earned the Devon Rex the nickname "poodle cat."

Litter of Devon Rex kittens

GERMAN REX

"Munk," the male cat born in 1930 in Königsberg, East Prussia, Germany

ORIGIN

EARLY ORIGIN

In 1930, two blue male kittens were born in Königsberg (East Prussia, Germany) to a Russian Blue father and to a mother described as a "brown Angora." Both had a curly-haired coat. It is known that one of them, "Munk," ran free outside as an adult and was not neutered. In this way, he could have contributed to the dissemination of the gene causing curly hair. Munk lived to the age of fourteen. Much later, after the Second World War, curly-haired cats were again discovered in Berlin in the 1950s. It is not known whether these cats were descended from Munk. As many people from Königsberg and the surrounding country worked in Berlin during the war, this could be a possibility. The recorded history of the German Rex breed only begins in 1951, however. In that year, Dr. Scheuer-Karpin, a vet, found a black female with a curly-haired coat living on the grounds of

"Lämmchen" with the first litter of German Rex kittens

a hospital. When she examined the animal more closely, it proved to have only a soft wavy undercoat comparable to that of the Cornish Rex and no (coarser) top coat. When Dr. Scheuer-Karpin took the animal into her house, it was probably already four years old. The vet named her

Mrs. O'Shea (U.S.) with "Christopher Columbus," the first German Rex in the United States

foundling "Lämmchen," meaning "lambkin." Lämmchen was covered by an ordinary house-cat called "Bläcki." The kittens born from this union all had normal coats. Dr. Scheuer-Karpin then wanted to have Lämmchen covered by one of her sons, to see whether the curly-haired coat was caused by a recessive gene, but Lämmchen would only accept Bläcki as her partner, and only after Bläcki's death would she allow her son "Fridolin" to cover her. That was in 1957, when Lämmchen was at least ten years old. Four kittens were born of this mating—two with a normal coat, and two with a curly-haired one. From this it could be concluded that Lämmchen's curly-haired coat could be inherited and that it would be inherited recessive.

MORE RECENT DEVELOPMENT HISTORY

Dr. Scheuer-Karpin wanted very much to perpetuate this mutation in a new breed, but found little support in her own country. This was understandable, considering the spirit of the time. A few of Lämmchen's descendants ended up in England, where they were used to bring new blood into the Cornish Rex—the gene that caused curly hair in the German Rex appeared after all to be the same as that of the Cornish Rex. Yet in Germany, particularly in East Germany, a few people could still be found who wanted to keep the new breed in existence. In that period, domestic cats, as well as Persians and Devon Rexes were crossed into the German Rex to broaden its genetic base. That was in fact necessary because there was little other material available behind the Iron Curtain, then in power. Nevertheless, now and then new curly-haired cats were discovered and included in the breeding program. In 1970 a German Rex female, "Jeannette vom Grund," was shown at a major exhibition in Prague, Czechoslovakia. In 1973, some German Rexes were exported to West Germany and a few more people began to be interested in perpetuating the cat breed. Although the breed was recognized by FIFé in 1983, it is still today in the development stage. The first breed association for it was set up in Germany in 2002.

German Rex kitten with the Tonkinese factor

TEMPERAMENT

The breed has a friendly, well balanced, and pleasant temperament. The animals are playful and affectionate and are very adaptable, but they find it really difficult to be on their own. If you want a German Rex, therefore, you are advised to provide it with a feline playmate as well. In spite of this, they can be a little domineering in the company of other cats; you should therefore try to choose a compatible playmate for them. They have a soft and melodious voice.

CARE AND MAINTENANCE

Because the coat of the German Rex is the same as that of the Cornish Rex, care of it is also the same. The coat of a German Rex needs little maintenance. Regular stroking is usually enough to keep it in good condition. A German Rex is normally washed before being shown and, just before it appears before the judges, is wiped over with a damp cloth, so that its coat curls up nicely again.

Black tortoiseshell German Rex, three-months-old female

Black tortoiseshell and blue tabby German Rex
kittens, ten days old

APPEARANCE

BODY
The German Rex is a muscular cat, without being heavy or plump. The body is medium-long and in all respects rounder and stockier in build than the elegant Cornish Rex. The German Rex has relatively elegant legs of medium length, with oval paws. The tail is medium length, powerful at its root, and runs gradually out to a point.

HEAD
The German Rex has a round head with firm cheeks and chin. The line of the nose has a slight indentation. The round eyes are medium large. The ears are large and have rounded tips.

COAT
The coat is soft, has a silky structure, and can be curly or wavy. There are no tough guard hairs in this breed.

COLORS
The German Rex may be bred in all possible colors, patterns, or combinations of these.

Black and white German Rex kitten,
three days old

REMARKS

- Occasionally longhaired German Rexes are born, a logical consequence of crossing Persians into the German Rex stock. These are not recognized, however.

German Rex with the Siamese factor

BOHEMIAN REX

ORIGIN

The Bohemian Rex is still today a very rare breed that is only bred in a few countries in the former Eastern bloc and in Russia. The history of the Bohemian Rex starts with that of the German Rex. In 1947, in Berlin, the female curly-haired kitten called "Lämmchen" was born, which was to become one of the most important ancestors of the German Rex. Breeders wanted to establish Lämmchen's exceptional coat in a breed, but had to cross in other breeds to avoid running into problems of inbreeding. In postwar

Bohemian Rex kitten

Berlin the political situation made it virtually impossible to exchange pedigree cats with countries on the other side of the Iron Curtain. East-German breeders therefore had to make do with the cats they had, and used Persians, among others, in the development of the German Rex. Normally it is the case with such crossings that descendents of an existing breed and of one still to be developed are not used for breeding the existing breed but only to develop the new one. Apparently this did not happen in East Germany. The recessive inherited curly-hair gene of the German Rex crept into the Persian stock in the former Eastern bloc. So it could happen that in 1965 in the East-German Von Sonneck Cattery of Persians, "suddenly" curly-haired Persian kittens were born. Later, more curly-haired Persian kittens were born, including some in Liberec, Czechoslovakia, in 1981. A few breeders tried to establish these curly-haired Persians in a new breed, but this proved a difficult task. Because of the fact that this curly-haired mutation among Persians was not commonly known, and the difficulties in communicating with cat breeders in other countries, it was left to just a handful of breeders to set up this breed. Nevertheless, they remained faithful to their new breed, and so far it has survived. In 1991 a provisional breed standard was drawn up, and three years later the breed name was accepted—Bohemian Rex, named after Bohemia, the region around Prague, the capital of the Czech Republic. Bohemian Rexes are still bred on a small scale today, particularly in the Czech Republic.

Cream Bohemian Rex

TEMPERAMENT

The temperament of the Bohemian Rex is similar to that of the Persian Longhair.

CARE AND MAINTENANCE

Caring for the Bohemian Rex is comparable to caring for the Persian Longhair (see: Persian Longhair). However, because of its curly coat, grooming this breed must be done very carefully because the coat can quickly become tufty.

APPEARANCE

BODY

The Bohemian Rex is medium to large, with a short, strong neck. The animal is stocky, stands low on its legs, and has a broad chest, massive shoulders, and a broad back. It is well-muscled.

Bohemian Rex

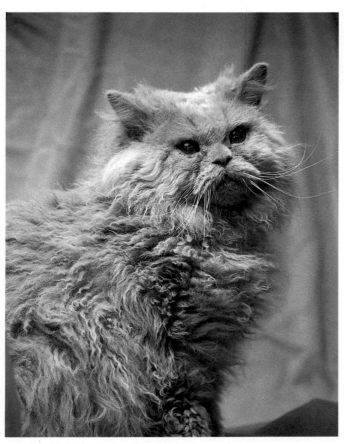

Bohemian Rex

The legs are short, thick, and strong. The large paws should preferably have tufts between the toes. The tail is fairly short in proportion to the body and has a slightly rounded tip.

HEAD

The head is round and massive and the skull broad. The forehead is round, with full cheeks. The nose is short and broad with a pronounced stop between the eyes. The stop (a dip in the line of the nose) should not be higher than the top eyelid nor lower than the bottom one. The chin is firm and the jaws broad and powerful. The large eyes are round in shape and set wide apart with a pleasant, open expression. The small ears are rounded, and set low in the skull.

COAT

The coat is medium to long, dense, with a prominent ruff and "breeches" covering the fore-legs. Except for the short hair on the face and ears, the hair is curly. The hairs on the chest, flanks, loins, and breeches are spiral shaped. On the shoulder blades, back, and tail the curls are less pronounced. The whiskers curl.

COLORS

The Bohemian Rex may be in any color recognized for the Persian Longhair; so far, breeders have concentrated mainly on red, cream, and bicolor.

REMARKS

- In April 1994, a Cornish Rex was experimentally crossed with a Bohemian Rex. The intention was to find out whether both breeds had the same curly-haired gene. Indeed, all the resulting kittens were curly-haired. This was proof that the curls of the Bohemian Rex are caused by the same gene (r) as the short curls of the Cornish Rex and therefore also the German Rex.
- Occasionally, a Persian with curly hair is born without provenance in countries outside the former Eastern bloc, as in The Netherlands in 2001. Most Persian breeders to whom this happens are not pleased, and sell the "rubbish" kitten as a pet. This is a pity because these curly-haired Persians could usefully contribute to building up the stock of Bohemian Rexes in the Czech Republic.

Bohemian Rexes have curly whiskers

AMERICAN WIREHAIR

ORIGIN

The progenitor of all American Wirehairs is found in Verona, New York. This red and white male, called "Council Rock Farmhouse Adam of Hi Fi," was born of two farm cats in a country barn in 1966. His brothers and sisters all had a normal hair structure, but Adam immediately attracted attention with his peculiar coat. Adam, with one of his litter sisters, went to live with a Mrs. O'Shea and the two animals were mated to each other. Two of the four resulting kittens proved to have the same wiry hair struc-

Black tortoiseshell and white American Wirehair, female

ture as Adam, and O'Shea started a breeding program to establish this mutation. To prevent excessive inbreeding, American shorthairs were regularly included in the breeding program. The C.F.A. cat organization began to register the animals in 1967, but it would be 1978 before the breed acquired championship status. American Wirehairs are on the whole only bred in the United States. Very few are encountered outside America.

TEMPERAMENT

The temperament of the American Wirehair is comparable to that of the American Shorthair. American Wirehairs, too, are friendly cats with a stable and easy temperament and they feel at home in the most diverse family situations. Their relations with other cats and pets are generally very good, and cats of this breed also get on well with children. They have a soft voice, which they do not use much.

CARE AND MAINTENANCE

The wiry coat of the American Wirehair is easy to care for. Apart from molting periods, a weekly brushing session is enough, after which the coat should be combed with a coarse comb. If an American Wirehair is shown, it makes sense to give the coat a wash at least a week before the show. This gives it the opportunity to recover.

APPEARANCE

BODY
The American Wirehair is a muscular cat, medium-sized to large, with a well-rounded body. The length of the sturdy, muscular legs is in proportion to the body. They have an average bone structure. American Wirehairs have strong, round paws, with firm paw pads. The length of the tail is in proportion to the body. The tail gets gradually thinner toward the end, and has a nicely rounded tip.

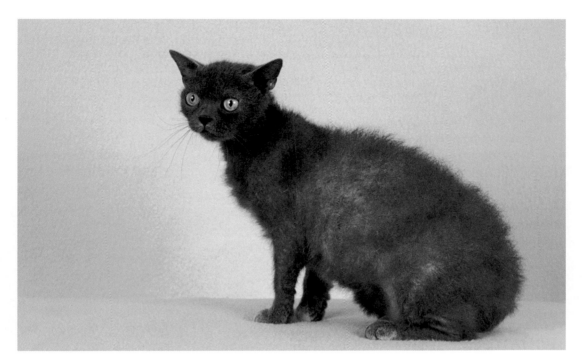

Blue American Wirehair

HEAD

The size of the head should be in proportion with the rest of the body and make a rather rounded impression. The cheekbones are prominent and the front of the muzzle and chin well developed. The American Wirehair has a slight pinch ("whisker break," or depression behind the whisker pads). The ears are medium large with slightly rounded tips. They are set wide apart. The large round eyes are set well apart. The line of the nose seen from one side has a slight curve, and should not have a stop.

COAT

The American Wirehair has a fuzzy coat with a coarse, hard structure, shorthaired, but not too much so. The hair on its belly is a little softer. Each separate hair can be spiral-shaped, or is bent back at the tip. The coat is resilient and should be full and dense, and is in no way comparable to the coats of most Rex cats that are much shorter and finer in structure and also feel softer. In no circumstances should the coat look too long, or be soft, so that it becomes wavy.

The American Wirehair's whiskers are curly and the same goes for the hairs in its ears.

COLORS

American Wirehairs are bred in the same colors as the American Shorthair. They should not be bred in colors that by their nature occur in the Far East, such as cinnamon, fawn, chocolate, lilac, ticked tabby, and partial albinism factors (Siamese, Tonkinese, and Burmese factors).

REMARKS

- The gene causing the wiry coat of the American Wirehair is inherited dominant.
- Its peculiar coat structure has given the cat the nickname "Punk of the Cat World."
- Mrs. O'Shea was not only the founder of the American Wirehair breed; she was also the first to breed the German Rex in the United States (see: German Rex).

SELKIRK REX

ORIGIN

The first Selkirk Rex was born in July 1987 in Sheridan, Montana, U.S. In a litter of house cats, there was a blue-cream and white female kitten with an unusual coat structure. In a roundabout way the animal reached a Persian breeder in Montana, Jeri Newman, who christened it "Miss DePesto of Noface." When it was fourteen months old, Jeri had the cat covered by her black Persian tom "Photo Finish of Deekay." Of the six kittens that were born of this union on 4th July 1988, there were three with the same curly coat as Miss DePesto—one black and white male, one black female, and one tortoiseshell female. This showed that the gene causing this coat structure was inherited dominant. Jeri Newman decided to build on this. She thought DePesto had a beautiful and unusual coat structure, but otherwise was not particularly good-looking. DePesto had a large heavy body on thin legs and a rather bad-tempered expression on her face. Jeri decided to establish the new curly-haired gene in a breed more like the round, friendly-looking British Shorthair. "NoFace Oscar Kowalski," the black and white male previously mentioned in DePesto's first litter, together with his mother, had a great deal of influence on the breed. DePesto herself had five litters, one by the Persian male, two by her son, "Oscar," one by a golden-shaded Persian and one by an unknown tom, after she managed to escape one day while in heat. The breed was later developed with the help of American Shorthairs, British Shorthairs, Persians, and Exotics. The first time that the Selkirk Rex was shown as a breed was in January 1990 at a C.F.A. show in Salt Lake City. In February 1992, the breed was accepted by the American C.F.A. Official recognition did not follow until May 1st 2000. Meanwhile, the Selkirk Rex has become a relatively popular breed that is still being developed. To expand the gene pool, use is still made of other breeds that approach the ideal type of the Selkirk Rex. Crossing in American Shorthairs is no longer allowed, but Persian Longhairs, Exotics, and British Shorthairs can still be used, although it is accepted that this is a temporary expedient. The intention is that by 2015, the breed will have such a wide genetic base and uniform type that no other breeds will need to be crossed in anymore. The breed is relatively popular in the U.S., but in Europe it is considerably less well-known among fanciers.

Colorpoint Selkirk Rexes

Selkirk Rex

TEMPERAMENT

If we look at the temperaments of the breeds from which the Selkirk has been developed, it will be plain why the Selkirk Rex, too, has a friendly, sociable, tolerant, and amiable disposition. The Selkirk Rex is affectionate, good-tempered, and loves the company of people. It can get on very well with children, as it can with other cats and with dogs. They enjoy playing and climbing, but are not overactive. If you accustom a kitten of this breed to an indoor life at an early age, there is a good chance that later in life it will no longer be interested in going outside. They often make their owners laugh with their sometimes rather rumpled appearance, funny, lovable glances, and their antics.

CARE

This breed has a soft-feeling coat consisting of untangled, loose curls. Selkirk Rex cats can have either longhaired or shorthaired coats, and neither variety needs much grooming. Unlike the Devon and Cornish Rexes, these cats molt in the same way as cats with a normal coat. In spring and early summer their coats will start to shed their hairs so that during this period you will need to give it some extra attention. Brushing will have to be kept to a minimum, because the coat can be damaged by too much brushing and pulling, and the curls will quickly get pulled out. If you show the cat, its coat will have to be washed. This is best done a few days before the show with a shampoo that should contain no "volumizing" ingredients. These in fact make the coat too heavy so that it does not fall loosely. After drying the cat with a towel, the coat can be given a good brush through. If you have used the right shampoo, then the curls—which are pulled out of shape by the brush—will spring back of their own accord in about half an hour. Finally, just before the cat appears before the judges, moisten the coat very lightly with a flower spray or special spray, after which the curls can be rubbed up by hand. Selkirk Rex owners claim that neutered cats, in general, have the best coats because they are not subject to hormones and hormone fluctuations.

APPEARANCE

BODY

The body of the Selkirk Rex makes a moderately compact impression, with a rectangular trunk. Cats of this breed are well-muscled and their bones relatively heavy. The legs are of medium length and have large round paws. The thick tail runs to a rounded tip.

HEAD

The Selkirk Rex has a round, broad skull of medium size and the line of the nose displays a stop. The ears are set far apart from each other, are medium sized, and should have rounded tips. The eyes of a Selkirk Rex are set far apart from each other. They are large and round.

COAT

There are shorthaired and longhaired Selkirk Rexes. The double coat of both short and longhaired Selkirk Rex cats feels nice and soft, fluffy, and springy. In fully-grown Selkirk Rexes, the coat on the tail and round the neck has more curls than on the rest of the body. On the back the coat is smoother. Very desirable are loose springy curls that do not get tangled with each other. The whiskers are always curly. This is also the most convenient way for breeders to distinguish between smooth and curly haired kittens in the first few days of their lives—from the whiskers, which in curly-haired kittens are not straight, but have kinks in them. Kittens are born with curls and usually lose them at about six months old. The curls come back when the animals are eight to ten months old. All in all, it might be two years before a Selkirk Rex develops its final coat. In young animals the emphasis at shows is on the build and the type, and less strictly on the coat. The structure and the quantity of curls vary and can change temporarily under the influence of hormones.

COLORS AND PATTERNS—GENERAL

Selkirk Rex cats may be and are bred in virtually all coat colors and patterns. Apart from the "natural" colors as we know them from ordinary non-pedigree farm cats, which include red, tortoiseshell, black, white, and blue, with or without white, silver, or smoke and tabby, we also meet Selkirk Rex cats with points and blue eyes like Siamese. With fully-grown animals, show judges pay more attention to the structure of their coat than to its color or the distribution of colors. All eye colors are allowed, but of course the preference goes to a color that is as expressive and deep as possible.

REMARKS

- Because the gene on which the Selkirk Rex's curly coat is based is inherited dominant, it is quite possible that from two Selkirk Rexes one or more normal-haired kittens will be born as well as curly-haired ones.
- The name Selkirk Rex was thought up by Jeri Newman—"Selkirk" was the surname of her stepfather and she named the breed in honor of her family. So the Selkirk Rex is not, as all the other Rex breeds are, named after the region from which the breed came.

Colorpoint Selkirk Rex

Red classic and white La Perm, male

Two La Perm kittens: black, and black tortoiseshell and white

LA PERM

ORIGIN

The history of La Perm starts in 1986 in Dallas, Oregon. There, Linda Koehl found a hairless female kitten in a litter of farm cats. The kitten grew up and at about the age of two months slowly but surely developed a curly coat. Linda kept the black tabby animal and called it "Curly"—it went on living on the farm and had a litter of kittens. Each year there were more curly-haired kittens to be found on Linda Koehl's farm, all descended from Curly. A breeding program was set up, in which apart from the curly-haired cats mainly house cats were involved, but also some pedigree cats, such as the Ocicat. In 1995, the cat organization T.I.C.A. admitted La Perm to the N.B.C. (New Breeder Color) class. In 1997 the L.P.S.A. (La Perm Society of America) was founded in the United States, with the object of promoting the breed and achieving official championship status. In subsequent years, La Perms were exported to many countries.

T.I.CA. granted the breed championship status in May 2003, by which time La Perm had already been recognized in several other countries. At present, the breed is bred in South Africa, The Netherlands, Germany, Russia, New Zealand, and Great Britain.

TEMPERAMENT

La Perms are friendly, active, and intelligent. They like attention and want to be involved in

Black tortoiseshell and white La Perm, female

everything. Their relations with other cats are good, as they are with dogs and children.

CARE AND MAINTENANCE

La Perms, both the shorthaired and the long-haired, need relatively little care in respect of their coat. The coat does not molt heavily, but like most other breeds becomes a little thinner, particularly in the spring. The coat is best left unbrushed. As with people whose hair has been permed, the curl tends to be pulled out by brushing. Owners of this breed use a revolving brush or very coarse comb to brush through the coat very carefully, little by little. In addition, cats of this breed are best washed every few months, dried lightly with a towel, and then left to dry in the air in a warm room without drafts. This will make the curls spring back beautifully again. A wash is also recommended before showing the cat, but do this at least several days before the show to give the coat the opportunity to recover.

APPEARANCE

BODY
The La Perm is a medium-large cat of a moderately Oriental type, which feels heavier than it looks. The legs are medium-large and in proportion to the body, with a medium-fine bone structure. The paws are rounded. The forelegs may be somewhat shorter than the hind legs. The neck is carried erect and has a medium length proportionate to the body. The tail is proportionate to the body in length and tapers gradually.

HEAD
The skull is slightly wedge-shaped with rounded outlines. The muzzle is somewhat broad, with a small pinch (a constriction behind the whisker pads). The muzzle is in proportion to the wedge shape. The chin is firm. Adult males may have heavy jowls. The medium to large ears are set so that they follow the lines of the wedge shape of the head. The eyes are medium large and expressive. When relaxed, they are almond shaped, but rounder when the cat is alert.

COAT

The La Perm has a medium-soft, loose-curling, and wavy coat which stands slightly away from the body. The breed can have either long or short hair. Both males and females can have a ruff—the more it curls the better they look—and the same goes for the density of the coat and its weight. With either length of hair, lynx tufts on the tips of the ears are very desirable.

La Perm

La Perm

COLORS AND PATTERNS

All colors, patterns, and combinations of them are recognized.

REMARKS

- Curly, the first La Perm kitten, was bald at birth, and this still sometimes happens in this breed. Sometimes fully grown La Perms temporarily lose their hair when they are on heat.
- Sometimes kittens without a curly coat are born to two La Perms. Very occasionally these kittens develop a curly coat later, but most of them stay smooth-haired.
- In this breed, the curly-hair mutation is inherited dominant.

La Perm

Sphinx mother and kitten

SPHINX

ORIGIN

EARLY HISTORY

The earliest known Sphinxes, at that time still called "Mexican Hairless," were two virtually bald cats living in Mexico around the year 1900. There are photographs of these cats, called "Dick" and "Nellie," in *The Book of the Cat*, published in 1903. There were, however, much earlier reports of hairless cats kept by the Aztecs. Although hard facts on this point are sparse, it is quite plausible as it is known that the Aztecs kept hairless dogs, the *Xoloitzcuintlis*. The genetic property that causes an almost hairless coat is not restricted, however, to any specific area or particular type of cat. The gene mutation that causes an almost hairless coat is in essence no different from the mutations that cause different colors or unusual hair structures. Gene mutations that influence appearance, so that the animal carrying the mutant gene differs totally in one or more points from its parents, occur in all

"Nellie" and "Dick," the first recorded hairless cats

animal species, e.g., white tigers, curly-haired dogs, short-legged breeds of chickens, albino mice, etc. Moreover, the gene causing hairlessness is not found only in cats. There are hairless dogs, mice, rats, and guinea pigs. Sparsely-haired cats turn up from time to time, throughout the world. In 1930, two hairless cats appeared at a show in Paris, the parents of which were ordinary farm cats. Over time, there have also been various reports of hairless cats in Morocco, the former Czechoslovakia, and Aus-

Sphinx kitten

tria. In 1987, a hairless cat was found in Russia and two new almost hairless breeds are based on it. Very rarely, hairless cats have also come to light in the United States.

RECENT ORIGINS

Many European Sphinxes are the descendants of two virtually hairless females, "Punkie" and "Paloma." These two cats were found roaming the streets of Ontario, Canada, in the 1970s. A cat lover took them home and contacted a breeder friend, who asked him to send the cats to The Netherlands where they were keen to find hairless cats. In The Netherlands, the cats went straight to Hugo Hernandez and Mrs. Hanny Natans, who wanted to breed back the Mexican Hairless Cat. With Punkie and Paloma they were able to make a start. They soon found support from other breeders. At first the base for breeding was, of course, very narrow. To prevent problems of inbreeding, non-hairless cats were also included in the program. For instance, in the early stages a number of

Devon Rexes were crossed in, because mostly hairless kittens were born in the first generation from them. Non-pedigree house cats approaching the ideal Sphinx type have also been crossed in, a practice that continues today. Many breeders prefer this last course. The road to their object, hairless kittens, is made rather longer by these crossings, but the much wider gene pool these cats contribute to the breed is seen as a major advantage. In addition to Punkie and Paloma, various other hairless kittens of unknown provenance have also been included in the breeding program. The breed was recognized in 1998 by the C.F.A. in America and later by several other coordinating cat organizations, so that it is to be found in virtually all countries where cats are shown and bred.

TEMPERAMENT

The temperament of the Sphinx is often described by cat fanciers as "part monkey, part dog, part cat, and part child." There is a core of truth in this, since the Sphinx is a very intelligent, affectionate, and playful cat that wants interaction with its owners. The animals are self-confident and self-assured. They are into everything. The average Sphinx will be very much at home even in a busy family. Apart from the fact that the animals like being with people and children, they also get on well with other cats. For a social animal such as a Sphinx, being alone is a real trial, and isolation can in some cases even make them ill. If you are interested in a Sphinx and work away from home, make sure that it has at least one other cat as playmate. The animals are generally extremely good-tempered and friendly. Aggression is alien to them. They do not need free

Sphinx

Sphinx kitten

Black tabby and white Sphinx male

access to the outside world to be happy, but you should then, of course, make sure that they have plenty of opportunity for amusement indoors, such as a good climbing pole and toys. They will make good use of these, since a Sphinx, when it is not sleeping, always wants to be doing something.

CARE AND MAINTENANCE

Anyone lazy by nature who thinks a Sphinx will need little maintenance is in for an unpleasant surprise. Sebaceous matter is produced on the skin of haired cats, forming a protective layer for the hairs, and Sphinxes produce no less of it. This greasy layer stays on

Sphinx cats have long, prehensile-looking toes

the skin, so that a Sphinx which is not washed enough soon gets "sticky" and starts to smell. The grease collects particularly in the ears, and also between the toes and round the claws. A weekly wash, preferably with a pH-neutral shampoo, keeps a Sphinx clean and fresh. Many breeders in fact successfully use lanoline infused baby wipes, intended for human use, to keep the area round the claws clean. Lotions or oils should never be used—the skin keeps supple naturally and such treatments block the pores. Well cared for Sphinxes seen at shows have almost all been "touched up." This means that the larger tufts of hair have been removed, and a Sphinx owner should also do that occasionally, because the hairs that from time to time grow locally do not improve its looks. Folds in the skin need no extra attention—they will not chafe because the skin is very flexible. Although the Sphinx is not a "maintenance-free" cat, it has the advantage that it leaves no hairs about the house or on clothes. In warm summers, sunburn can be a problem for Sphinxes with little pigment, or in places where there is little pigment. Make sure that your Sphinx can get into the shade or indoors.

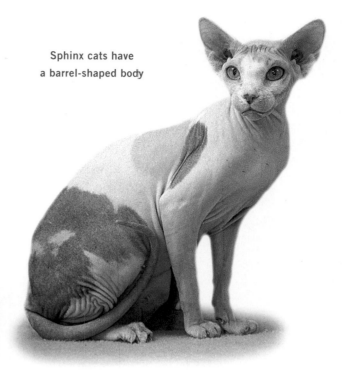

Sphinx cats have a barrel-shaped body

Blue Sphinx

APPEARANCE

BODY

The Sphinx is a muscular, medium-large cat with a broad chest and "barrel shaped" body. The length of the legs is in proportion to the body and the hind legs are slightly longer than the forelegs. The forelegs are set far apart and tend to be a little bowlegged. Sphinxes have medium-sized oval paws with long toes and thick paw pads. The tail tapers and is proportionate to the body in length.

HEAD

The medium-large head, which is rather longer than it is broad, has a moderate wedge shape with rounded outlines. The line of the nose has a moderate stop. The front of the muzzle should be strong and rounded, with a strong chin. The

The Sphinx's head is a moderate wedge-shape

Blue-cream Sphinx mother with kitten

their outer corners should point to the lower edge of the ears.

COAT

Although the Sphinx is not a completely hairless cat, preference is given at shows to those cats that look completely hairless. In kittens, the skin is very wrinkled and in adult animals wrinkles, especially on the head, are particularly valued. However, too much wrinkling is not desirable. Most Sphinxes have short curly whiskers, but the complete lack of whiskers does not count as a fault at shows.

COLORS

Because of the great diversity of their ancestors, Sphinxes come in all possible colors and combinations of these. The colors are, however, often a different shade than cats with hair. It is sometimes difficult for the amateur to determine what the color is. The color of the eyes goes with the color of the coat.

large ears are broad at the base. They should not be on top of the head, nor should they be set too low. The eyes are large and lemon-shaped, and

Sphinx cats

Sphinx kittens

Blue Sphinx

Sphinx cats

REMARKS ON "HAIRLESS" BREEDS

- Although the name suggests otherwise, such breeds are not completely hairless. These animals certainly have some hair, if only a little—usually soft, very short, downy hairs. Virtually all "hairless" cats also have longer hairs with a firmer structure at the base of the ears and on the tail, paws, and bridge of the nose. Many also have some hair on the back and flanks, although this is often seasonal. Really hairless kittens are sometimes seen, but over time and under the influence of hormones and so on they sometimes grow some hair (in places).

- It has occurred to breeders and fanciers that there are various kinds of hairlessness, and experimental crosses have shown that hairlessness, or partial hairlessness, can be caused by different genes that are inherited independently of each other. If, for example, two hairless cats are mated together, and their hairlessness is not founded on the same genetic basis, there is a high probability that only, or mainly, haired kittens will be born of the union.

- Various "myths" are created about hairless breeds, which are seldom based on hard fact. The alleged higher body temperature may be consigned to the realm of fancy—hairless cats have the same body temperature as other cats and only feel warmer because they have no coat. Neither are they choosy about their food, or liable to feel the cold, be sickly, or less fertile. Hairless cats are ordinary cats, the only difference being that they grow less hair.

- It is, of course, also sometimes thought that such cats cause no allergies. This, too, is false. For people who are allergic to cat hair, one of the hairless breeds may indeed be an option but, when the allergy is to skin flakes, they will cause an allergic reaction like any other cat.

DON SPHINX (DON HAIRLESS)

ORIGIN

In 1987, Jelena Kovaleva, a Russian, found an almost bald cat in the street in Rostov (Russia). Jelena kept this female, a blue tortoiseshell, which she called "Varya." As it grew up its coat became balder. Jelena concluded that the animal must be suffering from a fungal infection of the skin, and treated it with anti-fungal remedies. No matter what she tried, however, the balder it became. Finally it appeared that the cat simply had no coat—and never would have one—and that the cause should be sought elsewhere. Varya would become the ancestor of two different Russian breeds of hairless cats—the Peterbald and the Don Sphinx, also called the "Don Hairless." Varya roamed more or less at

Black and white Don Sphinx (harlequin markings)

Don Sphinx mother and her kittens

and Russian Blues were, and still are, included in this breeding program. In 1995 the breed was recognized by the W.C.F., with recognition by T.I.C.A. following two years later. Because breeders have based their selection on cats with as hairless a coat as possible, the kittens born nowadays of Don Sphinx bloodlines are more or less hairless at birth, with partially hairless cats hardly occurring any more.

will and had several litters by unknown fathers. In most of the litters, some of the kittens were hairless, or partly so, and became almost totally bald in later life. From this it followed that the gene that caused Varya's hairlessness was not the same as that of the Sphinx. In the Sphinx, baldness is inherited recessive, and if Varya's baldness was also based on a recessive gene, all Varya's kittens would have had to be haired, so Varya's baldness had to be inherited dominant. One of the kittens, called "Tschita," went to Irina Nemykina (Mythe Cattery) who started up a breeding program and thought up the breed name "Don Sphinx." Only ordinary house cats

Blue tabby Don Sphinx kitten

TEMPERAMENT

The Don Sphinx is an active, playful, and friendly cat that gets on excellently with other cats, dogs, and household pets. It enjoys company and likes to be near its owners.

CARE AND MAINTENANCE

The care of the skin in the absence of hair is similar to that of the Sphinx.

Litter of blue and white, and blue tabby and white, Don Sphinx kittens

APPEARANCE

BODY

The Don Sphinx is a medium-large, muscular cat with strong bones. The body is medium-long and the chest broad. The paws are oval in shape,

Blue and white Don Sphinx

Seal point Don Sphinx kitten

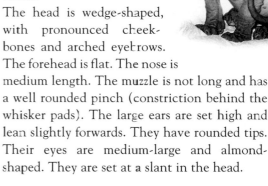

with long and agile toes. The long tail is strong and flexible.

HEAD

The head is wedge-shaped, with pronounced cheekbones and arched eyebrows. The forehead is flat. The nose is medium length. The muzzle is not long and has a well rounded pinch (constriction behind the whisker pads). The large ears are set high and lean slightly forwards. They have rounded tips. Their eyes are medium-large and almond-shaped. They are set at a slant in the head.

COAT/SKIN

The skin should be elastic and sit loosely. There is a demand for vertical wrinkling and horizontal lines in the skin on the forehead. Other good features are wrinkles in the neck, on the forelegs, and in the loins. There should be (sparse) hair only on the muzzle, ears, legs, and tail. In the winter the animal may be covered by a thin coat. A lightly haired tip of the tail is also allowed. Often kittens have some hair, but this coat disappears in the course of time. Usually these cats are virtually bald by the time they are two years old. The curly whiskers should be very short or broken.

Don Sphinx kitten, twelve days old

COLORS AND PATTERNS

All colors, patterns, and combinations of these are allowed.

Peterbald, male

PETERBALD

Peterbald

ORIGIN

The Peterbald is a very recent Russian breed of hairless cats that has been developed from the Don Sphinx. In 1993, after the breeding program for the Don Sphinx had been going for about ten years, a black-striped, elegantly built, Don Sphinx male, called "Afinguen Myth" and living in St. Petersburg, was mated to an Oriental-type, tortoiseshell female, "Radma Vom Jagerhof." The graceful kittens born from this combination were thought very beautiful in St. Petersburg, and gave the breeders the idea of developing a slim, elegant, hairless cat of Oriental type by making use of Don Sphinx, Siamese, and Oriental Shorthair Cats.

The existing Russian Don Sphinx was (and still is) developed mainly with the help of house cats, so that this breed is much coarser in type. The new, elegant type of hairless cat to be developed was called "Peterbald," a combination of the word "bald" and the place where the breed originated, St. Petersburg. Siamese and Oriental Shorthairs were, and still are, included in the breeding programs for Peterbalds, as is, on a smaller scale, the Russian Blue. In addition, slim, elegant Don Sphinx cats are included in the breeding program. The breed is mainly bred in and around St. Petersburg, but there are also some breeders in other countries, including Germany and the U.S., who are working on the breed.

Peterbald

TEMPERAMENT

This breed is known for its friendly, extrovert, and intelligent nature. It needs a great deal of attention from its owner if it is to feel happy. Peterbalds usually get on well with other cats, and also with dogs and other household pets.

CARE AND MAINTENANCE

Care and maintenance of these cats is the same as for the Sphinx.

Peterbald kitten

APPEARANCE

BODY

The body is robust, long, and muscular, yet gracefully built. The neck is slim and long and carried high. The legs are long with a strong, but fine, bone structure. The paws are oval-shaped. The tail is long and whip-like.

HEAD

The head is wedge-shaped with a flat forehead and the line of the nose is almost straight. The point of the muzzle is firm and there is no whisker break (pinch behind the whisker pads). The ears are pointed and large, broad at the base, and follow the lines of the wedge shape of the head. The eyes are oval in shape and medium-large. The chin is firm, but not exaggeratedly so.

COAT/SKIN

The skin is elastic, soft, and wrinkly. A light downy coat is allowed, as is rather longer hair on the ears, tail, paws, and muzzle, particularly in young animals less than two years old.

Peterbald kitten

COLORS AND PATTERNS

All colors and combinations are allowed, including Siamese markings. The color of the eyes is greenish-gold, except in "point" animals, which have blue eyes.

SCOTTISH FOLD & HIGHLAND FOLD

Cream and white Scottish Fold

ORIGIN

EARLY ORIGIN

In 1961, a Scottish shepherd called William Ross spotted in a neighbor's barn a white kitten that differed from its litter mates. The kitten had ears that folded forward instead of the normal erect ears. Some time later this cat, called "Susie," gave birth to a litter of which one, a white female kitten, was acquired by William and his wife Mary and called "Snooks." She had the same forward-folding ears as her mother. Snooks in turn had a litter in which there was a white male kitten with folding ears. It was named "Snowball" and was the first registered Scottish Fold. William and Mary Ross, with other interested parties and genetics experts, started a breeding program to establish the fold mutation in a breed. The G.C.C.F. in Britain recognized the breed quite quickly, and Scottish Folds were exported to other countries in Europe and particularly to the United States. The breeders came up against some unpleasant surprises, however. It seemed that a number of Scottish Folds had a thickening of the tail, and

Blue-cream and white Scottish Fold kitten

Black silver classic tabby Scottish Fold female

some of them had thickened legs, so that they had problems walking. As kittens, these cats were as healthy as any others, but from the age of about seven months these defects began to appear. Research showed that the gene responsible for changes to the cartilage of the ear in Scottish Folds also affected the cartilage in other parts of the body. It was discovered that these problems arose when two cats with folding ears were mated to each other. By only breeding from cats that showed no thickening or other irregularities in their tails, and consistently mating them with British Shorthairs, the

White Highland Fold, female

of Britain, but the largest coordinating cat organization in Britain, the G.C.C.F., has not yet reversed its earlier decision. The longhaired Scottish Fold, sometimes called the "Highland Fold," emerged rather later than its shorthaired ancestor. In the early days of Scottish Fold breeding, longhaired cats were also included in the breeding program. It was only a matter of

Black spotted Scottish Fold

breeders were able to overcome the problem. Nevertheless, in the early 1970s the G.C.C.F. decided to withdraw championship status from the breed. This meant that British breeders could no longer apply for pedigrees for their Scottish Folds, nor show their animals. At the time, the G.C.C.F. argued that the cats not only had bone problems, but also suffered from deafness. Since then it has become known that deafness in Scottish Folds has nothing to do with their cartilage, but with the fact that in the early days the breeding program used a large number of white cats—as is known, mating white cats to each other gives an increased risk of deafness, which is what had happened with the Scottish Folds.

RECENT DEVELOPMENT HISTORY

From the moment that the Scottish Fold was boycotted by the G.C.C.F. in Britain, it has been mainly American breeders who have been engaged in the further development of the breed. They, too, sometimes had to cope with cats displaying thickening of the tail or of the legs, and they, too, decided to stop breeding from such animals, and to keep the breed as healthy as possible by mating them consistently with American Shorthairs. In 1973, the Scottish Fold was officially recognized by the more progressive cat organizations in the United States, and the C.F.A. followed in 1978. In Europe, too, the breed was accepted by several organizations as a fully fledged breed. The breed was recognized in 1984 by the Cat Association

Black silver spotted Scottish Fold kitten

time before the first folded-ear cats with long hair were born. Particularly the Americans were very enthusiastic about the "Highland Fold" and the breed was recognized in the U.S. in 1987. Today we meet Scottish Folds in both short and longhaired versions in almost all countries where pedigree cats are kept, but because of the occasional occurrence of bone abnormalities the breed is regularly condemned.

The folded ears of the Scottish Fold give its head a particularly round look

Black silver tortoiseshell and white Highland Fold female

TEMPERAMENT

The temperament of the Scottish Fold and its longhaired peer is similar to that of the British Shorthair. They are predominantly quiet, well balanced, and sociable. They enjoy playing, but can also snooze for hours on a chair. Their adaptability makes cats of this breed feel at home in the most diverse situations.

Black silver classic tabby Scottish Fold, female

CARE AND MAINTENANCE

The coat of the shorthair can be kept in good condition with minimum attention. In molting periods loose, dead hair can easily be removed from the coat with a rubber massage glove. Outside the molting season the coat is better groomed with a bristle brush or (not too fine) comb, to prevent the undercoat from being damaged. Looking after a Highland Fold's coat demands rather more work. A good brush through with a wire brush once a week is necessary, with a particular focus on the

AMERICAN CURL

ORIGIN

EARLY HISTORY

The American Curl came about as a result of a natural mutation first discovered in June 1981 in Lakewood, in southern California. There Joe and Grace Ruga found two semi-longhaired, female kittens in their garden—one solid black and one black with white markings. The most noticeable feature of both was that their ears curled backward. Grace fed the kittens and they soon joined the young family. The black and white kitten got caught in the back door one day and ran away. The black one grew up with the Rugas and was given the name "Shulamith" (meaning "black but comely") from the *Song of Solomon*. In December of the same year, Shu-

American Curls

American Curl, shorthaired

lamith had her first litter by a neighboring tom. It was a litter of four kittens—black tabby, tabby point, black and white, and solid black. The kittens all had the same backward-curling ears as their mother. Grace gave the kittens away to friends. She and her husband did not at the time realize that the cats had a unique feature never observed before. Because they lived near a port to which ships came from all over the world, they thought that Shulamith might have come from somewhere abroad, where backward-turning ears were normal in the cat population. They searched through books on cats to find out whether there was any foreign breed with curled-up ears, but they could not find one. Neither could they find any information about "curly-eared" cats.

MORE RECENT HISTORY

Meanwhile, Shulamith from time to time had kittens that in their turn had litters with their new owners. The Rugas kept in contact with most of these, and exchanged their findings with them. Eventually the Rugas met a show judge who was able to convince them that curly ears were a unique feature in the cat world. In October 1983, Joe and Grace decided to show a number of their cats at a cat show in Palm Springs. Stimulated by the enthusiastic reactions at the show and with the help of, among others, a

American Curl kittens

breeder of Scottish Folds (a breed with forward-folding ears) it was decided to develop a new breed based on this ear shape mutation. A breed standard was drawn up and the new breed christened "American Curl." It was decided to allow crosses only with non-pedigree cats. This choice was not only made to prevent possible breed-related abnormalities being introduced into the new breed, but also to ensure as broad a genetic variation as possible. As the gene for curly ears was singly inherited dominant, crosses between a house cat and an American Curl produced kittens with curly ears in the first generation. Recognition of the American Curl came quickly. By 1987, the Curl had been granted championship status by T.I.C.A., and in 1993 this was followed with recognition by another, more conservative cat organization of American origin, the C.F.A. So far there has still been no suggestion of closing the

Black spotted American Curl

pedigree register. Crosses may still be made up to 2010, but only with non-pedigree cats, and subject to the condition that these non-pedigree cats approach as closely as possible the breed standard for build of body and type of head of the American Curl. The breed is after all still very young. In view of its American origin it is not surprising that a majority of its breeders—about a hundred of them—are in the United States, particularly in the breed's home state of California. Cats of this breed have also been exported to other countries, however, including Japan, South Africa, France, Germany, Belgium, and The Netherlands, and are now being bred in these countries on a small scale. Joe and Grace Ruga are still breeding and showing cats, under the cattery name "Curlnique."

TEMPERAMENT

The breed is in theory still in its infancy, and in the light of the enormous genetic variation in

Seal tabby point American Curl, male

its forebears it is as yet impossible to talk of a temperament associated with the breed. Most animals of the breed do have a people-oriented temperament, however. They are adaptable, friendly, and equable in mood. The average American Curl can get on well with children, dogs, and other cats. They are intelligent, playful, and inquisitive. They are moderately "talkative."

American Curls are sweet-tempered, inquisitive cats

CARE AND MAINTENANCE

Because the breed has virtually no undercoat, care of the coat is not too troublesome. It does not tend to tangle, and both short- and longhaired cats are easy to keep in good condition with a regular brushing session. Because of the typical bend in the ears, breeders recommend inspecting the auditory canal regularly for faults and cleaning it with a special ear cleaner for cats if necessary. An important point with this breed is that the ears should never be straightened; that is very painful for the cat, comparable to trying to straighten the curling hard cartilage edge of a human ear.

APPEARANCE

BODY

The American Curl is a well proportioned, normally muscular cat with a slim, rather than mas-

The typical "curled ears" do not require special care

Two white American Curls

American Curl, shorthaired

Longhaired American Curl

Seal tabby point American Curl, male

sive, build. Females weigh about five-and-a-half to eight pounds, and males eight to eleven pounds, but good proportions are thought more important than size. The length of the trunk is about half as long again as the height of the shoulders. The tail is wide at the root and tapers to the end. The legs are of medium length in proportion to the body. The bone structure is medium-heavy—not fine and not coarse. The paws are medium-sized and round in shape.

HEAD

The wedge-shaped head is in proportion to the body and rather longer than broad, with gentle transitions. The nose is medium in length and straight, but at the height of the lower edge of the eyes it runs up to the forehead. The muzzle is rounded, without an obvious pinch. The chin is firm and, seen from the side, lies in the same line as the upper lip and the nose mirror. The calculation of points shows the importance of the shape and location of the ears—the ears account for nearly thirty percent of the points a cat can be awarded at a show. The ears must never be angular, but always well rounded, and the curl should run in a fine, circular curve. The ears are medium-large and set at the corners of the head. They are wide and open at the base with rounded, flexible extremities. The fairly large eyes are walnut-shaped—oval at the top and round at the bottom, with an eye's width between them. They are set slightly slanting.

Tabby point and white American Curl kittens

Red spotted and white American Curl kitten

COAT

There are two varieties, the Longhair and the Shorthair American Curl. Longhairs have a fine, silky, and flat-lying semi-long coat with little or no undercoat and a full, bushy tail. Shorthairs have a soft, silky, close-lying shorthaired coat that should not feel fluffy; like the Longhairs, Shorthairs have very little or no undercoat.

COLORS AND PATTERNS—GENERAL

With the great variety of their ancestors, American Curls come in almost all colors. These vary from "farm-cat colors" such as black, red, blue, cream, and tortoiseshell, with or without a tabby pattern, silver undercoat, and any amount of white, or solid white, to Oriental colors and factors such as lilac, chocolate, and colorpoint. The breed is not really bred for color, so that many different colors and markings are possible in one and the same litter.

REMARKS

• It has meanwhile been discovered that the gene causing curly ears is singly dominant and variable in expression. To discover whether perhaps negative properties, too, are inherited with the gene causing curly ears, an experimental cross was made very early in the breeding program between a litter brother and litter sister from Shulamith's first litter. This cross resulted in healthy kittens, which should be a strong indication that no negative properties are associated with this mutation. Later crosses and research into abnormalities in, among others, the joints, tail, spine, and ears have, likewise, failed to surface any problems.

- The most important external feature of the American Curl is, without doubt, the shape of its ears. The ears can have several degrees of curl. A number of curly-eared cats have virtually uncurled ears, while others have ears with a degree of curl, and some have well curled ears. Kittens of this breed are born with normal ears, which begin to curl after ten days at the most. After that, the ears can become rather straight again, but they eventually reach their final shape by around the sixteenth week of their lives. In exceptional cases, an ear may in the end "uncurl" and stand straight up.

American Curl, longhaired

Black spotted American Curl kitten

MUNCHKIN

ORIGIN

EARLY HISTORY

In 1983 two shorthaired, female cats were found by Sandra Hochenedel, a music teacher, on the streets of Monroe, Louisiana. What was striking about both of them was that they had very short legs. Hochenedel kept the black kitten, which she called "Blackberry," and found a good home

Black ticked tabby Munchkin, shorthaired female

for the other. Blackberry had a litter by an unknown tom and bore four black kittens. Two of them also had short legs like their mother. Kay La France, a friend of Sandra Hochenedel, took several kittens home and gradually more were bred. Short-leggedness proved to be caused by a dominant inherited gene, which meant that Munchkins could never be born from two cats with normal legs, but only the other way round. It also meant only one of two parents need be a Munchkin for Munchkin kittens to be born. The kittens were always given away to friends. Eventually, a short-legged kitten turned up at a T.I.C.A. show in the "household pets" class. Dr. S. Pflueger, an all-round T.I.C.A. judge and member of the genetics committee, heard of it and wanted to know more. She wanted to study the short-legged animals on the assumption that they must be handicapped, because her earlier research into dwarfism in people had produced such a picture. The short-legged cats appeared to function like normal cats, however, and Pflueger soon wanted to establish this mutation in a breed.

RECENT DEVELOPMENTS

The breed name was thought up by Hochenedel, who called the animals "Munchkins" after the characters in the Wonderful Wizard of Oz. An application submitted by Pflueger for recognition by her cat organization was rejected. A number of interested people, however, including Hochenedel, La France, and Pflueger herself went on breeding these short-legged animals and entering them at shows. The animals were not only mated to each other, of course, but with many crosses to develop a wide pool of genes. It is known that, in addition to non-pedigree household cats, Abyssinians, Persians, and Ocicats were included in the breeding program. Eventually the breeders' efforts were rewarded and in 1995, Munchkins could be entered in the "New Breeds" class. A breed standard was also written, which among other things laid down that only crosses with non-pedigree cats were allowed, inspired by the fact

Munchkin

On a very small scale curly-haired (long and shorthaired) Munchkins are bred
under the breed name "Skookum"

that Munchkins had emerged naturally from household cats. These "dachshund cats" aroused great interest and even made the front page of the Wall Street Journal. Later it was found that there were more people in the United States who had short-legged house cats. The owners of these cats did not know that they were Munchkins until they saw the sudden publicity surrounding them. Very soon after they were first shown, Munchkin cats were exported to other countries. France was the first, but Munchkins were by now being admired in many other countries where pedigree cats are bred and shown. The Munchkin was given championship status by T.I.C.A. on May 1st 2002.

TEMPERAMENT

Munchkins are lively and playful cats that, apart from their short legs, are no different from any other "normal legged" one. They can climb, jump, and play, with their shorter legs in no way seeming to hinder them—even in heavily pregnant females the belly does not drag along the ground, as is sometimes thought. Munchkins are sociable pets that can get on very well with

Black tortoiseshell tabby and white
Munchkin kitten, longhaired

Ticked tabby Munchkin

other cats and mix happily with dogs. They are also very affectionate and like to be part of the family.

CARE AND MAINTENANCE

Neither the shorthaired nor the longhaired Munchkin needs much coat care. It is enough to groom the coat once a week with a bristle brush. The longhaired coat hardly ever tangles, but it is a good idea to comb it through with a coarse comb after it has been brushed.

APPEARANCE

BODY

The Munchkin is a medium-large cat with a broad, round chest, and a medium-thick tail that tapers slightly toward the end into a rounded tip. The muscular, straight legs are short, and the hind legs are longer than the forelegs. "Cow-heeled" Munchkins and cats with too cobby or too long a body are not appreciated at shows. Munchkins with paws turned inward or outward, an obvious dip behind the shoulders, or bowlegs win no prizes.

HEAD

The Munchkin has a medium-large, rather wedge-shaped head with large ears carried erect. The large, expressive eyes are walnut-shaped and set on a slight slant.

COAT

There are both long and shorthaired Munchkins. The Shorthair's coat should be

Black tortoiseshell tabby and white longhaired Munchkin female with Tonkinese factor

medium length with a moderately dense undercoat. The Longhair should feel silky and have an undercoat like the Shorthair, together with a ruff and bushy tail.

COLORS AND PATTERNS

The Munchkin is recognized in all coat colors and patterns. All eye colors are also recognized.

REMARKS

- Although Blackberry is regarded as the matriarch of the Munchkin breed, she is neither the only short-legged cat to be recorded, nor the first. In 1944 in a scientific monthly, Dr. H. E. Williams-Jones described four generations of short-legged cats that "progressed like ferrets." Twelve years later, the German Max Egon Thiel of Hamburg described a similar, stray cat that he had met playing with its normal-legged cousins in Stalingrad (now Volgograd), Russia. He called the animal a "Stalingrad Kangaroo cat" because it kept sitting up on its hind legs to look round, just like a kangaroo. Nobody knows what happened to these animals. Still later there were reports (and more keep coming) of short-legged cats in the United States and also in the Philippines, the Netherlands, and Belgium.
- At present, crosses are only allowed with ordinary domesticated short and longhaired house cats of no specific breed.
- The gene that causes short legs in this breed only works on the legs and toes, and does not affect other bones in the body. Recent radiological research on both young and older animals has revealed no abnormalities or other problems.
- Munchkin litters hardly ever consist one hundred percent of short-legged cats, but usu-

Munchkins with legs of a normal length are called "standards"

ally also contain kittens with legs of a normal length. These are called Munchkin non-standards and look like ordinary household cats. They are not shown, but if their type is good they might be used in the breeding program.
- The average Munchkin litter is three to four kittens. Because there do not appear to be any homozygous Munchkins (i.e., Munchkins that, when they are mated to a cat with normal length legs, only produce short-legged kittens) there is an indication that a homozygous Munchkin in the womb is not viable. This phenomenon, called a lethal factor, occurs in many other animals, such as the Rumpy White Mouse (where the lethal factor is associated with the white markings on the rump).

AMERICAN BOBTAIL

ORIGIN

The American Bobtail is an American breed rarely encountered outside its country of origin. The breed arose as a result of a spontaneous, natural mutation. For a long time, there had been reports of coarsely built, shorthaired cats living in semi-wild conditions in the United States. The first breeders of the American Bobtail were John and Brenda Sanders. In the late 1960s they were on vacation in a Native American reservation in Arizona. They found a black tabby kitten with a short tail and took it home with them. John and Brenda called the animal "Yodi" and

Black classic tabby young American Bobtail, longhaired

he became the ancestor of the American Bobtail breed. John and Brenda already had a female, colorpoint, non-pedigree household cat, "Mishi." When Yodi was old enough he covered Mishi and, in the resultant litter, all the kittens had their father's short tail. Two cat fanciers, Mindy Shultz and Charlotte Bentley, saw the kittens and wanted to establish the mutation in a breed. They took some of Mishi's and Yodi's kittens with them and in the course of time mated them both to each other and to other longhaired housecats. Other short-tailed cats, found all over America, were included in the breeding program. In the late 1970s the breed standard of the American Bobtail was written. Some ten years later, in 1989, the breed gained provisional recognition. By now it is recognized by almost all cat organizations in the United States, though the C.F.A. did not recognize the American Bobtail until 2001. The breed is reasonably well-known and popular in the U.S., but still rarely seen elsewhere.

TEMPERAMENT

American Bobtails are known for their well balanced, good tempered nature. They are friendly and sociable. They can get on very well with other cats as well as dogs and children. Because of their great adaptability, they will fit into the

American Bobtail, male

most divergent kinds of households. Many of them can at first be rather reserved when meeting people they do not know. Their short tail in no way hinders them in their freedom of movement, and cats of this breed are excellent climbers and hunters.

CARE AND MAINTENANCE

Caring for the coat of both shorthaired and longhaired American Bobtails is no trouble. A weekly grooming session is enough for both varieties of coat. American Bobtails sometimes have a tendency to get too fat, so it is important to ensure that they have enough exercise and not too many calories in their food.

APPEARANCE

BODY
The muscular and athletically built body gives a rectangular impression. The chest is broad and full. The hips are slightly higher than the shoulder blades and, seen from above, should look as broad as the shoulders. The legs are proportionate to the body and have sturdy bones with large round paws. The tail is an important feature of the breed. It is short and should reach no further than the heel, but should not be so short that it is hardly visible when the cat is alert (and holds its tail up). The tail can be straight, slightly bent, have a kink in it, or be thicker in parts, but must in any event be firm and flexible. The neck is of medium length but looks shorter because of its heavy musculature.

HEAD
The head is the shape of a broad wedge. The front muzzle is medium-long with fleshy whisker pads. Particularly in shorthairs the well-developed eyebrows are striking. The nose leather is large and the chin is strong. Seen from the side, the chin is in one line with the nose. The ears are medium-large with rounded tips. The large eyes are almost almond-shaped and deep-set. The outermost corners of the eyes point in the direction of the ears.

COAT
The breed is bred both with long hair and short hair. The American Bobtail has a double coat. The guard coat is hard in structure and water repellent. In colorpoints, silvers/smokes, and

Black spotted American Bobtail

American Bobtail

REMARKS

- The breed develops slowly—it may be two to three years before a cat is fully grown.
- The gene that causes the short tail of the American Bobtail is inherited dominant.
- Although no two tails are the same in this breed, it very rarely occurs that kittens are born either with a long tail or with almost no tail. In most American Bobtails the tail is about four inches long.

cats with dilute colors, the coat may be softer. The undercoat is beautifully dense. Lynx tufts and long hairs growing out of the ears are highly desirable, as are tufts between the toes in long-hairs.

COLORS AND PATTERNS—GENERAL

In this breed all colors and patterns are allowed. In tabbies a beautiful warm ground color gets high marks, and in tabby points (tabbies with the Siamese factor) clear tabby markings on the body are appreciated. All eye colors are allowed, apart from two differently colored eyes (odd eyes).

Black spotted American Bobtail, shorthaired

Glossary

A

Agouti gene: the tabby pattern inherited genetically by every cat becomes visible under the influence of the dominant inherited agouti gene (A).

American Lynx: in the 1980s, the American Joe Childers wanted to create a breed of cat with a short, stump tail, resembling the American Bobtail and Pixie-Bob. Very few breeders are involved in developing this breed and recognition has so far been withheld, so that there are doubts about the future development of this project.

Auburn: color term used particularly for the Turkish Van, synonymous with "chestnut."

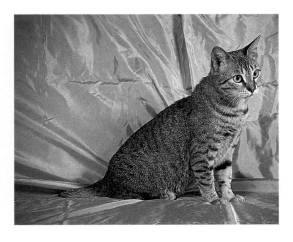

B

BAER-test: Brainstem Auditory Evoked Response test that enables a specialist veterinarian to diagnose lateral or bilateral deafness in animals.

Bicolor: literally, "two colors." Term used for cats of a single color and white. The term is also used for tabbies with white. The standard requirements for bicolor vary across the world, but mostly apply to cats with clear, white markings amounting to approximately one-third of the total surface.

Blotched tabby: term used in the U.K. for a "classic tabby," sometimes also called "marbled."

Blue: diluted version of black, which occurs if the recessive gene for dilution (d) is duplicated.

Blue-cream: diluted version of a black tortoiseshell. Also known as a "blue tortoiseshell" or "blue tortie."

Bronze: term for the color of the Egyptian Mau and synonym for black spotted.

Brown tabby: incorrect, but still frequently used term for a black tabby.

Burmese factor: one of the group of partial albino factors. The genetic code for this factor is cb.

C

Calico: U.S. term for a tortoiseshell and white cat

Californian Spangled: Spotted, shorthaired cat—so far not recognized as a breed—created by Paul Casey of the U.S.

Cameo: tabby cats with red or cream-colored coat tipping (phaeomelanin pigment). Under the influence of the Inhibitor gene, the hair shaft has been left without pigment about two-thirds upward from the root.

Ceylon: Originally a natural breed that from ancient times has existed in Sri Lanka and has now been recognized by several coordinating organizations. Resembles the Singapura and Abyssinian. Only appears as a ticked tabby in the following colors: black ticked, red ticked, blue ticked, cream ticked, tortoiseshell ticked, and blue-cream ticked. Now being bred on a modest scale.

Champagne: U.S. term for chocolate, used, among others, for the Burmese and Tonkinese.

Chimera: if two clusters of cells fuse at a very early embryonic stage, so that one instead of two kittens are born from these clusters, this phenomenon is called "chimera." A male cat from such a fusion can be a tortoiseshell and is normally fertile.

Chocolate: chocolate brown color, known as "Havana" in some breeds—a mutation of the black coat color in which the granules of black pigment have a different shape. The dilution of chocolate is lilac.

Chocolate tortoiseshell: a blended pattern of chocolate-colored and red hairs, also known as "chocolate tortie."

Cinnamon: a cinnamon-colored mutation of black. The dilution of cinnamon is fawn.

Classic: U.S. term for a marbled or blotched pattern.

Classic colors: term used for seal point, chocolate point, blue point and lilac point Siamese. Also another name for classic tabby.

Cobby: stocky, compact body shape, such as that of the British Shorthair.

Colorpoint: recessive mutation of complete coloring (C). Also known as the Siamese pattern—it is one of the partial albino factors. Colorpoint cats have blue eyes, a very light-colored body, and darker colored mask, ears, tail, legs, and, in males, scrotum.

Congenital disorder: a disorder or defect arising before birth. It can be an inherited condition, but not necessarily so.

Coupari: term sometimes used for a longhaired Scottish Fold.

Cream: diluted form of red, which occurs when the recessive gene for dilution (d) is duplicated.

Cross-breeding: mating two animals of different breeds.

Cypress: sometimes used as a popular name for a (black) striped cat.

D

Dilute: diluted (paler) version of a color.

Dilute calico: term for blue-cream and white.

Dilution: influenced by the presence of two genes for dilution (d), the pigment granules cluster together on the hair, causing the coat to fade optically. Black becomes blue, chocolate becomes lilac, cinnamon becomes fawn, and red becomes cream. The gene is inherited recessive.

Dominant gene: this gene will always show in the phenotype if it is present in the cat, even if the cat only has a single one.

Dutch Rex: former curly-haired Dutch breed of cat, no longer extant.

E

Ebony: little used synonym for black, mainly used for Oriental Shorthair and Longhair cats.

Eumelanins: pigment granules that cause a black coat color and all colors derived from it (blue, chocolate, lilac, cinnamon, and fawn). See also: phaeomelanins.

Extremities: a collective term for the parts of the body colored in colorpoints—the legs, muzzle, tail, and ears, and the scrotum in male cats.

F

Fawn: dilution of cinnamon that occurs if the recessive gene for dilution (d) is duplicated.

Fawn-cream: dilution of cinnamon tortoiseshell occurring if the recessive gene for dilution (d) is duplicated. A mixed pattern of cream and fawn-colored hairs is also sometimes called "fawn tortoiseshell."

Flame point: little used synonym for "red point."

G

Gene: carries information on inherited properties.

Genetics: the study of heredity.

Genotype: the genetic package of the cat. May differ from the phenotype (appearance).

Ghost marking: vague tabby markings in non-

agouti (solid color) cats, seen most clearly in kittens. These ghost markings usually disappear when the kittens get older. As every cat has a tabby pattern, but only shows it when the agouti gene is present, the ghost marking is a useful aid to determining what tabby pattern is carried by the animal and therefore can be passed on by it when it has an agouti partner. In cats with a phaeomelanin pigment (red and cream-colored cats) this ghost marking is almost always visible throughout their lives.

Golden: term for green-eyed tabbies that do not have a silver undercoat.

H

Harlequin: coat pattern in which only the top of the head, the tail, and about three patches on the body are colored.

Havana: another name for chocolate color, particularly in use for Oriental Longhairs and Shorthairs.

Honey Bear: Non-colorpoint Ragdoll created by Ann Baker (U.S.)

I

Inbreeding: term used for mating closely related animals, such as brother x sister or mother x son.

Inherited disorder: a disorder or abnormality that is inherited genetically.

Inhibitor gene: dominant inherited gene (I) that inhibits the pigmentation of part of the hair from the root upward, so that a silver-white undercoat comes into being. Tabby cats with the inhibitor gene are called "silvers," and "solid" or "self" cats are called "smokes."

Heterozygous: term used for a cat with two different genes for a specific property, so that this property is not purebred. In this case, the phenotype (appearance) of the cat is not the same as its genotype (genetic make-up).

Himalayan: U.S. term for colorpoint Persian Longhairs.

Himalayan pattern: another term for colorpoint.

Homozygous: Purebred. This term is used when both genes for a specific property are the same.

J

Jowls: prominent, rounded cheeks of mature, entire male cats, which develop under the influence of hormones and gradually disappear after neutering.

K

Kink in the tail: polygenetically inherited malformation of the tail bones.

L

Lavender: sometimes used as a synonym for lilac.

Lilac: dilution of chocolate resulting from the presence of two recessive genes for dilution (d).

Lilac-cream: also known as "lilac tortoiseshell" or "lilac tortie." Dilution of chocolate tortie.

Lynx point: another name for tabby point.

M

Mackerel tabby: another term for striped tabby.
Mandalay: Australian equivalent of the Asian.
Mandarin: another name for the Oriental Longhair.
Marbled: another term for classic or blotched.
Melanocyte: cells that are responsible for pigmentation.
Mink: synonym for Tonkinese factor.
Mutation: spontaneous changes in inherited material. Often used for noticeable, visible changes such as ear folds or hairlessness, but covers all possible genetic changes that occur spontaneously.

N

Natural color: term for colors that traditionally occur in non-pedigree farm cats in Europe—

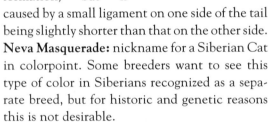

red, cream, black, blue, tortoiseshell, and blue tortoiseshell with or without blotched, spotted, or striped tabby patterns and any amount of white in their coats. Solid white also belongs to this group of natural colors, including a smoke or silver undercoat.

Nervous kink: term used if the tip of the tail forms a kink when the cat becomes excited. This is not a malformation, but is caused by a small ligament on one side of the tail being slightly shorter than that on the other side.

Neva Masquerade: nickname for a Siberian Cat in colorpoint. Some breeders want to see this type of color in Siberians recognized as a separate breed, but for historic and genetic reasons this is not desirable.

Non-agouti colors: also known as "solid" (U.S.) or "self" (U.K.) black, blue, and chocolate. The inability to express the underlying tabby pattern. The non-agouti gene is recessive (a).

Non-natural colors: colors and markings that have been introduced more recently into farm cats in Europe, such as the partial albino factors (Siamese, Burmese, and Tonkinese factors);

chocolate, lilac, cinnamon, and fawn; and also the ticked tabby pattern.

O

Odd-eyed: two differently colored eyes, with one eye being blue. Cats with odd eyes are usually either solid white or have a substantial amount of white in their coat.

Ojos Azules: Spanish for "blue eyes" and a name for a now rarely encountered group of cats that combines blue eyes with little or no white. Attempts in the 1980s to establish this property in a new breed failed. Normally blue eyes only occur in colorpoints, solid white cats, and cats with a large amount of white in their coats.

Oriental body structure: term for fine-boned, lithe, and elegant cats.

Out-cross: term used for mating two cats that are entirely or virtually unrelated.

P

Partial albino factors: group of recessive mutations of complete coloring (C). This covers the Siamese factor (cscs), the Burmese factor (cbcb), and the Tonkinese factor (cbcs).

Particolor: term for the group of cats with white markings. It covers bicolors, tricolors, vans, and harlequins.

Patched tabby: another name for a tortie tabby.

Phaeomelanin: granules of pigment that cause a red (or its dilution, cream) coat color.

Phenotype: external appearance—that which can be seen.

Piebald spotting: unpigmented parts of the coat (white patches) caused by the dominant S-gene.

Pinch: tuck behind the whisker pads.

Platinum: U.S. term for the lilac coat color, particularly used for Burmese and Tonkinese.

Points: The darker-colored extremities in colorpoints—tail, legs, ears, muzzle, and (in males) scrotum.

Polygenetic inheritance: term denoting that

the inheritance is not based on a single gene, but on more factors.

Poodle cat: nickname for the Devon Rex. Also for a German breed of cat that has both folded ears (Fd-gene) and a curly-haired coat, and is becoming fairly rare.

R

Ragamuffin: a breed that derives from the Ragdoll and is being bred on a small scale in the United States. All colors are permissible.

Recessive gene: genes that can only be revealed phenotypically if there are two of them, such as

the gene for dilution (d) and blotched or classic tabbies (mc). A recessive property can be "handed down" for generations, without showing itself. A cat displaying a recessive property always inherits this from both parents.

Ruddy: term for the natural wild color (black ticked tabby) in Abyssinians and Somalis.

S

Seal: another name for black, used for colorpoints.

Self: term used in Britain for an evenly-colored cat.

Seychelles: term used for a Siamese or Balinese with white patches.

Shaded: term used for tabbies in which the tabby pattern has faded to a shadow. The stronger form of "tipped."

Shell: term for red and cream-colored (phaeomelanin pigment) tabby cats whose coat has been left unpigmented for approximately seven-eighths of each hair, from the root upward, under the influence of the Inhibitor gene. As only the tips of the hair shafts are colored, the cat presents as virtually white.

Siamese factor: one of the group of partial albino factors. Recessive factor (cs) that passes on the colorpoint pattern and

accompanying blue eye color, provided the factor is duplicated. The cat's basic color only shows itself in its extremities.

Smoke: non-agouti (and therefore solid-colored) cat with a silver-white undercoat, caused by the Inhibitor gene. Usually the coat is left unpigmented about halfway up from the root of each hair, but the extent of the loss of color is inherited polygenetically and can manifest itself in different ways.

Sorrel: alternative term for cinnamon in Abyssinians and Somalis.

Spotted tabby: the dominant gene causing spots in a tabby (Sp) breaks up the underlying marbled or striped tabby pattern into spots. Ocicats are, for instance, classic or blotched cats with the Sp-gene. Spotted tabbies can, however, also occur without the Sp-gene by repeated selection of striped tabbies with an interrupted stripe pattern.

Stop: Abrupt interruption in the line of the nose, so that it does not run smoothly.

Stud tail: sticky, brown secretion around the root of the tail of an unneutered male cat, caused by an overproduction of the scent gland.

T

Tabby: coat pattern which is expressed by the presence of the dominant inherited agouti gene (A). This gene is inherited independent of color—the tabby pattern shows the actual color of the cat.

Thai blue point: term for a Korat with Siamese markings.

Ticked tabby: one of the four tabby patterns occurring among cats. Known as the "Abyssinian tabby" pattern, being typical of the Abyssinian, but also seen in several other breeds. Originally from the Middle and Far East and inherited dominant (Ta) over other tabby patterns. The coat consists of hairs that have two or three dark bands, similar to those of a wild rabbit. The stripes are sometimes more defined and some-

Tortie: another name for tortoiseshell.

Tortie tabby: a combination of tabby and tortoiseshell.

Tortoiseshell: term for cats with a pattern resembling tortoiseshell, sometimes shortened to "tortie," combining eumelanins and phaeomelanins. Tortoiseshell cats are almost always females.

Type: a complex of external properties that determine the total image of a breed.

U

Ural Rex: Russian breed of cats with curly-haired coat. Still being developed.

times very vague to almost invisible on the legs and tail.

Tipped: term used for a tabby pattern that has been faded to a haze by selection. Combined with the Inhibitor gene, a tipped cat will at first sight look almost white, since only the tips of the hairs contain any pigment. The difference with real white cats is clearly visible from the pigmented rims around the nose leather and eyes. A slightly stronger form of tipped is called "shaded." Shaded and tipped cats can often be encountered in the same litter, as this property is passed on polygenetically. See also: Cameo and Shell.

Tonkinese factor: one of the group of partial albino factors. An intermediate form between the Burmese factor (cb) and the Siamese factor (cs), which occurs when the factors for Siamese and Burmese are combined (cbcs). The Tonkinese is not purebred—mating two Tonkinese-colored cats passes on the Tonkinese factor (cbcs), as well as the Burmese factor (cbcb) and the Siamese factor (cscs).

V

Van: term for a coat pattern, named after the Turkish Van, which is only recognized in this specific pattern. It describes cats with a white body, a colored tail, and one or two colored patches on their heads. Some associations accept or demand another small colored patch elsewhere on the body.

Y

York chocolate: new breed of longhaired cat created by Janet Chiefari and currently being developed. It is either white with solid chocolate or lilac-colored patches, or solid chocolate or lilac. The breed enjoys provisional recognition by some associations, but is only bred, in small numbers, in the United States, Canada, and Europe (in Italy).

W

Weaning: making kittens independent of their mother's milk.
White patches: unpigmented parts of the coat, caused by the dominant inherited S-gene (piebald spotting).

Acknowledgments

The publisher and author extend their thanks to all the breeders, show judges, cat owners, and cat fanciers who have contributed to the production of this book.

Special thanks are due to a number of professional photographers, without whose help this book could never have been produced, and in particular to Linda Beatie (Paradox, U.S.) who provided all the pictures of American breeds. Many thanks also to Diana van Houten, veterinarian, for reading the medical chapters of the original Dutch text; Tjerk Huisman for reading the chapters on color and genetics; Francien Verspui, cat owner and breeder, for reading the general chapters and those on breeding; and to Cécile Gautier for organizing photographic sessions with breeders and owners in France, where part of the photography for this encyclopedia took place. Finally, my thanks to Mimy, for the good old times.

Photo credits

All photographs were taken by Esther Verhoef/ Furrytails.nl, with the exception of:

Priscilla van Andel: p. 103 above, 202 above.

G. Anderiesen: p. 406 below.

Günther Ardon: p. 304 below right.

Ineke Blokker: p. 78 above, 99, 203 left, 215 above, 316 both, 317 below left and center, 318 all.

W. Böhr (D.): p. 422 above.

Marianne Booij: p. 317 above left.

The Book of the Cat (Frances Simpson, 1903): p. 8 below, 12 left, 13 right, 222 below, 229 right, 230 above left and below left, 239 above right, 269 below (both), 270 above, 291 left, 292 all, 302 below left, 326 right (both), 354 below (both) and center, 403 above right, 434 below.

Jason Couvier: p. 442 and 443.

Mevr. A. Edel (D.): p. 421 above.

Robert Fox (G.B.): p. 403 below, 404 below, 405 below left, 405 below.

Glück family (D.): p. 422 below.

Wilfred and Carla Groeneveld: p. 53 below, 54 below left, 185 above, 270 below, 271 below, p. 274 above right.

M. van Hulst: p. 162 below, 163 all, 164 all, 165 right.

I. Jänicke (D.): p. 421 below, 422 right.

T. Jensen: p. 331 above.

N. Kovaleva (D.): p. 440 and 441.

Monique Knook: p. 234 above.

Mark Lathouras (AUS.): p. 406 center right.

Lüning family: p. 407 below left.

Paradox Photography/Linda Beatie (CAN., U.S.): p. 223-227 incl., 240 left, 243 above, 245 above right, 257-259 incl., 260 above, 261 right, 269 above, 270 center, 272 above, 273 below left, 275 above, 279 above, 288 above and below left, 289 all, 293 below and center, 295 above and center, 296 above and center, 299 center, 310-312 incl., 319 below left, 320 right, 321 below right, 330 below, 334 below, 336 below, 359 and 360, 361 above, 362 above, 363 left, 364 below, 386 above left, 387 all, 388 above, 389 right, 390 above, 398 below (both), 402 above, 406 above left, 407 above right and center, 408 below right, 409 below, 426-430 incl., p. 439 all, 444 above left, 449 above, 451 below left, 452 above, 453 above, 459-461 incl.

Pemmie Molle: p. 147 right and 168 above.

O'Shea (U.S.): p. 420 right.

Marijke Pel: p. 288 below right, 290 both, 362 below, 363 below right, 365 above.

D. Pribylová (CZ.): p. 307 left, 309 below left.

Chris Puddephatt (CAN.): p. 361 below.

Cheryl Sarges (U.S.): p. 212 above.

Foto Scheffer: p. 302 above and center, 303 both, 304 left, 305 both, 306 above.

Dr. Scheuer-Karpin (D.): p. 420 below.

Maureen Shackell (G.B.): p. 404 below left.

Valeriy Sinitcin (RUS.) (with thanks to Svetlana Ponomareva): p. 323 both, 324 and 325.

Z. Slunecko (CZ.): p. 307 right, 308 right, 309 right and above.

Mollie Southall (G.B.): p. 403 center right, 404 above right, 405 above right.

Hans van Spaandonk: p. 74 above.

Francien Verspui: p. 20 above, 54 below, 60 below, and 61 below.

J. Versteeg: p. 92 above.

N. Volkova (CZ.): p. 308 left.

Leslie Wal: p. 246 left, 343 below, 344 all, 346 below, 347 above.

Mrs Wöllner (private archive) (with thanks to I. Jänicke, D.): p. 420 above left.

Index